Linux Security

Linux Security

Ramón J. Hontañón

SYBEX

San Francisco   Paris   Düsseldorf   Soest   London

Associate Publisher: Richard J. Staron
Contracts and Licensing Manager: Kristine O'Callaghan
Acquisitions and Developmental Editors: Maureen Adams, Tom Cirtin
Editor: Sarah Lemaire
Production Editor: Jennifer Campbell
Technical Editor: James Eric Gunnett
Book Designer: Bill Gibson
Graphic Illustrator: Tony Jonick
Electronic Publishing Specialist: Jangshi Wang
Proofreaders: Emily Hsuan, Laurie O'Connell, Nancy Riddiough
Indexer: Ted Laux
Cover Design: Ingalls + Associates
Cover Illustration: Ingalls + Associates

Library of Congress Card Number: 2001088117

ISBN: 0-7821-2741-X

To Stacia, my wife and my best friend.

Foreword

According to legend, security threats come from sophisticated code hackers who have a deep understanding of networks and operating systems. These legendary characters are motivated by a noble desire to force unresponsive computer corporations to improve their software. If this were true, Linux would not be a target for security attacks. After all, Linux is open-source code. No one can claim that a corporate monolith is keeping the code hidden. If these legendary characters were truly rebels against the corporate system working to improve the security of operating system software, they would be writing new Linux code. Unfortunately this is not true, and Linux is one of the most popular targets for attack.

The reality of network attacks is both more sordid and more mundane than the mythology. Some attacks come from petty criminals out to steal credit card numbers. But most attacks come from unskilled people running canned attack scripts that are so simple to use they are called "kiddie scripts."

Clearly, open-source code is no deterrent. The people who run attack scripts are not motivated to "fix" the system; they are just looking for easy targets. Your job is to make sure that your system isn't an easy target. *Linux Security*, by Ramón Hontañón, can help you do that job.

Good security is a fundamental part of good system administration. Security is essential to running a reliable Linux system. Your computer will be attacked and compromised by people on the network. To reduce the number of successful attacks, limit the amount of damage done, and quickly recover from the attack, you need the right tools and the skills to use them. *Linux Security* shows you those tools and teaches you how to use them effectively.

Craig Hunt

March, 2001

Acknowledgments

Back in June of 2000, Craig Hunt offered me the opportunity to write a book on Linux security. When I agreed to take on the project, I never imagined how much I would learn from this experience. Over the course of the last seven months, I've had the privilege to meet and work with a number of Sybex publishing professionals who took me under their wing from the start and helped me write a better Linux security book. I'd like to take this opportunity to thank each of them individually.

As the editor for the Linux Library series, Craig Hunt is the one who made it all possible. His depth of knowledge in the TCP/IP and Linux arenas is simply humbling. I have learned from his dedication, tenacity, and especially from his relentless pursuit of perfection.

Neil Edde, an associate publisher at Sybex, helped me draft a schedule that allowed me to shuffle book writing with the responsibilities of a full-time job. He patiently answered all my novice questions and offered the direction I needed to get this project underway.

As the development editor, Tom Cirtin guided me through the initial chapters and helped me get the book in shape for its launch. He encouraged me when I felt overwhelmed and was always there for me when I needed his advice. He made the process much more bearable during the initial stages, which I found to be the most difficult.

Jennifer Campbell was the production editor for this book. She helped me stay on schedule and always kept me informed of what was coming next. It was through her that I got to see the "light at the end of the tunnel." Thanks Jennifer!

The acquisitions editor for the Linux Library series is Maureen Adams. She made sure this book hit the bookstands on schedule while accommodating the need to extend interim deadlines to allow for late-breaking content to be added.

Sarah Lemaire edited the final text and allowed me to concentrate on the book's content by helping out with the format. Her edits were thorough and consistent, and her writing style significantly improved the flow of the material. This book is just as much hers as it is mine. I'd also like to thank Dale Good for editing the first two chapters of the book.

Throughout the writing and editing process, I received assistance from Carl Montgomery, Dan Mummert, Kristine O'Callaghan, Senoria Bilbo-Brown and Tami Crady, most from Sybex headquarters in Alameda, CA. Thank you all for lending a hand!

I could not have written this book without a number of people who influenced my life both on a personal level (Tom, Peggy, Dubie, T-Jay, Kerry, and Suzie Dailer, Art Mezerski, Dr. John Atkins, and Dr. Frank Hiergeist) as well as on a professional level (Mike Jaskowiak, Carl Humes, Julia Walsh, Rick Weldon, Farrel Johnson, and Lisa Deming). I'm very lucky to have crossed paths with all of you.

Finally, I'd like to thank my father, Ramón, for giving me the opportunity to travel abroad and pursue an education in the field that I love, as well as my mother, María José, and my brother, Carlos, for providing me with constant moral support. Last, but certainly not least, I'd like to thank my wife, Stacia, for her unconditional love, for her boundless patience, and for letting me get out of home improvement for the last seven months.

Ramón J. Hontañón
Ashburn, VA
May, 2001

Contents at a Glance

Contents

Introduction

With the advent of the Internet revolution came the ability of hundreds of geographically dispersed software developers to collaborate on projects that would had been inconceivable just years before. It was the fall of 1991, and while the Internet hadn't yet become the household name that it is today, a global team of talented software junkies was hard at work crafting what would become the most successful public-domain software offering of all time: the Linux operating system. Ten short years after the first 0.*x* release, the "Volkswagen of operating systems" enjoys an increasingly strong foothold in the workstation marketplace and stands above all other server platforms as one of the most robust, and certainly the most cost-effective, operating systems.

Ironically, the same Internet explosion that helped usher in the development of the Linux operating system is also to blame for the climate of lawlessness that has forced network administrators to re-examine their network security postures. As corporations large and small look to the Internet as a necessary way to conduct business, network managers become instant security experts, and what once was the distant threat of malicious intrusion is now the order of the day.

While there is no such thing as a *secure* network server, the Linux operating system was designed with a strong focus on security, and its open-source nature allows administrators, developers, and end users to constantly audit it for vulnerabilities. It's precisely this ability to look "under the hood" that makes Linux the platform of choice in environments where security is just as important as high availability and ironclad stability.

This book concentrates on what it takes to make your Linux servers as secure as possible, and how to ensure that your servers continue to be secure, even in the face of the ever-mutating array of malicious threats that plague the Internet today. It contains practical, step-by-step advice on how to harden a Linux installation, starting with a "stock" distribution using freely available software tools. The tips and techniques described in this book are equally relevant to installations of one or one thousand Linux servers. The advice that you'll find here is the result of over ten years of experience that includes Linux systems, large-scale TCP/IP network administration, security consultation, and security product development for a leading Internet service provider.

Who Should Buy This Book

This book goes well beyond a simple introduction to Linux security. Instead, it offers a comprehensive reference that is tailored for network administrators and experienced Linux users. While it does describe in detail all the security concepts that are introduced, this book assumes that the reader already has a basic understanding of operating system principles, server administration, and TCP/IP networking fundamentals.

Security topics are presented using a pragmatic approach, briefly describing the theory behind each concept, but with a strong emphasis on their direct application in Linux server administration, including examples and sample configurations. The idea is simple: Empower system administrators to secure Linux servers without compromising their performance and level of service.

While all of the security tools are described in the context of the Linux operating system, most topics introduced in this book are also relevant to any other Unix variants because most Unix system tools are source-compatible across different flavors of the operating system.

How This Book Is Organized

This book is divided into six parts:

- System Security
- Network Security
- Application Security
- Perimeter Security
- Remote Access and Authentication
- Appendices

The security topics introduced in this book are organized in order of proximity to the Linux kernel, starting with the core (system security), moving outward toward the network layer, application layer, and finally to the perimeter, where the private network meets the public Internet. In addition, this book discusses remote access to the network using dial-up networking and strong user authentication. At each of these layers, the reader will find references to several choices of publicly available utilities and native Linux tools, including complete instructions for their successful installation and configuration.

The goal of this book is to provide a comprehensive how-to guide for building security into Linux servers from the ground up. However, the more experienced network administrator who has already mastered security at the system and network levels can use this book as a reference to deploy application and perimeter security mechanisms and to rationalize the security tools already implemented.

Part 1: System Security

Part 1 provides the information you need to understand security at the operating system level. Chapter 1 introduces the basic building blocks of Linux security. Chapter 2 describes the security considerations in the installation and setup of a Linux system. Chapter 3 discusses system monitoring and auditing.

Chapter 1: Understanding Linux Security

This chapter explains the basic ideas behind system security in general and Linux security in particular. It introduces security concepts that will be used throughout the rest of the book and discusses their role in a comprehensive Linux security solution.

Chapter 2: System Installation and Setup

This chapter describes the process of installing and configuring the base Linux server software with an emphasis on security, highlighting the areas that are critical for the protection of the system against potential vulnerabilities. It also introduces the concept of encrypted filesystems and presents several alternatives for their implementation.

Chapter 3: System Monitoring and Auditing

The security process doesn't stop at implementation. This chapter explains how to monitor and audit Linux server installations for hidden security vulnerabilities. It also describes a number of public-domain utilities that can be used for monitoring and auditing at the operating system level.

Part 2: Network Security

Part 2 builds on the practices introduced in the previous section by discussing a secure approach to configuring and managing Linux network servers (daemons) and the resources associated with them. Chapter 4 focuses on the /etc/inetd.conf configuration file. Chapter 5 explores a number of utilities available for monitoring and auditing network layer vulnerabilities.

Chapter 4: Network Services Configuration

Linux systems are network-ready by default. Careful management of network services is paramount to a secure server installation. This chapter explores the configuration of the inetd and xinetd Internet *super-servers*, the spawning of stand-alone servers, and the installation and configuration of TCPWrappers, a transport layer filtering tool.

Chapter 5: Network Monitoring and Auditing

Continued monitoring is just as important at the network level as it is at the system level. This chapter provides details on several network layer auditing utilities and surveys the current state of Linux-based intrusion detection and network forensics.

Part 3: Application Security

Part 3 covers the security considerations of a number of popular server-class Linux applications. Chapter 6 discusses electronic mail transport agent security. Chapter 7 introduces the security issues associated with Apache, the most widely deployed HTTP server in the world. Chapter 8 discusses the security implications of file-sharing services and network print daemons.

Chapter 6: Electronic Mail

This chapter focuses on the two most prevalent mail transport agents used in Linux servers: Sendmail and Qmail. In addition, the ever-popular Pretty Good Privacy (PGP) package is introduced, as is its public domain counterpart, the Gnu Privacy Guard (GnuPG).

Chapter 7: HTTP Services

If the Web browser is the Internet's "killer app," the Apache HTTP server is, without a doubt, the Internet's "killer server." This chapter explores Apache's security vulnerabilities and offers an in-depth look at its security configuration. In addition, two Apache-based implementations of Secure Sockets Layer (SSL) are introduced: Mod_SSL and Apache-SSL.

Chapter 8: Samba Security

Central to any Linux server is its ability to share files with other Linux servers (via NFS) and with Windows clients (via Samba/SMB). This chapter offers a rare look into the security measures that should be taken when implementing these utilities, as well as the perils of offering Unix printing via LPD.

Part 4: Perimeter Security

Part 4 goes "outside the box" to explore practical methods of protecting your Linux server network from Internet threats while still offering users an acceptable level of service and connectivity. Three types of firewalls are described: network layer firewalls (Chapter 9), transport layer firewalls (Chapter 10), and application layer firewalls (Chapter 11).

Chapter 9: Network Layer Firewalls

This chapter explains the ubiquitous packet-filtering firewall and its native support in the Linux kernel. This chapter describes the user-space tools (IPfwadm, IPchains, IPtables) that Linux provides to manage network layer rules. It also offers a look into IP masquerading and network address translation.

Chapter 10: Transport Layer Firewalls

Chapter 10 introduces the SOCKS5 system, a public-domain, transport layer firewall that allows a Linux server to proxy all public network communications on behalf of a number of diverse clients sitting behind the firewall in the private network.

Chapter 11: Application Layer Firewalls

The Trusted Information Systems (TIS) Firewall Toolkit takes the concept of transport layer proxying a step further. Chapter 11 explains in detail the installation, configuration, and maintenance of the application-specific proxies that make up the TIS toolkit.

Part 5: Remote Access and Authentication

Part 5 complements the discussion of Linux security by examining remote access to the network from the public Internet. Chapter 12 provides a comprehensive view of virtual private networking support in the Linux system. Chapter 13 outlines the S/KEY and Kerberos authentication utilities. In addition, Chapter 13 surveys the Plug-in Authentication Module support in the latest Linux kernels.

Chapter 12: Virtual Private Networking

Virtual private networks (VPNs) are all the rage in networking today, and Linux has historically been in the forefront of standards-based virtual private network support. Chapter 12 focuses on Free S/WAN, a public-domain, full-featured IPsec implementation, and PoPToP, a server implementation of the PPTP protocol made popular by Microsoft. The chapter also discusses the Secure Shell (SSH), a secure replacement for the standard Linux shell.

Chapter 13: Strong User Authentication

Secure remote access hinges on the Linux server's ability to authenticate the user who is requesting access. Chapter 13 explains the S/Key system for one-time password generation and the Kerberos suite of secret-key-based authentication. This chapter also describes the current kernel support for Plug-in Authentication Modules (PAMs).

Appendices

The two appendices that come with this book provide you with information that supplements what you've learned in the chapters that precede them.

Appendix A: Other Sources of Information

This appendix contains a list of selected Web references containing useful information on Linux security. These Web sites should be part of your daily morning Web-browsing routine. This appendix also identifies some mailing lists that focus on security information that you should subscribe to for regular updates.

Appendix B: PAM Module Reference

Appendix B expands on the Pluggable Authentication Modules (PAM) discussion in Chapter 13 by providing detailed references to the most important PAM modules available for Linux.

Conventions

This book uses the following typographical conventions:

- `Inline_Program_Font` is used to identify the Linux commands, filenames, and domain names that lie within the body of the text.
- `Program_Font` is used in listings and examples.
- **Bold** is used to indicate something that must be typed as shown. This might be user input in a listing, a recommended command line, or fixed values within the syntax of a command. For example, command syntax written as **key** *key_id* means that the command key must be typed exactly as shown.
- *Italic* is used in command syntax to indicate a variable for which you must provide the value. For example, command syntax written as **key** *key_id* means that the variable name *key_id* must not be typed as shown; you must prove your own value for *key_id*.
- Square brackets ([ ]) are used in a command's syntax to indicate that the item enclosed in square brackets is optional. For example, `ls [-1]` means that `-1` is an optional part of the `ls` command.
- | is a vertical bar that indicates you need to choose one keyword or the other in a command's syntax. For example, yes | no means choose either yes or no.

Help Us Help You

Things change. In the world of computers, things change rapidly. Facts described in this book will become invalid over time. When they do, we need your help locating and correcting them. Additionally, a 400-page book is bound to have typographical errors. Let us know when you spot one. Send your improvements, fixes, and other corrections to support@sybex.com. If you'd like to offer the author some feedback directly, send mail to linux_security@hotmail.com.

Part 1

System Security

Featuring:

- A Security Primer
- The Layered Approach to Information Security
- Choosing a Linux Distribution
- Building a Secure Kernel
- File System Encryption
- Techniques for Monitoring and Auditing

1

Understanding Linux Security

Information security has become a topic of increasing interest, not only in the Linux community but in all other areas of information technology. As potential threats materialize and become headline news, network and systems administrators are forced to wear other hats, as part-time police officers, as investigators, and, in a few unfortunate instances, even as forensics experts, so to speak. As the Internet continues to experience mind-boggling growth, fueled by, among other factors, the ubiquity of Linux servers, so grows the number of published Linux vulnerabilities and the complexity of defending your network and Linux servers against malicious attacks and so-called benign intrusions.

While the mission is a challenging one, it is by no means impossible. A Linux administrator has access to a wide variety of tools and techniques to protect against *most* types of intrusions. It is indeed true that there is no such thing as a completely secure system. But it is just as true that by increasing the security measures in your server network, you are making your system a much more difficult target, and, with the right implementation of these features, your chances of becoming a victim are going to decrease dramatically.

This book is a road map to aid you in your quest to secure your production servers from harmful attacks. In addition, it will help you make sure that the servers stay secure throughout their useful life and during the course of normal operation, including maintenance, upgrades, expansions, and other system administration tasks.

The first section of this chapter introduces the concept of security and defines some important terms that will be used throughout this book.

An Information Security Primer

There is nothing mystical about information security. At times overly glorified, and rarely well understood, the concept of information security cuts across many other disciplines, including network and system administration, programming, configuration management, and even documentation, auditing, and training. As a Linux server administrator, you will find that securing your network is an exercise in versatility. Very few corporations are large enough to justify the additional expense of having an information security expert on staff, and yet, practically all corporations would be adversely affected by even the most casual intrusion.

This section starts by defining a set of working terms commonly used when discussing information security and then moves on to define the process of information security, detailing each of the steps that make up this process.

Security Terminology

Throughout this book, I will use several terms that are often not well understood, or that are open to interpretation. This section provides working definitions for these security-related concepts.

Bastion Host

While the general aim of securing your network is to keep unauthorized personnel out of your servers, there is an increasing need to allow public access to some of these servers. At the very least, you will be asked to maintain a public Web and FTP server, and perhaps even a publicly available DNS server. A *bastion host* is one that should be publicly available enough that you don't feel comfortable placing it in the same segment as your private servers. It's a fortified host, hence the name. A bastion host is typically designed and maintained by the system administration staff who are knowledgeable about the security issues involved in setting up public servers such as these.

Think of the bastion host as the mailbox in front of a house, next to the curb. It's available to anybody, but it is at a safe distance and it is physically separated from the house. Or you may prefer to think of a bastion host as a scout in a military unit, securing the route ahead of the main group. Figure 1.1 shows the typical placement of a bastion host.

Figure 1.1   Placing bastion hosts on a dedicated firewall segment

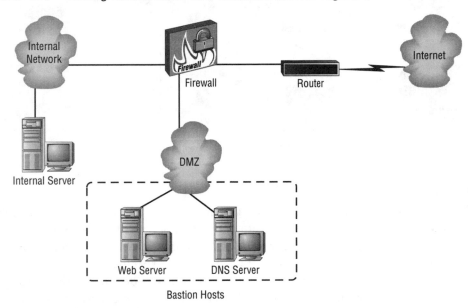

Demilitarized Zone (DMZ)

You want to establish a network segment that is under your administrative control, but is physically separate from your protected network. This segment is referred to as a *demilitarized zone (DMZ)*. The DMZ is typically a small network, comprising up to a half-dozen or so bastion hosts. Note that a DMZ is often connected to a separate network interface through a firewall, as shown in Figure 1.1. However, a DMZ can also be positioned as an intermediate segment between the firewall and the Internet access router. Figure 1.2 shows this configuration.

Figure 1.2   Placing bastion hosts on an intermediate DMZ segment between a firewall and an Internet access router

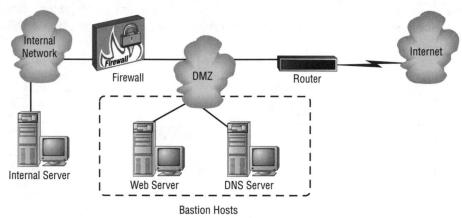

Extranet

The term *extranet* refers to a network segment dedicated to provide services to a set of users who are known to your organization, but are not trusted at the same level as your internal users. For example, you may be asked to offer extranet services to business partners so that you can share proposals and system specification documents. Or perhaps your company is a subcontractor in a multi-vendor integration effort, and needs to make many large files available to other development partners.

Access to extranet servers often requires some form of authentication, although the appropriate access control measurements should be in place to ensure that extranet users do not gain access to internal network services. Note that it is perfectly acceptable to place extranet servers in the same DMZ segment as the more public bastion hosts. By doing this you allow outside people access to the material they need to see, but they do not gain access to the internal information of the company that needs to be kept confidential. Figure 1.3 shows the placement of extranet hosts on a DMZ.

Figure 1.3 Placing extranet hosts on a demilitarized zone (DMZ)

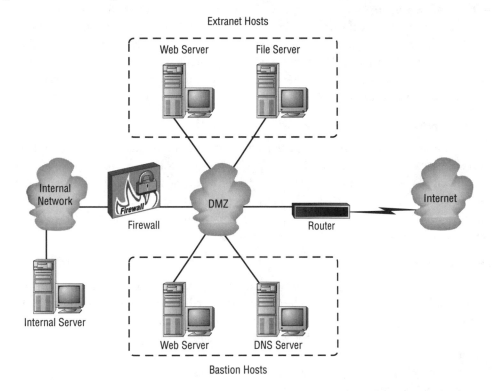

Firewall

In general, a *firewall* is a logical entity or physical device that controls public access to a private network. This is often accomplished by deploying a computing device with physical connections to both the private and public networks. This device can run either special-purpose software or a common operating system, with the appropriate packages needed to support the firewall feature. While its primary purpose is to grant or deny network access in and out of the private network, a firewall can also log traffic statistics, authenticate users, and even detect intrusions by identifying suspicious usage patterns. This is a very important part of securing your network.

Intranet

The term *intranet* means a private network. When we speak of an intranet, we're referring not only to the physical network segment, but also to a collection of servers (Web, mail, multimedia) that are meant to be accessed exclusively by internal users. These are different and are physically separated from the extranet and public servers. Typically, intranets include content that is confidential, data that is mission critical, or data that is appropriate only for internal use by company employees.

Packet Filter

Running on a firewall appliance, a *packet filter* program makes decisions on whether to forward or block a packet based on the packet's source, destination, or payload type. The most popular packet filters are those that operate at the network (IP) layer and act on a set of rules based on the packet's source and destination IP address, as well as on the source and destination transport (TCP) layer number. The original, first-generation firewalls were simple packet filters.

Proxy Server

Acting as a specialized type of firewall, a *proxy server* accepts Internet connection requests from internal network clients, and forwards them to the target Internet host as if the originator of the request were the proxy server itself. The Internet host then responds to the proxy server, which then forwards the response to the appropriate internal network client. Proxy servers typically operate at the transport (TCP) layer and above, and can be used for enforcing access rules, logging connection requests, and even for caching commonly accessed public content.

Security by Obscurity

Security by obscurity is the practice by which internal services are not protected from the public network, but their access is purposely obscured by cryptic addresses, or resource identifiers, or both. For example, you may choose to make sensitive information available to your business partners using an anonymous FTP server, but naming the file with a leading period (.) so that the name does not show up on a regular directory listing. This is a questionable practice. Intruders are not easily deterred by obscurity, and automated scanning tools are especially good at finding this type of hidden information. The security by obscurity practice keeps only the least experienced hackers out of your system.

The Process of Information Security

Plain and simple, you need to protect the resources that are important to your organization to the extent that a compromise of these resources would negatively impact the operation of your organization. You need to decide what data must be secured and what data should be secured if you have the resources. You also need to know what the cost to the company will be if the network is cracked and the data is stolen or maliciously changed. For some organizations, their public Internet presence is meant to complement the information available through other means, and a compromise of this information would not have any serious consequences for its operation. For example, it would not be a good use of security resources to ensure the privacy of the transmission of weather data for a free Internet portal, or the integrity of a streaming video feed to a Web site displaying several traffic cameras. We are, however, in the Information Age, and an increasing number of companies are built exclusively on the integrity and availability of information that needs to be exchanged over the public network. Those organizations rely on their Internet-exchanged data as much as on their bricks-and-mortar presence. This includes online banks, investment and benefits management firms, and the overwhelming majority of business-to-business transactions conducted over the Internet. These enterprises must spare no expense to ensure that the data on their servers is always private and available, and that the integrity of its data is beyond reproach.

Security is not a product. It is not software, and it is also not simply an excuse for a consulting engagement. It is a discipline that needs to be taken into consideration in any decision that you make as a network and system administrator. Security does not start or stop. You cannot install security, and you can't even buy security. Security is training, documentation, design decisions, and appropriate implementations. And the most important aspect of security is monitoring and honing your security policies as needed.

The fundamental steps in the process of information security are described in the next subsection.

Security Policy Development

A security policy is your master document, your mission statement, and the ultimate source that tells the rest of your coworkers *what* you're protecting and *how* you intend to protect it. While some companies might hire an outside consultant to draft this policy, this often falls on the plate of the network administrator. There are several good online sources for help on this topic:

- The Internet Engineering Task Force's (IETF's) *Site Security Handbook* (RFC 1244) is a comprehensive guide to security policy and procedure development.

- Purdue University's COAST Project offers a number of sample, real-life security policies at `ftp://coast.cs.purdue.edu/pub/doc/policy`.

- A good Web site with general security policy information is `www.sans.org/newlook/resources/policies/policies.htm`.

The basic building blocks of a security policy are as follows:

Version   The revision number and date of the policy.

Introduction   Briefly describes the company's history, its purpose, and its mission, including references to the company's current Internet service provider (ISP), and the provider of any managed or outsourced security applications and mechanisms, such as firewalls, virtual private networks (VPNs), or content filters.

Network Diagram   Shows the basic building blocks of both the intranet and the extranet (if any). Make sure that the diagram clearly shows the border where the internal network connects to the Internet service provider's edge router.

Physical Security   Defines the areas that are off-limits for general employees and the roles and identities of employees who are allowed to enter them. This should include physical specifications for server platforms, such as front panel configuration, power connections, UPS systems, and console access. This section should also address the type of access control used to enter data centers and network closets.

WARNING It is critically important to restrict unauthorized and inexperienced people from gaining access to the data center or server room. To do otherwise is to invite damaging and expensive accidents or sabotage.

Intranet and Extranet Services   Services allowed *in* and *out* of the intranet/extranet, including service type, source, destination, time of day, and user authentication. Include allowable content for electronic mail exchanges, as well as for HTTP and FTP downloads.

TIP You may want to know the ports for the services you would like to allow and the ports for the services you do not want to allow here, so that you can reference them later on.

Remote Access   Special restrictions for remote users (via dial-up or dedicated VPN) who gain access to the Intranet using dial-up and/or encryption clients from the Internet.

Firewall Configuration   Detailed configuration reference of your perimeter defense devices, including access control rules, logging facilities, and authentication methods.

User Account Policy   User account creation and maintenance policy, including choice of usernames, password expiration/termination rules, and disk and process quotas.

Data Use Policy   This section should cover the types of user and data files on the server and how they should be handled. It should include initial permissions, access control, and group creation criteria.

Auditing, Monitoring, and Enforcement   A security policy is useless if it's not actually enforced. In this section, you should clearly define the tools and methodology you'll employ to monitor servers and network resources to ensure that the policy is being followed. Be sure to clearly include the types of punitive and/or corrective actions to be imposed on violators.

NOTE   You must follow through on the auditing part of the policy document or else it is pointless to create it. It may sound obvious, but you cannot have a secure network if you are not monitoring it for security.

Official Assent   This is the section where you clearly state who is directly responsible for the writing and continued enforcement of the policy. It should include signatures from IT officers, corporate counsel, and the developer or developers of the policy itself. Be sure to date the signatures.

Even the most clear, concise, and complete security policy will be ineffective if it is not accessible to employees. Be sure to include a hard copy of this policy with the new employee orientation packet, and remind your employees periodically of its location online so they can consult it as it evolves. In addition, conduct periodic training sessions on its use and compliance, and set up a mechanism by which users and IT staffers alike can submit suggestions for improvement.

Security Mechanism Implementation

Once you have an agreed-upon security policy, it's time to implement the mechanisms necessary to enforce it. This is often a combination of system configuration changes, tool installation, user procedure development, and monitoring. To implement mechanisms for the policy outline used in the previous section, you need perform the following tasks:

Physical Security   Install UPS devices, combination locks, and physical environment alarms in the data center, if they are not already provided for you. Configure Linux servers so root access is only allowed at the console.

Intranet and Extranet Services   Install and configure a perimeter defense device (firewall, router with access lists, and so forth) to enforce restrictions on extranet and intranet services. (Chapter 9, "Network Layer Firewalls," covers the topic of Linux firewalls in detail.)

Remote Access   Install and configure a virtual private network endpoint (see Chapter 12, "Virtual Private Networking") and/or a network device to support strong remote authentication and authorization (see Chapter 13, "Strong User Authentication").

User Account Policy   Configure the /etc/login.defs configuration file to force users to change their passwords periodically. I recommend that you set PASS_MAX_ DAYS to a maximum of 90, which forces your users to change passwords every three months. This amount of time keeps users on their toes and reminds them that the password is a very important part of network security, even though changing it every 90 days may be viewed as a hassle. Write a script that periodically executes the last and finger commands to find out how long users have been inactive and inserts an asterisk (*) in their /etc/passwd entries, if appropriate. In addition, you should train your users in the art of choosing a good, unpredictable password, one that includes alphanumeric characters and is not related to a user's environment, such as the name of their spouse, the street they live on, or the car they drive.

Data Use Policy   Use the right global umask permissions for initial file creation and execute a script periodically to ensure that you have no rogue setuid/setgid exe- cutables. (See Chapter 2, "System Installation and Setup," for a full discussion of system security configuration and monitoring.)

Auditing, Monitoring, and Enforcement   Install an auditing and monitoring tool such as Satan, COPS, or PortSentry and use it periodically to ensure that your net- work defenses still comply with your security policy. (See Chapter 5, "Network Monitoring and Auditing," for a comprehensive discussion of network auditing and monitoring tools.)

Periodic Policy Editing and Security Auditing

Much like the Internet, your network is probably changing all the time. Make sure you review your security policy to ensure that it still reflects the needs of your network. Have you added any new servers recently? Has your user population grown substantially as a result of your company's latest merger? Has there been a recent round of layoffs, with a lot of disgruntled employees leaving? Even if your network hasn't changed significantly, you need to play the part of an intruder and try to break into your server from the outside. Make sure you're a step ahead of the real bad guys who are constantly trying to do the same thing.

An area of your security policy that deserves special attention is remote access. With the recent advent of VPN technology, it is easier than ever to provide universal access to trav- eling users using a simple Point-to-Point Tunneling Protocol (PPTP) or Internet Protocol Security (IPSec) client installed on their laptops. It is important to realize the implications of allowing this type of access. While you used to be able to physically see the bounds of your network, remote access extends the perimeter of your intranet to places that you may not necessarily wish to trust completely. You may want to retool your security policy to include restrictions on such areas as the following:

- Version of the IPSec/PPTP client to use.

- Timeout setting of the client. A user who has been idle for 15 minutes typically does not mind re-establishing the remote connection.

- Type of authentication used. Username/password is no longer enough for secure remote access.

- Type of screensaver and idle length. Demand the use of screensavers that password-lock after the idle timeout is reached.

In addition, this book introduces a number of software utilities that can be used to automate some of the auditing and monitoring that are necessary to ensure policy compliance. Chapter 3, "System Monitoring and Auditing," discusses auditing at the system level, while Chapter 5 extends the discussion to the network layer.

The Goals of Information Security

You can map all the security needs for your Linux server into one of four basic goals:

- Data confidentiality

- Data integrity

- User authentication and access control

- Data and service availability

The ultimate purpose of your security policy, tool and policy implementation, and configuration management is to address each of these goals. The following sections examine each goal in more detail.

Data Confidentiality

In this increasingly public world, maintaining the confidentiality of the data in your Linux servers is a full-time task of its own. As your users rely on network servers for more aspects of their everyday work routines, they also trust more confidential and private information to these services. The advent of cryptography has provided the Linux systems administrator with an invaluable tool to ensure confidentiality by allowing users to encrypt sensitive data stored on the servers. Linux supports both private-key and public-key encryption, the two primary types of cryptographic encryption.

Private-Key Encryption

Also referred to as *symmetric-key* encryption, private-key encryption allows users to select a secret key that can then be used to seed an algorithm that converts the sensitive data (plaintext) into the scrambled, or encrypted data (cyphertext). This process is reversible, so the same user can then decrypt the cyphertext into the original plaintext, provided that he or she can produce the original encrypting key. The longer the key, the harder it is for an attacker to derive the plaintext from the cyphertext.

The de facto standard for private-key encryption is the Data Encryption Standard (DES), developed by IBM for use by the U.S. Government in 1977. Although its 56-bit key was believed to be more than adequate at the time, the DES algorithm has been cracked several times. This has prompted the National Institutes for Standards and Technology (NIST) to coordinate the development of the next-generation DES, called AES (Advanced Encryption Standard), which uses much longer key lengths and is substantially more robust.

There are several Linux security applications that make use of private-key encryption, including the Kerberos suite of authentication tools. Chapter 13 covers this topic in more detail.

Public-Key Encryption

While private-key encryption is an effective way to protect sensitive data, it lacks the versatility necessary to protect data exchanges between two parties, especially when those two parties have no prior knowledge of each other. This led Martin Hellman and Whitfield Diffie to develop the concept of public-key encryption, in their landmark 1976 paper, "New Directions in Cryptography," *IEEE Transactions on Information Theory*. The idea is surprisingly simple: The sender encrypts a message with the well-known public key of the receiver. The receiver (and nobody else) can then decrypt the message into the original plaintext. This ensures confidentiality of the message without the need for sender and receiver to share a common private key. Not surprisingly, public-key encryption is a common technique used to protect the content of electronic mail messages as they travel over the Internet.

The Linux-supported Pretty Good Privacy (PGP) package, and its open-source equivalent, GNU Privacy Guard (GPG) offer two examples of public-key-driven security applications. Chapter 6, "Electronic Mail," describes both PGP and GPG.

Data Integrity

Once an attacker has gained access to your information as it is being transmitted over the Internet, the attacker can do any of the following:

- Use the content for nefarious purposes, such as extortion or competitive advantage.

- Modify the content before it reaches its intended destination.
- Destroy the data altogether.

Preserving the integrity of the data as it travels via the Internet is often a priority even when confidentiality is not. For example, consider a Web-driven service through which your customers can download security patches to your company's software products. While the patches themselves can be downloaded in the clear, it is critical that the customer be assured that the patch has not been maliciously modified.

Once again, cryptography comes to the rescue. By using *digital signatures* attached to the patch distribution, your users can verify the validity of the software that they're about to install. Before making the patch available, the digital signature tool obtains a *digest*, a summary of the data that composes the patch. You then sign this digest with your private key and make your public key available to your users. They can then reverse the process by verifying the signature of the digest using your public key. If a single bit has been modified during transmission, the signature fails verification and your users know that tampering has occurred.

A popular application of data integrity checking in Linux systems security is found in the Tripwire suite of file integrity tools. This is one of the topics of discussion in Chapter 3.

User Authentication and Access Control

The need for authentication is as old as humankind itself. As long as there have been groups with different rights and privileges, humans have been required to authenticate themselves as legitimate members of those groups. The most basic form of authentication is visual inspection (you look like the Alice I know, therefore, you must be Alice). A slightly more sophisticated form of authentication relies on the subject's possession of a token that is unique to the subject's identity and that only the subject should be able to produce (for example, a secret word or a driver's license). In Internet terms, this translates to simple username/password authentication, which remains the primary means of online authentication.

However, there are two fundamental vulnerabilities inherent in this type of authentication:

- People tend to choose easy-to-guess passwords when they're forced to memorize them, and they tend to write them down when they're forced to choose good passwords.
- Passwords are easy to sniff. Every time a password is used, it is sent out over the network, typically in the clear, which exposes it to a malicious intruder who is simply monitoring the public medium.

To address the first vulnerability, you should make use of the `npasswd` utility, which forces users to choose good passwords. You should also use `crack` tool, which attempts to guess poor passwords that your users may have chosen. (Chapter 3 discusses both of these utilities in detail.) To protect passwords from being sniffed, you must ensure that all remote access takes place either via Secure Shell (SSH), or using one-time passwords through an S/KEY login session. These tools are discussed in detail in Chapters 12 and 13 respectively.

The advent of e-commerce on the Internet has brought about the need for a way to authenticate truly anonymous parties—i.e., those who are totally unknown to us prior to the transaction. Public-key cryptography once again provides a solution to this problem. By using certificates carrying the digital signature of a well-known *certificate authority (CA)*, anonymous parties can be authenticated based on the transitive nature of trust in the CA. That is, if I trust the CA, and the CA can vouch for the fact that this person is whom he or she claims to be, then I should believe it.

The Linux implementation of *Secure Sockets Layer (SSL)* includes the tools necessary to implement a simple *Public Key Infrastructure (PKI)* that you can use to provide strong authentication of anonymous subjects. This is topic is discussed in detail in Chapter 7, "HTTP Services."

Data and Service Availability

It has been said that in the age of networking and wireless communications that the only truly secure system is a brick—nothing goes in and nothing comes out. While this may be true, Linux administrators don't have the luxury of taking this radical approach. In fact, the performance of most system administrators is often measured by their ability to keep the systems always up and accessible from the public network. There are obvious reasons why you would want to make sure that your Linux servers are up all of the time (your corporation does want to make a profit, right?), but there are more subtle reasons why high availability is important to information security.

Chances are that your users rely on your online systems for authentication and private communication of sensitive data. In the absence of these systems—i.e., if they're not available—users are likely to use less secure methods to transmit and store data, which often results in compromising the company's security policy. For example, consider a user who needs to send an encrypted proposal to the legal department in the next five minutes. If the PGP key server is down and the user is faced with a substantial delay, the user is more likely to send the document unencrypted, rather than face a potential loss of an important sale.

The next section examines the types of vulnerabilities that are often found in Linux servers, including a specific type of vulnerability that can open the door to *denial of service* attacks, which aim to disrupt the availability of your Linux server.

Linux Security

Linux is no more susceptible to attacks than any other Unix variant. As an open-source product, it's up to the development and user communities to ensure that whenever a vulnerability is found, it is made public and a fix is made available in a timely manner. Linux has an outstanding track record in this regard. This, along with the constant scrutiny to which the source code is subject every day, make Linux an excellent choice of platform for the security-conscious system administrator.

But the cold reality is that no matter how diligently you go about securing your Linux server, chances are that you're going to get attacked. The following sections dig into the character of the prototypical malicious attacker, and provide a comprehensive list of the types of attacks that you're likely to be subject to, as well as the consequences of each one. We'll also look at ways you can protect your server installation from these attacks.

Types of Attackers

Just as there are varying types of security incidents, there are also a variety of types of perpetrators. While attackers hail from all sorts of backgrounds, there are four broad types of characters that can be used to typify the attacker population as a whole. Let's take a closer look at each of these categories.

Joyriders

Often high school or college students, joyriders have time on their hands. They choose their victims at random, and they have no ulterior motive to focus on a specific target other than easy availability. Joyriders get discouraged relatively easy, don't use confidential information, and are not likely to tamper with its integrity. Joyriders confide the details of a successful attack only to their immediate peer group.

You can protect yourself from joyriders by making sure your Linux server is not subject to any obvious vulnerability, and by keeping up with the security patches available for your distribution of Linux. The joyrider is the easiest attacker to defend against.

Cult Members

The Internet has proven to be fertile ground for semi-organized groups that share a common interest in orchestrating network attacks. These groups often conduct themselves as cults, use cryptic names for their members, and communicate using a characteristic jargon that is often hard to decipher for the uninitiated. The most prevalent cults embrace particular sociopolitical causes and pick their victims among those whom they perceive to be the enemy of such causes. Not surprisingly, a number of federal government Web sites have been the target of these cults, who typically deface the site to include a carefully worded protest message.

Cult members are not as easily deterred as joyriders and share a common pool of skills and resources that makes them challenging to defend against. If your company or agency could be the target of a political movement, you should take extraordinary steps to ensure that your hosts, especially your Web and file servers, are protected against defacing and content modification.

Spies

Unlike joyriders and cult members, corporate spies target their victims very carefully and often gather information about the target for a long period of time before orchestrating the attack. The attack of choice is usually unlawful intrusion into confidential resources for financial or political gain. Spies are very well financed, and they often have an impressive array of skills and resources available. They aim to be as stealthy as possible and will attempt to cover their tracks after a successful break-in.

You should protect your servers against spies by guarding your confidential data with access control as well as intrusion detection mechanisms (more on this in Chapter 5). You should also offer decoys, or false confidential information, to keep the spies guessing which file contains the real information. This is similar to the presidential motorcade with four identical black limousines, only one of which actually contains the president.

Insiders

Attacks by insiders are by far the hardest attacks to counter because the potential attackers already possess a wealth of information about the target. Insiders do not have to jump through any hoops to gain access to the Linux server. The only challenge left for them is to bypass the basic system security mechanisms that keep them from accessing someone else's information.

Not only is this type of attack hard to prevent, but it's also hard to detect once it has taken place. Chapter 2 offers a great amount of detail on how to make sure that users stay within their bounds and that permissions and access controls are not violated.

Common Attacks against Linux Servers

So now you know *whom* you should be defending against, but *what* is it exactly that you need to be afraid of? You've heard of the most newsworthy security incidents, like the defacing of the U.S. Department of Justice's Web site or the widespread disruption of service at E*TRADE and others. But how exactly do they do that? It pays off to dig deep below the headlines and find out exactly how attackers can exploit Linux vulnerabilities in order to wreak havoc on our servers.

The following is a fairly comprehensive list of the types of attacks seen on Linux servers in the last five years.

Web Server Attacks

As the most popular service offered on the Internet today, the HTTP server has become the most vulnerable daemon running on a Linux server today. Note that I'm not implying that Web servers are fundamentally weak. It's a simple case of exposure; as the most ubiquitous service, a Web server is also the most frequently attacked. In addition, Web servers use a complex set of configuration parameters and are prone to subtle configuration errors, which makes them even more vulnerable. Web server attacks on Linux hosts fall under two categories: Common Gateway Interface (CGI) script intrusions and buffer overflows, as described in the following sections.

CGI Script Intrusions   The `cgi-bin` directory houses executable scripts that can be invoked from the server on behalf of a user. There is nothing inherently insecure about the way Web servers handle these scripts, but the fact that you're allowing remote users to execute code in the local server is, by itself, dangerous. When misconfigured, certain Web servers even allow remote users to execute these script with `root` permissions, which can be used by attackers to grant themselves access to the system via other means at a later time. A recent attack managed to simply gain read-only access to the CGI scripts. Although this sounds like an innocent intrusion, in reality users often keep passwords and other sensitive data hard-coded in the CGI scripts, so the user managed to gain access to the system using this information.

In general, you can prevent CGI script intrusions by configuring the Web server to prevent the execution of CGI scripts in random locations. You should train your users in proper programming techniques and provide them with plenty of secure sample CGI script code that they can use.

Buffer Overflows   Although buffer overflows have been around since the genesis of the Internet (remember Robert Morris' worm in 1988?), they have become more prevalent with the advent of the World Wide Web, and more important, Web browsers. By entering an unusually large URL containing actual computer code, the attacker causes the data structure that was meant to hold the URL to overflow, thereby invading the portion of memory where the actual Web server instructions "live," and replacing them with the instructions included in the URL. This allows the attacker to execute random code with the same permissions as the Web server itself.

Make sure that your Web server is not being executed with `root` permissions. Instead, most Linux Web servers start as root (so they can listen on TCP port 80, which is a privileged port), but then fork a nonprivileged child process to provide the actual Web service. Most servers use the username nobody for this purpose.

root Compromises

This is one of the most devastating attacks on a Linux server and one of the most common. The intruder manages to gain root privileges by using one of the following approaches:

- Sniffing the root password
- Guessing the root password
- Browsing through system logs looking for accidental appearances of the root password
- Staging a buffer overflow attack on a vulnerable application to gain root access

It's hard to ensure that the root password is kept under lock and key, so you should simply disable root logins, except perhaps on the system console in the data center (see the discussion in the section "Physical Security" later in this chapter). Instead of logging on as root to do administrative work, use the sudo command that allows regular users to assume root privileges temporarily. Chapter 2 discusses sudo and other system security commands.

TIP It is a good idea to change the root password often and make sure it is not easy to guess. Using a string of random uppercase and lowercase letters with a few numbers thrown in, such as IRGrh954E45ejh, will make it very hard for someone to hack the root password.

Denial of Service (DoS) Attacks

Denial-of-service (DoS) attacks have received global attention in the media lately due to the increasing incidence of attacks on high-profile Web sites. The aim of such attacks is not to steal or modify any private server content, but rather to disabled a public server that offers public content. The preferred method of bringing down a Linux server is to overwhelm it with a large amount of fabricated traffic. A variation on the plain DoS attack is the *distributed DoS* (DDoS) attack, where a large number of traffic sources are used to generate this bogus traffic. These sources are often hijacked systems belonging to unsuspecting users.

Examples of DoS attacks include:

The teardrop attack The attacker floods the victim with a large number of improperly fragmented IP packets.

The synflood attack The attacker opens a large number of TCP connections halfway until the victim's network buffers, which are tied up waiting for the connection to complete, become unavailable.

While there is little that you can do to protect your Linux server from a new DDoS attack, you can prevent it from being hijacked and becoming one of the attackers. By implementing *egress filters* in your Internet routers, you can make sure that the traffic that leaves your network does not have a source address outside of the subnets that make up your private network.

Address Spoofing

This is the attack of choice for packet-filter firewalls. These types of filters are typically configured to ensure that only private—i.e., known—addresses are allowed to initiate connections through the device. It is then relatively easy for attackers to forge their source IP addresses to appear as if they were coming from the inside. Although the return packets will not be forwarded to the attackers (they are pretending to have an internal address, and that's where the response will go), attackers can do plenty of damage by sending packets in the blind. In fact, the point of the attack is usually to set up a root compromise or buffer overflow that allows attackers to open up a back door that they can use to access the system later.

To combat IP address spoofing, you should set up *ingress filters* on your packet-filtering device. (For more information, see Chapter 9.) This ensures that you do not accept packets coming in through the public interface of your firewall with a source that falls within your block of internal addresses. But this defense is a stopgap tactic at best. The real solution is to avoid using address authentication (packet filtering) and resort to cryptographic authentication instead, as for example, SSH.

Session Hijacking

In this specialized form of address spoofing, a TCP session hijacker observes the sequence of numbers in a TCP conversation and impersonates one of the participants by providing the other party with the expected sequence number. The attacker stages a DoS attack on the impersonated party in order to prevent it from continuing to take part in the conversation. When successful, the attacker can issue commands on the remote host as if it were the impersonated party.

You should teach your users to recognize the symptoms of a hijacked session so that they can report these incidents. Most often, they notice that one of their sessions is no longer responding, while other sessions that have been idle for some time are showing unsolicited command output. As with address spoofing, the real solution to the threat of session hijacking is to use an authentication method that is not based solely on IP addresses.

Eavesdropping

One of the most difficult challenges in the expansion of the Internet as a global medium is its public nature, where the privacy and reliability of communications is never guaranteed.

It is surprisingly easy to sniff a network segment and fish for confidential information. In fact, the Linux revolution has exacerbated this problem, since even the most naïve user can use Linux's ability to promiscuously inspect every packet that it sees on the wire. Not only can intruders capture the payload of network packets flying by, but they can also capture password information that they can use to stage a root compromise of the unsuspecting server.

> **WARNING**   You should never, under any circumstance, allow the root password of your Linux server to traverse the network unencrypted.

To protect your root password, you should:

- Disable root logins over the network.
- Disable `telnet`, `rsh`, `rlogin`, and `ftp`.
- Only use Secure Shell (`ssh`) for interactive logins.
- Only use Secure Copy (`scp`) to transfer files to and from the server.

In addition, you should make use of Linux's support for VPN technology, which uses strong cryptography to protect the entire conversation between your Linux server and any other host with which you need to exchange confidential information. Chapter 12 is devoted to the topic of VPNs in the Linux environment.

Trojan Horses

You've all downloaded seemingly useful free software from the Internet, only to find out that its features were largely exaggerated. However, an increasing number of Linux servers are being infected by software that performs a very different task from the one it advertises. These so-called *Trojan horses* are programs that, though disguised as harmless applications, open up a back door through which intruders can exploit the system, often with root privileges. Just like the wooden artifact used by the Greeks to break into Troy during the war, the Trojan horse presents itself as a useful tool and is often partially functional. But even as it appears to serve its advertised purpose, it can cripple or destroy your server and often your entire network.

Trojan horses can be extremely difficult to detect. In fact, they are often disguised as security applications, so you can be shooting yourself in the foot while thinking you're improving the overall security of the server. A good example of this surfaced in January 1999, when it was discovered that a widely distributed version of TCP-Wrappers was actually a Trojan horse. (See Chapter 4, "Network Services Configuration," for a detailed description of TCPWrappers.) While originally designed to monitor and filter transport layer connections, the Trojan horse version of TCPWrappers had been modified to provide root access to would-be intruders.

Another feature common to most Trojan horse programs is their ability to inform attackers of the intrusion, providing them enough detail about your system so that they can stage a successful attack. The Trojan TCPWrappers was designed to send an e-mail to the intruder's address that includes information about the infected system and about the unsuspecting user who installed the program.

You can protect yourself against Trojan horses by following these simple recommendations:

- Download all your software from well-known Internet sites, or well-published mirrors of these primary sites.
- Before you install the software, look for digital signatures or checksums to assure the integrity of downloaded package.
- Make as much standard software as possible available to your users (as long as your security policy allows it). Keep it up to date.
- Periodically monitor Trojan horse advisories from the CERT Coordination Center (www.cert.org).

In addition, you should conduct periodic scans of your server and look for suspicious network ports that are active or in LISTEN state. Listing 1.1 shows an execution of the netstat command that shows a server with a suspicious port (555) in LISTEN state. Note that the command has not been able to resolve port number 555 to a well-known number in the /etc/services file. This is an indication that the daemon is not a standard one and should be investigated further.

Listing 1.1 Execution of the *netstat* command showing a suspicious daemon running on TCP port 555

```
[ramon]$ netstat -a
Active Internet connections (servers and established)
Proto Recv-Q Send-Q Local Address           Foreign Address State
tcp        0      0 *:555                   *:*             LISTEN
tcp        0      0 *:ssh                   *:*             LISTEN
tcp        0      0 *:ftp                   *:*             LISTEN
udp        0      0 *:snmp                  *:*
raw        0      0 *:icmp                  *:*             7
raw        0      0 *:tcp                   *:*             7
Active UNIX domain sockets (servers and established)
Proto RefCnt Flags       Type       State         I-Node Path
```

```
unix  0      [ ACC ]     STREAM      LISTENING     491     /dev/log
unix  1      [ ]         STREAM      CONNECTED     985     @0000003d
unix  1      [ ]         STREAM      CONNECTED     886     @00000039
unix  1      [ ]         STREAM      CONNECTED     959     @0000003c
unix  1      [ ]         STREAM      CONNECTED     554     @00000021
unix  1      [ ]         STREAM      CONNECTED     740     @00000035
unix  0      [ ]         STREAM      CONNECTED     117     @00000013
unix  1      [ ]         STREAM      CONNECTED     744     @00000036
unix  1      [ ]         STREAM      CONNECTED     986     /dev/log
unix  1      [ ]         STREAM      CONNECTED     960     /dev/log
unix  1      [ ]         STREAM      CONNECTED     887     /dev/log
unix  1      [ ]         STREAM      CONNECTED     745     /dev/log
unix  1      [ ]         STREAM      CONNECTED     741     /dev/log
unix  1      [ ]         STREAM      CONNECTED     588     /dev/log
```

Chapter 5 contains a more detailed look into the tools available for monitoring your Linux server for this type of intrusion.

Cryptanalysis and Brute Force Attacks

Most of the cryptographic algorithms in use today have proven to be robust enough to provide an appropriate level of confidentiality, integrity, and authentication. However, there have been several cases where some of these algorithms have been found to be vulnerable to attacks or mathematical exploits where the keyspace (the average number of combinations before the algorithm can be cracked) has been proven to be much smaller than initially thought. (By "mathematical exploits" I mean exploits that take advantage of flaws present in the functions used by the algorithm designers to derive prime numbers, generate keys, add entropy, and so on.)

In 1998 we saw a highly publicized case of cryptanalysis, where renowned security experts Bruce Schneier and "Mudge" discovered a number of security flaws in Microsoft's authentication algorithm for PPTP, a VPN protocol used in the Windows operating system). The MS-CHAP v.1 authentication algorithm was found to be vulnerable to password eavesdropping. In addition, the Microsoft Point-to-Point Encryption Algorithm (MPPE) was also found to be much less effective than the 128-bit key strength that the vendor advertised, thereby exposing the user to eavesdropping attacks on the transmitted data. In 1999, Microsoft released MS-CHAP v.2 as an enhancement of the original version. However, a fundamental flaw still remains; the confidentiality of the VPN transmission is only as strong as the password that users choose for authentication.

There is a Linux version of PPTP (PoPToP, discussed in Chapter 12) that is fully interoperable with the Microsoft implementation and is, therefore, subject to the same password-guessing weakness.

This leads us to our last type of attack: brute force guessing of passwords and keys. As the computing power available to the average user increases at exponential rates, so does the potential for an intruder to guess your password or key. By employing a *brute force* approach, would-be attackers use idle computing power available to them in order to attempt to guess encryption keys until the correct one is found. These are also called *dictionary attacks*, because the attacker often uses a well-known dictionary to try to guess a password, based on the fact that most users tend to choose real words as their passwords.

The power of brute force attacks on cryptographic algorithms was best illustrated in the summer of 1998 when the Electronic Frontier Foundation (EFF) was able to crack the 56-bit key of the DES algorithm using a purpose-built computer at a cost of $250,000. The feasibility of these types of attacks has raised the bar for cryptographic strength, and has raised the awareness of the limitations of even the strongest cryptography in use today.

Now that you've seen who the enemies are and have taken a peek at their weapons of choice, let's take a look at how you can orchestrate an appropriate defense, using some of the layers in the Open Systems Interconnect (OSI) model as a point of reference.

The Layered Approach to Information Security

A lot of work has been devoted to the topic of adding security to the Linux kernel. There is now native kernel support for packet filtering, packet logging, masquerading, and even defense against denial of service attacks. This goes a long way toward securing the system itself, but are you willing to let intruders get all the way into the portals of your servers? An effective security policy is one that starts at the core of the Linux server, but keeps moving outward by including protection mechanisms outside of the system itself. Your defense should cover the network configuration of the server, the network applications that run on the server, the perimeter of the corporate network, and even the remote access clients used by road warriors to access corporate resources from the public Internet.

Let's take a closer look at the considerations that apply to each of these layers. Note that this discussion will work its way outward from the Linux kernel toward the Internet.

Physical Security

This is the most fundamental and often the most overlooked type of Linux server security. Physical security starts with the surroundings of the server itself. Is the room to the data center kept under lock and key? If so, who is allowed to enter the room? Are contractors and maintenance workers escorted? If you're building a new installation or moving into a new location, follow this simple set of guidelines when designing the physical layout of your data center:

- Install magnetic card readers to access the data center. Review the access logs periodically. Look for unusual patterns of access. Ask the users for verification of their log entries.

- Escort maintenance workers and field technicians at all times while in the data center.

- Change the default passwords on terminal servers, remote control devices, and power distribution units. Create accounts for each administrator. Monitor their use.

- Choose Linux servers with a front panel lock to keep intruders from rebooting the machine and from inserting foreign media into the drives.

- Avoid using incoming phone lines to console ports unless it's strictly necessary. Use dial-back modems.

- Enable password-protected screensavers, like xlock and vlock on the X-displays of Linux servers.

- Install a good monitoring device that alerts a human in the event of excessive temperature, smoke, or humidity in the data center.

It's important to keep in mind that the main goal of physical security is to maintain high availability of your server installation. Make sure that your servers are not on the same electrical circuits as receptacles and appliances that are accessible from outside the data center. You would be surprised how much downtime I can create by sticking a screwdriver in an electric receptacle or light socket in the middle of a three-day weekend.

TIP   Providing redundant power supplies is the answer to a lot of these types of problems. If the servers support it, use it!

I don't recommend that you set BIOS and boot-loader passwords, because they will prevent the system from coming up from a reboot without human intervention. This could seriously jeopardize availability unless you have staff available to care for your servers 24/7.

System Security

The most fundamental security requirement of a Linux server is the guarantee that an active nonprivileged user cannot gain access to another user's protected resources or more important, to areas of the system reserved for privileged system accounts. More subtle vulnerabilities include users' abilities to overextend their file quota, CPU use, or maximum number of active processes. All of these violations could constitute the seed of a potential DoS attack, which could render the system or some of its parts temporarily unavailable, or even permanently disabled. Part 1 of this book (Chapters 1 through 3) is devoted to the topic of Linux system security.

Network Security

Securing the system from the potential mischief of employees or users who are otherwise in good standing is a great step forward, but it only covers the case where the system is isolated from the outside world. This is clearly not a realistic prospect, since most Linux servers are deployed to serve the user population over a network that is often public. Thus, the diligent Linux administrator should carefully evaluate the server's physical connection to the network, including all its interfaces, their TCP/IP configurations, and, most important, the configuration of the server's active network daemons. Part 2 of this book, "Network Security" (Chapters 4 and 5), describes the details of network security, including practical strategies and the tools available for securing your network.

Application Security

Some of the daemons that come standard in today's Linux distributions are actually full-fledged applications with a fairly complex set of configuration files. Unlike simple `telnet` and FTP daemons, Web, mail, and file servers use complex protocols. In order to protect these services, network administrators must deploy a security defense particular to each protocol. These application-specific mechanisms are the topic of Part 3 of this book, "Application Security" (Chapters 6 through 8).

Perimeter Security

The firewall is the workhorse of network security. Firewalls are a pivotal part of a complete security solution, protecting the perimeter of the local area network where it connects to the public Internet. While the main purpose of a firewall is to keep unwanted traffic out of the local network, this is also the place where you can log all the traffic going into and out of the network. While most firewalls are dual-homed (two network interfaces), some have additional interfaces that you can use to attach bastion and extranet servers, whose access permissions are such that they need to be physically segregated from the local area network. Firewalls and their role in perimeter security are covered in Part 4 of this book, "Perimeter Security" (Chapters 9 through 11).

Remote Access and Authentication

Just about the time when system administrators managed to get a handle on network security, virtual private networks appeared on the scene, and administrators' jobs got a whole lot tougher. The network perimeter now extends to all the systems that connect to it remotely, at least for the duration of the dial-in session. VPN standards like IPSec and PPTP provide a common framework for data privacy, but they do not completely address the issue of authentication, and they fail to cover the issue of authorization and access control. Part 5, "Remote Access and Authentication" (Chapters 12 and 13), discusses the topic of virtual private networking and remote access security.

Human Security

Regardless of how much time and energy you devote to developing a sound security strategy, humans are ultimately at the controls, and they are often the weakest link in the information security chain. The most air-tight of perimeter defenses can be rendered totally useless by an insider with an axe to grind, and the strongest password policy cannot cope with users who write their passwords on yellow sticky notes and paste them on their monitor.

Conducting security awareness training and monitoring security policy compliance is a step in the right direction, but as is often the case, there are many other less tangible factors that contribute to the security of your server installation. Employees who are disgruntled or just bored present a considerable risk to your enterprise, especially those who have access to sensitive information that could be used by a competitor.

There is no substitute for a satisfied employee who is challenged by the work and rewarded for his or her effort. While ethics and behavior are difficult to monitor and enforce, it is just as effective to ensure employees' good morale and motivation. A yearly company picnic and a generous performance incentive bonus program could be your company's best investment in information security.

> ***WARNING*** If you have to fire disgruntled employees, you or a member of the security staff should escort them out of the building and make sure that they are not permitted to touch any computer before they leave. Even before you fire them, you should have their access removed and passwords changed. Otherwise, you are inviting disaster.

In Sum

Security is often a poorly understood topic. There is often too much emphasis on tools and not enough emphasis on procedures and methods. An efficient security defense should start with a comprehensive security policy upon which you can build an appropriate set of mechanisms. Remember that security is a process!

The goal of information security is to ensure confidentiality, integrity, authentication, and availability of the data on your servers. Cryptography is the only viable way to ensure that data is properly protected as it is exchanged over the Internet.

There is a diverse array of vulnerabilities and types of attacks that you need to be prepared to defend against. The only way to put up and maintain an effective defense is to start with the system and work your way out toward the perimeter, considering each layer separately. Don't forget to account for remote access to your Linux server.

We'll start the detailed discussion of this layered approach by taking a close look at system security in the next chapter.

2

System Installation and Setup

The previous chapter, "Understanding Linux Security," offers an overview of the most important concepts in information security in general, and Linux server security in particular. This chapter starts drilling into the details by discussing the security implications of the following Linux server administration tasks:

- Choosing a Linux distribution
- Building a secure kernel
- User account security
- File and directory permissions
- `syslog` security
- Filesystem encryption

Note that you will be taking on these tasks before you even connect your server to the network. Although most of us associate security with network layer services, a number of important security issues must be decided during the setup and configuration of the system itself. This chapter guides you through the process of choosing the distribution that is best suited for your security needs and goes on to offer specific advice on how to configure your kernel to maximize system and network security. Finally, this chapter gives you practical advice on securing the accounts and the filesystem to ensure that you can offer your users an adequate level of protection against attacks from other legitimate, or seemingly legitimate, system users. You'll learn how to minimize the exposure of your root user, and you'll learn about the tools available to implement filesystem encryption on your Linux server.

Let's start by taking a look at the process of selecting a Linux distribution that's right for you.

Choosing a Linux Distribution

A crucial step in building a secure Linux server is selecting the distribution that best fits the needs outlined in your security policy. This decision is going to determine much of your success in installing and maintaining a secure Linux server. But what exactly makes a distribution "secure?" Here is a set of criteria to consider before making that decision:

- Does the vendor have a well-known mechanism to report security vulnerabilities found in its distribution?
- Does the vendor issue periodic security advisories that warn users of vulnerabilities found in its distribution?
- How often are security issues resolved? Does the vendor devote a well-delineated portion of its Web or FTP site to security information (patches, security updates, etc.)?
- How often does the vendor release general distribution upgrades? A slow-moving release schedule is likely to prolong the exposure of known vulnerabilities.
- Does the vendor offer an intuitive, easy-to-use tool for installing and updating software packages?
- Does the vendor support open source efforts to improve Linux security or to create vendor-neutral security scripts and tools?
- How long has the vendor has been in existence?
- Have the previous versions been secure and well maintained?

As with any other choice of Linux software, there is no clear winner here, but you can make a more educated decision by finding out the vendor's general stance in these areas. The following sections look at the most prominent Linux distributions and examine the security features of each one.

Red Hat

As the most successful Linux vendor to date, Red Hat has been able to devote considerable resources to the tracking, dissemination, and resolution of security flaws in the packages that it distributes. However, as of the writing of this book, their Web site still lacks a separate security section where Linux administrators can see all of Red Hat's security patches at a glance. That said, they do seem to keep up to date on the security issues that come up in their versions.

Their RPM package management system is the industry standard, and their release schedule calls for a major revision every six months or so, which ensures that you're always running recent (and often more secure) software packages. This schedule is a good compromise between having up-to-date software and avoiding the "bleeding edge" of the latest (and often unstable) versions of most tools.

Red Hat's numbering scheme seems to make use of the .0 minor number for an initial major release (e.g. 7.0) and .1 and .2 for the subsequent maintenance updates. If you opt for Red Hat, I recommend that you try to upgrade up from a .0 release as soon as the update is available. You may want to wait until they release the 7.1 or later version to make sure that any critical bugs have been fixed in the previous version.

Caldera

Rivaling Red Hat's success, Caldera's OpenLinux has grown into a major player in the Linux distribution market. Unlike Red Hat, Caldera maintains two separate release lines for clients (eDesktop) and servers (eServer). Both of these packages are now in a stable release line, although new versions are usually not available as often as Red Hat's.

Like Red Hat, Caldera offers a well-laid-out mechanism for updating releases by downloading the appropriate packages (also in RPM format) from its FTP site. Caldera seems to be increasingly committed to offering a security-minded distribution, and most vulnerabilities are addressed by software updates within one or two days of being identified.

Security advisories for OpenLinux can be found at `http://www.calderasystems.com/support/security/` (see Figure 2.1). This is the longest running resource of its kind, and it includes a chronological list of advisories for all OpenLinux packages and all the available patches or solutions.

Figure 2.1 OpenLinux security advisories

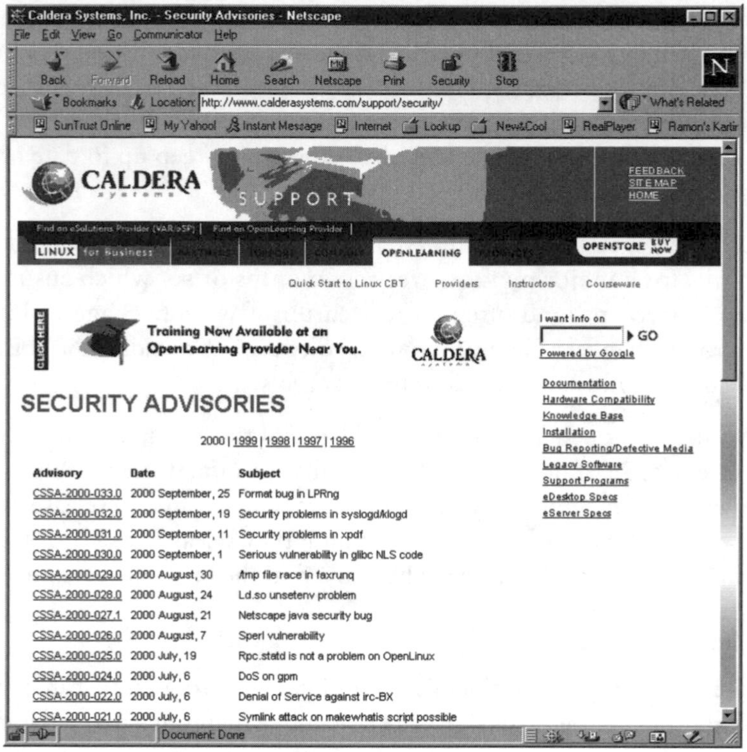

SuSE

An extremely popular distribution in the European market, SuSE offers a full-featured set of supported packages (six CDs worth of them!) and also uses the RPM package management system. Their release schedule is similar to Red Hat's with the .0 minor numbers signaling the initial offering of a major release. However, they typically offer up to four minor releases (e.g., 6.4) before moving on to another major version. Red Hat, on the other hand, generally has only two minor releases with each version.

One of SuSE's distinguishing characteristics is the inclusion of the `seccheck` script that can be periodically invoked from `cron`, to test the overall security of the system in a number of areas. The vendor also includes a utility that you can use to "harden" your server installation (`harden_suse`). This is a sign that this vendor is concerned with security and is willing to spend development and maintenance resources to prove it.

You can find this vendor's security clearinghouse at `http://www.suse.de/security` (see Figure 2.2), including a comprehensive list of advisories and pointers to their two security-related mailing lists.

Figure 2.2   SuSE security page on the World Wide Web

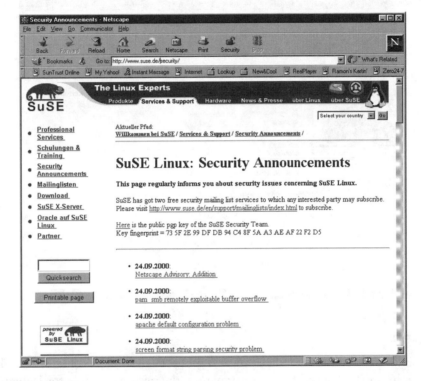

Turbolinux

This vendor has been in the Linux market since 1992 and has had a great deal of success in the Asian and European markets. Even though it has not been embraced as widely as Red Hat and Caldera in the U.S., it has gained a lot of momentum in recent months, especially in the high-end server application market.

The Turbolinux release schedule is significantly longer than Red Hat's and Caldera's, but they maintain a list of security updates for each release at `http://www.turbolinux.com/security` (see Figure 2.3). They also include a separate security subdirectory for each release update section in their FTP site.

Figure 2.3 Turbolinux Security Center page on the World Wide Web

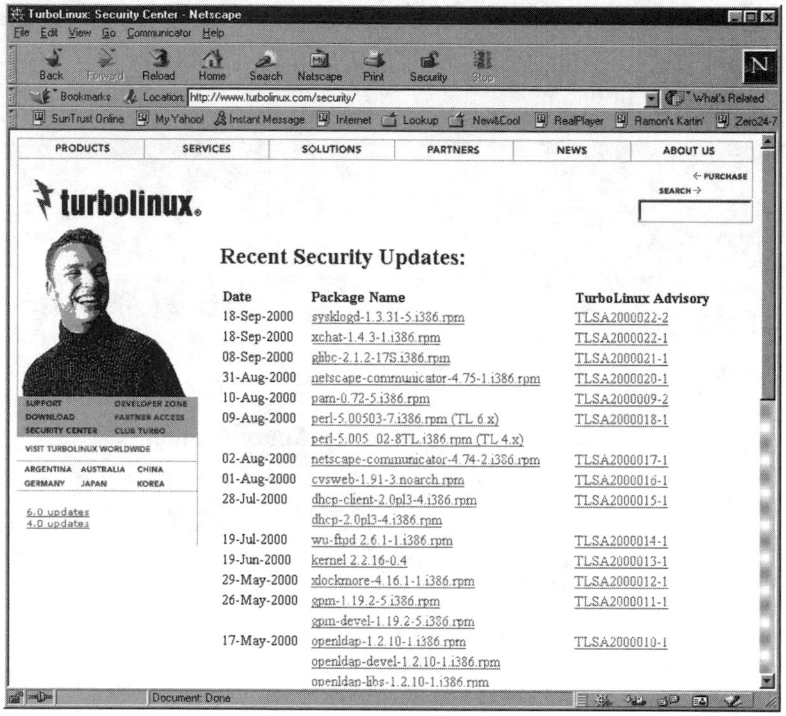

Debian

This Linux distribution is maintained by a group of about 500 volunteer developers around the world. Due to its nonprofit nature, the release schedule for Debian's Linux distribution is different from most commercial vendors', focusing on small interim minor releases rather than major updates. These small releases are often driven by a number of security fixes, and are usually about 100 days apart.

Unlike most commercial vendors, Debian has a clearinghouse for security information at http://security.debian.org that you can use for this purpose (see Figure 2.4). This is one of the most straightforward vendor security sites available. The content is well organized, and the security advisories are easier to find than those of the other vendors. In addition, the page includes links to the archives of the Debian-specific security mailing list going back at least two years.

Figure 2.4   Debian's security page on the World Wide Web

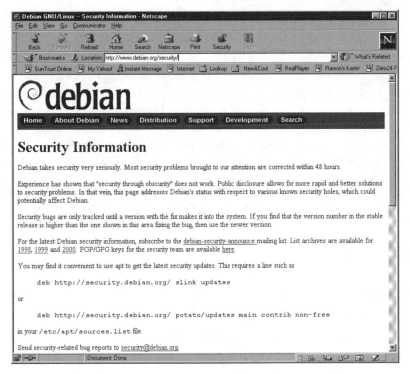

And the Winner Is...

All Linux distributions can be made secure, and all vendors are making an effort to keep users informed of vulnerabilities and patch availability. Although each vendor seems to excel in a different aspect of security, there are no clear winners or losers here.

Your choice of a Linux distribution should depend on your administration style. If you're willing to spend some time every few days catching up with the latest vulnerabilities, and you're willing to install incremental patches as needed, Debian is a good choice for you. If instead you prefer to bundle security updates with vendor releases, I recommend that you opt for a more actively updated distribution, such as Red Hat, Caldera, SuSE, or Turbolinux.

In either case, you should plan to make use of the security resources of your vendor of choice, including a daily scan through their Web page and a subscription to their security mailing list. In addition, you should monitor the BugTraq mailing list (`http://www.securityfocus.com/forums/bugtraq/`) for vulnerabilities common to all Linux vendors.

Building a Secure Kernel

While most Linux users are content to run the standard kernel provided in the latest distribution, you'll need to become familiar with the process of downloading the kernel sources, modifying their configuration, and building a custom kernel. The advantages of building a custom kernel are twofold: You're specifying the security options that you want, and you are also building a lean kernel, compiling only the driver support that you need. Another benefit to compiling your own kernel is that you know what is in it and can see any security holes that may need to be addressed in the future or immediately (if the holes are big enough). In addition, the solution to many security vulnerabilities comes in the form of a patch to be applied to the Linux kernel, which requires you to recompile the kernel.

The first step in building a custom kernel is to obtain the kernel sources. If you're using Red Hat, you need both the `kernel-headers` and `kernel-source` RPM packages. To install either of those packages, use one of the following commands:

```
[root]# rpm -q kernel-headers
kernel-headers-2.2.12-20
[root]# rpm -q kernel-source
kernel-source-2.2.12-20
```

These two packages populate the `/usr/src/linux` directory, which should contain all the source and configuration files necessary to compile the Linux kernel from scratch.

TIP Before you install your new kernel, create an emergency boot disk in case the new kernel has problems booting. On Red Hat, use the command: `mkbootdisk --device /dev/fd0 2.2.12-20` (assuming that your system modules directory is `/lib/modules/2.2.12-20`).

Logged on as root, go to the Linux source directory and clean up any lingering configurations from previous kernel builds using the following commands:

```
[root]# cd /usr/local/linux
[root]# make mrproper
```

At this point, you're ready to specify the options that you'd like to build into the kernel using this command:

```
[root]# make config
```

This command prompts you for a series of options that you can choose to add to your kernel (Y), leave out (N), or add as a dynamically loaded module (M). Table 2.1 shows the 2.2.X kernel options that have security implications, and should be set to the appropriate value during the make config step.

Table 2.1   Kernel Configuration: Recommended Security Options

Configure Option	Description	Recommendation
CONFIG_PACKET	Protocol used by applications to communicate with network devices without a need for an intermediate kernel protocol	Y
CONFIG_NETLINK	Two-way communication between the kernel and user processes	Y
CONFIG_FIREWALL	Firewalling support	Y
CONFIG_INET	Internet (TCP/IP) protocols	Y
CONFIG_IP_FIREWALL	IP packet-filtering support	Y
CONFIG_SYN_COOKIES	Protection against synflooding denial of service attacks	Y
CONFIG_NET_IPIP	IP inside IP encapsulation	N
CONFIG_IP_ROUTER	IP routing	N
CONFIG_IP_FORWARD	IP packet forwarding (routing)	N
CONFIG_IP_MULTICAST	IP Multicast (transmission of one data stream for multiple destinations)	N

NOTE   These are the recommended settings for a typical Linux single-homed server. Later on in this book, you'll learn about the concept of Linux firewalls, which are typically multi-homed and often require a different kernel configuration. We will discuss these special systems, including their kernel configurations in Part 4 of this book, "Perimeter Security."

System Security

PART 1

The CONFIG_SYN_COOKIES option prevents the kernel from entering a deadlock state whenever its incoming connection buffers are filled with half-open TCP connections. Note that in the 2.2.X kernels, setting CONFIG_SYN_COOKIES simply enables the option, but does not actually activate it. You must enter the following to activate SYN_COOKIES support:

```
[root]# echo 1 > /proc/sys/net/ipv4/tcp_syncookies
```

The CONFIG_IP_ROUTER and CONFIG_IP_FORWARD options allow a multi-homed Linux server to forward packets from one interface to another. This option should be disabled because there is a possibility that an intruder could use your Linux server as a router, circumventing the normal path of entry into your network (the one you are policing).

The final step before actually compiling the kernel sources is to build a list of dependencies using this command:

```
[root]# make dep
```

Now you're ready to compile your new kernel. Execute the following command to compile and link a compressed kernel image:

```
[root]# make zImage
```

If you have chosen loadable module support during the make config step above, you'll also need to execute the following commands:

```
[root]# make modules
[root]# make modules_install
```

To boot the new kernel, you must first move it from the source directory to its final destination. Make a backup of the old image first using these commands:

```
[root]# cp /zImage /zImage.BACKUP
[root]# mv /usr/src/linux/arch/i386/boot/zImage /zImage
[root]# /sbin/lilo
```

Re-run lilo every time you update the kernel image on your hard drive. In addition, it is a good idea to create a separate lilo.conf entry for your backup kernel (/zImage.BACKUP), even though you have an emergency boot diskette, because planning for disasters is an important part of security. When you are updating your version of Linux, it is always good to be able to go back to the old version if the newer one does not work as it should. See *Linux Network Servers 24seven* by Craig Hunt (Sybex, 1999) if you need more information about lilo and lilo.conf.

You should now restart your system to make sure that you can boot the new kernel. Don't forget to have your emergency boot disk close by in case there are problems.

> **WARNING**   Be prepared for the worst, because if you aren't prepared, the worst is going to happen to you.

User Account Security

The CSI/FBI Computer Crime and Security Survey (http://www.gocsi.com/prelea_000321.htm) shows, year after year, that the overwhelming majority of successful system attacks come from insiders—that is, disgruntled (or just bored) nonprivileged users who manage to gain root authority through subversive means. Even when the attack comes from the outside, seizing a misconfigured or stagnant user account is one of the easiest ways to crack access to root. It's also important to protect against your own mistakes, since root access can be a powerful and dangerous tool, even in the proper hands.

You should pay special attention to the part of your security policy that regulates the creation and maintenance of user accounts. Here is my recommended set of considerations for managing your Linux server accounts:

Disable inactive accounts.   Attackers look for accounts that have not been accessed for awhile in order to seize them for their nefarious ends. This gives attackers the luxury of being able to "squat" the account and hide their exploits without being noticed or reported. Most Linux distributions allow you to specify the conditions under which an account should be disabled. I recommend that you disable all accounts as soon as the password expires (more on password expiration later), while allowing users a week to change their passwords before they expire. Red Hat's linuxconf provides a graphical interface to specify this policy (see Figure 2.5).

I usually set passwords to expire every 4 months (120 days), and allow users 7 days to change their passwords. The 0 value under Account Expire After # Days simply directs the system to disable the account if the password expires. The default value of –1 directs the system never to cause the account to expire, so make sure you change this default.

Figure 2.5 Setting user account expiration parameters with *linuxconf*

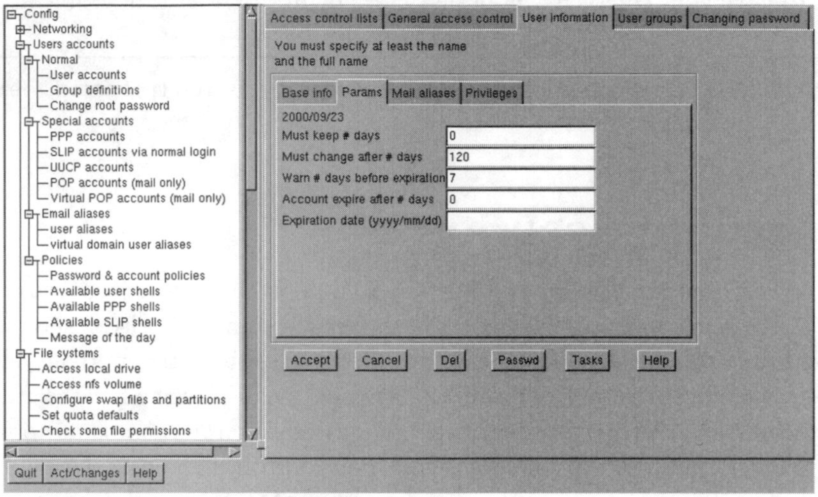

Disable root access across NFS mounts. Pay special attention to the /etc/exports file, where you declare the local filesystems that you'd like to share via Network File System (NFS). By default, the NFS server on most Linux distributions maps user ID 0 (root) to a nonprivileged user, like nobody. This behavior, however, can be overridden by the no_root_squash option in the NFS server's /etc/exports file. Avoid this option at all costs. It leaves your entire NFS server at the mercy of a root user on any of your clients.

See *Linux NFS and Automounter Administration* by Erez Zadok (Sybex, 2001) if you have set up your Linux clients to mount remote NFS shares automatically.

Restrict the use of your root user to when it's absolutely necessary. You should resist the temptation to log on to root to execute an administration command, and stay logged on to execute other user-level commands. The longer you're logged on as root, the longer you're exposed to a number of vulnerabilities, such as Trojan horses and session hijacking.

Use a descriptive root prompt. Sometimes you are your worst enemy. When you have several terminals active on your X-display, it's important to be able to tell at a glance which ones are root terminals. This helps you avoid executing a user-level command on a root window by mistake. Make sure the root prompt is distinctive enough and that it includes a root-specific character, such as a sharp sign (#).

Use a minimal *$PATH* for your root account. A common attack on the root account is to place Trojan horse versions of frequently used utilities in a directory that is included in the root $PATH. This is a very subtle attack, and the only way to protect against it is to ensure that you know the contents of your $PATH variable, and the contents of the directories included in the variable. To minimize the chance of running a Trojan horse, avoid having directories in your $PATH that are writeable by any user other than root.

Use special-purpose system accounts.   An operator who simply needs to shut down the system does not need full root privileges. That's the purpose of default Linux accounts such as operator and shutdown. In addition, I recommend that you install and use sudo, which is described in detail in the section "The sudo Utility" later in this chapter.

Use group memberships.   As a Linux administrator, you'll often be asked to make a file or directory available for reading and writing to several users who are collaborating on a single task. While it is easy to simply make these resources world-writeable, don't do it. Take the time to add a new group, make each of the users a member of this group, and make the resources accessible only to members of the group. Think of files with wide-open permissions as vulnerabilities waiting to be exploited.

Restrict root logins to the system console.   To monitor who is logging in as root, configure the /etc/securetty file to allow direct root access only from the console. This action forces authorized root users to use su or sudo to gain root privileges, thus allowing you to easily log these events. The standard Linux default is to allow root logins only from the eight virtual system consoles (function keys on the keyboard):

```
[root]# more /etc/securetty
tty1
tty2
tty3
tty4
tty5
tty6
tty7
tty8
```

Aside from the logging advantage, this is an extra hurdle in the event that the root password becomes compromised. Intruders would have to first gain access to a regular user's account (or to the physical console) to exploit their finding.

Using good user account practices is paramount in ensuring the security of your system, but by choosing a poor password, users can undermine all the work you have done to protect their accounts. The next section offers some practical advice on choosing strong passwords and enforcing their use.

Good Passwords

While stronger modes of authentication are becoming increasingly commonplace, the username and password remain the most widely used method of authentication for Linux servers. Much has been said and written about the importance of password security, so I'll keep this discussion brief and to the point. There are some very simple rules to follow that can go a long way toward locking down your password policy:

Don't set your system to cause passwords to expire too quickly.   If the period between password expirations is too short, users are more likely to feel that they'll forget their passwords, so they will write them down. In addition, users will use cyclic, predictable password patterns. When it comes to password expiration, anything less than three months should be considered too short.

Don't allow your passwords to get stale.   Conversely, if you allow your users to have the same password for a year, they're exposing it for a longer time than is safe. Four months is a good compromise, but six months is not an unreasonably long expiration period.

Avoid short passwords.   Force your users to pick passwords that are at least six characters in length. Anything shorter than that is too easy to guess using brute force attacks, even if random characters are chosen. Figure 2.6 illustrates how you can enforce a password length minimum using a systems administration tool like Red Hat's `linuxconf`. Note that in addition to enforcing the six-character limit, this page forces the user to use a minimum of two non-alphanumeric characters.

Crack your own passwords.   As part of your periodic system security audit, use password-guessing tools to look for weak passwords in your `/etc/passwd` file. Contact the guilty users directly and suggest to them that they use longer passwords, with more non-alphanumeric characters, with a mix of uppercase and lowercase characters. Chapter 3, "System Monitoring and Auditing," discusses this topic in more detail, when it formally introduces the `crack` utility.

Delete unused accounts.   Most Linux servers don't offer UUCP, PPP, NNTP, Gopher, or Postgres services, yet most Linux distributions ship with these accounts. Completely remove these accounts, and any others that don't make sense in your environment.

Figure 2.6   Setting password length parameters with *linuxconf*

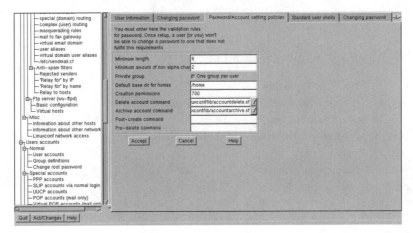

Avoid empty password fields.   Never set up users with no password, even if their shell is highly restricted. Gaining access to any user on your system gets intruders halfway to their destination.

An effective way to minimize the risk associated with user passwords is to configure support for shadow password and group files. This is the topic of the next section.

Shadow Passwords

One of the easiest system vulnerabilities to overlook is the ability by any user to *crack* another user's password. This can be done quickly and easily, using tools readily available on the Internet. To prevent this, enable *shadow passwords*. Shadow passwords split the password files into two: the /etc/passwd file, which contains a place-holder in the actual password field entries, and the /etc/shadow file, which contains the encrypted password. The /etc/shadow file does not need to be readable by anyone except root, which makes it more difficult for a regular user to attempt to crack another user's password (including root).

Most Linux distributions also support the concept of *shadow groups*, where the actual members of each group are not listed in the main /etc/group file, but rather, in the /etc/gshadow file, which, like the /etc/shadow file, is readable only by root.

TIP   Some Linux distributions do not have shadow passwords enabled by default; if your distribution is one of these, enable this feature right away.

Listing 2.1 shows how you should look for the existence of the /etc/shadow file. If it does not exist, simply create it with the pwconv command. Note the change in the /etc/passwd file after the conversion:

Listing 2.1   Creating a shadow password file

```
[root]# ls -l /etc/shadow
ls: /etc/shadow: No such file or directory
[root]# more /etc/passwd
root:PV/67t9IGeTjU:0:0:root:/root:/bin/bash
bin:*:1:1:bin:/bin:
daemon:*:2:2:daemon:/sbin:
adm:*:3:4:adm:/var/adm:
lp:*:4:7:lp:/var/spool/lpd:
sync:*:5:0:sync:/sbin:/bin/sync
shutdown:*:6:0:shutdown:/sbin:/sbin/shutdown
halt:*:7:0:halt:/sbin:/sbin/halt
mail:*:8:12:mail:/var/spool/mail:
operator:*:11:0:operator:/root:
ftp:*:14:50:FTP User:/home/ftp:
nobody:*:99:99:Nobody:/:
ramon:aa1g0.pAVx2uA:501:100:Ramon J. Hontanon:/home/ramon:/bin/bash
[root]# pwconv
[root]# ls -l /etc/shadow
-r--------   1 root     root            563 Sep 23 15:27 /etc/shadow
[root]# more /etc/passwd
root:x:0:0:root:/root:/bin/bash
bin:x:1:1:bin:/bin:
daemon:x:2:2:daemon:/sbin:
adm:x:3:4:adm:/var/adm:
lp:x:4:7:lp:/var/spool/lpd:
sync:x:5:0:sync:/sbin:/bin/sync
shutdown:x:6:0:shutdown:/sbin:/sbin/shutdown
halt:x:7:0:halt:/sbin:/sbin/halt
mail:x:8:12:mail:/var/spool/mail:
operator:x:11:0:operator:/root:
ftp:x:14:50:FTP User:/home/ftp:
nobody:x:99:99:Nobody:/:
ramon:x:501:100:Ramon J. Hontanon:/home/ramon:/bin/bash
[root]# more /etc/shadow
root:PV/67t9IGeTjU:11223:0:99999:7:::
bin:*:11223:0:99999:7:::
```

```
daemon:*:11223:0:99999:7:::
adm:*:11223:0:99999:7:::
lp:*:11223:0:99999:7:::
sync:*:11223:0:99999:7:::
shutdown:*:11223:0:99999:7:::
halt:*:11223:0:99999:7:::
mail:*:11223:0:99999:7:::
operator:*:11223:0:99999:7:::
ftp:*:11223:0:99999:7:::
nobody:*:11223:0:99999:7:::
ramon:aa1g0.pAVx2uA:11223:0:99999:7
```

The next section of this chapter discusses the sudo utility, a useful tool to minimize the exposure of the root password to your Linux server.

The *sudo* Utility

During the normal course of administering my Linux systems, I often go several weeks before actually logging on as the root user. In fact, there have been times when I have come close to forgetting the root password. The sudo utility affords me this luxury, and I recommend that you install this tool on every system that you administer. By allowing the system administrator to predefine root access for regular users, sudo can be used to execute commands with root privileges in lieu of actually logging in as root, and exposing the root password on the network. In general, the less often the root password is actually typed, the more secure it will be.

Installing *sudo*

You can download sudo in both RPM and source format. I recommend that you use the RPM package system to install it, since the default compilation parameters are typically rational, and there is very little need for customization.

Let's start the installation by ensuring that sudo is not already present:

```
[root]# rpm -q sudo
sudo-1.5.9p4-1
```

In this case, you do have a previous installation of sudo, but it's out of date, so delete it and install a more current version using the following commands:

```
[root]# rpm -e sudo
[root]# rpm -i ./sudo-1.6.3p5-1rh62.i386.rpm
[root]# rpm -q sudo
sudo-1.6.3p5-1
```

You now have installed the sudo utility. Make sure you take a look through /usr/doc for the documentation that comes with the source package before you start using the tool.

The *sudoers* file

As with any Linux utility, sudo comes with a configuration file where you can customize its operation. This file is in /etc/sudoers by default, and contains, among other things, the list of users who should be allowed to run the sudo command, along with the set of commands that each sudo user is allowed to execute.

The general format used to add users to this file is as follows:

```
userhost(s)=command(s)[run_as_user(s)]
```

For example, if you'd like to grant user alice permission to run the shutdown command, you specify the following:

```
alice ALL = /etc/shutdown
```

Note that the ALL directive can be used as a wildcard for any fields in the sudoers file. Let's consider another example where user bob is given access to all root commands, as any user:

```
bob ALL = ALL
```

And finally, let's consider the case where you'd like user charlie to be allowed to run su to become user operator:

```
charlie ALL = /bin/su operator
```

> **WARNING** If you're using sudo to grant a user root access to a limited set of commands, make sure that none of these commands allow an "escape" to a Linux shell, because that would give the user unrestricted root access to *all* system commands. Note that some Linux editors (e.g., vi) include this shell escape feature.

Using *sudo*

The basic usage of the sudo command is as follows:

```
sudo [command line options] [username] [command]
```

Table 2.2 contains a summary of the most important sudo command-line options.

Table 2.2   *sudo* command-line options

Option	Parameter	Purpose
-v	N/A	Prints out the current version.
-l	N/A	Lists the allowed and forbidden commands for this user.
-h	N/A	Prints usage message.
-b	N/A	Runs command in the background.
-u	username	Runs the command as the specified username (default is root).

For example, to show the contents of the shadow password directory, simply use:

```
sudo cat /etc/shadow
```

To edit a file in a user's directory preserving his or her permissions:

```
sudo -u fred vi /export/home/fred/.forward
```

I recommend that you use the sudo command strictly to log the root activity of users who are fully trusted to execute any root command on your Linux server (including yourself), rather than using it to allow certain users the execution of a small set of system utilities. It is relatively easy for a user to maliciously extend the privilege of a given command by executing an escape command to the root shell.

The following section describes sudo's logging features, as well as the format of the sudo log file.

The *sudo.log* file

By default, sudo logs all its activity to the file /var/log/sudo.log. The format of entries into this file is as follows:

date:*user*:HOST=*hostname*:TTY=*terminal*:PWD=*dir*:USER=*user*:COMMAND=*cmd*

Each of these fields has the following meaning:

- *date*: the timestamp of the log entry
- *user*: the username that executed sudo
- *hostname*: the host address on which the sudo command was executed
- *terminal*: controlling terminal from which sudo was invoked
- *dir*: current directory from which the command was invoked

- *user*: username that the command was run as
- *command*: the command that was executed through sudo

For example, Listing 2.2 illustrates a typical sudo.log file showing six entries, all executed by username ramon, invoking commands to be run as root.

Listing 2.2   Contents of the *sudo.log* file

```
Sep 23 14:41:37 : ramon : HOST=redhat : TTY=pts/0 ; PWD=/home/ramon⤶
; USER=root ; COMMAND=/bin/more /etc/shadow
Sep 23 14:43:42 : ramon : HOST=redhat : TTY=pts/0 ; PWD=/home/ramon⤶
; USER=root ; COMMAND=/usr/sbin/pwconv
Sep 23 14:43:51 : ramon : HOST=redhat : TTY=pts/0 ; PWD=/home/ramon⤶
; USER=root ; COMMAND=/bin/more /etc/shadow
Sep 23 14:55:30 : ramon : HOST=redhat : TTY=pts/0 ; PWD=/home/ramon⤶
; USER=root ; COMMAND=/bin/cat /etc/securetty
Sep 23 15:12:27 : ramon : HOST=redhat : TTY=pts/1 ; PWD=/home/ramon⤶
; USER=root ; COMMAND=/bin/linuxconf
Sep 23 15:23:37 : ramon : HOST=redhat : TTY=pts/0 ; PWD=/home/ramon⤶
; USER=root ; COMMAND=/usr/sbin/pwunconv
```

File and Directory Permissions

Perhaps one of the most difficult aspects of Linux administration, file permissions are a vital aspect of system security, and as such, an entire section of this book is devoted to their discussion. Linux (like all Unix variants) treats most resources as files, whether they're directories, disk devices, pipes, or terminals. While this makes for straightforward software architecture, it also introduces a fundamental challenge to the Linux administrator charged with ensuring the security of these resources.

Permissions on files and directories have a direct effect on the security of your system. Make the permissions too tight and you limit users' ability to get their work done. Make permissions too lax and you invite unauthorized use of other users' files and general system resources.

The next subsection of this book examines the specifics of suid and sgid permissions on the Linux operating system.

suid and *sgid*

Linux supports device and file permissions for three distinct groups of users, each of which is represented by three bits of information in the permissions mask, in addition to two special-purpose high-order bits, for a total of 12 bits:

AAABBBCCCDDD

Each of these bits has the following meaning:

AAA   setuid, setgid, sticky-bit

BBB   user (read, write, execute)

CCC   group (read, write, execute)

DDD   other (read, write, execute)

Thus, if we have a new executable file called report that we want read, written, and executed only by the file's owner, but read and executed by everybody else, we would set its permissions to the appropriate bit-mask value as follows:

```
[ramon]$ chmod 0755 report
[ramon]$ ls -l report
-rwxr-xr-x  1 ramon    users        19032 Sep 25 19:48 report
```

Note that 7 is the octal representation of the binary number 111. The permissions displayed include only three bits per portion (user, group, other), while in reality, Linux allows you to specify four bits for each of the groups. This is addressed by overloading the representation of the third bit with the following values:

x   execute

s   execute + [setuid or setgid] (applicable only to the user and group portions)

S   [setuid or setgid] (applicable only to the user and group portions)

t   execute + sticky (applicable only to the other portion)

T   sticky (applicable only to the other portion)

Now consider the case where you'd like this file to be executed with root permissions because it has to read and write to privileged areas of the filesystem, but you would like nonprivileged users to be able to execute it. You can achieve this by setting the very first bit of the permissions mask as follows:

```
[ramon]$ sudo chown root:root report
[ramon]$ sudo chmod 4755 report
[ramon]$ ls -l report
-rwsr-xr-x  1 root     root         19032 Sep 25 20:30 report
```

As discussed earlier, s in the user portion of the permissions mask denotes that the setuid and execute bits are set for the user (file owner). This means that the file will execute with the user permissions of the file owner (root) instead of the executing user (ramon). In addition, you can set the setgid bit in order to have the file execute with the group permissions of root, as follows:

```
[ramon]$ sudo chmod 6755 report
[ramon]$ ls -l report
-rwsr-sr-x   1 root      root          19032 Sep 25 20:30 report
```

The third bit in the permissions mask is often referred to as the *sticky bit,* and is used in directories to signal the Linux kernel that it should not allow a user to delete another user's files, even if the directory is world-writeable. This is most often used in the /tmp directory, which has wide-open permissions:

```
[ramon]$ ls -ld /tmp
drwxrwxrwt   7 root      root           1024 Sep 25 21:05 /tmp
```

Note the final t in the mask. This prevents you from deleting your fellow user's files in that directory unless they explicitly allow you to do so by setting write permissions for others.

In general, use of setuid and setgid should be restricted to those partitions that are only writeable by root. I recommend that you explicitly disallow use of setuid/setgid on the /home directory, by specifying the nosuid option in the /etc/fstab file, as shown in Listing 2.3.

Listing 2.3 Contents of the */etc/fstab* file

```
[ramon]$ cat /etc/fstab
/dev/sda8          /            ext2    defaults             1 1
/dev/sda1          /boot        ext2    defaults             1 2
/dev/sda6          /home        ext2    exec,nodev,nosuid,rw 1 2
/dev/sda5          /usr         ext2    defaults             1 2
/dev/sda7          /var         ext2    defaults             1 2
/dev/sda9          swap         swap    defaults             0 0
/dev/fd0           /mnt/floppy  ext2    noauto               0 0
/dev/cdrom         /mnt/cdrom   iso9660 noauto,ro            0 0
none               /proc        proc    defaults             0 0
none               /dev/pts     devpts  mode=0622            0 0
```

Figure 2.7 illustrates how this option can be specified from Red Hat's linuxconf utility.

Figure 2.7   Setting the nosuid option on a local filesystem with *linuxconf*

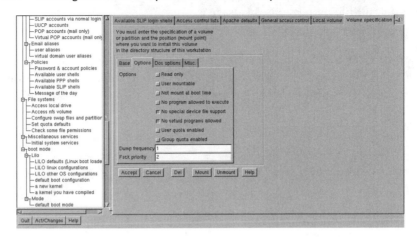

Also, note that the No Special Device File Support option (option nodev in /etc/fstab) is selected. This effectively prevents a user from creating a block device in the /home filesystem, which would be considered a highly suspect action by a nonprivileged user.

Having taken these precautions, you still need to be vigilant of the setuid/setgid present in your Linux server. I suggest that you run this command in cron, piping its output to an e-mail report to your mailbox every morning, as follows:

```
find / -type f \( -perm -04000 -o -perm -02000 \) -exec ls -l {} \;
```

This command should report on all the scripts that have either the setuid or the setgid bit set in the permissions mask. Compare the current report with the previous day's report, and ensure that any new files have been created by the administration staff. At the very least, you should have the output of this command written to a separate file within /var/log.

> **NOTE**   The Linux kernel allows you to use setuid/setgid permissions only on binary executables, not on shell scripts. This restriction protects against malicious tampering with shell scripts, a common occurrence that can result in a serious compromise of root.

The *umask* setting

The default permissions for new files created on your server can have a profound impact on its overall security. Users who create world-writeable files by default are effectively poking tiny holes in your system security. Linux uses the umask configuration setting to control default file permissions. Its usage is

```
umask AAA
```

where AAA is the octal complement of a default permissions mask of 666 (777 for directories). For instance, a umask of 022 would yield a default permission of 644 for files (the result of subtracting 022 from 666). Let's look at an example in Listing 2.4.

Listing 2.4 *umask* configuration examples

```
[ramon]$ umask 000
[ramon]$ touch example1
[ramon]$ ls -l example1
-rw-rw-rw-   1 ramon     users            0 Sep 25 22:08 example1
[ramon]$ umask 022
[ramon]$ touch example2
[ramon]$ ls -l example2
-rw-r--r--   1 ramon     users            0 Sep 25 22:08 example2
[ramon]$ umask 66
[ramon]$ touch example3
[ramon]$ ls -l example3
-rw-------   1 ramon     users            0 Sep 25 22:08 example3
```

I recommend that you edit your /etc/profile file to assign a mask of 066 to the root user and assign a mask of 022 to your regular users. This ensures that root-created files have no permissions for group and others, while any other files are created with world-read permissions only.

Limiting Core Dump Size

A common means for a local user to gain root privileges is to force a setuid/setgid program to dump a core file (upon crashing) in a specific location within the filesystem. By using this method to overwrite arbitrary files anywhere on the server, including /etc/passwd, /etc/hosts.equiv, or .rhosts, intruders can effectively create for themselves a user with root privileges. With today's servers having gigabytes of physical memory available, these core files could potentially fill an entire disk, which would result in a denial of service (DoS) attack for other users relying on the same filesystem.

There is an effective way to keep core files under control. Using the ulimit command, you can control the resource utilization limits of any user, including the maximum size of a core dump file. You should simply set this size to 0, using the following command:

```
ulimit -c 0
```

You can include this command in the global /etc/profile configuration file also.

syslog Security

One of the most significant skills of sophisticated intruders is their ability to clean up all evidence that an attack has taken place. This is the electronic equivalent of a criminal using gloves at the scene of the crime, and it's a constant source of frustration for those who make a living out of tracking down the actions of these intruders.

You should go to whatever lengths are necessary to make sure that you can safeguard *some* evidence that your system was tampered with. The problem is that it's very difficult to guarantee that your log files are correct when attackers could be modifying them with their root privileges. You should take advantage of the syslog program's ability to send a copy of all log events to a remote server.

For example, in order to send all your kernel, mail, and news messages to a remote syslog server (hostname "zurich"), add the following line to your /etc/syslog.conf configuration file:

```
kern.*, mail.*, news.*[TAB]@zurich
```

(Don't forget that the syntax of this file calls for a tab character to be inserted between fields.)

After making this modification, you must send the -HUP (hang-up) signal to the syslog daemon to force it to read its configuration:

```
[ramon]$ sudo killall -HUP syslogd
```

Keep in mind, however, that some services may not be configured or able to log events via syslog. You should use cron to move those services' log files to a remote server several times throughout the day—the more often the better.

Filesystem Encryption

However strong your physical and system security measures are, you need to be ready for the time when a user gains access to some other user's files. Cryptography is your last line of defense. By encrypting the contents of sensitive directories, users can protect the privacy of their data even after an intrusion has succeeded.

This section describes two different ways to do this, both of which are based on secret-key technology using standard encryption algorithms. Let's take a look at each of them in more detail.

The Cryptographic File System

The Cryptographic File System (CFS) was developed by Unix pioneer Matt Blaze and constitutes the first full-blown integration of secret-key encryption into the Linux filesystem. One of the most important advantages of CFS is its support of both local filesystem types (e.g., ext2) as well as remote filesystems such as NFS. This support protects your data as it sits in your server, and also as it travels through the network whenever you share an NFS mount point. CFS supports several encryption algorithms including DES, 3DES, MacGuffin, SAFER-SK128, and Blowfish.

CFS's main drawback, however, is performance. If you elect to use 3DES encryption (which I recommend, since DES is barely adequate nowadays), you will pay a price, and you'll see a noticeable delay in your disk access, especially for large files. This is partly due to the fact that CFS operates in user space (outside of the kernel.) However, running in user space can actually be an advantage, because other cryptographic filesystem modules are offered as a patch to particular versions of Linux kernels, and they're often not available for the latest stable kernel.

Let's start by installing the software on our server.

Installing CFS

While the package can be obtained in source form, it's also available from www.zedz.net (or ftp.zedz.net) in RPM format, as shown in Listing 2.5.

Listing 2.5   Downloading the CFS distribution in RPM format

```
[ramon]$ ftp ftp.zedz.net
Connected to ftp.zedz.net.
220 warez.zedz.net FTP server ready.
Name (ftp.zedz.net:ramon): anonymous
331 Guest login ok, send your complete e-mail address as password.
Password: rhontanon@sybex.com
230 Guest login ok, access restrictions apply.
Remote system type is UNIX.
Using binary mode to transfer files.
ftp> cd /pub/crypto/disk/cfs/
250 CWD command successful.
ftp> get cfs-1.3.3bf-1.i386.rpm
local: cfs-1.3.3bf-1.i386.rpm remote: cfs-1.3.3bf-1.i386.rpm
200 PORT command successful.
150 Opening BINARY mode data connection for cfs-1.3.3bf-1.i386.rpm (194436
bytes).
226 Transfer complete.
```

```
194436 bytes received in 22.7 secs (8.4 Kbytes/sec)
ftp> quit
221-You have transferred 194436 bytes in 1 files.
221-Total traffic for this session was 197280 bytes in 2 transfers.
221-Thank you for using the FTP service on warez.zedz.net.
221 Goodbye.
[ramon]$ sudo rpm -i cfs-1.3.3bf-1.i386.rpm
```

At this point you have installed CFS on your system (note that there is no need to rebuild the kernel or reboot the server). Let's take a look at configuring CFS in the next step.

Configuring CFS

The first step is to make sure your server is configured to run NFS services (statd, portmapper, and mountd). This is a requirement for CFS to work correctly. Since CFS actually protects the privacy of NFS shares, perhaps this is just the tool you were looking for to add NFS back into your security policy. You can verify that NFS is running on your system by looking for the mountd line with the following command:

```
[ramon]$ ps aux | grep mountd
root      5756  0.0  0.7  1132  456 ?    S    19:15   0:00 rpc.mountd
```

Next, create a /null directory. CFS refers to this directory as the *bootstrap mount point*. In addition, you need to create the directory that you want to use as the root for all encrypted data (I chose /crypt for this purpose):

```
[ramon]$ sudo mkdir /null
```

```
[ramon]$ sudo chmod 0000 /null
```

```
[ramon]$ sudo mkdir /crypt
```

Add the /null directory to the list of exported filesystems using the following command:

```
[ramon]$ echo "/null localhost" >> /etc/exports
```

Add the following commands to the end of /etc/rc.d/rc.local:

```
if [ -x /usr/sbin/cfsd ]; then
        /usr/sbin/cfsd && \
                /bin/mount -o port=3049,intr localhost:/null /crypt
fi
```

That's the end of the installation. You're now ready to try out CFS. You can either restart your system or type the commands that you just added in the rc.local file by hand.

Using CFS

There are three commands that support the operation of the CFS package:

```
cmkdir [-1] [private_directory]
cattach [private_directory] [cleartext_directory]
cdetach [private_directory]
```

Start by creating a directory that is going to contain all your confidential information:

```
[ramon]$ cmkdir secret
```

The command prompts you for a passphrase, which is then used to hash out an appropriate secret encrypting key. You'll need this passphrase to be able to get at the data in this directory.

WARNING Note that by default, CFS uses the 3DES algorithm for encryption. This is noticeably slower than the DES variant that can be specified using the -1 switch: (# **cmkdir -1 secret**). I strongly recommend against this option, because the DES algorithm has been known to be vulnerable to brute force attacks. If you're encrypting data that you expect to keep around for a while, you should make it as resistant as possible to cryptanalysis.

The next step is to attach this newly created directory to the master CFS tree:

```
[ramon]$ cattach secret decrypted
```

You are then prompted for the same passphrase that you provided when you created the directory. If you authenticate successfully, the secret directory will be available to you as /crypt/decrypted in cleartext form. Once you're done working with the clear text directory, simply make it unavailable using the following command:

```
[ramon]$ cdetach secret
```

As with any other encryption, CFS is only as strong as your ability to protect the passphrase used to encrypt the data. In addition, you should ensure the integrity of the CFS utilities themselves (cmkdir, cattach, cdetach) to be sure that they have not been replaced with Trojan horse versions. Chapter 3 shows you how to use file integrity tools to ensure that these and other important system utilities have not been tampered with.

Practical Privacy Disk Driver

A more recent alternative to CFS is Allan Latham's Practical Privacy Disk Driver (PPDD). Unlike CFS, this utility actually creates a disk driver similar to a physical disk device, but its behavior is controlled by the PPDD software. Also unlike CFS, there is built-in support for only one encryption algorithm: Blowfish. This shouldn't be considered a drawback because Blowfish has fared well so far in the many attempts to crack it via both cryptanalysis and brute force.

The goal of this utility is to provide an encryption device that is totally transparent to the user, who can access the PPDD-protected directories without the need for any special procedures.

Let's take a closer look at PPDD, starting with its installation.

Installing PPDD

As of this writing, there is no RPM package for PPDD, probably because the installation requires a kernel patch and rebuild. So you need to download the package in source format from ftp.gwdg.de (see Listing 2.6).

Listing 2.6   Downloading the PPDD distribution

```
[ramon]$ ftp ftp.gwdg.de
Connected to ftp.gwdg.de.
220 ftp.gwdg.de FTP server (Version wu-2.4.2-academ[BETA-18](1) Mon Jul 31
14:25:08 MET DST 2000) ready.
Name (ftp.gwdg.de:ramon): anonymous
331 Guest login ok, send your complete e-mail address as password.
Password:rhontanon@sybex.com
230-Hello User at 204.254.33.77, there are 44 (max 250
230-Local time is: Wed Sep 27 03:00:15 2000
230 Guest login ok, access restrictions apply.
Remote system type is UNIX.
Using binary mode to transfer files.
ftp> cd /pub/linux/misc/ppdd
250 CWD command successful.
ftp> get ppdd-1.2.zip
local: ppdd-1.2.zip remote: ppdd-1.2.zip
200 PORT command successful.
150 Opening BINARY mode data connection for ppdd-1.2.zip (198959 bytes).
226 Transfer complete.
198959 bytes received in 28.4 secs (6.9 Kbytes/sec)
ftp>
```

Once you have verified that the file has been successfully downloaded (and it is of the right size), you need to unzip it and extract the tar file, as shown in Listing 2.7.

Listing 2.7 Installing the PPDD distribution

```
[ramon]$ unzip ppdd-1.2.zip
Archive:  ppdd-1.2.zip
 extracting: tmp/ppdd-1.2.tgz.sig
  inflating: tmp/ppdd-1.2.tgz
[ramon]$ tar zxf tmp/ppdd-1.2.tar
```

At this point you should have a new subdirectory called ppdd-1.2 in your current directory. Since the PPDD distribution will be applying a patch against the current Linux sources, make sure that you have a good set of kernel source and header files in /usr/linux and that you have been able to successfully build a working kernel from these files. Don't forget to make a backup copy of the kernel before patching it.

Next, go into the PPDD source directory and apply the kernel patches:

```
[ramon]$ cd ppdd-1.2
```

```
[ramon]$ sudo make apply_patch
```

This results in a modification to the Linux sources, so you should rebuild your kernel and install the resulting boot file at this point. Don't forget to reconfigure lilo, or to have an emergency boot disk handy!

If the new image boots without any errors, you're ready to create the encryption device. The following command assumes that you'll be using /dev/hdc1 as your encrypted disk partition:

```
[ramon]$ sudo ppddinit /dev/ppdd0 /dev/hdc1
```

It is at this stage that you'll be prompted for a passphrase, whose hash will constitute the secret key used in the Blowfish algorithm.

Next, you need to set up the newly created device, and you need to write an ext2 filesystem on it using the following commands:

```
[ramon]$ sudo ppddsetup -s /dev/ppdd0 /dev/hdc1
```

```
[ramon]$ sudo mkfs /dev/ppdd0
```

Using PPDD

To use PPDD, simply mount the encrypted device on a real mount point (I'll use /crypt for consistency):

```
[ramon]$ sudo mount /dev/ppdd0 /crypt
```

From this point on, your users can access resources within /crypt transparently, as if it were a regular filesystem.

Before you shut down the server, you should unmount the /crypt filesystem as you would any other partition, and you should also disconnect the ppdd0 driver, as follows:

```
[ramon]$ sudo umount /crypt
[ramon]$ sudo ppddsetup -d /dev/ppdd0
```

PPDD encrypts an entire filesystem with a key derived from a single passphrase and allows users to access the files within the filesystem using the standard Linux permissions model. This makes PPDD a good candidate for protecting a server's disk from being read by an intruder who has physically seized the system, as well as for protecting backup media that have fallen into the wrong hands.

In Sum

This chapter examines the issues involved in system-level Linux security and provides a set of recommended configurations and utilities that can aid in protecting your server from unauthorized access by local users. While all the popular Linux distributions are becoming increasingly security conscious, there are still a staggering number of vulnerabilities being reported daily.

It's important to understand the impact of all kernel parameters and recognize which ones can have a direct influence on the security of your server. You should build your own custom kernel for efficiency, but also for security and accountability.

You should protect your server against root exploits. One way to do this is by constantly monitoring the permissions of your system files, and by guarding against the perils of setuid/setgid executables. Setting the correct default umask for your users ensures that they're creating files with a safe set of permissions. Also, limiting the size of core files with the ulimit command can prevent a common type of root compromise attack.

When all else fails, filesystem encryption can protect the data that has been compromised. The Cryptographic File System (CFS) provides good granularity for individual protection of user information, while the Practical Privacy Disk Driver (PPDD) is an efficient, transparent method for encrypting filesystems (and backups) in bulk.

The next chapter, Chapter 3, covers the monitoring and auditing of your system and describes the tools that you can use to ensure the integrity of your system files. This is an essential part of system security, and should be used in conjunction with the recommendations in this chapter.

3

System Monitoring and Auditing

Monitoring your system for abnormal behavior is an essential task in both system administration and information security. Most attackers leave their "fingerprints" in the system log files, and examining these logs is a fundamental step in the process of network forensics. More important, examining log files on a regular basis, looking for erratic or suspicious user behavior, can prevent attacks and enhance the overall security of your server.

There are attackers who may be able to penetrate your system without leaving any evidence in the log files. However, even the best attackers will not be able to delete or modify a history file without being noticed. Examining log files is just one critical part of your overall security plan.

You should be looking at the system log files for

- Repeated authentication failures
- Unusual shutdowns
- Attempts to relay messages through your mail server
- Any events that seem out of the ordinary

A single authentication failure for a single user can be attributed to a mistyped password. Multiple authentication failures for a single user can be attributed to an acute case of "fat-finger" syndrome. Multiple authentication failures for multiple users, however, are a clear sign of an attack in the making, or a sign that one of your internal users may be trying to guess the root password in an effort to gain greater access to your server.

Through the use of the centralized `syslog` facility, Linux offers a wealth of real-time diagnostics that are often not used to their full extent, not because they don't offer the right kind of information, but because most system administrators don't know exactly how to use these diagnostics. The problem is that the standard Linux `syslog` files are too verbose to be of any value. A typical `/var/log/messages` file on a standard Red Hat or Caldera distribution can grow by 500–600K bytes in a typical day for a average-load server.

Human inspection of log files has two major shortcomings:

- The task is tedious and expensive because it has to be performed by a (highly paid) system administrator who is trained to recognize the trouble signs.
- Humans are prone to error, especially when scanning large text files full of repetitive sequences.

Luckily, the Linux community has responded to the challenge and has developed a number of useful log-monitoring tools that can be run batch style to identify certain keywords or patterns that are known to spell trouble. The section "System Log Monitoring" later in this chapter illustrates the concept of log monitoring using two such tools: `swatch` and `logcheck`.

System Logging with *syslog*

The `syslog` utility allows the system administrator to configure and manage log files generated by heterogeneous system utilities and applications from a central location. Linux comes standard with the `syslog` utility configured and the `syslogd` daemon active upon startup. The system administrator specifies in the `/etc/syslog.conf` file which messages they would like to see logged, and the application directs the messages to the appropriate log file. Most generic messages are directed to the `/var/log/messages` file, although the system administrator can choose any arbitrary file as the destination. In general, Linux uses the following initial log files:

`/var/log/messages`   This is the primary Linux log file, used for recording most common system events.

`/var/log/secure`   Authentication failures for daemons started from `/etc/inetd.conf` are logged here. (Chapter 4, "Network Services Configuration," discusses the `inetd` utility.)

/var/log/maillog   The *sendmail* daemon is notoriously verbose (and often very busy), so it makes sense to dedicate this separate log file to keep track of mail-delivery messages.

/var/log/spooler   This is the log file where other daemons such as UUCP and News (NNTP) log their messages.

/var/log/boot.log   The boot-up messages displayed when the system is coming up are typically logged in this file.

These five log files are automatically rotated by the system via the /etc/logrotate.d/ syslog script. Rotating essentially means renaming the current log file to something like logfile.1 while creating a new (empty) file called logfile to record only those events that took place since the last rotation. At the next rotation, the logfile.1 file is renamed to logfile.2 and the logfile.11 file (if you're only keeping 10 log files) is deleted.

syslog.conf File

Listing 3.1 shows a typical syslog.conf file on a Linux system. It includes references to the five log files described earlier in this section.

Listing 3.1   A typical Linux */etc/syslog.conf* file

```
# Log all kernel messages to the console.
# Logging much else clutters up the screen.
kern.*                                  /dev/console

# Log anything (except mail) of level info or higher.
# Don't log private authentication messages!
*.info;mail.none;authpriv.none          /var/log/messages

# The authpriv file has restricted access.
authpriv.*                              /var/log/secure

# Log all the mail messages in one place.
mail.*                                  /var/log/maillog

# Everybody gets emergency messages, plus log them on another
# machine.
*.emerg                                         *
*.emerg                                         @loghost
```

```
# Save mail and news errors of level err and higher in a
# special file.
uucp,news.crit                                    /var/log/spooler

# Save boot messages also to boot.log
local7.*                                          /var/log/boot.log
```

The general format of the entries in the `syslog.conf` file is as follows:

facility.priority[;*facility.priority*][TAB]*action*

Each field is defined as follows:

facility   The *facility* field is the subsystem that you want to log events from. The current supported subsystems are

- `auth`: secure and authentication messages
- `authpriv`: private secure and authentication messages
- `cron`: clock/scheduler daemon
- `daemon`: other system daemons
- `kern`: Linux kernel messages
- `lpr`: line printer system messages
- `mail`: mail system
- `news`: network news subsystem
- `sysloguser`: internal `syslog` messages
- `uucp`: Unix-to-Unix copy subsystem
- `local0`–`local7`: reserved for local use

The special character * can be used to denote any (and all) facilities.

priority   The *priority* field specifies the priority level of the message within a given subsystem. The current priorities are (in ascending order of criticality)

- debug: debug-level messages for troubleshooting
- info: informational messages
- notice: normal messages of special interest
- warning: abnormal messages signaling impending failure
- error: failure condition messages
- crit: critical error-condition messages
- alert: condition needing immediate action
- emerg: error condition leading to system failure

The special character * can be used to denote any (and all) priorities.

destination   The *destination* field defines the destination for log messages that match the given facility and priority combination. This can be either a filename, or a host name when the @ sign precedes the keyword. The * character takes on a special meaning here, denoting all users; in other words, all users who are currently logged on will receive a copy of the message on their active terminals. Needless to say, you should only use this for absolutely critical messages that might impact the user's ability to continue to work on the system.

action   The *action* field can be one of the following:

- A regular file. In this case, all messages will be appended to the end of the file. The file must be specified with a full path name, starting with the / character.
- A named pipe. In this case, the messages are used as the standard input to the pipe.
- A terminal or console. In this case, the messages are displayed over the given device.
- A remote machine. In this case, the messages are sent to a remote host's `syslogd` daemon.
- A list of users. In this case, the messages are broadcast to the terminals owned by any active users. The special character * is used to send messages to all users that are currently logged on.

Applying these facility, priority, destination, and action values, you can see that the `syslog.conf` file in Listing 3.1 is instructing the `syslogd` daemon to:

- Log all kernel messages to the console.
- Log `authpriv` and `mail` messages to `secure` and `maillog` respectively.
- Log `emergency` messages to all the users' terminals and to the remote system `loghost`.
- Log `uucp` and `news` messages (critical and above) to `spooler`.
- Log `local7` (boot) messages to `boot.log`.
- Log the remaining messages (info and above) to `messages`.

Some messages are critical enough to the system that they should be stored outside the system itself. This is necessary to make sure that you can continue to log events, even when the local disk is full or is otherwise unavailable. Keeping a set of log files on a separate system also has clear security advantages, since a sophisticated attacker will most likely delete or otherwise tamper with the log files on the attacked system. An attacker would have to repeat all the steps he used to get on the first server to get on the second server in order to completely erase his trail.

The next section describes the operation of remote `syslog` and discusses the security implications of running this service on the remote server.

syslog Server Security

The Linux model is one where services can easily transcend physical servers, and the `syslog` facility is no exception. When the action `@loghost` for kernel emergency messages is specified in Listing 3.1, the implication is that there is a system named (or aliased to) `loghost` that is actively listening on UDP port 514 for incoming `syslog` requests.

While this facility makes a more robust logging mechanism, it also introduces a known vulnerability, where attackers can target port 514 UDP by sending very large files to this service to fill up the disks and make the server unavailable. This can then be followed by a stealth attack on the servers that this `loghost` was logging for in the first place.

If you deploy remote `syslogd` servers, I recommend that you take at least one of the following precautions:

- Protect access to port 514 UDP by ensuring that only authorized servers are allowed to write to that service (see Chapter 9, "Network Layer Firewalls").

- Deploy your remote `syslogd` server on a separate, dedicated network segment that is exclusive for this use (e.g., a 10.0.0/24 management network).

- Use a dedicated partition to write remote `syslogd` messages. This partition could fill up completely without having any other adverse effect on the system. (Note, however, that when the log files fill up, the system is really no longer useful.)

TIP In order to allow your remote `syslogd` server to accept messages from other machines, don't forget to use the -r flag when invoking `syslog`.

System Log Monitoring

The basic idea behind log file monitoring is to define a set of system log files of interest, and a set of *triggers,* or regular expressions, to monitor for. When the tool finds a trigger in the appropriate log file, it executes a specified action (sends an e-mail, executes a command, pages the administrator, etc.). Two full-featured system log monitoring tools are `swatch` and `logcheck`.

swatch

The Simple WATCHer (`swatch`) is a monitoring tool developed by Todd Atkins at University of California, Santa Barbara (UCSB). It is composed of a large Perl script that

System Security

PART 1

does all the monitoring and a configuration file where you can specify your triggers and a set of actions for each trigger. The following sections describe the installation, configuration, and use of swatch.

Installing *swatch*

While swatch is readily available in RPM format, be aware that most Linux distributions lack three of the Perl packages required by swatch:

- perl-File-Tail: a Perl module for reading from continuously updated files
- perl-Time-HiRes: a Perl module for handling high-resolution time variables
- perl-Date-Calc: a Perl module for Gregorian calendar date calculations

These modules are part of the CPAN Perl archive that is also available in RPM format. Once you have downloaded these three Perl packages, as well as the latest swatch RPM, then install all four packages in the order shown in Listing 3.2.

Listing 3.2   The *swatch* installation process

```
[ramon]$ ls -l *.rpm
-rw-r--r--   1 ramon    users        55922 Sep 30 22:49 ⏎
perl-Date-Calc-4.2-2.i386.rpm
-rw-r--r--   1 ramon    users        12280 Sep 30 22:49 ⏎
perl-File-Tail-0.91-2.i386.rpm
-rw-r--r--   1 ramon    users        12500 Sep 30 22:49 ⏎
perl-Time-HiRes-01.20-2.i386.rpm
-rw-r--r--   1 ramon    users        28279 Sep 30 22:45 ⏎
swatch-3.0b4-1.noarch.rpm
[ramon]$ sudo rpm -i perl-Date-Calc-4.2-2.i386.rpm
[ramon]$ sudo rpm -i perl-File-Tail-0.91-2.i386.rpm
[ramon]$ sudo rpm -i perl-Time-HiRes-01.20-2.i386.rpm
[ramon]$ sudo rpm -i swatch-3.0b4-1.noarch.rpm
```

If there are no errors during these installation steps, you are now ready to configure and use the swatch utility.

Configuring *swatch*

There is only one swatch configuration file, typically called .swatchrc or swatchrc. This file contains a definition of the triggers that you'd like to monitor, as well as the appropriate action that you would like taken in the presence of each of the triggers. The file should have one keyword per line, with an optional equal sign (=) and an optional value for the keyword.

The following section defines the keywords used in the swatchrc configuration file.

Pattern-Matching There are two options available in swatchrc for specifying triggers, or patterns, to watch out for:

Watch for *regex* Take the appropriate action when the regular expression specified in *regex* is found within the file or command being monitored.

Ignore *regex* Take the appropriate action when there is any activity within the file or command being monitored, except for events that match the expression specified in *regex*.

Pattern-Matching Action Once the pattern has been identified, you must specify the action to be taken. Here are the options available:

echo Write the event that matches the pattern being monitored.

bell Ring a bell by printing the appropriate ASCII character. This action is only appropriate if you're directing the output of swatch to stdout.

exec *command* Executes the specified command as if it were typed in at the command line. You can pass positional variables from the matched line to the command. For example, $1 is the first character in the line, $2 for the second character, and so on. $* is the entire line.

mail[=address:*address*:...][,subject=*your_subject*] Sends an electronic mail message to the address you specify (*address*), with an optional subject header (*your_subject*). Note that if the recipient is omitted, the message is sent to the user who owns the swatch process on the local server.

Pipe *command* Pipe the matched lines from the monitored file as input to the specified command.

throttle *hours*:*minutes*:*seconds* This option is useful for patterns that appear repetitively. Rather than taking action on each appearance of the trigger, swatch can signal the event only periodically. However, you will get a report of how many times the event occurred during that time.

when *day*:*hour* This option is used to restrict the use of an action to a day of the week and an hour of the day. It's useful to configure swatch to page the system administration staff in some instances or to simply e-mail them in other instances, depending on their availability.

swatch Configuration File Examples

The following is a sample swatch configuration file to alert the system administrator of any user authentication failures in the last 30 minutes. This example specifies that you'd like to be notified by pager whenever one of the filesystems has reached capacity. You are instructing swatch to look for the expression "authentication failure," and you are specifying an e-mail message that indicates what action to take. The e-mail message will have the subject "Auth Failure Report." The echo directive instructs swatch to include the offending message in the e-mail. The throttle directive ensures that you are only alerted once every 30 minutes, regardless of the frequency of the message within the 30-minute period.

```
watchfor /authentication failure/
        echo
        bell
        throttle 00:30
        mail=sysadmin@example.com,subject=Auth Failure Report
```

If it's after hours, the following configuration file entry indicates that the staff should also be paged. This example looks for occurrences of the string "filesystem full" and sends two separate e-mail messages, one to sysadmin@example.com, and another to sysadmin-pager@example.com, but only during the hours of 5 P.M. to 9 A.M.

```
watchfor /filesystem full/
        echo
        mail=sysadmin@example.com,subject=Filesystem Full
        mail=sysadmin-pager@example.com,when=1-7:17-9
```

Finally, consider the following example of a swatch configuration file that triggers corrective action at the same time that the administration staff is informed of the condition. This example is similar to the previous two, except that it invokes the execution of a script (cleanup_old_files) whenever the string "filesystem full" is encountered.

```
watchfor /filesystem full/
        echo
        mail=sysadmin@example.com,subject=Cleaning Files
        exec "cleanup_old_files"
```

Running *swatch*

The swatch script accepts several command-line options. Table 3.1 describes the ones that you need to be most interested in.

Table 3.1   *swatch* Command-Line Options

Configure Option	Description	Default
`--config-file=`*filename*	Location of the configuration file.	`$HOME/.swatchrc`
`--help`	Display a short help summary.	N/A
`--version`	Display swatch script version.	N/A
`--tail-file=`*filename*	Examine lines of text as they're added to the file.	*Note: Only one of these options can be specified at any one time. The default is:* `--tail-file=/var/log/messages`.
`--read-pipe=`*command*	Examine input piped in from the specified command.	
`--examine=`*filename*	Examine specified filename in a single pass.	

I recommend that you always include the `--config-file` option, and that you place the configuration file in an obvious place, like `/etc/swatchrc`, where it's easier to track and manage. When no command-line options are specified, the default `swatch` command is

```
swatch --config-file=~/.swatchrc --tail-file=/var/log/messages
```

More typical invocations of the `swatch` command would be

```
swatch --config-file=/etc/swatchrc.messages --tail-↵
file=/var/log/messages
```

```
swatch --config-file=/etc/swatchrc.htmlaccess.log --tail-↵
file=/var/log/htmlaccess.log
```

```
swatch --config-file=/etc/swatchrc.authlog --tail-↵
file=/var/log/authlog
```

Note that these commands specify separate configuration files for each system log file to be monitored. I recommend that you invoke each of these `swatch` commands (or whichever commands you find useful) on a separate virtual terminal (or `xterm` in the system console) and review the output periodically. As always, the severity of the alert (`echo`, `mail`, `page`, etc.) should be in accordance with the type of event and its recommended handling as stated in your security policy.

logcheck

Maintained by Craig Rowland of Psionic, logcheck is an adaptation of frequentcheck.sh, a log-monitoring package that once accompanied the Gauntlet firewall from Trusted Information Systems, although some of the most important components have been totally rewritten. Unlike swatch, the logcheck design is such that you don't have to have a constantly running process scrutinizing your log files, which should cut down on overhead on the server. In addition, logcheck can alert you of unusual events, even if you have not defined them as triggers to look for.

The logcheck package contains two executables: logtail and logcheck.sh. logtail keeps track of how much of the log file was monitored last time, and it is written in C for performance reasons. logcheck.sh controls all processing and inspects the contents of the log files. It is meant to be invoked from cron and should be configured to run at least hourly.

Installing logcheck

Fortunately, the RPM version of the logcheck package is ubiquitous, and I recommend that you use the following installation method, since there is no need for special configuration of the sources. Once you have obtained the .rpm file, simply install it using the rpm utility:

```
[ramon]$ ls -l logcheck-1.1.1-1.i386.rpm

-rw-r--r--   1 ramon users  33707 Sep 28 20:04 logcheck-1.1.1-i386↩
rmp

[ramon]$ sudo rpm -i logcheck-1.1.1-1.i386.rpm
```

TIP Don't forget to erase any previous or outdated versions of logcheck before running the command that installs logcheck.

Configuring logcheck

Upon installation, logcheck writes a number of reference files in the /etc/logcheck directory, which it uses for default pattern matching. The most interesting of these files is logcheck.hacking (shown in Listing 3.3), in which the author has placed a number of regular expressions that are often associated with documented attacks on Linux servers, such as

- VRFY root
- EXPN root

- A sendmail command that is used to obtain more information on legitimate mail users (EXPN, VRFY), as well as login failure attempts from accounts that enjoy system privileges (root), or should not be attempting interactive logins (uucp, bin, sync).

- The command login.*; .*LOGIN FAILURE.* FROM .*root, which signals a root login with the wrong password

Listing 3.3 The standard */etc/logcheck/logcheck.hacking* reference file

```
"wiz"
"WIZ"
"debug"
"DEBUG"
ATTACK
nested
VRFY bbs
VRFY decode
VRFY uudecode
VRFY lp
VRFY demo
VRFY guest
VRFY root
VRFY uucp
VRFY oracle
VRFY sybase
VRFY games
vrfy bbs
vrfy decode
vrfy uudecode
vrfy lp
vrfy demo
vrfy guest
vrfy root
vrfy uucp
vrfy oracle
vrfy sybase
vrfy games
expn decode
expn uudecode
expn wheel
expn root
EXPN decode
```

```
EXPN uudecode
EXPN wheel
EXPN root
LOGIN root REFUSED
rlogind.*: Connection from .* on illegal port
rshd.*: Connection from .* on illegal port
sendmail.*: user .* attempted to run daemon
uucico.*: refused connect from .*
tftpd.*: refused connect from .*
login.*: .*LOGIN FAILURE.* FROM .*root
login.*: .*LOGIN FAILURE.* FROM .*guest
login.*: .*LOGIN FAILURE.* FROM .*bin
login.*: .*LOGIN FAILURE.* FROM .*uucp
login.*: .*LOGIN FAILURE.* FROM .*adm
login.*: .*LOGIN FAILURE.* FROM .*bbs
login.*: .*LOGIN FAILURE.* FROM .*games
login.*: .*LOGIN FAILURE.* FROM .*sync
login.*: .*LOGIN FAILURE.* FROM .*oracle
login.*: .*LOGIN FAILURE.* FROM .*sybase
kernel: Oversized packet received from
attackalert
```

In addition, the /etc/logcheck directory includes a file named logcheck.violations that contains patterns that, although they should be flagged as suspicious, don't quite constitute evidence of an attack in progress. For example, a line such as

```
RETR passwd
```

indicates that someone tried to retrieve the password file via FTP. While this is not an illegal action per se, you should at least question the motive of the user who performed this transfer.

The logcheck.violations file also contains references to failed login attempts and other system access diagnostics, such as file transfers and kernel warnings, that are less critical than the logcheck.hacking file but still warrant further investigation.

Listing 3.4 shows the contents of the logcheck.violations file.

Listing 3.4   The standard */etc/logcheck/logcheck.violations* reference file

```
!=
-ERR Password
ATTACK
BAD
```

```
CWD etc
DEBUG
EXPN
FAILURE
ILLEGAL
LOGIN FAILURE
LOGIN REFUSED
PERMITTED
REFUSED
RETR group
RETR passwd
RETR pwd.db
ROOT LOGIN
SITE EXEC
VRFY
"WIZ"
admin
alias database
debug
denied
deny
deny host
expn
failed
illegal
kernel: Oversized packet received from
nested
permitted
reject
rexec
rshd
securityalert
setsender
shutdown
smrsh
su root
su:
sucked
unapproved
vrfy
attackalert
```

You should update the `logcheck.hacking` and the `logcheck.violations` files regularly with newly discovered log message patterns, or, better yet, make sure that you always have an up-to-date `logcheck` installation on all your servers. In addition, take the time to add items to these files that are specific to your server and your system needs. For example, add message patterns from Apache if you're running an HTTP server, or from `sendmail` if you're running a mail server.

Note that by default, the Linux version of `logcheck` scans the `/var/log/messages` file for all events, so make sure that this file is indeed seeing all application log messages. Your `/etc/syslog.conf` file should have the following line in it:

```
*.info          /var/log/messages
```

While there are no real configuration files, the actual `logcheck` shell script (`/usr/sbin/logcheck`) is very readable, and it has a few variable definitions toward the front. I recommend that you only change the line

```
SYSADMIN=root
```

to a username other than root, if you have a special account to which the logs should be e-mailed instead.

Running *logcheck*

`logcheck` uses `cron` to schedule periodic runs. Make sure that your system is indeed running `crond` (the `cron` daemon) by issuing the following command:

```
[ramon]$ ps aux | grep cron
root        403  0.0  0.4  1284  304 ?          S    Sep24   0:00 crond
```

Upon installation, the `logcheck` RPM distribution creates the following file in the `/etc` directory:

```
/etc/cron.hourly/logcheck
```

This file forces the `cron` job on your server to execute `logcheck` at the top of the hour, resulting in hourly e-mail messages to the root account on the server. This e-mail message includes a report on the security violations and any unusual system events recorded during the last hour.

Listing 3.5 shows an example of this hourly report. In this report, `logcheck` reports that there was a SOCKS5 client that failed to properly authenticate to the local server, as well as a regular user (ramon) who performed a `su` command to inspect the `/var/log/messages` file.

Listing 3.5 Sample e-mail sent by *logcheck* to the local root user

```
From: root <root@redhat.example.com>
Message-Id: <200010012201.SAA16387@redhat.example.com>
To: root@redhat.example.com
Subject: redhat.example.com 10/01/00:18.01 system check
Status: RO
Content-Length: 222
Lines: 8
Security Violations
=-=-=-=-=-=-=-=-=-=
Oct  1 17:28:14 redhat Socks5[16296]: Auth Failed: (204.168.33.2:↩
1196)
Unusual System Events
=-=-=-=-=-=-=-=-=-=-=
Oct  1 17:28:14 redhat Socks5[16296]: Auth Failed: (204.168.33.2:↩
1196)
Oct  1 18:17:15 redhat sudo:    ramon : TTY=pts/3 ; PWD=/usr/doc/↩
logcheck-1.1.1 ; USER=root ; COMMAND=/usr/bin/tail/var/log/messages
```

swatch vs. *logcheck*

Both swatch and logcheck have a place in your system defense. While swatch makes for a better real-time log notification tool, logcheck provides a straightforward, easy-to-install tool that you can use to create custom reports that can be periodically examined by the administration staff.

Whichever tool you choose to implement, it's crucial to choose a recipient who will have enough time and dedicate enough energy to read the reports thoroughly. These tools are meant to help in one of the most tedious aspects of systems security, but ultimately, there is no substitute for human scrutiny and appropriate response.

File Integrity Auditing

Ensuring the integrity of system executables, configuration files, and log files is paramount to a successful security defense. Consider the case where an intruder manages to replace a commonly executed file (like login) with a Trojan horse version. If the attacker manages to create a Trojan horse login that performs just like the original, this attack could go undetected forever. Since you can't easily "look" inside executables, the only way you can flag such a compromise is by comparing the current *signature* of the current login utility to the signature taken when the system was first installed.

These signatures are cryptographic hash functions whose properties ensure that two different files can never yield the same hash. Therefore, the slightest modification in one of these files can cause the signature to be drastically different. This is the fundamental principle behind most file integrity assurance tools. By taking a *signature snapshot* of all the executable files before the system goes on the network, you create a baseline that can be stored in a database, preferably on a write-once, read-many-times medium (to ensure that it cannot be tampered with). You can then periodically compare these signatures to the current state of the files and deal with any changes appropriately.

The following section introduces tripwire, the most popular Linux file integrity assurance utility, and explains its installation, configuration, and use as part of a comprehensive system security strategy.

tripwire

Born in 1992 under the auspices of Dr. Gene Spafford at Purdue University, tripwire was the first tool to be offered in the field of file integrity assurance. In 1999, the maintenance and development of the tool was taken over by Tripwire, Inc., a commercial endeavor spearheaded by Gene Kim, one of tripwire's original developers, while working for Dr. Spafford back at Purdue.

Installing *tripwire*

Although they offer a fully supported line of commercial products based on the tripwire concept, Tripwire, Inc. makes the Linux version of their tool available for free download. You can obtain a gnu-zipped file containing the distribution at www.tripwire.com/downloads. Once you have downloaded the archive file, decompress it and extract the contents of the resulting .tar file to the current directory using the following commands:

```
[ramon]$ gunzip Tripwire_221_for_Linux_x86.tar.gz
[ramon]$ tar xf Tripwire_221_for_Linux_x86.tar
[ramon]$ rm Tripwire_221_for_Linux_x86.tar
[ramon]$ ls -l
total 8814
-r--r--r--   1 ramon     users      9825 Jan 11  2000 License.txt
-r--r--r--   1 ramon     users      7060 Jan 11  2000 README
-r--r--r--   1 ramon     users     23065 Jan 11  2000 Release_Notes
-r--r--r--   1 ramon     users      3300 Jan 11  2000 install.cfg
-r-xr-xr-x   1 ramon     users     31919 Jan 11  2000 install.sh
drwxr-xr-x   2 ramon     users      1024 Jan 11  2000 pkg
```

Before proceeding with the installation, take a look at the install.cfg file, which contains a number of environment variables that control the installation process. Table 3.2 shows the options that you should examine, along with their default settings. I recommend that you change the value of TWROOT to the location where you normally install system tools (for example, /usr/local/tripwire) because most other environment variables build on this base directory.

NOTE   Despite my suggestion, I use /usr/TSS in these examples to make the text more compatible with other tripwire documentation.

Table 3.2   *tripwire install.cfg* Environment Variables

Variable	Description	Default
TWROOT	The root directory	/usr/TSS
TWBIN	Location of the program executables and configuration files	${TWROOT}/bin
TWPOLICY	Location of policy files	${TWROOT}/policy
TWMAN	Location of the man pages	${TWROOT}/man
TWDB	Location of the databases	${TWROOT}/db
TWSITEKEYDIR	Location of key used to secure the configuration and policy files	${TWROOT}/key
TWLOCALKEYDIR	Location of key used to secure database files and reports	${TWROOT}/key
TWREPORT	Location of results of integrity checks	${TWROOT}/report

Next, simply execute the supplied install.sh script as the root user:

```
[ramon]$ sudo ./install.sh
```

During the installation process, you are prompted to enter a passphrase to protect the confidentiality and integrity of the configuration and policy files. You are also asked to enter the name of the database that will eventually contain the signatures to the system files that you choose to monitor. Choose a good passphrase composed of at least 16 characters. (tripwire accepts passphrases of up to 1023 characters!)

> **NOTE** If you choose to accept the installation directory default of /usr/TSS, you should at least include /usr/TSS/bin in your PATH environment variable if you want to execute tripwire commands without supplying a fully qualified file path. Do not include this path in root's PATH variable, however. You may also want to include /usr/TSS/man in your MANPATH environment variable so you can display the supplied man pages.

Configuring *tripwire*

Once the package has been installed in the appropriate directory, you must create a configuration file, as well as a default policy, that will also be stored in a text file. After these two files are created, use the twadmin utility to encode and sign both files to ensure that their contents are not modified. The next step is to initialize the signature database, which allows you to run your first integrity check.

The following sections explain in more detail the process of creating a tripwire configuration file and a policy file.

The *tripwire* Configuration File   The tripwire configuration file is typically found at the following location:

```
${ROOT}/bin/twcfg.txt
```

The purpose of this configuration file is to control the location of all the other files in the tripwire distribution after it has been installed. Listing 3.6 contains the default contents of the file.

Listing 3.6   Initial contents of the *tripwire* configuration file (*twcfg.txt*)

```
ROOT            =/usr/TSS
POLFILE         =/usr/TSS/policy/tw.pol
DBFILE          =/usr/TSS/db/$(HOSTNAME).twd
REPORTFILE      =/usr/TSS/report/$(HOSTNAME)-$(DATE).twr
SITEKEYFILE     =/usr/TSS/key/site.key
LOCALKEYFILE    =/usr/TSS/key/redhat.example.com-local.key
EDITOR          =/bin/vi
LATEPROMPTING =false
LOOSEDIRECTORYCHECKING =false
MAILNOVIOLATIONS =true
EMAILREPORTLEVEL =3
REPORTLEVEL     =3
MAILMETHOD      =SENDMAIL
SYSLOGREPORTING =false
MAILPROGRAM     =/usr/lib/sendmail -oi -t
```

If you specified a custom value for TWROOT before the installation, the paths in this file should reflect that fact. Note that the first six variables in the twcfg.txt file are needed for tripwire operation, while the rest are optional. Table 3.3 contains a description of the environment variables in this file that are different from the ones in the installation configuration (see Table 3.2 for those). Unless you have a very specific need to do so, I recommend that you do *not* change the default contents of this configuration file.

Table 3.3   *tripwire twcfg.txt* Environment Variables

Variable	Description
EDITOR	Editor for interactive reports.
LATEPROMPTING	Delay the prompting of the passphrase to minimize exposure.
LOOSEDIRECTORYCHECKING	Don't check file for properties that are likely to change often.
MAILNOVIOLATIONS	Send e-mail report even if no violations occurred.
EMAILREPORTINGLEVEL	Default verbosity level of e-mail report (0 through 4).
REPORTLEVEL	Default verbosity level of printed report (0 through 4).
MAILMETHOD	Choice of mail transport (SMTP or Sendmail).
SYSLOGREPORTING	Send user.notice reports through syslog.
MAILPROGRAM	Program invoked for mailing Tripwire violation reports.

The next section describes the syntax and maintenance of the policy file and the last steps needed to get tripwire up and running.

The *tripwire* Policy File   Now that you have defined the operational parameters of tripwire, you're ready to tell it which files to watch. This is done in the policy file, which is located by default in /usr/TSS/policy/twpol.txt.

A typical tripwire policy file has three distinct sections:

- Global definitions of variables whose scope includes the entire policy file
- File severity levels that allow you to prioritize the execution of policies
- Rules or group of properties to be checked for each file or object

Consider the sample (partial) policy of the tripwire policy file (twpol.txt) in the examples in this section. This example contains the global variables that determine the location of the tripwire root directory (TWROOT), binary directory (TWBIN), policy (TWPOL), database (TWDB), key files (TWSKEY, TWLKEY), and report (TWREPORT).

```
@@section GLOBAL
TWROOT="/usr/TSS";
TWBIN="/usr/TSS/bin";
TWPOL="/usr/TSS/policy";
TWDB="/usr/TSS/db";
TWSKEY="/usr/TSS/key";
TWLKEY="/usr/TSS/key";
TWREPORT="/usr/TSS/report";
HOSTNAME=redhat.example.com;
```

The next example shows the file severity level section of the tripwire policy file. This example defines a number of macros to be used later in the policy. It uses several built-in property masks that tell the policy which events to examine or ignore (IgnoreNone, ReadOnly, Dynamic, Growing), as well as some user-defined property masks (+pug, 33, 66, 100). These masks direct tripwire to look for certain types of changes in a given file or directory. (See Table 3.4 for a complete list of the characters used in tripwire's property masks.)

```
@@section FS
SEC_CRIT       = $(IgnoreNone)-SHa;    # Critical files - we can't
                                       # afford to miss any changes.

SEC_SUID       = $(IgnoreNone)-SHa;    # Binaries with the SUID or SGID
                                       # flags set.

SEC_TCB        = $(ReadOnly);          # Members of the Trusted
                                       # Computing Base.

SEC_BIN        = $(ReadOnly);          # Binaries that shouldn't
                                       # change.

SEC_CONFIG     = $(Dynamic);           # Config files that are changed
                                       # infrequently but accessed
                                       # often.

SEC_LOG        = $(Growing);           # Files that grow, but that
```

```
                                          # should never change ownership.
        SEC_INVARIANT = +pug;             # Directories that should
                                          # never change permission or
                                          # ownership.
        SIG_LOW       = 33;               # Non-critical files that are
                                          # of minimal security impact.
        SIG_MED       = 66;               # Non-critical files that are
                                          # of significant security impact.
        SIG_HI        = 100;              # Critical files that are
                                          # significant points of
                                          # vulnerability.
```

Table 3.4   *tripwire* Policy File Property Mask Characters

Property	Description
-	Ignore properties
+	Record and check properties
p	File permissions
I	Inode number
n	Number of links
u	User id of file owner
g	Group id of file owner
t	File type
s	File size
l	File is expected to grow
d	Device number of disk
I	Device number to which inode points

Table 3.4   *tripwire* Policy File Property Mask Characters *(continued)*

Property	Description
b	Number of blocks allocated
a	Access timestamp
m	Modification timestamp
c	Inode creation/modification timestamp
c	Cyclic redundancy check

The Tripwire Binaries rule instructs `tripwire` to watch the binaries themselves and tag any violation with the highest severity value:

```
# Tripwire Binaries
(rulename = "Tripwire Binaries", severity = $(SIG_HI))
{
   $(TWBIN)/siggen    -> $(ReadOnly);
   $(TWBIN)/tripwire -> $(ReadOnly);
   $(TWBIN)/twadmin  -> $(ReadOnly);
   $(TWBIN)/twprint  -> $(ReadOnly);
}
```

The Tripwire Data Files rule also instructs `tripwire` to watch the policy configuration and key files. Note that in the file severity section earlier, SEC_BIN was defined to be ReadOnly, so you're telling `tripwire` that the policy, configuration, and key files should not change at all. Here's an example of the Tripwire Date Files rule:

```
# Tripwire Data Files - Configuration Files, Policy Files, Keys, ⏎
Reports, Databases
(rulename = "Tripwire Data Files", severity = $(SIG_HI))
{
$(TWDB)                         -> $(Dynamic) -i;
$(TWPOL)/tw.pol                 -> $(SEC_BIN) -i;
   $(TWBIN)/tw.cfg               -> $(SEC_BIN) -i;
```

```
$(TWLKEY)/$(HOSTNAME)-local.key    -> $(SEC_BIN) ;
$(TWSKEY)/site.key                 -> $(SEC_BIN) ;


#don't scan the individual reports
$(TWREPORT)                            -> $(Dynamic) (recurse=0);
}
```

Make sure to define rules to monitor the integrity of the policy directory, the key files, and the reports, as in the previous example. Note that the content of the report files is considered to be dynamic, and the recurse=0 directive instructs tripwire not to go into any of the report subdirectories.

The following is an example of a medium severity rule that defines a set of files that can change on a regular basis, but must retain their user and group ownership:

```
# Commonly accessed directories that should remain static with↵
regards to owner and group
(rulename = "Invariant Directories", severity = $(SIG_MED))
{
  /      -> $(SEC_INVARIANT) (recurse = 0);
  /home  -> $(SEC_INVARIANT) (recurse = 0);
  /etc   -> $(SEC_INVARIANT) (recurse = 0);
}
```

After you have edited the textual policy file to make any necessary additions or modifications, encrypt it and sign it with the following command:

```
[ramon]$ sudo /usr/TSS/bin/twadmin --create-polfile↵
/usr/TSS/policy/twpol.txt
```

This results in the creation of a binary file called /usr/TSS/policy/tw.pol. At this point, you have a valid configuration file and an initial policy file in place.

The next section explains how to initialize the tripwire database and how to start using the application.

Running *tripwire*

You're almost ready, but before you start comparing file signatures to look for tampering, you need to snap a baseline of what the signatures should look like on all the files in your policy. This takes place when you first initialize the signature database using the following command:

```
[ramon]$ /usr/TSS/bin/tripwire --init
```

Whenever you want to check the integrity of the current state of the files, simply issue the command

[ramon]$ **/usr/TSS/bin/tripwire --check**

which results in a report being written to stdout and saved to the file location specified in the REPORTFILE environment variable (see Listing 3.6).

If you would like the report to be e-mailed to you instead, use the following variant of the previous command:

[ramon]$ **/usr/TSS/bin/tripwire --check --email-report**

Once you have reviewed the report, you can confirm that any integrity differences have been acknowledged by writing the new integrity results to the database. Do this by using the following command:

[ramon]$ **/usr/TSS/bin/tripwire --update**

Finally, as you make changes to the policy file, you need to force tripwire to reload its policy definitions using the following command:

[ramon]$ **/usr/TSS/bin/tripwire --update-policy**

TIP I recommend that you run tripwire at least twice a day and examine the integrity reports carefully before updating the signature database. Ideally, you should simply add the tripwire --check --email-report command to a cron job. This command should be executed first thing in the morning and shortly before the system administration staff goes home for the day.

Password Auditing

Keeping track of logs and ensuring the integrity of your files can significantly strengthen your server, but it's easy to fall prey to the "crunchy on the outside, chewy on the inside" syndrome. The weakest link in most of today's Linux servers is the users and more specifically, their choice of passwords. While your security policy should always include a section outlining the properties of good passwords, you should also take a proactive approach to password security and conduct periodic audits of all your users' passwords.

As with any other Unix system, the Linux passwords are stored as the result of a one-way DES encryption operation on the original cleartext password. (Some Linux systems also support MD5 hashing for password protection.) This means that the actual password is never stored in the clear. Whenever a user attempts to log on to the system, the login program encrypts the password entered and compares the result to the one found in `/etc/passwd` (or `/etc/shadow`). Only if the two passwords match is the user allowed access to the system.

There are several password-auditing tools available for Linux. These tools take as input the encrypted password file, and they attempt to guess each user's password by staging a *dictionary attack*, where a collection of commonly used words is DES-encrypted one by one and the results are compared to the `/etc/passwd` entries. If a match is found, the username is recorded and included in the output report for the security administrator.

This section describes one of these tools, John the Ripper, developed as part of the Openwall project (`www.openwall.com`).

John the Ripper

An alternative to the original `crack` program, John the Ripper is a robust password-guessing tool that uses its own routines to attempt to crack passwords, rather than using the Linux `crypt(3)` system call. This results in a noticeable performance advantage over the earlier version of the `crack` tool. Another advantage is that John the Ripper runs on a variety of platforms (most Unix, DOS, and Windows systems), so you can use other machines in your network to try and crack your Linux servers' passwords.

By using John the Ripper to try to guess your own users' passwords, you can alert them that they have chosen too short or too weak a password and exhort them to change it before an attacker with the same tool guesses it and breaks into their account.

Installing *john*

The `john` installation is trivial. Download it from `www.openwall.com/john` (it's not available in RPM form), decompress it, and expand the archive (see the steps in Listing 3.7). Once you have expanded the sources into their own directory, go to the `src` directory and run the `make` command. Note that you have several options for the target executables (type **make** with no arguments to see the options). Listing 3.7 shows a build for an ELF format executable on the i386 architecture.

Listing 3.7   Installing and compiling *john*

```
[ramon]$ ls -l john-1.6.tar.gz
-rw-r--r--   1 ramon    users        497354 Oct  3 19:27 john-⤸
1.6.tar.gz
[ramon]$ gunzip john-1.6.tar.gz
[ramon]$ tar xf john-1.6.tar
[ramon]$ cd john-1.6
[ramon]$ ls
```

```
README  doc  run  src
[ramon]$ cd src
[ramon]$ make
To build John the Ripper, type:
        make SYSTEM
where SYSTEM can be one of the following:
linux-x86-any-elf         Linux, x86, ELF binaries
linux-x86-mmx-elf         Linux, x86 with MMX, ELF binaries
linux-x86-k6-elf          Linux, AMD K6, ELF binaries
linux-x86-any-a.out       Linux, x86, a.out binaries
linux-alpha               Linux, Alpha
linux-sparc               Linux, SPARC
generic                   Any other UNIX system with gcc
[ramon]$ make linux-x86-any-elf
ln -sf x86-any.h arch.h
make ../run/john ../run/unshadow ../run/unafs ../run/unique \
JOHN_OBJS="DES_fmt.o DES_std.o BSDI_fmt.o MD5_fmt.o MD5_std.o↵
BF_fmt.o BF_std.o AFS_fmt.o LM_fmt.o batch.o bench.o charset.o↵
common.o compiler.o config.o cracker.o external.o formats.o↵
getopt.o idle.o inc.o john.o list.o loader.o logger.o math.o↵
memory.o misc.o options.o params.o path.o recovery.o rpp.o↵
rules.o signals.o single.o status.o tty.o wordlist.o unshadow.o↵
unafs.o unique.o x86.o" \
        CFLAGS="-c -Wall -O2 -fomit-frame-pointer -m486"
make[1]: Entering directory `/home/ramon/john-1.6/src'
gcc -c -Wall -O2 -fomit-frame-pointer -m486 -funroll-loops DES_fmt.c
gcc -s DES_fmt.o DES_std.o BSDI_fmt.o MD5_fmt.o MD5_std.o BF_fmt.o↵
BF_std.o AFS_fmt.o LM_fmt.o batch.o bench.o charset.o↵
common.o compiler.o config.o cracker.o external.o formats.o↵
getopt.o idle.o inc.o john.o list.o loader.o logger.o math.o↵
memory.o misc.o options.o params.o path.o recovery.o rpp.o↵
rules.o signals.o single.o status.o tty.o wordlist.o unshadow.o↵
unafs.o unique.o x86.o -o ../run/john
ln -s john ../run/unshadow
ln -s john ../run/unafs
ln -s john ../run/unique
make[1]: Leaving directory `/home/ramon/john-1.6/src'
[ramon]$ ls -l ../run/john
-rwxr-xr-x   1 ramon    users      148428 Oct  3 19:59 ../run/john
```

There is no make installation step, so simply copy the executable to the appropriate place in your filesystem using the following command:

```
[ramon]$ sudo cp ../run/john /usr/local/bin
```

Configuring *john*

All configuration parameters are kept in the file ~\john.ini, which must be present in the current directory when john is invoked. There are four environment variables that can be configured in this file:

wordfile   The wordfile variable is the file that contains the word list to be used to crack passwords in batch style.

idle   When set to Y, the idle variable forces john to use only idle CPU cycles. I recommend this setting if you need to run john on a production server. The default value is N.

save   The save variable is the delay (in seconds) of the crash recovery file. This file contains checkpoints of the work done so far in case of an interruption. The default value is 600.

beep   When the beep variable set to Y, john beeps every time a password is successfully cracked. The default value is N.

The following is the [options] portion of a sample john.ini file containing these environment variables:

```
[ramon]$ more john.ini
#
# This file is part of John the Ripper password cracker,
# Copyright (c) 1996-98 by Solar Designer
#
[Options]
# Wordlist file name, to be used in batch mode
Wordfile = ~/password.lst
# Use idle cycles only
Idle = N
# Crash recovery file saving delay in seconds
Save = 600
# Beep when a password is found (who needs this anyway?)
Beep = N
```

Running *john*

By invoking john with no options, you can allow john to come up with enough random tries to crack the passwords:

```
[ramon]$ john /etc/passwd
```

Alternatively, you can supply a list of commonly used words for john to try. The word list can be a file; the following example uses the file my_guesses:

```
[ramon]$ john -wordfile:my_guesses /etc/passwd
```

As a third option, the word list can be piped in via the stdin, as in the following command:

```
[ramon]$ cat my_guesses | john -stdin /etc/passwd
```

Note that in general, john runs for a long time, and it writes its findings as it goes along into the ~/john.pot file. If you wish to see the passwords that john has cracked so far, issue the following command:

```
[ramon]$ john -show /etc/passwd
```

Also, if you are using shadow passwords, you need to merge /etc/passwd and /etc/shadow into a single file for john to work properly. (See Chapter 2, "System Installation and Setup," for information about shadow passwords. The john executable can do this conversion when invoked as unshadow. Start by creating a symbolic link using the command

```
[ramon]: sudo ln -s /usr/local/bin/john /usr/local/bin/unshadow
```

and then invoke the unshadow script with both files using the command

```
[ramon]$ unshadow /etc/passwd /etc/shadow > mypasswd
```

You now have a file (mypasswd) that you can try and crack through john:

```
[ramon]$ john mypasswd
```

Although it's very stable in its current form, the john utility is still being actively developed, and new versions often introduce a dramatic increase in performance. Check the Web site www.openwall.com periodically to look for updates.

In Sum

Security is a process, and putting up a strong defense is virtually useless unless you're willing to monitor your system for intrusions and stay vigilant. The `syslog` facility is a powerful system security tool, especially when the resulting log files are periodically monitored for abnormal behavior. This chapter describes two such tools: `swatch` and `logcheck`.

The value of examining log files, however, is greatly diminished if you can't be sure that their contents haven't been modified by an intruder in order to cover his/her tracks. Part of your security-monitoring procedures should include an integrity check on both log files and important system executables. This serves to assure you that the log files haven't been tampered with and that the executables haven't been replaced by Trojan horse versions.

Finally, it's easy to underestimate the importance of using good passwords that can stand up to naïve intrusion attempts. Among the password-auditing tools currently available for Linux, John the Ripper stands out as a clear winner because of its performance and its ease of use.

Once you have implemented your system security measures and established procedures for system monitoring and auditing, it's time to consider your network layer defense. The next part of this book, Part 2, "Network Security," describes the server configuration issues that impact network security and introduces monitoring and auditing tools and procedures that apply to the network layer.

Part 2

Network Security

Featuring:

- Understanding `inetd` and `xinetd` and Their Configurations
- Starting Network Services from the `/etc/rc.d` Directory
- Protecting Your Network Services with TCP Wrappers
- Understanding the `/etc/services` File
- Using the `netstat` Command for Network Connection Monitoring
- Using the `nessus` Package for Network Security Auditing
- Scanning Your Own Systems Using `nmap`
- Conducting Host-Based Security Audits Using TARA
- Detecting Port-Scan Attacks in Real Time Using PortSentry
- Dissecting Ethernet Packets Using Ethereal

4

Network Services Configuration

Part 1, "System Security," described the concepts that you need to master in order to secure your Linux installation and configuration before connecting your server to the public network. It explored the process of choosing a Linux distribution, configuring password authentication, and ensuring the confidentiality and availability of the data kept on the filesystems. In addition, it showed you how to ensure the integrity of system utilities and configuration files.

Part 2, "Network Security," takes the discussion one step away from the system itself and deals with the issues associated with connecting a Linux server to a network. Native support for a wide range of TCP/IP services has always been one of the strongest qualities of the Linux operating system. Configuring these services with security in mind, however, is an increasingly difficult challenge for system administrators as new network services are demanded of their servers.

This chapter begins Part 2 by discussing network services configuration on a Linux server. It includes a detailed description of

- The issues associated with the `inetd` daemon
- The `/etc/rc.d` startup files
- TCP Wrappers, a tool for enforcing access control on network daemons
- The commands that are available to show network activity on your server

Let's start by introducing a simple set of rules to apply when configuring Linux network daemons.

Securing Network Services

Once you feel comfortable with your system setup, it's time to take the next step: configuring the network interface(s) of the server and connecting them to your network. Whether this is an intranet server targeted for internal users or an Internet bastion host for public (and anonymous) use, there are some important issues for you to consider:

- Which network services are strictly necessary?
- Should other services be present, but inactive?
- Should I allow any client to connect to the server?
- Should certain clients be allowed to connect to *all* services?
- Do I need to maintain a log of service activity?

As always, it's imperative to run the minimum number of services and to ensure that the services that you need to offer don't introduce any of the vulnerabilities described in Chapter 1, "Understanding Linux Security." The bad news is there are literally hundreds of network services available (although they are not always enabled) on a typical Linux distribution. What is the good news, you ask? Well, there are only two places to look for these services: the inetd daemon and the /etc/rc.d directories.

The next section offers a detailed look at the inetd daemon and explains the syntax of its configuration file, /etc/inetd.conf.

Spawning Internet Daemons with *inetd*

All Linux distributions (and all Berkeley-style Unix variants for that matter) include a central network service utility controlled by the inetd process. This "super-server" acts as the clearinghouse, or central point of administration, for all Internet services running on the server. You can verify that the master inetd process is running on your system by entering the following command:

```
[ramon]$ ps aux | grep inetd
root        421  0.0  0.0  1232   60 ?          S     Sep24   0:00 inetd
```

The inetd daemon is started by Linux at system startup, and it immediately listens for the network ports listed in the /etc/inetd.conf file, the main configuration file for the inetd daemon (more on that in the next section). If an incoming request matches a network port number specified in its configuration, inetd assigns the appropriate listener application to the incoming socket and continues to listen for future connections. This is done in order to optimize system resources, because having a single process listen for several ports represents a lighter load on the system than having each process listen on its own port.

The only `inetd` command-line option of interest is `-d`. This option starts the daemon with debugging enabled, as in the following command:

```
[ramon]$ sudo /usr/sbin/inetd -d
```

Note that you have to stop the `inetd` daemon manually (because it gets started by default), and then re-invoke it with the debug option enabled, as shown in Listing 4.1.

Listing 4.1   Execution of *inetd* with the debug option enabled

```
[ramon]$ sudo killall inetd
[ramon]$ sudo /usr/sbin/inetd -d
ADD : ftp proto=tcp, wait.max=0.40, user.group=root.(null)↵
builtin=0 server=/usr/sbin/tcpd
ADD : telnet proto=tcp, wait.max=0.40, user.group=root.(null)↵
builtin=0 server=/usr/sbin/tcpd
ADD : login proto=tcp, wait.max=0.40, user.group=root.(null)↵
builtin=0 server=/usr/sbin/tcpd
someone wants telnet
accept, ctrl 3
24257 execl /usr/sbin/tcpd
24257 reaped
someone wants ftp
accept, ctrl 3
24259 execl /usr/sbin/tcpd
24259 reaped
someone wants pop-3
accept, ctrl 3
24261 execl /usr/sbin/tcpd
...
```

Keep in mind that, when invoked with the `-d` option, `inetd` displays its diagnostics to the `stderr` process (the controlling `tty` by default), making this option useful only when you're trying to troubleshoot a problem. Listing 4.1 shows a debug session during which three requests are received (`telnet`, `ftp`, and `pop-3`).

The next section discusses `/etc/inetd.conf`, the configuration file used by the `inetd` daemon.

Configuring *inetd* with */etc/inetd.conf*

As with any Linux facility, the `inetd` daemon consults a plain-text configuration file upon startup. The `/etc/inetd.conf` contains one line for each of the services that `inetd` is to listen for. Each line contains seven positional fields, separated by a tab character or a space, as described in this section. Note that each field must be included on each line. These seven fields are as follows:

Service Name   The *service name* field is the actual name of the service to listen for (e.g., telnet, ftp, finger, etc.). These services should correspond to a TCP or UDP port number, and this mapping should be present in the /etc/services file (discussed later in this chapter) or in the /etc/rpc file for RPC-style services. In both cases, the service name is the first field in those files.

Socket Type   The *socket type* field has a value of stream, dgram, raw, rdm, or seqpacket. In a typical Internet Linux server, you should only see stream (for TCP sockets) and dgram (for UDP sockets).

Protocol   The *protocol* field denotes the type of transport layer protocol that the daemon uses. It is one of the choices in the /etc/protocols file (e.g., tcp, udp).

Wait/Nowait[.max]   This field applies to dgram services only and refers to the dae-mon's ability to process incoming requests with multiple threads (nowait) or a single thread (wait). The optional [.*max*] field is an integer that denotes the maximum number of server instances to spawn in a 60-second interval. You should have no reason to change this from the default of 40. Increasing this value does not enhance the performance of most services and could open the door to a denial-of-service (DoS) attack.

User [.group]   The inetd daemon can spawn a service with ownership other than the root user. You can specify both the *user* and the optional *group* as the service to be run. I recommend that you never run a service as root unless strictly necessary (use the nobody username when possible). If running as root, make sure to configure swatch or logcheck (see Chapter 3, "System Monitoring and Auditing," for more information on those utilities) to monitor its messages as closely as possible.

Server Program   The *server program* field specifies the actual executable that is spawned when a request is received. Make sure that you specify the entire path to avoid attacks that may change the default $PATH variable in the system. Also, apply good integrity-assurance techniques (see the discussion of the tripwire utility in Chapter 3) to this executable, in order to avoid Trojan horse attacks. Note that the keyword internal can be used if the inetd daemon handles this request by itself (e.g., echo, time, chargen, and discard).

TIP In a security-minded Linux server, the server program should always be tcpd. (See the section "TCP Wrappers" later in this chapter.)

Server Program Arguments   The *server program arguments* field is the place to specify arguments that you would like to pass to the server program. Note that you must start with the program name itself (argv[0] in Linux programming terms).

inetd Configuration Examples

By default, Linux distributions are shipped with a generous set of daemons in the inetd.conf file. Consider, for instance, the standard /etc/inetd.conf file that is shipped with the SuSE 7.0 distribution, as shown in Listing 4.2. (The comment lines in this etc/inetd.conf file have been removed for simplicity.)

Listing 4.2   A typical default */etc/inetd.conf* file

```
[ramon]$ grep -v "^#" /etc/inetd.conf
time      stream  tcp  nowait  root    internal
time      dgram   udp  wait    root    internal
ftp       stream  tcp  nowait  root    /usr/sbin/tcpd  in.ftpd
telnet    stream  tcp  nowait  root    /usr/sbin/tcpd  in.telnetd
shell     stream  tcp  nowait  root    /usr/sbin/tcpd  in.rshd -L
login     stream  tcp  nowait  root    /usr/sbin/tcpd  in.rlogind
talk      dgram   udp  wait    root    /usr/sbin/tcpd  in.talkd
ntalk     dgram   udp  wait    root    /usr/sbin/tcpd  in.talkd
pop3      stream  tcp  nowait  root    /usr/sbin/tcpd  /usr/sbin/popper -s
finger    stream  tcp  nowait  nobody  /usr/sbin/tcpd  in.fingerd -w
http-rman stream  tcp        nowait.10000    nobody  /usr/sbin/tcpd↵
/usr/sbin/http-rman
swat      stream  tcp        nowait.400      root    /usr/sbin/swat  swat
```

The system administrator has some work to do on this file. First of all, very few Linux servers need to provide time services, and the talk/ntalk services are of questionable use for most of today's server installations. The same applies to the finger service. The POP3 daemon should only be present if your server is meant to house user mailboxes, and I recommend that such a server be dedicated exclusively to that purpose.

Both the shell and login services are RPC-based daemons, and, along with the telnet and ftp services, they should be replaced with a secure equivalent, like Secure Shell (ssh). The ssh application is discussed in detail in Chapter 12, "Virtual Private Networking."

http-rman is a tool that converts Linux man-format manual pages to HTML on the fly for real-time perusal via a Web server. Finally, the swat service is the Samba Web Administration Tool (SWAT). If you have a legitimate need for either of these services, be sure that TCP Wrappers is properly configured to restrict their access to only authorized clients. Make sure you see the following response from this grep command:

```
[ramon]$ grep http-rman /etc/hosts.allow
http-rman : ALL EXCEPT LOCAL
```

The syntax of the /etc/hosts.[allow|deny] file is described in the "TCP Wrappers" section later in this chapter.

xinetd: The Next Generation *inetd*

When Panos Tsirigotis of the Computer Science Department at University of Colorado at Boulder realized that most Linux network administrators were using TCP Wrappers in conjunction with inetd, he set off to come up with a tool that would offer the features from both applications. The result was xinetd, the extended Internet services daemon.

On the surface, xinetd works just like inetd, acting as a super-server that inspects all incoming connections and spawns the appropriate server program to handle each connection. Like inetd, xinetd can also be started with a -d option to force more verbose output for debugging purposes:

> [ramon]$ **sudo /usr/sbin/xinetd -d**

But the real advantage of xinetd over its predecessor is its security features. While inetd with TCP Wrappers can block incoming connections based on source/destination IP addresses and port numbers, xinetd allows the screening of connections based on

- Rate of incoming connections (useful to thwart denial-of-service attacks)
- Total number of connections for a particular service
- Number of incoming connections from specific hosts
- Time of the day

In addition, you can define limits on the size of the log files that the service creates so that a potential attacker can't stage a denial-of-service attack on your server by filling your disk with logging information. Finally, xinetd lets you define a forwarding rule by which incoming connections can be redirected to other hosts in the private network (for example) that need not be reachable from the public Internet.

Installing *xinetd*

While Red Hat Linux 7.0 includes xinetd as part of the standard distribution, most Linux vendors have not yet bundled xinetd into their product. You can easily obtain the RPM version of the xinetd package from a trusted archive like www.rpmfind.net. To install xinetd, enter the following command:

> [ramon]$ **sudo rpm -i xinetd-2.1.8.9pre9-6.i386.rpm**

This package installs the server executable (/usr/sbin/xinetd), as well as the man pages and a startup file (/etc/rc.d/init.d/xinetd).

Configuring *xinetd* with */etc/xinetd.conf*

The xinetd daemon is started by Linux at system startup, and its configuration is obtained from /etc/xinetd.conf, as well as from all the files in the /etc/xinetd.d/

directory. Each file in this directory contains the xinetd configuration for a particular service. (Each file is the equivalent of a single line of /etc/inetd.conf.) For example, the following directory listing of /etc/xinetd.d/ shows that this system has been configured to offer telnet, tftp, and imap services via xinetd:

```
[ramon]$ ls -l /etc/xinetd.d/*
-rw-r--r--    1 root      root              169 Feb  3 17:18 tftp
-rw-r--r--    1 root      root              322 Mar 16 23:28 imap
-rw-r--r--    1 root      root              318 Feb  3 17:18 telnet
```

A typical file in this directory looks like the following:

```
service service_name
{
keyword = value value value ...
keyword += value value value ...
keyword -= value value value ...


...
}
```

service_name is the actual name of the service to listen for (for example, telnet, ftp, finger, etc.), as defined in the /etc/services file. The *keyword* field defines a set that can be assigned one or more values (=), appended one or more values (+=), or reduced by one or more values (-=). The following are some of the most useful keywords supported by the xinetd utility:

disable Setting the disable keyword to yes results in the service not starting. Set this keyword to no to enable the service to listen for. This keyword is useful for temporarily disabling a service without having to delete the file from the /etc/xinetd.d/ directory.

socket_type The socket_type keyword can have a value of stream, dgram, raw, rdm, or seqpacket. In a typical Internet Linux server, you should use only stream (for TCP sockets) and dgram (for UDP sockets).

protocol The protocol keyword is the type of transport layer protocol that the daemon uses. It is one of the choices in /etc/protocols (e.g. tcp, udp).

wait The wait attribute determines whether the service is single-threaded or multithreaded. If its value is set to yes, the service is single-threaded; this forces xinetd to start the server and stop handling requests for the service until the server dies. If the value is set to no, xinetd continues to handle new requests after starting the server.

Network Security

PART 2

user   The user keyword defines the uid to use for the server process.

group   The group keyword defines the gid to use for the server process.

instances   The instances keyword defines the maximum number of server instances that can be active concurrently for this service. The value can be either a number or the value UNLIMITED (no limit).

server   The server keyword is the fully qualified location of the server program to handle this service.

server_args   The server_args keyword specifies the set of arguments passed to the server. Unlike inetd, the server name itself should not be included in the list of arguments.

only_from   The only_from keyword specifies the remote hosts or networks from which the given service is available. Its value can be a host name (host.example.com), a domain (.example.com), a single-host IP address (63.75.44.67), a network address (63.75.44.0), or an IP address with a netmask range description (63.75.44.0/24).

no_access   The no_access keyword specifies the remote hosts or networks to which the particular service is unavailable.

access_times   The access_times keyword specifies the time intervals when the service is available. Time periods are specified using the syntax: *hour*:*min*-*hour*:*min* (e.g., 09:00-17:00).

log_on_type   The log_on_type keyword defines the destination of the log messages. The value can be one of the following:

- SYSLOG *syslog_facility* [*syslog_level*]: Send the output to the specified syslog facility with the specified level.
- *FILE* [*soft_limit* [*hard_limit*]]: Send the output to *FILE*. Once the file size has reached *soft_limit*, a message is logged. Once the file size has reached *hard_limit*, logging ceases.

log_on_success   The log_on_success keyword defines the type of information to be logged when the remote client connects to the server and when the connection is torn down. The value can be one of the following:

- PID: Log the server's process ID.
- HOST: Log the remote host address.
- USERID: Log the user ID of the remote process.
- EXIT: Log the fact that the service exited, including the exit status.
- DURATION: Log the duration of a service session.

log_on_failure   The log_on_failure keyword defines the type of information to be logged when the remote client cannot connect to the server, either because of access control or because of limits imposed on resource allocation. The value can be one of the following:

- HOST: Log the remote host address.
- USERID: Log the user ID of the remote process.
- ATTEMPT: Log the fact that the attempt was made.

bind   The bind keyword specifies the interface or IP address to listen on. This lets you run a server on only the secure interface of a multi-homed server, for example.

redirect   The redirect keyword specifies the IP address and port number to which xinetd should forward incoming connections. When a connection is received for the specified service, xinetd spawns a process to forward the connection to the given IP address and an optional TCP port.

xinetd Configuration Examples

The main xinetd configuration file resides in /etc/xinetd.conf, and typically contains a defaults section with parameters that affect all services, along with an includedir statement that effectively pulls in all service-specific files in the target directory (/etc/xinetd.d, in this case). Listing 4.3 illustrates a typical /etc/xinetd.conf file.

Listing 4.3   A typical default */etc/xinetd.conf* file

```
#
# Simple configuration file for xinetd
#
# Some defaults, and include /etc/xinetd.d/

defaults
{
        instances           = 60
        log_type            = SYSLOG authpriv
        log_on_success      = HOST PID
        log_on_failure      = HOST
}


includedir /etc/xinetd.d
```

Note that the file in Listing 4.3 limits the total number of concurrent xinetd instances for a given service to 60. In addition, it requests that logging be performed via the authpriv facility of the standard syslog system. Successful connection attempts log the connecting host and the process ID, and failed connection attempts log the host name only.

The following excerpt is an example of a `telnet` configuration in the `/etc/xinetd.d/` directory, included by the main `/etc/xinetd.conf` file:

```
[ramon]$ sudo more /etc/xinetd.d/telnet
service telnet
        {
                socket_type     = stream
                wait            = no
                user            = root
                server          = /usr/sbin/in.telnetd
                redirect        = 10.0.0.2 23
                bind            = 127.0.0.1
                log_on_failure += USERID
                disable         = no
        }
```

This `telnet` service defines the stream (TCP) socket type, specifies multi-threaded operation (`wait` = no), uses the root username as the owner of the service, and logs the user ID when there is an unsuccessful login. Note that this file uses the += operator to add USERID to the set of values already defined for the `log_on_failure` variable (`/etc/xinetd.conf` defined `log_on_failure` = HOST). This file also includes a `redirect` statement to forward all `telnet` connections to host 10.0.0.2 (standard `telnet` port 23), while only listening for connections on the `loopback` interface (127.0.0.1).

Consider a slightly different example:

```
[ramon]$ sudo more /etc/xinetd.d/imap
service imap
        {
                socket_type     = stream
                wait            = no
                user            = root
                server          = /usr/local/sbin/imapd
                only_from       = 204.154.22.0/24 localhost
                disable         = yes
        }
```

In this case, the file defines a listener for the IMAP service (Internet Mail Access Protocol), where only hosts in the 204.154.22.0 class C domain and on the local host are allowed to request service. Note that this file temporarily disables the service by setting the disable keyword to yes.

Let's look at one more example:

```
[ramon]$ sudo more /etc/xinetd.d/tftp
service tftp
        {
                socket_type   = dgram
                wait          = yes
                user          = nobody
                server        = /usr/sbin/in.tftpd
                server_args   = /tftpboot
                access_times  = 01:00-23:00
                disable       = no

        }
```

This is an illustration of a server (tftpd) that takes a command-line argument (/tftpboot, or the location of the TFTP directory). This is handled by adding the argument to the server_args keyword. Note that this example restricts the access times to this service from 1 A.M. to 11 P.M., perhaps due to the fact that there is a scheduled maintenance period from 11 P.M. to 1 A.M. every day.

Starting Network Services from */etc/rc.d*

While most of the core Linux network services are started from inetd, an increasing number of daemons are being configured to start independently upon system startup. This gives application programmers tighter control over the execution of their services, and allows them to spawn additional instances of certain daemons, sometimes even in advance of receiving a request. This is especially useful for high-volume and high-overhead services, like WWW, Sendmail, SSH, etc.

It is important, however, to maintain all the startup scripts in a central location within the filesystem, and Linux uses the /etc/rc.d directory as the default for this purpose. Within this directory, there are a number of subdirectories named in a similar manner:

```
[ramon]$ cd /etc/rc.d
[ramon]$ ls -ld rc*.d
```

```
drwxr-xr-x  2 root    root      4096 Jul 29 14:30 rc0.d
drwxr-xr-x  2 root    root      4096 Oct 21 13:42 rc1.d
drwxr-xr-x  2 root    root      4096 Oct 22 15:40 rc2.d
drwxr-xr-x  2 root    root      4096 Oct 22 15:40 rc3.d
drwxr-xr-x  2 root    root      4096 Jul 29 14:30 rc4.d
drwxr-xr-x  2 root    root      4096 Jul 29 14:30 rc5.d
drwxr-xr-x  2 root    root      4096 Jul 29 14:30 rc6.d
drwxr-xr-x  2 root    root      4096 Oct 21 13:41 rcS.d
```

Each of these directories contains scripts to be executed when the system enters a particular runlevel (0–6 and S). Table 4.1 shows the significance of each runlevel. The system's init process (always the first process to be executed) invokes the actions found in the /etc/inittab file, which in turn, invokes the appropriate file in /etc/rc.d as the system enters each runlevel.

Table 4.1   The Linux Runlevels and Their Meanings

Runlevel	Meaning
0	Halt the system (shutdown)
1	Multi-user mode without network
2	Multi-user mode with network
3	Multi-user mode with network and xdm (X-display manager)
4	Reserved (not used by Linux)
5	Reserved (not used by Linux)
6	System restart (reboot)
S	Single-user mode

Each directory contains both start scripts (filename starts with S) and kill scripts (filename starts with K), as shown in Listing 4.4.

Listing 4.4   Partial contents of the *etc/rc.d/rc3.d* directory

```
[ramon]$ cd rc3.d
[ramon]$ ls -l
total 0
lrwxrwxrwx 1 root root  8 Oct 21 13:45 K20rwhod -> ../rwhod
lrwxrwxrwx 1 root root 11 Oct 21 13:45 K20sendmail -> ../sendmail
lrwxrwxrwx 1 root root 13 Oct 21 13:45 K22wvdial.dod ->↵
../wvdial.dod
lrwxrwxrwx 1 root root 12 Oct 21 13:45 K23nfsserver -> ../nfsserver
lrwxrwxrwx 1 root root  9 Oct 21 13:41 K23pcnfsd -> ../pcnfsd
lrwxrwxrwx 1 root root  9 Oct 21 13:44 K24autofs -> ../autofs
lrwxrwxrwx 1 root root 11 Oct 21 13:45 K24ypclient -> ../ypclient
lrwxrwxrwx 1 root root  9 Oct 21 13:41 K30random -> ../random
lrwxrwxrwx 1 root root  9 Oct 21 13:41 K35routed -> ../routed
lrwxrwxrwx 1 root root  9 Oct 21 13:42 K35syslog -> ../syslog
lrwxrwxrwx 1 root root  6 Oct 21 13:41 K36nfs -> ../nfs
lrwxrwxrwx 1 root root  8 Oct 21 13:41 K38route -> ../route
lrwxrwxrwx 1 root root 11 Oct 21 13:45 K40dhclient -> ../dhclient
lrwxrwxrwx 1 root root 10 Oct 21 13:41 K40network -> ../network
lrwxrwxrwx 1 root root  8 Oct 21 13:41 K45dummy -> ../dummy
lrwxrwxrwx 1 root root 17 Oct 21 13:45 K45irda -> /sbin/init.d/irda
lrwxrwxrwx 1 root root 11 Oct 21 13:45 K51firewall -> ../firewall
lrwxrwxrwx 1 root root 10 Oct 21 13:41 K99kerneld -> ../kerneld
lrwxrwxrwx 1 root root  8 Oct 21 13:45 S20rwhod -> ../rwhod
lrwxrwxrwx 1 root root 11 Oct 21 13:45 S20sendmail -> ../sendmail
lrwxrwxrwx 1 root root  7 Oct 22 14:54 S20sshd -> ../sshd
lrwxrwxrwx 1 root root  7 Oct 21 13:41 S21cron -> ../cron
lrwxrwxrwx 1 root root  8 Oct 21 13:45 S21smbfs -> ../smbfs
lrwxrwxrwx 1 root root 13 Oct 21 13:45 S22wvdial.dod -> ../wvdial.dod
lrwxrwxrwx 1 root root  6 Oct 21 13:41 S30xdm -> ../xdm
lrwxrwxrwx 1 root root 11 Oct 21 13:45 S99firewall_final ->↵
../firewall
```

Note that both the start and kill scripts are really just symbolic links to the same script, which lives in the /etc/rc.d directory (in the case of SuSE) or in the /etc/rc.d/init.d directory (in the case of Red Hat and other Linux distributions). When the system is coming up, the S scripts are invoked with a command-line argument of start. When the system is coming down, the K scripts are invoked instead, with a command-line argument of stop. The two numbers after the first letter of the script determine the order in which the script is executed. For example, the S20at script is executed before the S21cron script.

Although judging by the size of the /etc/rc.d directory, there are a large number of daemons started, in reality, most of these scripts check for the existence of a specific configuration before starting the service. This means that unless you have explicitly asked your server to offer a specific service (such as rwho, for example), the daemon is not started by the script. The S20rwhod script, shown in Listing 4.5, first checks the /etc /rc.config file and only starts the rwho daemon if it detects that the $START_RWHOD environment variable has been set to yes.

Listing 4.5   The *S20rwhod* startup script

```
[ramon]$ more S20rwhod
#! /bin/sh
# Copyright (c) 1998, 2000 SuSE GmbH Nuernberg, Germany.All rights⤦
reserved.
#
# /sbin/init.d/rwhod
#

. /etc/rc.config

base=${0##*/}
link=${base#*[SK][0-9][0-9]}

test $link = $base && START_RWHOD=yes
test "$START_RWHOD" = yes || exit 0

return=$rc_done
case "$1" in
    start)
        echo -n "Starting rwho daemon"
        startproc /usr/sbin/rwhod || return=$rc_failed
        echo -e "$return"
        ;;
    stop)
        echo -n "Shutting down rwho daemon"
        killproc -TERM /usr/sbin/rwhod || return=$rc_failed
        echo -e "$return"
        ;;
    reload|restart)
        $0 stop && $0 start || return=$rc_failed
        ;;
    status)
        checkproc /usr/sbin/rwhod && echo OK || echo No process
```

```
        ;;
    *)
        echo "Usage: $0 {start|stop|reload|restart}"
        exit 1
esac

test "$return" = "$rc_done" || exit 1
exit 0
```

Note that the S20rwhod script can be used to start and kill the rwho daemon, since it checks for the command-line argument with which it was called.

The first time that you boot up your system, make sure to record which daemons get started to ensure that you are not running anything that you don't intend to run. The trusty ps command is the right tool to verify which /etc/rc.d services are running on your server, as shown in Listing 4.6.

Listing 4.6   Looking for active network services in the process table

```
[root]$ ps aux
root    1  0.0  0.0   400  280  ?    S   15:02 0:03 init
root    2  0.0  0.0     0    0  ?    SW  15:02 0:00 [powerd]
root    3  0.0  0.0     0    0  ?    SW  15:02 0:00 [kflushd]
root    4  0.0  0.0     0    0  ?    SW  15:02 0:00 [kupdate]
root    5  0.0  0.0     0    0  ?    SW  15:02 0:00 [kpiod]
root    6  0.0  0.0     0    0  ?    SW  15:02 0:00 [kswapd]
root    7  0.0  0.0     0    0  ?    SW  15:03 0:00 [md_thread]
root   86  0.0  0.2  1384  808  ?    S   15:03 0:00 /usr/sbin/syslogd
root  190  0.0  0.2  1632 1064  ?    S   15:03 0:00 /usr/sbin/klogd -c 1
root  270  0.0  0.6  7264 2336  ?    S   15:03 0:00 /usr/sbin/httpd -f⤸
/etc/httpd/httpd.conf -D SUSEHELP
root  292  0.0  0.1  1280  648  ?    S   15:03 0:00 /usr/sbin/gpm -t sun⤸
-m /dev/mouse
root  301  0.0  0.1  1344  704  ?    S   15:03 0:00 /usr/sbin/inetd
root  341  0.0  0.4  2632 1600  ?    S   15:03 0:00 sendmail: accepting⤸
connections
root  343  0.1  0.3  2376 1184  ?    S   15:03 0:11 /usr/local/sbin/sshd
root  352  0.0  0.2  1552  880  ?    S   15:03 0:00 /usr/sbin/cron
root  398  0.0  0.1  1224  632 tty2  S   15:03 0:00 /sbin/mingetty tty2
root  399  0.0  0.1  1224  632 tty3  S   15:03 0:00 /sbin/mingetty tty3
root  400  0.0  0.1  1224  632 tty4  S   15:03 0:00 /sbin/mingetty tty4
root   01  0.0  0.1  1224  632 tty5  S   15:03 0:00 /sbin/mingetty tty5
root  402  0.0  0.1  1224  632 tty6  S   15:03 0:00 /sbin/mingetty tty6
root  420  1.0  2.0 14144 7848  ?    SL  15:03 1:57 /usr/X11R6/bin/X :0
```

Network Security

PART 2

```
root 471  0.0  0.6  4024 2328 ?    S  15:05 0:01↵
/usr/local/sbin/sshd
root 472  0.0  0.1  1392  736 ?    S  15:05 0:00 /usr/bin/lpd
root 369  0.0  0.0     0    0 ?    Z  18:14 0:00 [cron <defunct>]
```

There are several noteworthy daemons in the process table in Listing 4.5:

- A `sendmail` process listening on TCP port 25
- A line-printer daemon (`lpd`) listening for network print requests from remote clients
- A Web server (PID 270) listening on TCP port 80
- A `syslogd` process accepting remote `syslog` requests on UDP port 514
- A Secure Shell (SSH) process listening for client requests on port TCP 22

Let's say that you don't want to run a specific service. In this case, you need to modify the `/etc/rc.d` directory accordingly. There are several ways to prevent these services from starting, and each Linux distribution has a system tool (`linuxconf`, `yast`, etc.) that provides you with this capability. But it's important to know how to do it "under the hood," because all of these tools are just modifying these script directories anyway.

You start by identifying during which runlevel the service is started; let's use `apache` as an example. The following `find` command walks through the `/etc/rc.d` directory tree and identifies in which subdirectory the `apache` script is present. For example, if you find a startup script in `/etc/rc.d/rc3.d`, you know that the service in question is being started when the server enters runlevel 3.

```
[ramon]$ find /etc/rc.d/* -name "*apache" -print
/etc/rc.d/rc2.d/K20apache
/etc/rc.d/rc2.d/S20apache
/etc/rc.d/rc3.d/K20apache
/etc/rc.d/rc3.d/S20apache
```

You can see that the `apache` daemon gets invoked during both runlevel 2 and runlevel 3. You can then move to delete these files because they're simply symbolic links to `/etc/rc.d/apache`:

```
[ramon]$ sudo find /etc/rc.d/* -name "*apache" -exec rm {} \;
```

Note that the previous command prevents `apache` from coming up the next time you restart the system. In order to terminate the current process, execute the following command:

```
[ramon]$ sudo killall httpd
```

By cleaning out your `/etc/inetd.conf` and `/etc/rc.d` files, you have gone a long way toward keeping your network daemons under control. The next section describes how to go the distance by also controlling some of the configuration files that unwanted daemons tend to leave behind.

Additional Network Security Considerations

While most daemons are started from inetd and /etc/rc.d, there are also a number of places within your server that you should be watching. These include mostly configuration files for network services, which should be audited in the event that a service is unintentionally started. For example, special attention should be paid to rhosts authentication, the portmapper daemon, and services started as chroot. The next three sections of this chapter describe each of these topics in detail.

Disabling *rhosts* authentication

Although most current Linux distributions no longer come configured for this type of authentication, a few older systems may still be vulnerable. First and foremost, make sure that your inetd.conf file does not include support for the rlogin daemon. The command

```
[ramon]$ grep rlogin /etc/inetd.conf
```

should not return anything. If you do have rlogin enabled, simply delete (or comment out) the offending line and restart the inetd daemon. The r series of remote access commands (rsh, rlogin, rcp) are riddled with security holes and should not be used.

In addition, look for the /etc/hosts.equiv file, or an .rhosts file in any home directory. If there is one, remove or rename it immediately. If this file contains a host name definition (or IP address), users on that host will be able to rlogin to your server without being prompted for a password if you accidentally leave rlogin running. This is the ultimate vulnerability, and it's the main reason why the r commands should never be used.

Use the following command as the root user to periodically weed out all .rhosts files from users' home directories:

```
[ramon]$ sudo find /home -name ".rhosts" -exec rm {} \;
```

The *portmap* Daemon and RPC Services

The *portmapper (*portmap*)* is the network service that enables remote procedure call (RPC) facilities such as Network File Systems (NFS) for file sharing and Network Information Services (NIS or "yellow pages") for name resolution. Started from /etc/rc*.d, the portmap daemon listens to local RPC servers, which register their port numbers with the portmap services. (Unlike regular inetd-driven services, RPC programs don't bind to a fixed TCP/UDP port.) Remote clients that wish to use an RPC service contact the portmap first, which then returns the port number where the RPC daemon can be reached.

RPC-based services can be extremely vulnerable to malicious attacks, especially when the intruder registers a bogus RPC service remotely and asks portmap to listen for requests to this service. In addition, it is very difficult to enforce access control on RPC-based services, especially since their associated ports change each time the system is rebooted. This makes the portmap daemon a security liability.

If you are using a Linux distribution that's over two years old, I recommend that you disable it as soon as you build your system and leave it disabled until you come up with an alternative.

TIP If your Linux distribution is more than three years old, I also recommend that you upgrade your Linux system altogether. Just make sure that you test the upgrade on a practice server and not on a development server; otherwise you could run into a lot of trouble.

In most Linux distributions, portmap is started or stopped from one or more of the following files:

- /etc/rc.d/rc2.d/S11portmap
- /etc/rc.d/rc3.d/S11portmap
- /etc/rc.d/rc4.d/S11portmap
- /etc/rc.d/rc5.d/S11portmap

Since 1996, Linux distributions have included a secure version of the portmap service that can enforce access-control rules on the same files as TCP Wrappers (/etc/hosts.allow and /etc/hosts.deny). To find out if you're running this version of portmap, insert the following line into the /etc/hosts.deny file:

    portmap: ALL

In addition, insert the following line into the /etc/hosts.allow file:

    portmap: <a trusted hostname>

Then, proceed to mount an NFS share from the trusted host and from a different host. If you can mount the share from the trusted host but not from the different host, you're running a version of portmap that enforces access control. You can go ahead and enable it by putting the startup script back in /etc/rc.d/rc*.d/S11pormap.

Note, however, that securing the portmap service is only one step toward enhancing the security of your system. If you must use RPC services, make sure that each of them (NIS, NFS, etc.) is secure and up to date, because an intruder can always simply brute-force guess which port the service is running on.

Running Network Services as *chroot*

Linux allows you to run a command with a modified root directory such that directory references are relative to the path specified in the chroot command. This allows you, for example, to run several instances of an HTTP server, each with its own set of configurations and executables. The idea is an attractive one: allow the process to believe that it has free reign of the server while confining it to a small "sandbox." However, the chroot protection can be easily circumvented, especially when the application runs with root privileges.

Limit chroot execution of network services to instances when the daemon runs under a nonprivileged user, and ideally, to when the daemon operates in read-only mode. chroot is especially useful for non-interactive Web servers whose content stays static over time.

TCP Wrappers

Developed by Wietse Venema during his tenure at The Netherlands' Eindhoven University, the TCP Wrappers package has quickly become a standard tool included in all of today's Linux distributions. Furthermore, this is arguably the most useful network security tool to come along since the dawning of the operating system.

By interposing itself between the inetd daemon and the server application itself, TCP Wrappers adds a layer of access control to an otherwise wide-open inetd facility. The real beauty of this tool, and the main reason for its popularity, is its simple design. There is no need to recompile (or even modify) either the inetd daemon or the server applications themselves. Instead, you simply modify your /etc/inetd.conf file to include the TCP Wrappers application instead of the real server name. The TCP Wrappers application receives and examines every connection request and decides to grant it or deny it based on a set of criteria specified by the network administrator.

The next two sections describe the TCP Wrappers installation and configuration.

Installing TCP Wrappers

The success of TCP Wrappers has resulted in its widespread use on the majority of production Linux servers today. In fact, most distributions even come outfitted with a default configuration for TCP Wrappers. If you need to install TCP Wrappers on an older Linux installation, or you would like to upgrade your existing installation, simply find the .rpm distribution of the tool in your favorite archive. Listing 4.7 shows you how to install TCP Wrappers using the RPM facility.

Listing 4.7   Installing TCP Wrappers via RPM (Upgrade option)

```
[ramon]$ rpm -q tcp_wrappers
tcp_wrappers-7.6-7
[ramon]$ sudo rpm -U tcp_wrappers-7.6-10.i386.rpm
```

Network Security

PART 2

```
[ramon]$ rpm -q tcp_wrappers
tcp_wrappers-7.6-10
```

Listing 4.7 shows a system that was running version 7.6.7 and has been upgraded to the more recent version 7.6.10.

WARNING Trojan horse versions of TCP Wrappers were placed on a number of public FTP servers around January 21, 1999. The offending file was labeled as version 7.6, and it introduced a root vulnerability on the systems where it was installed. I strongly discourage you from downloading this file (the tar archive was named tcp_wrappers_7.6.tar.gz). Obtain it in RPM format from a well-known and trusted repository instead. Refer to CERT Advisory CA-1999-01 for more detailed information.

Once you have verified your TCP Wrappers installation, it's time to look at the configuration files that you need to edit. This is the topic of the next section.

Configuring TCP Wrappers

The first step in configuring the TCP Wrappers package is to make sure it is being properly invoked. This is done by ensuring that the service name field in /etc/inetd.conf is set to the location of the tcpd binary (/usr/sbin/tcpd in Listing 4.2). This allows the TCP Wrappers daemon to intercept all incoming requests and to examine them before passing them on to the real server application. The name of this application is specified in the server program arguments field of /etc/inetd.conf.

The real power of the TCP Wrappers tool is the fine-grain level of access control that it provides. The system administrator can define a set of allowable clients for each network service. To do this, you must edit two configuration files that are typically found in the /etc directory: /etc/hosts.allow and /etc/hosts.deny. These files are already included in most Linux distributions, but make sure that they exist and edit them to reflect your site's security policy.

These two files are consulted by the TCP Wrappers application in that order (first hosts.allow, then hosts.deny) and can contain rules specifying access-control directives. The connection request is granted unless there is a specific deny directive found in one of these files. I recommend that your /etc/hosts.deny file have a catchall rule at the end that denies all requests. This forces you to have to enter specific allow directives for those services that should be permitted.

The basic syntax for the rules in the /etc/hosts.allow and /etc/hosts.deny files is as follows:

```
daemon_list : client_list [: shell_command]
```

These fields have the following meanings:

- *daemon_list* is a comma-separated list of server names.
- *client_list* is a comma-separated list of patterns matching one or more clients.
- *shell_command* is the action to execute when the rule has found a match.

Table 4.2 describes the types of expressions that can make up one of these rules.

Table 4.2   TCP Wrappers Configuration: Access Control List Patterns

Pattern	Meaning
.example.com	Any host name that ends with .example.com.
134.33.	Any host address whose first two octets are 134.33.
10.0.0.0/255.0.0.0	The class-A network 10.0.0.0.
ALL	A true wildcard (i.e., *any* host).
LOCAL	Host name that contains no period (.).
KNOWN	Both host name and address are resolved (via DNS).
UNKNOWN	Both host name and address are not resolved (via DNS).
PARANOID	Host name does not match the address (via DNS).

In addition, shell commands can make use of a number of supplied variables whose instance gets replaced on the fly according to the current context. Table 4.3 summarizes the most significant of these variables.

Table 4.3   TCP Wrappers Configuration: Shell Command Expansion

Pattern	Meaning
%a	Client host address
%A	Server host address
%h	Client host name

Network Security

PART 2

Table 4.3   TCP Wrappers Configuration: Shell Command Expansion *(continued)*

Pattern	Meaning
%H	Server host name
%p	Daemon process ID
%d	Daemon process name (`argv[0]`)

TCP Wrapper Configuration Examples

The following commands illustrate some of the access-control configurations for TCP Wrappers. This example is a limited setup, where you are denying everything except access to the `finger` daemon (wide open) and access to the `telnet` daemon (to local hosts, hosts within the `.sybex.com` domain, and hosts in the 192.168.0.0/16 block).

```
[ramon]$ more /etc/hosts.allow
in.fingerd:ALL
in.telnetd:LOCAL, .sybex.com, 192.68.
[ramon]$ more /etc/hosts.deny
ALL: ALL
```

The next example is similar to the previous example; it adopts a deny-all stance, but it does allow `ftp` connections from anywhere except the host `badguy.example.com`.

```
[ramon]$ more /etc/hosts.allow
in.ftpd:ALL EXCEPT badguy.example.com
[ramon]$ more /etc/hosts.deny
ALL: ALL
```

The following example is a simple configuration with a "booby trap." You're allowing all traffic coming from internal hosts to all servers. You're disallowing any external traffic, and a notice of every unsuccessful connection is e-mailed to the root account. Note that you're actually mailing the results of the `safe_finger` command, applied against the offending host. This command is supplied with TCP Wrappers, and it acts as a bare-bones `finger` client, much leaner (and more secure) than the standard Linux `finger` client.

```
[ramon]$ more /etc/hosts.allow
ALL:LOCAL
[ramon]$ more /etc/hosts.deny
ALL: ALL (/usr/sbin/safe_finger -l @%h |/bin/mail -s %d-%h root) &
```

Testing Your TCP Wrappers Configuration

Aside from man pages and documentation, the TCP Wrappers RPM file installs four executables as part of the TCP Wrappers package. You have already seen two of these:

/usr/sbin/tcpd   The tcpd file is the main daemon executable, which is invoked by the inetd daemon before dispatching the appropriate network server application.

/usr/sbin/safe-finger   The safe-finger file is the finger application often used to obtain information across the network from the client that is attempting to establish an inbound connection.

Two other tools are important for testing your TCP Wrappers configuration. They are tcpdchk and tcpdmatch and they are described in the following two sections.

Using *tcpdchk*

The executable /usr/sbin/tcpdchk is the TCP Wrappers configuration "checker." The tcpdchk script examines the configuration files and reports any potential problems that may lie therein. It reports on the following types of conditions:

- Nonexistent path names in /etc/inetd.conf
- Services configured by tcpd but not in /etc/inetd.conf
- Services that cannot be protected with TCP Wrappers
- Syntax errors in /etc/inetd.conf and/or the tcpd configuration files

The tcpdchk command can be invoked with the -v option for a verbose, tabular output. I strongly recommend that you run this command before you go live with your TCP Wrappers setup and that you don't run it on a production server.

Listing 4.8 contains sample output from the tcpdchk command.

Listing 4.8   Running the *tcpdchk* utility

```
[ramon]$ tcpdchk -v
Using network configuration file: /etc/inetd.conf

>>> Rule /etc/hosts.allow line 1:
daemons:  ALL
clients:  LOCAL 208.203.255. 153.39. 63.64.73. 204.177.181.↵
204.254.33.
access:   granted

>>> Rule /etc/hosts.allow line 2:
daemons:  finger
warning: /etc/hosts.allow, line 2: finger: no such process name↵
in /etc/inetd.conf
```

Network Security

PART 2

```
clients:  LOCAL
access:   granted

>>> Rule /etc/hosts.allow line 3:
daemons:  pop-3
warning: /etc/hosts.allow, line 3: pop-3: no such process name in↵
/etc/inetd.conf
clients:  LOCAL 208.255.255.256
warning: /etc/hosts.allow, line 3: 208.255.255.256: not an internet↵
address
access:   granted
>>> Rule /etc/hosts.deny line 1:
daemons:  ALL
clients:  ALL
access:   denied
```

In the example in Listing 4.8, the tcpdchk script found two rules in one of the tcpd configuration files that refer to the ftp and pop-3 service, neither of which are found in the /etc/inetd.conf file. In addition, the tcpdchk script found a syntax error in our tcp configuration (host 208.255.255.256); an IP address octet cannot go higher than 255.

Using *tcpdmatch*

The /usr/sbin/tcpdmatch script predicts whether a request from a specific client to a given service would be granted or denied. The command syntax of the tcpdmatch script is

> tcpdmatch *service client*

where *service* is the server name, and *client* is an IP address or a host name corresponding to the host requesting the service. For example, consider the three invocations of the tcpdmatch script shown in Listing 4.9.

Listing 4.9   Running the *tcpdmatch* utility

```
[ramon]$ tcpdmatch in.ftpd local.example.com
client:   hostname local.example.com
client:   address  10.0.0.2
server:   process  in.ftpd
matched:  /etc/hosts.allow line 1
access:   granted
[ramon]$ tcpdmatch in.ftpd 143.45.22.3
client:   address  143.45.22.3
server:   process  in.ftpd
matched:  /etc/hosts.deny line 1
access:   denied
```

```
[ramon]$ tcpdmatch in.telnetd remote.example.com
client:    hostname remote.example.com
client:    address  207.55.44.67
server:    process  in.telnetd
matched:   /etc/hosts.deny line 1
access:    denied
```

In the first two commands in Listing 4.9, you're testing access to the ftp server, first using a local host as the destination and then using an external address as the destination. Given the tcpd configuration, the first request would be granted, while the second request would be denied. The third command example in Listing 4.9 probes access to the telnet daemon from a remote address, which is rightfully denied.

TCP Wrappers Event Logging

One of the most useful features of TCP Wrappers, second to address-based filtering (filtering based on the IP address of the requesting client), is the ability to log every incoming network request, along with the result (grant/deny). As is the case with most Linux applications, TCP Wrappers uses the syslog facility to record events of interest. Examine your /etc/syslog.conf settings and look for the TCP Wrappers log events on the file where the authpriv.* facility gets directed (typically /var/log/secure):

```
[ramon]$ sudo tail -f secure
Oct 24 08:05:47 buggs in.telnetd[24257]: connect from elmer
Oct 24 08:06:07 buggs in.ftpd[24259]: connect from elmer
Oct 24 08:07:10 buggs in.rlogind[24261]: connect from elmer
Oct 24 21:04:42 buggs in.ftpd[25220]: connect from localhost
Oct 24 21:05:34 buggs in.telnetd[25228]: connect from goodguy
Oct 24 21:06:03 buggs in.fingerd[25232]: refused connect from badguy
```

Note that each entry in the output from this sudo command contains

- a datestamp
- the name of the host (buggs)
- the name of the network server
- the action, whether it was an accept (elmer, localhost, goodguy), or a denial (badguy)

It's generally a good idea to configure swatch and/or logcheck to look for the keyword refused, and alert the staff of repeated unsuccessful connection requests, a sure sign of a brute-force attack.

The */etc/services* File

The /etc/services file is found in every Linux installation, and it provides a mapping between a numeric transport layer port number (TCP/UDP) and a character string used to refer to this service. For example, the /etc/services file is where the system utilities find that ftp uses port 21/TCP while snmp uses 161/UDP. The general syntax of the file is

> *service-name* *port*/*protocol* *#comment*

The meanings of these fields are as follows:

- *service-name* is the string to be looked up (ftp, snmp, telnet, etc.)
- *port* is the numeric port number (21, 161, etc.).
- *protocol* is either TCP or UDP.
- *#comment* can also be a list of aliases for the given *service-name*.

Listing 4.10 lists the top of a typical /etc/services file found on a Linux system.

Listing 4.10   Partial detail of a Linux */etc/services* file

```
[ramon]$ more /etc/services
# /etc/services:
# $Id: services,v 1.4 1997/05/20 19:41:21 tobias Exp $
#
# Network services, Internet style
#
# Note that it is presently the policy of IANA to assign a
# single well-known port number for both TCP and UDP; hence,
# most entries here have two entries even if the protocol
# doesn't support UDP operations. Updated from RFC 1700,
# ``Assigned Numbers'' (October 1994).  Not all ports
# are included, only the more common ones.


tcpmux          1/tcp           # TCP port service multiplexer
echo            7/tcp
echo            7/udp
discard         9/tcp           sink null
discard         9/udp           sink null
systat          11/tcp          users
daytime         13/tcp
daytime         13/udp
netstat         15/tcp
qotd            17/tcp          quote
```

msp	18/tcp	# message send protocol	
msp	18/udp	# message send protocol	
chargen	19/tcp	ttytst source	
chargen	19/udp	ttytst source	
ftp-data	20/tcp		
ftp	21/tcp		
fsp	21/udp	fspd	
ssh	22/tcp	# SSH Remote Login Protocol	
ssh	22/udp	# SSH Remote Login Protocol	
telnet	23/tcp		

While it's not a requirement that service names be used, avoid using service numbers in /etc/inetd.conf because they are not as readable, and they are more prone to errors than a character string. Conversely, the netstat command (described in the next section) is much more readable if you create service names for all the service numbers in use.

The *netstat* Command

The netstat command is one of the most powerful utilities available to you in your quest for a secure network configuration. While the process table shows you which daemons have been started from the command line, and the /etc/inetd.conf file shows you the ones that are inetd-controlled, the netstat command is the ultimate authority on diagnosing which ports your Linux server is listening on.

The netstat command is very broad in function, but it is the --inet and -a options that show you the current state of your network configuration. Consider the sample output in Listing 4.11.

Listing 4.11 Output of the *netstat --inet -a* command

```
[ramon]$ netstat --inet -a
Active Internet connections (servers and established)
Proto Recv-Q Send-Q Local Address     Foreign Address       State
tcp        0      0 buggs:ssh         elmer:1186            ESTABLISHED
tcp        0      0 *:telnet          *:*                   LISTEN
tcp        0      0 *:ftp             *:*                   LISTEN
tcp        1      0 buggs:2148        226.146.218.1:www     CLOSE_WAIT
tcp        1      0 buggs:2146        226.148.218.1:www     CLOSE_WAIT
tcp        0      0 *:www             *:*                   LISTEN
tcp        0      0 buggs:1335        elmer:6000            ESTABLISHED
tcp        0      0 buggs:ssh         elmer:39470           ESTABLISHED
tcp        0      0 *:smtp            *:*                   LISTEN
```

```
tcp       0        0 *:ssh                *:*                      LISTEN
tcp       0        0 *:socks              *:*                      LISTEN
raw       0        0 *:icmp               *:*                      7
raw       0        0 *:tcp                *:*                      7
```

The netstat --inet -a command in Listing 4.11 shows the connections that are currently active (ESTABLISHED) or in the process of being torn down (CLOSE_WAIT), as well as those services that are currently awaiting new connections (LISTEN). You need to focus on this latter category and look for those services that appear after the host name (and the period) under the Local Address column. In fact, I often create a script that e-mails me the output of the following netstat command periodically:

```
[ramon]$ netstat --inet -a | grep LISTEN
tcp       0        0 *:telnet             *:*                      LISTEN

tcp       0        0 *:ftp                *:*                      LISTEN

tcp       0        0 *:www                *:*                      LISTEN

tcp       0        0 *:smtp               *:*                      LISTEN

tcp       0        0 *:ssh                *:*                      LISTEN

tcp       0        0 *:socks              *:*                      LISTEN
```

The previous output from the netstat command is the most accurate picture of what your Linux server looks like to a potential intruder. There are a total of six services active, and there are service names for all of them. (I had to add the service name socks to /etc /services by hand; otherwise I would simply see port 1080.)

The challenge is to make sure that the services listed by this command are those that your security policy currently allows, and to make sure that you have TCP Wrappers configurations for all these services.

Also, make sure to update the daemons that serve these ports with the latest security fixes and monitor their log files several times daily. If you follow these basic guidelines, you'll have a very close grip on the network configuration of your server.

In Sum

Network security goes a step beyond system security by examining the current configuration of the daemons on the Linux server. This chapter provides a detailed discussion of the configuration of the `inetd` daemon, as well as the directory structure of the startup network daemons. Both of these must be considered in order to ensure a secure network configuration.

The TCP Wrappers utility is an essential addition to all Linux distributions because it provides a flexible, unintrusive tool to enforce access controls on incoming network connections. In addition, TCP Wrappers affords you the capability to maintain detailed logs of all network activity at the TCP/UDP layer. The `netstat` command should also be used as an aid in the process of securing the network layer because it offers a succinct view of the ports that are currently active on the server.

The next chapter, Chapter 5, "Network Monitoring and Auditing," concludes Part 2 with a comprehensive look at the monitoring and auditing tools that the administrator can use to ensure the continued security of his/her system. Chapter 5 also introduces the topic of intrusion detection and discusses the concepts behind digital forensics.

Network Security

PART 2

5

Network Auditing and Monitoring

Chapter 4, "Network Services Configuration," kicked off Part 2, "Network Security," with a detailed discussion of security at the network layer by examining the configuration of the Linux network services and discussing the daemons that control these services. Chapter 4 outlined some important configuration guidelines and showed you how to get a handle on the network services running on your Linux server.

This chapter concludes Part 2 by introducing the concept of network monitoring and auditing. We'll start by defining those terms in detail and by identifying where they fit in the overall security process. We'll then describe a representative sample of tools that are available to conduct network audits and to monitor the network activity surrounding your Linux server.

Network Auditing

The aim of network auditing is to ensure that the security mechanisms you have implemented are effective in addressing the requirements of your security policy. By staging the very same break-ins that your policy is trying to guard against, you'll learn just how vulnerable you are, and you'll be able to predict and quantify your security risks, as well as their likely consequences. Make sure to tell the other network and system administrators in advance that you are going to be staging break-ins on your server.

The most effective approach to network auditing is to play the role of an intruder, attempting to gain unauthorized access to your Linux server from the public network. In almost every instance, this experiment reveals "holes" that weren't apparent when you implemented your security mechanisms. Whenever you meet system security administrators who talk about their *impenetrable* defense, always assume that the reason why they don't know of any holes is because they have not conducted any security audits. Chances are that a bored high school kid half a world away with a cable modem and a lot of time on his hands is "auditing" their network defenses at 4 A.M.

Network auditing tools provide a layer of automation to the process of exploring network vulnerabilities on a server. These tools fall into two general categories:

- *Network-based* auditing tools are tools that attempt to find vulnerabilities by scanning your server from the public network.

- *System-based* auditing tools are tools that attempt to find system vulnerabilities by executing on the server itself.

The next two sections introduce some noteworthy examples of both of these two types of auditing tools.

Network-Based Auditing Tools

While there have always been attempts to build a comprehensive tool for exposing network vulnerabilities on a system, it wasn't accomplished until 1995, when Dan Farmer and Wietse Venema (who also created TCP Wrappers) released the first version of SATAN (Security Administrator's Tool for Analyzing Networks). This network-based auditing tool quickly became a household word among network and systems administrators. In their 1993 landmark paper, "Improving the Security of Your Site by Breaking Into It," Farmer and Venema capitalized on the concept of building an application that would systematically attempt to break into a target system, or even a range of systems within a subnet. Two years later, SATAN was born, and the initial response from the Linux community was overwhelmingly positive.

However, the release of SATAN did not come without some controversy. Although this was clearly a useful tool for uncovering your own host's vulnerabilities, it could also be used by intruders to find their way into just about any system on the Internet, as long as perimeter defenses permitted it. However, this did not diminish SATAN's usefulness, and soon thereafter there were two more SATAN follow-ups, SAINT (Security Administrator's Integrated Network Tool) and SARA (Security Auditor's Research Assistant).

SAINT provides improved vulnerability testing and detection, an improved user interface, and the capability to specify multiple levels of security. SAINT is much more robust than the original SATAN was, fixing a number of important bugs. SARA is a more modular package, with interfaces to third-party products such as Nmap and Samba. SARA also features an advanced report writer to document the vulnerabilities that it finds.

The latest evolution of this series of tools is Nessus, which, just like its predecessors, is a Web-driven application with a sophisticated back end that attempts to exploit and report on a number of known security vulnerabilities. The next section describes the Nessus application in more detail.

Nessus

The Nessus project was born in April 1998 as an initiative to replace the aging SATAN package with another free, Unix-based auditing toolkit. While a few commercial offerings were starting to become available at that time, these packages focused more on the style of their reports and on their network discovery abilities instead of on the robustness and completeness of their auditing features. In addition, the price of commercial auditing tools was (and still is) prohibitive for most companies.

Nessus erupted as a free, open-source, full-featured, security-auditing tool that continues to see active support by developers around the world. New attack definitions are added daily, often just hours after being publicly announced. But if that's not up-to-the-minute enough, the modular architecture of Nessus allows you to write your own customized *attack-check plug-in* that can be seamlessly integrated into the system without the need for recompilation. For example, Listing 5.1 contains a plug-in that instructs Nessus to check whether the target system's Sendmail installation allows for anonymous mail relaying, a technique often used for spamming.

Listing 5.1 *smtp_relay.nasl:* Nessus plug-in script to check for Sendmail mail relaying

```
fake = get_kb_item("Sendmail/fake");
if(fake)exit(0);

# can't perform this test on localhost
if(islocalhost())exit(0);

port = get_kb_item("Services/smtp");
if(!port)port = 25;
if(get_port_state(port))
{
 soc = open_sock_tcp(port);
 data = recv(socket:soc, length:1024);
 crp = string("HELO nessus.org\n");
 send(socket:soc, data:crp);
 data = recv_line(socket:soc, length:1024);
 crp = string("MAIL FROM:test_1@nessus.org\n");
```

Network Security

PART 2

```
        send(socket:soc, data:crp);
        data = recv_line(socket:soc, length:1024);
        crp = string("RCPT TO: test_2@nessus.org\n");
        send(socket:soc, data:crp);
        i = recv_line(socket:soc, length:4);
        if(i == "250 "){
                security_warning(port);
                set_kb_item(name:"Sendmail/spam", value:TRUE);
                }
        close(soc);
    }
```

There are two components to the Nessus system: the client (`nessus`) and the server (`nessusd`). You can control the server with a variety of different clients since these components are offered for Linux (X11/GTK), Windows32, and even as a Java application. The server maintains a list of users with an associated set of permissions, so it's possible for two clients to log on to the server to perform a separate set of auditing tasks at the same time. The privacy of the communication between the client and the server can be protected with one of a number of encryption protocols; payload compression can even be added.

The Nessus Attack Scripting Language (NASL) allows you to automate predefined security scans that can then be run periodically out of `cron`. The scripts simply select the server and plug-ins to be used, the security tests to be applied, and the range of addresses that you want to audit.

While the Nessus software remains in the public domain under the GPL agreement, `nessus.com` offers fee-based professional auditing services using the same code base. This ensures the continued development of the system and keeps its quality and usability high.

Installing Nessus   The Nessus system can be installed from both the sources and from the RPM package distributions. I recommend that you install it using the RPM distributions, which are available from the same site as the sources. You need three separate RPM packages to build the entire Nessus distribution:

- `nessus-X.X.X-X.i386.rpm` (the base system, including the server)
- `nessus-client-X.X.X-X.i386.rpm` (the Linux client)
- `nessus-plugins-X.X.X-X.i386.rpm` (the plug-ins)

The latest version of these files is always available from the RPM directory of `ftp.nessus.org`. Listing 5.2 shows how this is done.

Listing 5.2 Downloading Nessus RPM packages via *ftp*

```
[ramon]$ ftp ftp.nessus.org
```

```
Connected to ftp.cis.fed.gov.
Name (ftp.nessus.org:ramon): anonymous
331 Guest login ok, send your complete e-mail address as password.
Password:
230 Logged in anonymously.
Remote system type is UNIX.
Using binary mode to transfer files.
ftp> cd /pub/nessus/nessus-1.0.6/RPMS/i386
250 "/pub/nessus/nessus-1.0.6/RPMS/i386" is new cwd.
ftp> get nessus-1.0.6-1.i386.rpm
local: nessus-1.0.6-1.i386.rpm remote: nessus-1.0.6-1.i386.rpm
200 PORT command successful.
150 Opening BINARY mode data connection for nessus-↵
1.0.6-1.i386.rpm (462536 bytes).
226 Transfer completed.
462536 bytes received in 31 secs (15 Kbytes/sec)
ftp> get nessus-client-1.0.6-1.i386.rpm
local: nessus-client-1.0.6-1.i386.rpm remote: nessus-client-↵
1.0.6-1.i386.rpm
200 PORT command successful.
150 Opening BINARY mode data connection for nessus-client-↵
1.0.6-1.i386.rpm (333438 bytes).
226 Transfer completed.
333438 bytes received in 22.6 secs (14 Kbytes/sec)
ftp> get nessus-plugins-1.0.6-1.i386.rpm
local: nessus-plugins-1.0.6-1.i386.rpm remote: nessus-plugins-↵
1.0.6-1.i386.rpm
200 PORT command successful.
150 Opening BINARY mode data connection for nessus-plugins-↵
1.0.6-1.i386.rpm (390005 bytes).
226 Transfer completed.
390005 bytes received in 26.1 secs (15 Kbytes/sec)
ftp> bye
221 Goodbye.
[ramon]$
```

In addition to the Nessus software itself, make sure that your system has the following two packages (required by Nessus):

GTK   GTK is The Gimp Toolkit, a set of Motif-like widgets that are used by the Nessus client's windowing system. Most Linux distributions install GTK by default.

Network Security

PART 2

Run the following command to find out if your distribution includes GTK (you'll also need glib):

```
[ramon]$ rpm -q glib gtk+
glib-1.2.1-2
gtk+-1.2.1-10
```

Nmap   Nmap (The Network Mapper) is a port scanner that is discussed later in this chapter. The detailed installation instructions are described in the section "Nmap" later in this chapter.

Once you have verified that you have these two packages on your system, simply install the Nessus packages you downloaded using the rpm command (don't forget to use sudo to obtain root privileges):

```
[ramon]$ sudo rpm -i nessus-1.0.6-1.i386.rpm
[ramon]$ sudo rpm -i nessus-plugins-1.0.6-1.i386.rpm
[ramon]$ sudo rpm -i nessus-client-1.0.6-1.i386.rpm
```

The Nessus software is now installed in your system. The next section will guide you through the process of configuring Nessus for use.

Configuring the Nessus Server   Since a single Nessus server can be accessed from multiple clients, the server keeps its own database of users and performs its own authentication and authorization. So, the first step in configuring Nessus is to create a user account for the client. The utility /usr/sbin/nessus-adduser allows you to do just that, as shown in Listing 5.3.

Listing 5.3   Creating a user account on the Nessus server

```
[ramon]$ sudo /usr/sbin/nessus-adduser
Using /var/tmp as a temporary file holder

Add a new nessusd user
----------------------
Login : ramon
Authentication method (cipher/plaintext) [cipher] : cipher

Source restriction
------------------
Source host or network [anywhere] : 192.168.1.0/24
One time password : mySeCreT

User rules
----------
```

```
Enter the rules for this user, and hit ctrl-D once you are done :⏎
(the user can have an empty rules set)
accept 192.168.1.0/24
accept 10.0.0.0/24
default deny
^D
Login              : ramon
Auth. method       : cipher, can connect from anywhere
One time password  : mySeCreT
Rules              :
accept 192.168.1.0/24
accept 10.0.0.0/24
default deny

Is that ok ? (y/n) [y] y
Generating primes: ......q...................pg
user added.
[ramon]$
```

In the example in Listing 5.3, you have created a new username, ramon, who will use encryption (`cipher`) when attempting to connect to the Nessus server.

***

> **NOTE** Note that encryption is only available from the Unix version of the Nessus client at the moment. I recommend that you only use this client because strong authentication and protection of the client-server communication is a crucial component of the security of this tool.

User ramon is only allowed to connect to the Nessus server from a client with an IP address in the 192.168.1.0/24 block, and ramon is only allowed to scan target hosts that fall within 192.168.1.0/24 and 10.0.0.0/24 IP blocks. The general syntax of the `User Rules` section is

```
[accept|deny]  ip/mask
default [accept|deny]
```

The fields in this section have the following meanings:

- `ip` is a numeric IP address.
- `mask` is a decimal notation subnet mask (e.g., 24 for a full class C).
- The [accept|deny] lines grant or deny access rights to a specific block of IP addresses.

- The default line (usually at the end) defines the default action to take for IP blocks that don't fit any specific rule.

The nessusd server reads a configuration file upon startup. This file is typically located at /etc/nessus/nessusd.conf. Each line in this file can be a comment (starting with the # sign) or a definition of the following format:

variable-name = value

I recommend that you use the configuration file defaults to start out with, unless you decide to move some of the Nessus files from the place where RPM drops them. Listing 5.4 shows the variables in the nessusd.conf file that contain the paths of the Nessus files.

Listing 5.4   *nessus.conf* directory path definitions

```
# Path to the security checks folder :
plugins_folder = /usr/lib/nessus/plugins

# Log file (or 'syslog') :
logfile = /var/log/nessus/nessusd.messages

# Dump file for debugging output, use `-' for stdout :
dumpfile = /var/log/nessus/nessusd.dmp

# Rules File :
rules = /etc/nessus/nessusd.rules

# Users Database :
users = /etc/nessus/nessusd.users
```

The variables in Listing 5.4 are used as follows:

- The plugins_folder variable specifies the folder that contains the plug-ins Nessus uses to check for vulnerabilities on the target system.
- The logfile variable specifies the file where the Nessus application will direct all log events. If the value of logfile is syslog, all events will be logged using the Linux syslog facility.
- The dumpfile variable specifies the target file of the debugging output.
- The rules variable points to the location of the Nessus daemon's rulesets.
- The users variable stores a reference to a file containing the users that are allowed to log on to the Nessus application.

Once you have edited the nessusd.conf file, it's time to start the nessusd daemon. The next section describes the details of this operation.

Running the Nessus Daemon   By default, the RPM installation of Nessus creates a daemon called /usr/sbin/nessusd. The nessusd daemon listens for client requests to scan one or more target hosts.

NOTE   The nessususd daemon *must* be started by the root user.

The command-line usage for the nessususd daemon is as follows:

```
nessusd [--background] [--config-file=config_file] [--listen=IP_
address] [--port=port]
```

Table 5.1 describes the nessusd command-line options, their meanings, and their default values.

Table 5.1   Nessus Daemon Command-Line Options

Option	Meaning	Default
--background	Run as a daemon (start and send to background).	N/A
--config-file=config_file	Use an alternate configuration file.	/etc/nessus/ nessusd.conf
--listen=IP_address	Address from which to accept requests. This overrides any rules that a given user may have associated with them.	N/A
--port=port	Listen on an alternate port.	3001

In general, you start the nessusd daemon by simply issuing the following command; the -D option in this command instructs the daemon to run in the background, giving you back control of the terminal session:

```
[ramon]$ sudo /usr/sbin/nessusd -D
```

At this point, you're ready to fire up the Nessus client and start scanning some of your Linux servers to look for security vulnerabilities. The next section guides you through that process.

Configuring and Running the Nessus Client   Since you're a Linux administrator, you'll probably feel comfortable running the Linux client, which is the most robust of the clients by far. To invoke it for the first time, simply type the following command:

[ramon]$ **/usr/bin/nessus**

At this point, a dialog box appears asking you to create a new passphrase (see Figure 5.1). This is the secret that protects your private key. Once your private key is unlocked, the client and the server use public-key authentication to come up with a symmetric key to protect all subsequent communication. If this is not the first time you invoke Nessus from your account, the client simply asks you to provide the passphrase that you specified the first time (Figure 5.2).

Figure 5.1   Creating a new Nessus client passphrase

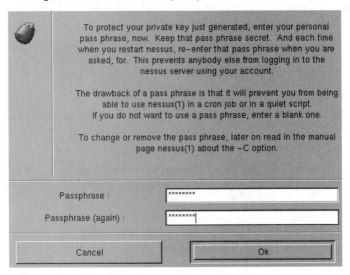

Figure 5.2   Entering the Nessus client passphrase

If the passphrase is correct, the client displays the main menu, which is open to the Nessusd Host tab by default. This is where you point the client to the appropriate server. In the example in Figure 5.3, the server is `nessus.example.com` and the username being used to log on is ramon.

Figure 5.3   Logging on to the Nessus server

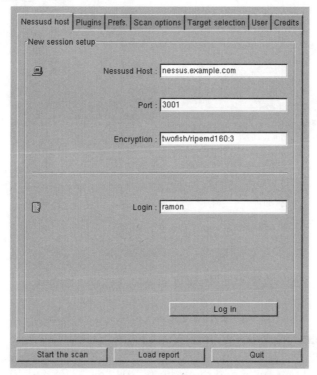

The next tab in the main Nessus client window is the Plugins tab, shown in Figure 5.4. On this screen, you can choose among all the plug-ins that are currently present in the plug-ins folder (`/usr/lib/nessus/plugins`, by default). I recommend that you click the Enable All But Dangerous Plugins button. This disables the Denial of Service plug-in at the bottom of the list. If you opt to run this attack as well, make sure you do it during a maintenance window of the target server, since it will be rendered useless at least momentarily.

Figure 5.4   Selecting Nessus plug-ins

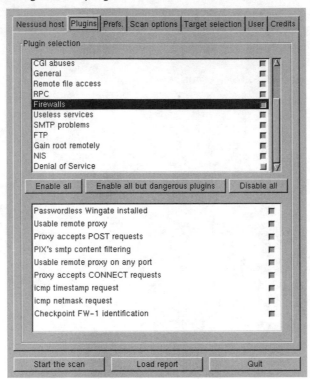

The next tab of interest is the Target Selection tab. On this screen you can specify the servers to be scanned for vulnerabilities. You can use comma-separated notation, including host names, IP addresses, or networks with a /subnet notation (e.g., 192.168.1.0/24). Figure 5.5 shows a scan of two target hosts, 204.254.33.75 and 204.254.33.76.

Figure 5.5   Specifying target hosts to be scanned

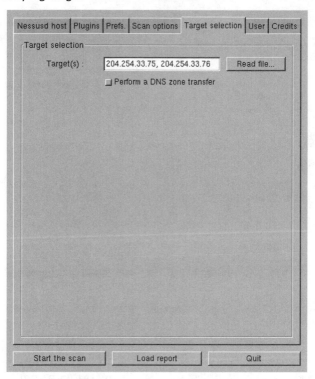

To start the testing, simply click the Start the Scan button. The status screen appears, as illustrated in Figure 5.6. The scan continues for as long as it takes the Nessus server to complete all the tests specified on the Plugins tab screen. The total duration of the scan will vary widely, depending on the number of hosts to be scanned and the complexity of the tests.

Figure 5.6 Nessus scanning: status window

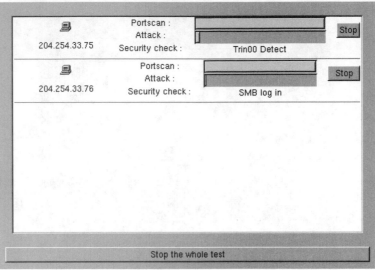

At the conclusion of the test, Nessus provides you with a summary window (see Figure 5.7) that displays the list of target hosts and a quick synopsis of the security holes, warnings, and notes found on each of the hosts. Simply select the host of interest and click the Save As pull-down. Select your format of choice (HTML is a good candidate), and click the Save As button. You can then view the complete vulnerability report with your favorite Web browser, as shown in Figure 5.8.

Figure 5.7 Nessusd report summary

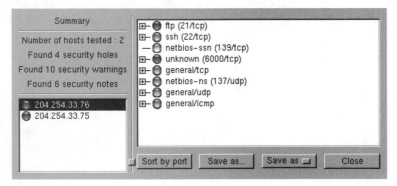

Figure 5.8 Viewing an HTML Nessus report

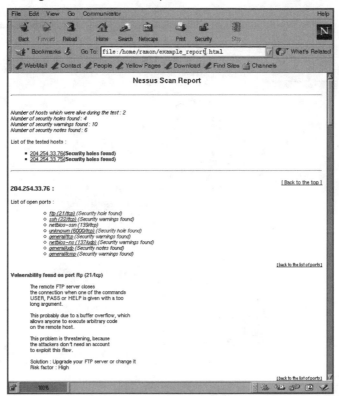

Alternatively, you can get more information about each of the vulnerabilities found by Nessus by expanding on each of the lines under the Summary section on the left-hand side of the screen (see Figure 5.9).

Look at the report in Figure 5.9. In this example, Nessus has identified a problem with the FTP server on the target machine in which an intruder could cause a buffer overflow, leading to the execution of arbitrary code on the server. In addition, Nessus has identified another associated vulnerability whereby the intruder could use a dump core on the FTP server to write portions of the /etc/shadow file on a world-readable part of the filesystem.

These conditions are tagged as high and medium priority, and a solution is even suggested (to upgrade to a more recent and secure version, not surprisingly).

Figure 5.9 Viewing details on a Nessus report

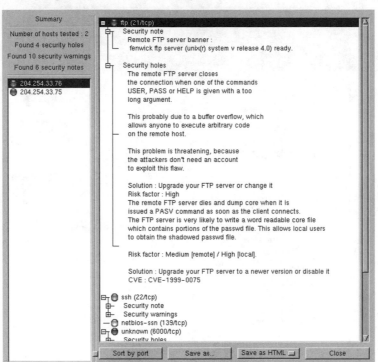

Nmap

While the Nessus philosophy was to provide a polished front end and a scalable client-server architecture to allow multiple users to audit the network at the same time, the Nmap tool offers a powerful, versatile network-scanning tool for the more experienced network administrator. I have found Nmap to be a great tool for quickly assessing:

- Which hosts are up in a certain subnet
- Which ports (TCP, UDP) are open on a range of target systems
- What operating system is running on those systems

I use the first two capabilities areas to make sure that there aren't any rogue systems up and running on my local area network (LAN), and to make sure that my Linux servers are not running any services that I'm not aware of. The third capability allows me to find out exactly what type of system a suspected intruder is coming from. This is part of the information that I send back to the authorities of the intruder's domain when I report an access violation or an attack.

The next section explains how to download and install the latest version of the Nmap package.

Installing Nmap   The main source of Nmap distribution is `www.insecure.org`. You can download both the full sources or the RPM packages from this site. The simplest way to install it is by using the remote source, as follows:

```
[ramon]: rpm -vhU http://www.insecure.org/nmap/dist/nmap-2.53-
1.i386.rpm
```

Once installed, you'll use the main Nmap executable, located at `/usr/bin/nmap` by default. The following section describes some common uses of the Nmap tool.

Using Nmap   Although Nmap is a comprehensive network-auditing tool, its discussion in this book focuses on its ability to identify live hosts, active network services, and remote operating system type because these are the areas where Nmap is most useful.

The simplest use of Nmap is to identify which hosts are *live* (up and available) on the network at any one time. This task is called a *port scan*. Listing 5.5 illustrates an example of using Nmap to perform a port scan on a subnet.

Listing 5.5   Using Nmap to perform a port scan on an entire subnet

```
[ramon]$ sudo nmap -sP 192.168.1.0/24

Starting nmap V. 2.53 by fyodor@insecure.org↵
( www.insecure.org/nmap/ )
Host pluto (192.168.1.5) appears to be up.
Host donald (192.168.1.7) appears to be up.
Host minnie (192.168.1.44) appears to be up.
Host dumbo (192.168.1.67) appears to be up.
Nmap run completed - 256 IP addresses (4 hosts up) scanned in 9↵
seconds
```

Nmap considers a host to be *up* if it responds to either an ICMP Echo request or to a TCP ACK.

Another popular use of Nmap is to identify which ports (TCP, UDP) are open on a remote host. This is called a *TCP scan*. A port is *open* when there is a listener daemon that responds to network requests to that port on the target system.

Listing 5.6 illustrates an example of using Nmap to perform a TCP scan. In this example, Nmap has found that the target hosts have a total of three TCP ports open: Secure Shell (TCP service number 22), SMTP Mail (TCP service 25) and Secure HTTP (TCP service 443). Note that by default, Nmap only scans the first 1500 or so TCP ports.

Network Security

PART 2

Listing 5.6 Using Nmap to perform a TCP scan on a single target host

```
[ramon]$ sudo nmap -sS target.example.com

Starting nmap V. 2.53 by fyodor@insecure.org↵
( www.insecure.org/nmap/ )
Interesting ports on target.example.com (192.168.1.1):
(The 1520 ports scanned but not shown below are in state: filtered)
Port       State       Service
22/tcp     open        ssh
25/tcp     open        smtp
443/tcp    closed      https
Nmap run completed -- 1 IP address (1 host up) scanned in 178 seconds
```

The third example illustrates Nmap's ability to identify the type of operating system running on a remote host and to examine the particularities of the host's TCP implementation. The Nmap authors call this *TCP fingerprinting,* and their implementation is fairly sophisticated, using a constantly updated file containing fingerprint templates that it compares to the target's TCP responses.

Listing 5.7 shows a sample run of Nmap to identify the operating system for three target hosts: a Lucent Pipeline PL75 router, a Solaris 2.5.1 workstation, and a Linux server. Note that part of the output in Listing 5.7 includes the degree of difficulty (`Difficulty=`), which tells you how hard it is to identify the target operating system over the network. Note that Linux earned the highest degree out of the three targets!

Listing 5.7 Using Nmap to Identify a remote host's operating system

```
[ramon]$ sudo nmap -O 192.168.1.1 192.168.1.100 192.168.1.200

Starting nmap V. 2.53 by fyodor@insecure.org↵
( www.insecure.org/nmap/ )
Interesting ports on router (192.168.1.1):
(The 1522 ports scanned but not shown below are in state: closed)
Port       State       Service
23/tcp     open        telnet

TCP Sequence Prediction: Class=random positive increments
                        Difficulty=15144 (Worthy challenge)
Remote OS guesses: Ascend P130 Router, Ascend P75
Interesting ports on fantasia (192.168.1.100):
(The 1519 ports scanned but not shown below are in state: closed)
Port       State       Service
21/tcp     open        ftp
```

Network Security

PART 2

```
22/tcp      open       ssh
139/tcp     open       netbios-ssn
6000/tcp    open       X11


TCP Sequence Prediction: Class=random positive increments
                        Difficulty=23419 (Worthy challenge)
Remote operating system guess: Solaris 2.5, 2.5.1


Interesting ports on penguin (192.168.1.200):
(The 1516 ports scanned but not shown below are in state: closed)
Port        State      Service
21/tcp      open       ftp
22/tcp      open       ssh
23/tcp      open       telnet
80/tcp      open       http
989/tcp     open       ftps-data
1080/tcp    open       socks
3001/tcp    open       nessusd


TCP Sequence Prediction: Class=random positive increments
                        Difficulty=2630920 (Good luck!)
Remote operating system guess: Linux 2.1.122 - 2.2.14


Nmap run completed -- 3 IP addresses (3 hosts up) scanned in 10
seconds
```

As always, the use of Nmap is a double-edged sword. Although this utility should be in every security administrator's toolkit, always be vigilant and look for evidence of an Nmap scan on your network because that is typically the precursor of an attack. The swatch and logcheck utilities discussed in Chapter 3, "System Monitoring and Auditing," are well suited for this purpose.

Both Nessus and Nmap identify potential exploits on a target system by contacting it via the network. An alternative class of host-based auditing tools accomplishes the same task, but the tools are executed on the target system itself. The next section in this book explores host-based auditing in more detail and introduces some examples of the host-based approach to network security auditing.

Host-Based Auditing Tools

While Nessus and Nmap allow you to play the part of the "bad guy" attempting to break into your Linux server from the public network, the majority of successful network attacks are actually staged from the inside. This fact prompted the Unix community to design a tool that could be used on the system itself, to identify vulnerabilities from inside attacks.

In 1993, Dan Farmer, who is also the author of the SATAN network-based audit tool, released a utility called COPS (Computer Oracle and Password System). A pioneer in the field of host-based security auditing, COPS is actually a collection of smaller tools, each of which targets a specific vulnerability in a typical Unix system that can lead to a network attack. These checks extend to areas like the anonymous FTP server, the /etc/rc.* directories, cron entries, and NFS and Sendmail vulnerabilities.

Texas A&M University released a set of host-based auditing scripts (code-named Tiger) as a follow-up to COPS, but stopped developing new features in 1994. Both COPS and Tiger are now hopelessly out of date, but a worthy successor has emerged. The next section describes the Advanced Research Corporation's TARA package.

TARA

TARA (Tiger Auditors Research Assistant) is a 1999 update of the Tiger system from Texas A&M by a private company (Advanced Research Corporation) working under funding from the National Institutes of Health (NIH). The resulting package was released to the public domain under the auspices of the GNU General Public License (GPL).

As was the case with Tiger, TARA is a set of shell scripts controlled by a central utility, which is still named `tiger` to honor its direct ancestor. The main goal of this tool is to identify settings on your Linux server that would make it easier for an intruder to gain root privileges over the network. TARA is meant to be run both interactively and periodically in batch mode. Either way, the result is a report of the potential vulnerabilities found at the time of its execution.

The next section explains how to download and install the latest versions of the TARA scripts on your Linux server.

Installing TARA

The TARA distribution can be obtained directly from the ARC Web site at http:// www-arc.com/tara/. There is no RPM package available, so you have to download the source archive. Simply decompress and extract the archive as shown in Listing 5.8.

Listing 5.8 Extracting the TARA archive

```
[ramon]$ ls -l tara-2.0.9.tar.gz
-rw-r--r--   1 ramon     users        355267 Nov 18 17:13 tara-↵
2.0.9.tar.gz
[ramon]$ gzip -dc tara-2.0.9.tar.gz | tar -xf -
[ramon]$ cd tara-2.0.9
[ramon]$ sudo mkdir -p /usr/spool/tiger/work
```

```
[ramon]$ sudo mkdir -p /usr/spool/tiger/logs
[ramon]$ sudo mkdir -p /usr/spool/tiger/bin
[ramon]$ sudo make install
```

The steps in Listing 5.8 install the appropriate TARA files in the /usr/local/tiger
directory, including the main tiger executable, /usr/local/tiger/tiger. Note that
you have to create the following three directories outlined in the Makefile file that comes
standard with TARA:

TIGERWORK=/usr/spool/tiger/work   This directory is used for temporary scratch
files by the tiger executable. The default directory is something other than /tmp so
you can easily identify (and clean up) the temporary files created by the application.

TIGERLOGS=/usr/spool/tiger/logs   This directory is where the tiger reports are
saved.

TIGERBIN=/usr/spool/tiger/bin   This directory is where the TARA auxiliary
executables go.

NOTE   You have to add /usr/local/tiger to your PATH environment variable if
you want to invoke the tiger executable without specifying the complete file path.

The next section explains how to use the TARA configuration file.

Configuring TARA

The TARA configuration file resides in /usr/local/tiger/tigerrc. TARA ships with
a default tigerrc file, but I recommend that you make the following changes before using
the application:

Tiger_Check_CRON=Y   Setting this option to Y causes TARA to check cron entries
for all users and identify possible vulnerabilities in the commands contained in them.
The default value is N.

Tiger_Check_KNOWN=Y   Setting this option to Y tells TARA to check for indications
of known break-in attempts. The default value is N.

Tiger_Check_PERMS=Y   Setting this option to Y tells TARA to check permissions
and ownership of system files, looking for directories that are wide open. It also
directs Tiger to check permissions and ownership of the setuid/setgid files. The
default value is N.

Tiger_Check_FILESYSTEM=Y   Setting this option to Y directs TARA to perform
filesystem checks, including checking the ownerships of the mount points and the
permissions of the NFS exports. The default value is N.

Tiger_Check_PATH=Y   Setting this option to Y tells TARA to check the PATH settings for system accounts and to look for directories that would normally not be
in a privilege user's PATH. The default value is N.

These options are turned off in the default `tigerrc` file in order to save time because some of these checks could take several minutes, depending on the speed and complexity of the filesystem on your Linux server. However, it's important to the security of your server that these checks take place so make sure to modify the `tigerrc` file appropriately.

Using TARA

Once TARA has been installed and configured, you invoke it by simply typing the name of the main executable (you'll need root privileges), as shown in Listing 5.9.

Listing 5.9   TARA execution

```
[ramon]$ sudo tiger
Tiger Analytical Research Assistant (TARA)
    Developed by Texas A&M University, 1994
    Updated by the Advanced Research Corporation, 1999
    Covered by GNU General Public License (GPL)

Using configuration files for Linux 2
18:42> Beginning security report for redhat.hontanon.com.
18:42> Starting file systems scans in background...
18:42> Checking password files...
18:42> Checking group files...
18:42> Checking user accounts...
18:42> Checking .rhosts files...
18:42> Checking .netrc files...
18:42> Checking ttytab, login, securetty, and ftpusers files...
18:42> Checking PATH settings...
18:42> Checking anonymous ftp setup...
18:42> Checking mail aliases...
18:42> Checking cron entries...
18:42> Checking 'inetd' configuration...
18:42> Checking NFS export entries...
18:42> Checking permissions and ownership of system files...
18:42> Checking for indications of breakin...
18:42> Performing system specific checks...
18:42> Waiting for filesystems scans to complete...
18:45> Filesystems scans completed...
18:45> Security report completed for redhat.hontanon.com.
Security report is in `/usr/spool/tiger/logs/security.report.↵
goofy.001118-18:42'.
```

As you can see by the last line in Listing 5.9, the result of the TARA run is a textual report that is stored in a file called `security.report.goofy.001118-18:42`. The name of the file includes the host name (goofy) date in *YYMMDD* format, as well as the time of day (*HH:MM*) when the command was executed. The contents of this file are shown in Listing 5.10.

NOTE   For an HTML-formatted report, simply type **tiger -H**.

Listing 5.10   A typical TARA report

```
[ramon]$ cd /usr/spool/tiger/logs
[ramon]$ sudo more security.report.goofy.001118-18:42
18:42> Beginning security report for goofy (i686 Linux 2.2.12-20).
# Checking accounts from /etc/passwd.
--WARN-- [acc001w] Login ID postgres is disabled, but still has a
valid shell.
--WARN-- [acc001w] Login ID uucp is disabled, but still has a
valid shell.
# Performing check of PATH components...
--WARN-- [path002w] /usr/bin/actived in root's PATH from default
is not owned by root (owned by news).
--WARN-- [path002w] /usr/bin/actmerge in root's PATH from default
is not owned by root (owned by news).
# Checking services from /etc/services.
--FAIL-- [inet003f] The port for service imap is assigned to service
imap2.
--FAIL-- [inet003f] The port for service irc is assigned to service
ircd.
# Performing check of system file permissions...
--WARN-- [perm001w] /etc/exports should not have group read.
--WARN-- [perm001w] /etc/exports should not have world read.
# Performing checks for Linux/2...
--ERROR-- [misc005w] Can't find check_sendmail'...
# Checking symbolic links...
--WARN-- [xxxxx] The following files are unowned:
/usr/local/netscape/netscape
```

The report in Listing 5.10 has unveiled a number of warnings and errors that could lead to security vulnerabilities:

- Two usernames in /etc/passwd (postgres and uucp) are accounts that have been disabled, but they still have a valid shell. The implication here is that you should assign a non-working shell to accounts that have been deactivated.

- Two executables were found on root's PATH that are not actually owned by root. This leaves the window open for root to accidentally execute code that is controlled by a regular user, which clearly represents a vulnerability.

- Two services (imap and irc) are not using well-known TCP port numbers.

Network Security

PART 2

- The /etc/exports file, which specifies the filesystems that the server will be exporting via NFS, has the wrong permissions.
- The check_sendmail script is missing.
- The file /usr/local/netscape/netscape is owned by a user ID that is not present in /etc/passwd. This typically means that a valid username has been deleted from the password file (by mistake, if you're lucky).

If you would like more information on any of these diagnostics, TARA offers the tigexp utility, which can be invoked with the corresponding diagnostic code. Listing 5.10, a security report produced by TARA, contains the diagnostic codes in brackets []. The following command shows how to use tigexp using one of the diagnostic codes from the report in Listing 5.10:

```
[ramon]$ tigexp perm001w
```

```
The owner of the indicated file is not what is considered best for
security reasons.  Unless you have a specific reason for not changing
the ownership, this should be corrected.
```

As you can see, TARA offers a wealth of diagnostic information on your system's configuration, and it allows a Linux system administrator to mitigate some of the well-known network attacks before they happen. However, network auditing is a sometimes tedious and always time-consuming activity. Not even the most diligent system administrator can rely on the systems being secure by simply auditing them regularly.

The next section in this book explores the concept of network monitoring, which, along with auditing, constitutes the basis of your ongoing defense against intrusion.

Network Monitoring

The previous section presented some very effective tools and techniques for scanning, strobing, and poking at random systems, looking for half-open doors and misconfigured systems that might invite break-ins. While the aim of these tools is to enhance the security of your system, it is naïve to assume that they are not going to be used for nefarious actions by a would-be intruder.

The challenge is on you as a security administrator to

- Look for signs that you are being scanned by tools like Nessus and Nmap.
- Hope that the versions of these tools that the intruder is using are at least as old as the one you used during the last audit.

In actuality, even if the intruder is a joyrider casually scanning your subnet looking for an open door, and even if you have made sure that your system is secure, the intruder's activity is consuming precious bandwidth on your Internet connection. In addition, that activity could eventually lead to a denial of service (DoS) attack on your entire network, or at least on the system that is currently being targeted by the intruder.

Clearly, the job of the security administrator is both a proactive and a reactive one. Network auditing aims at preventing an attack, and it should be your primary focus. However, network monitoring also has just an important a role in helping you react to an attack. The next two sections describe two popular Linux network-monitoring tools available in the public domain: PortSentry and Ethereal.

PortSentry

Part of Psionic Software's Abacus suite of security software, PortSentry is a real-time monitoring tool designed to detect a port scan directed at your system, and to respond to it appropriately. These responses are configurable and they vary in nature, from adding the offender's IP address to your TCP Wrappers' /etc/hosts.deny file, to modifying the local routing table to divert responses to that host.

One of PortSentry's strongest suits is its *Advanced Stealth Scan Detection Mode*, which is the capability to learn the ports that your Linux server is listening on and only to look for connections to the ports that are not currently in service. This makes for light operation that uses precious little CPU cycles. This is very important because you do not want to compromise the performance of your Linux server when you run a network monitor on it. If you have to compromise your server performance when running a network scan, perform the scan during off-peak hours to make sure that your users are not affected by it.

Another advantage of PortSentry over most other network monitors is its ability to keep track of intruders' IP addresses as a function of time. This allows you to only react to a port scan when the intruder is a repeat offender, or to take specific action based on the frequency at which a particular address is attempting to perform a port scan on your system.

The next section describes the installation of the PortSentry application on your Linux server.

Installing PortSentry

You can download the latest version of PortSentry from Psionic's Web site, www.psionic.com, in source distribution format. In addition, the RPM version is also available from the usual archives. Simply download the appropriate RPM package and install it on your system using the following command:

```
[ramon]$ sudo rpm -i portsentry-1.0-4.i386.rpm
```

This command installs the main executable (`/usr/sbin/portsentry`) as well as the configuration file `/etc/portsentry/portsentry.conf`).

Configuring PortSentry

Before start up PortSentry, edit the main configuration file, `/etc/portsentry/portentry.conf`, and assign the following environment variables in it:

ADVANCED_PORTS_TCP (ADVANCED_PORTS_UDP)   This variable determines the highest port that PortSentry will monitor. Since Nmap typically scans the first 1500 ports or so, I recommend that you set this value to 1500. Note that there are two applicable variables, one for TCP and another for UDP. Also note that by default, PortSentry does not listen for scans on the ports that are active on your Linux server.

ADVANCE_EXCLUDE_TCP (ADVANCED_EXCLUDE_UDP)   Initialize this variable with the port numbers that should not cause an alarm, even though the system is not currently listening for them. These should be port numbers that are typically used by mistake, like port 80 (HTTP) on an HTTPS server.

BLOCK_TCP (BLOCK_UDP)   This variable instructs PortSentry to not block any hosts that are found guilty of perpetrating TCP (or UDP) scans. This can be useful to avoid a subtle type of attack where the intruder spoofs their address to be that of a legitimate host in order to force your Linux server to block traffic from that host. Forging the source is relatively easy to do, especially within a UDP packet.

KILL_ROUTE   This variable allows you to specify the command that PortSentry should use in order to kill the local route to a port scan perpetrator. The $TARGET$ placeholder can be used to pass the IP address of the offending host to the command. I recommend that you take less drastic action than routing this address into a black hole, such as adding their address to an `ipchains` block list, as in the following example:

```
KILL_ROUTE="/sbin/ipchains -I input -s $TARGET$ -j DENY -l"
```

NOTE   See Chapter 9, "Network-Layer Firewalls," for a full discussion of this type of perimeter security devices.

KILL_RUN_CMD   This variable allows you to specify the command that PortSentry should use just before applying the command defined in KILL_ROUTE. Resist the temptation to use this command to take automatic retaliatory action against the (alleged) intruder. This action can be used as a denial of service against you, as mentioned in the discussion of the BLOCK_TCP variable. I thereby recommend that you comment out this option.

KILL_HOSTS_DENY   This variable allows you to specify the syntax of the `/etc/hosts.deny` entry that PortSentry should add in order to block the offending host from TCP Wrappers. The $TARGET$ placeholder can also be used here. I recommend that you use a setting similar to the following:

```
KILL_HOSTS_DENY="ALL: $TARGET$ : $DENY"
```

SCAN_TRIGGER   Setting this variable to something higher than 0 gives an offender a number of "free" scans before you take action. I recommend setting this variable to 1 in order to weed out the one-off casual port scanner.

In addition to the /etc/portsentry/portsentry.conf file, always edit the /etc/ portsentry/portsentry.ignore file and add any hosts (one per line) that you want PortSentry to ignore altogether. I recommend that you limit this to the local host (127.0.0.1) and to the addresses of all the interfaces on your Linux server.

Using PortSentry

The Linux version of PortSentry has the capability to use advanced port-scan detection even for the more sophisticated port scans. For example, it will detect a *SYN flood* attack, where an intruder initiates a large number of half-open TCP connections against your server.

The two command-line options of the portsentry command that are of interest are:

```
portsentry -atcp
```

```
portsentry -audp
```

The first command-line option, -atcp, listens for TCP scans starting with TCP port 1 and ending with the port number specified in the ADVANCED_PORTS_TCP variable of the configuration file. Conversely, the second command-line option, -audp, listens for scans from UDP port 1 to ADVANCED_PORTS_UDP.

A typical attack is logged by PortSentry directly to syslog, where it appears (typically on /var/log/messages) in the following format:

```
Nov 18 21:11:49 mickey portsentry[19891]: attackalert: Connect from↩
host: badguy/192.168.100.100 to TCP port: 900

Nov 18 21:11:49 mickey portsentry[19891]: attackalert: Host↩
192.168.100.100 has been blocked via wrappers with string: "AL

L: 192.168.100.100"

Nov 18 22:11:32 mickey portsentry[19891]: attackalert: Host: badguy/↩
192.168.100.100 is already blocked Ignoring
```

In this example, PortSentry was started with the line

```
portsentry -atcp
```

and instructed to watch for all TCP connections below port 1500. The intruder (192.168.100.100) attempted to connect to TCP port 900, which does not have a daemon associated with it. This triggered action by PortSentry, which is configured to add a line of the type

```
ALL: 192.168.100.100
```

to the /etc/hosts.deny file in order to deny TCP Wrappers access to the offending host. Note that the intruder attempts a second scan an hour later, but this time PortSentry does not add the entry to /etc/hosts.deny, since the intruder has already been blocked.

While PortSentry is obviously a powerful tool for detecting (and even countering) port scans, its usefulness can be enhanced by a robust syslog-checking tool such as swatch and logcheck, as described in Chapter 3 of this book.

Ethereal

PortSentry is a useful tool for detecting port-scan attempts at the transport layer (TCP or UDP), but system administrators often find themselves in need of a tool that allows them to examine the content of network packets as they fly through the wire. Ethereal is the optimal tool for this kind of application.

Offered under the GNU GPL, Ethereal is the product of a large collaborative effort by a group of developers who were unhappy with the high price of commercial packet analyzers. The result is a robust packet sniffer that can capture and analyze packets natively, and that can read and display stored capture files created by a number of other (even commercial) analyzers.

Due to its open-source nature and its modular design, it's easy for programmers to add their own protocol support to Ethereal by writing their own protocol interpreters (or *dissectors,* as they're called in this program). Before reaching version 1.0, Ethereal already included support for over 100 protocols.

Installing Ethereal

The latest Ethereal distribution is available in RPM format from any of the usual outlets. To install, simply download the RPM file and execute a command like the following:

```
[ramon]$ sudo rpm -i ethereal-0.8.12-1.i386.rpm
```

NOTE Ethereal RPM has a dependency on libpcap. It requires libpcap of release level 0.4 or greater.

Using Ethereal

You can display the main Ethereal window by just entering the executable name with no command-line options. (You'll have to be root to use the network interfaces in promiscuous mode). Use a command like the following:

[ramon]$ **sudo ethereal**

Shortly after invoking this command, a window appears on your X display, consisting of three separate panes (see Figure 5.10).

Figure 5.10   The three panes of the main Ethereal window

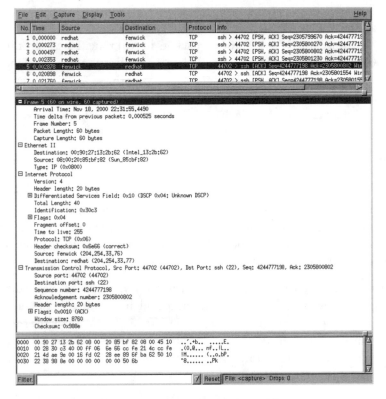

The top pane displays a summary line for each packet that is captured on the wire, including a packet sequence number, the lapsed time at which it was captured (starting at 0 as the capture start time), the source, destination addresses, and the transport layer protocol type (TCP, UDP, etc.)

The middle pane displays a detailed view of the selected packet from the top pane. In Figure 5.10, you have stopped the packet capture and have drilled down on a packet found in a conversation between hosts fenwick and redhat. The frame is an Ethernet II frame carrying an IP packet, which in turn carries a TCP packet in its payload. Ethereal provides a fine level of detail at each of the layers, including source and destination TCP ports, sequence and ACK numbers, and flags and checksums found at the end of the TCP packet.

The bottom pane shows a dump of the payload found on the TCP packet. Since the application type of this TCP packet is Secure Shell (SSH), the payload is encrypted, so it is not decipherable.

As you can see, Ethereal is a powerful tool that provides a level of detail that is often hard to correlate, especially when capturing packets in real time. However, this is an appropriate tool to use in a reactive situation, when an application like PortSentry has already alerted you to the fact that you're under attack. After the session has been captured, Ethereal allows you to save the file and stow away the entire capture for later examination or as forensic evidence after the attack.

In Sum

Network security is a game of intelligence and counterintelligence. Each minute spent trying to break into your own system is worth an hour of pouring through the unfortunate aftermath of an intrusion. While network auditing should be part of your periodic system and network maintenance routine, network monitoring should be given an even higher priority, especially when you have reasons to suspect that you may be under attack.

It's imperative to make sure that your security policy includes a clear statement of how often, and under what circumstances, auditing and monitoring should take place. Decide how you are going to deal with port-scanning offenders, and apply the same standards to all perpetrators. Avoid retaliatory action; instead, log all the details of the scan and attempt to gather as much information about their source so you can contact the appropriate authority to report the incident.

Part 3, "Application Security," expands the discussion away from the network layer to cover security issues associated with the use of the most common Linux server applications, including Sendmail, Apache, and a variety of file servers. The next chapter begins that discussion with a look at the security issues behind Sendmail.

Part 3

Application Security

Featuring:

- Using Sendmail for Secure Mail Relaying
- Adding Privacy and Strong Authentication to Your Sendmail Server
- A Security Overview of Qmail and Postfix
- Protecting POP and IMAP Mail Servers
- Using GnuPG for Mail Application Privacy and Authentication
- Securing the Apache HTTP Server
- Protecting Your Web Traffic with mod_ssl
- Understand Samba Access Control and Authentication

6

Electronic Mail

Parts 1 and 2 of this book explore the security challenges associated with the systems and network layers of the Linux server. The next step in this progression is to examine the security issues inherent to the application layer. This chapter kicks off Part 3, "Application Security," by taking a close look at a number of electronic mail server applications, their installation, setup, and their impact on the overall security of your server.

While the World Wide Web has seen its traffic (HTTP) grow faster than any other protocol in recent Internet history, electronic mail (SMTP) packets still outnumber any other protocol in usage today. With recent legislative decisions in favor of the validity of electronic signatures, you're likely to see the amount of electronic mail use grow at an even faster rate as companies start using the Internet for the distribution and signature of legally binding documents and their supporting materials.

However, electronic mail is one of the most challenging applications to secure due to the public and widespread nature of the service. Mail servers often must handle messages of very disparate sizes, origin, and composition. Electronic mail is easily the part of your server to which you should devote the most attention on a day-to-day basis, since it's the application that will experience the most amount of traffic.

This chapter will explore three popular mail transport agents (MTAs), Sendmail, Qmail, and Postfix, and will describe two types of mail-retrieval protocols, Post Office Protocol v.3 (POP3) and Internet Mail Access Protocol (IMAP). In addition, this chapter will take a look at Pretty Good Privacy (PGP) and its open source cousin, Gnu's GNU Privacy Guard (GnuPG).

Let's kick off the discussion with an in-depth look at Sendmail, the daemon application that provides the transport for the majority of today's Linux e-mail servers.

Sendmail

Sendmail has been the de facto standard for Unix-based Internet MTAs ever since the first TCP/IP-enabled version of Berkeley Unix came out in 1984. The Sendmail agent is still in use today, fueled by a well-organized group of dedicated developers that make up the Sendmail Consortium (`www.sendmail.org`).

While the first few Sendmail versions were robust enough to perform in production environments, even under extremely heavy loads, they were not designed with security in mind because the Internet hadn't yet become the ubiquitous (and risky) medium that it is today. However, starting with version 8.9, the Sendmail developers have adopted a more defensive philosophy in light of an increasing incidence of documented security exploits, mostly fueled by its expanding popularity. The result was a much more secure default distribution, almost pedantic in the way that it safeguarded against misconfigurations that can lead to security holes.

Versions 8.10 and 8.11 of Sendmail have gone a step further, implementing a comprehensive defense against unsolicited commercial e-mail (UCE), otherwise known as *spam*. In addition, Sendmail version 8.11 was the first version to incorporate support for SMTP authentication, the topic of the next section.

Secure Mail Relaying via SMTP Authentication

Mail server administrators are being asked to ensure the security of their mail server while still providing an acceptable level of service to legitimate users. This typically means disabling all mail relaying through the corporate mail server, except for those addresses that are known to belong to the company's remote access users. The problem with this approach is that with the advent of universal remote access and broadband technology, it's increasingly difficult to know the addresses of the legitimate users.

The focus has shifted toward a just-in-time authentication of the mail client, whereby remote system users identify themselves as corporate users before being granted the ability to relay mail through the server. The Internet Engineering Task Force (IETF) has proposed SMTP authentication (RFC2554) as the standard protocol to enable secure mail relaying, and Sendmail 8.10 now incorporates native support for SMTP authentication.

If you have a large mobile work force and you find yourself having to allow mail-relay connections from otherwise anonymous destinations, I recommend that you upgrade to Sendmail 8.11 right away. Red Hat 7.0 comes standard with Sendmail 8.11.0, and also includes Cyrus' implementation of Simple Authentication and Security Layer (SASL), which is used by Sendmail to implement SMTP authorization.

Listing 6.1 shows the steps you need to take to add SMTP AUTH support to a standard Red Hat 7.0 installation.

Listing 6.1   Configuring Sendmail for SMTP authorization per RFC2554

```
[ramon]$ rpm -q sendmail
sendmail-8.11.0-8
[ramon]$ rpm -q cyrus-sasl
cyrus-sasl-1.5.24-6
[ramon]$ sudo saslpasswd ramon
Password: mypass
Again (for verification): mypass
```

As you can see in Listing 6.1, first make sure that you have both a recent version of Sendmail (SMTP AUTH support is implemented as of Sendmail 8.10), as well as a recent version of cyrus-sasl (more recent than 1.5.10). Next, use the saslpasswd utility to create the secret password for each remote user who will be using SMTP AUTH. In Listing 6.1, a new user named ramon is created, whose password will be mypass.

In addition, you must modify the standard Red Hat 7.0 /etc/mail/sendmail.mc file to include the provision to allow relaying when SMTP AUTH is successful. To accomplish this, simply add the line:

```
TRUST_AUTH_MECH(DIGEST-MD5 CRAM-MD5)
```

to the options section of /etc/mail/sendmail.mc. Don't forget to recreate the /etc/sendmail.cf file from the updated macro configuration file using the following command:

```
[ramon]$ sudo m4 sendmail.mc > /etc/sendmail.cf
```

At this point, the local sendmail daemon allows relaying to only those SMTP clients that authenticate themselves using either DIGEST-MD5 or CRAM-MD5. (CRAM stands for Challenge/Response Authentication Mode. MD5 is a popular one-way hashing algorithm.) There are a number of mail user agents (MUAs) that support CRAM-MD5 authentication natively, such as Pine, Mulberry, Eudora, Pegasus, and Akmail. You should make sure that one of these mail clients is used and that they are configured with the username and password that you specified with the saslpasswd command.

Application Security

PART 3

Once you have successfully added strong authentication to your Sendmail service, the next step is to add privacy to the mail transport communications. This is the topic of the next section.

SMTP over TLS

Sendmail version 8.11 introduces support for secure SMTP over TLS (STARTTLS) per RFC2487. The term *STARTTLS* simply refers to the new SMTP command that is used to initiate the TLS-enabled mail transport session. This extension allows you to set up a secure bridge from two SMTP (Sendmail) servers that can communicate using TLS (also known as Secure Sockets Layer, or SSL). This ensures the privacy and integrity of the exchange and strongly authenticates the identity of the two communicating peers. To add STARTTLS support to a stock installation of Sendmail, start by ensuring that you have installed both Sendmail 8.11 or above and OpenSSL using the following command:

```
[ramon]$ rpm -q sendmail openssl
sendmail-8.11.0-8
openssl-0.9.5a-14
```

> **NOTE**   Chapter 7, "HTTP Services," explains in more detail the nature and purpose of the SSL protocol.

Next, you need to create your own certificate authority (CA) using OpenSSLø so that you can sign (and verify) the X.509 digital certificates of your remote peers. Listing 6.2 shows the commands needed to create the CA.

Listing 6.2   Creating a certificate authority for Sendmail STARTTLS

```
[ramon]$ sudo mkdir /etc/mail/CA
[ramon]$ cd /etc/mail/CA
[ramon]$ sudo mkdir certs crl newcerts private
[ramon]$ echo "01" > serial
[ramon]$ cp /dev/null index.txt
[ramon]$ cp /usr/share/ssl/openssl.cnf openssl.cnf
[ramon]$ sudo openssl req -new -x509 -keyout private/cakey.pem -out⤵
cacert.pem -days 365 -config openssl.cnf
```

The commands in Listing 6.2 perform the following tasks:

1. Create a directory (/etc/mail/CA) where you will be storing your Sendmail Certificate Authority information.

2. Create four subdirectories where you will store the CA certificates (certs), the certificate revocation lists (crl), new certificates signed by the CA (newcerts), and the CA's private key (private).

3. Initialize two housekeeping files (serial and index.txt) and copy the standard configuration file (/usr/share/ssl/openssl.cnf) into the current CA directory.

4. Use the openssl command to create a new CA private key (private/cakey.pem) and a new CA certificate (cacert.pem) that is valid for the next 365 days.

Next, you need to create a certificate for the Sendmail server using the following command:

```
[ramon]$ sudo openssl req -nodes -new -x509 -keyout newreq.pem -out ↵
newreq.pem -days 365 -config openssl.cnf
```

And finally, you need to sign the new certificate (newreq.pem) with the CA's private key, as follows:

```
[ramon]$ sudo openssl x509 -x509toreq -in newreq.pem -signkey ↵
newreq.pem -out tmp.pem

Getting request Private Key

Generating certificate request

[ramon]$ sudo openssl ca -config openssl.cnf -policy policy_anything ↵
-out newcert.pem -infiles tmp.pem

Getting request Private Key

Generating certificate request

[ramon]$ sudo openssl ca -config openssl.cnf -policy policy_anything ↵
-out newcert.pem -infiles tmp.pem

Using configuration from openssl.cnf

Enter PEM pass phrase:

Check that the request matches the signature

Signature ok

The Subjects Distinguished Name is as follows
countryName           :PRINTABLE:'US'
stateOrProvinceName   :PRINTABLE:'Virginia'
localityName          :PRINTABLE:'Ashburn'
organizationName      :PRINTABLE:'Ramon J. Hontanon'
organizationalUnitName:PRINTABLE:'Ramons Pile O Bits'
commonName            :PRINTABLE:'redhat.example.com'
emailAddress          :IA5STRING:'rhontanon@sybex.com'
```

Application Security

PART 3

```
Certificate is to be certified until Nov 27 01:03:45 2001 GMT (365
days)
Sign the certificate? [y/n]:y

1 out of 1 certificate requests certified, commit? [y/n]y
Write out database with 1 new entries
Data Base Updated
[ramon]$ sudo rm -f tmp.pem
```

As you can see, the signing operation actually takes three separate commands, with an extra one to clean up the temporary file (tmp.pem) used by the first three commands. The result is an X.509 certificate, written to the file newcert.pem, which is in Privacy Enhanced Mail (PEM) format.

NOTE The X.509 standard defines the format of digital certificates and certificate revocation lists. Aside from the digital signature, an X.509 certificate includes fields for its version, the serial number, the issuer's (CA) name, the validity period, and the subject (owner) name. Another IETF standard, the PEM definition is often used to exchange X.509 certificates inside files as PEM-encoded text messages.

Next, you need to modify sendmail.mc to add CA support to your Sendmail installation. Listing 6.3 contains the exact commands that you need to add to the sendmail.mc file.

Listing 6.3 Adding certificate support to sendmail.mc

```
define(`CERT_DIR', `MAIL_SETTINGS_DIR`'CA')dnl
define(`confCACERT_PATH', `CERT_DIR')dnl
define(`confCACERT', `CERT_DIR/cacert.pem')dnl
define(`confSERVER_CERT', `CERT_DIR/newcert.pem')dnl
define(`confSERVER_KEY', `CERT_DIR/private/cakey.pem')dnl
```

The commands in Listing 6.3 are pointing Sendmail to the appropriate files in the CA that you built back in Listing 6.2:

- CERT_DIR (and CERT_PATH): The directory where the CA is located (/etc/mail/CA)
- CACERT: The root CA certificate (cacert.pem)
- SERVER_CERT: The certificate for the Sendmail server (newcert.pem)
- SERVER_KEY: The private key for the Sendmail server (private/cakey.pem)

If your version of Sendmail has STARTTLS support configured, it should appear as 250-STARTTLS when you execute the following command (note the third line from the bottom):

```
[ramon]$ telnet localhost 25
Trying 127.0.0.1...
Connected to localhost
Escape character is '^]'.
220 redhat.example.com ESMTP Sendmail 8.11.0/8.11.0; Sun, 26 Nov 2000
21:04:55 -0500
ehlo localhost
250-local.sendmail.COM Hello localhost [127.0.0.1], pleased to meet you
250-ENHANCEDSTATUSCODES
250-DSN
250-STARTTLS
250 HELP
quit
```

Using STARTTLS

There are two useful applications for Sendmail's STARTTLS support:

- Allowing relaying based on successful certificate authentication
- Restricting SMTP connections to those who are valid certificate holders

By requesting a CA-signed X.509 certificate from all SMTP users requesting mail relaying, the local Sendmail agent can ensure that only authenticated users are allowed to relay through your server, regardless of what IP address they may be coming from.

In addition, STARTTLS can be used to allow SMTP connections to your mail server only in the event that the remote system has presented a valid certificate that can be verified by the local server's CA. You can either restrict incoming connections to those clients holding a valid certificate, or you can force outgoing mail connections to only succeed if the remote end can accept your certificate and agree to establish a secure (encrypted) SMTP session. You can use this last feature to set up a virtual private SMTP link over the public Internet, where you can share sensitive information via e-mail with a greater degree of confidentiality.

Application
Security

PART 3

As you can see, STARTTLS addresses the three main concerns of information security as a whole (confidentiality, integrity, and authentication), and it does this using standard open-source software components. It is not a substitute for a network layer virtual private network (VPN) system that guarantees the privacy of all traffic, regardless of application. This concept is discussed in detail in Chapter 12, "Virtual Private Networks."

STARTTLS is, however a good first step toward the adoption of a full-fledged VPN, especially if your security policy is such that only SMTP traffic needs to be protected while travelling outside your network. In fact, it's generally a good idea to protect the content of SMTP packets, even as they traverse the internal network, where they can be subject to unauthorized eavesdropping by insiders.

> **NOTE** For in-depth information on the installation, configuration, and administration of Sendmail on a Linux server, please refer to *Linux Sendmail Administration* (Sybex, 2001), part of the Craig Hunt Linux Library.

You can also find more information on Sendmail and the Sendmail consortium at www.sendmail.org.

The next two sections describe two alternative MTAs that have been gaining popularity in the last few months. Let's kick off the discussion with Qmail.

Qmail

While Sendmail is responsible for carrying over two-thirds of the e-mail traffic exchanged over the Internet on a daily basis, it does have some worthy competitors. In fact, one alternative to Sendmail is gaining popularity at an unprecedented pace: Qmail. Developed by Dan Bernstein at the University of Illinois at Chicago, Qmail aims to address the security issues found in Sendmail by offering an MTA designed from the ground up with security in mind. From its inception, Qmail followed some very fundamental rules, such as

- Avoid running the main MTA daemon as root. Instead, only two of its auxiliary scripts need root privileges.
- Avoid the use of setuid. Only one Qmail script, qmail-queue, is setuid.
- Treat addresses differently than programs and files. This is done to avoid a common vulnerability of Sendmail's where users were feeding the Sendmail daemon shell scripts in place of addresses, only to have the server execute them (often with root privileges).

In addition to this design philosophy, Qmail has a few circumstantial advantages over Sendmail:

- Qmail is more recent. Hindsight is 20/20, and Qmail has learned a lot of the vulnerabilities that are inherent to MTAs in general and that were only discovered because Sendmail was deployed first.

- Qmail was born in a different climate. The Internet of 1984 was very different from the Internet of 1996. This forced Qmail developers to write applications that would withstand the risks of today's brave new public networks. Sendmail has been keeping up with the new vulnerabilities, but it's done it via patches and slight enhancements to the original design.

- Qmail is a simpler (and smaller) program. In the 15+ years that Sendmail has been used in a production environment, the feature requests have never stopped flowing. The result is a very complete, but very complex MTA. As is the case with any piece of server software, complexity breeds vulnerability.

However, there are certain areas where Sendmail still has the upper hand:

- Sendmail is more mature. It still moves the overwhelming majority of SMTP traffic over the Internet and is a much better known quantity. There is extensive Sendmail documentation, including books and tutorials, as well as training and certification.

- Sendmail's installation procedure is robust and well automated, whereas Qmail still requires a number of manual steps to be executed.

- Sendmail is more scrutinized, with an installed base that is orders of magnitude larger than Qmail's. This leads to much quicker identification of security vulnerabilities, and prompt availability of the appropriate security fix.

When it comes to advocating the security of the package, the Qmail community backed up their claims with one of the now infamous financial "challenges." The contest started in April of 1997 and ended in April of 1998, and aimed to find a security vulnerability in the Qmail software that would give a remote user unauthorized access to the target system. The contest period ended and no one was able to find a legitimate vulnerability on the software, so the $1,000 prize went unclaimed.

Putting aside the result of this challenge, I recommend that you don't base your decision about which MTA to use solely on Qmail's claims of proven security. Both Qmail and Sendmail can be made secure enough to meet the requirements of any security policy. If you are already using Sendmail in your mail server installation and you have built some core expertise on it, you may want to stay with that package. The danger in changing MTAs is that you'll almost always need a learning period during which you are more prone to making simple configuration mistakes that may lead to a security vulnerability.

Application Security

PART 3

If you are building an SMTP server from the ground up and have no previous Sendmail experience, review the features that Qmail offers and make sure that it can meet your overall mail-handling needs. If the answer is yes, then Qmail is a better fit for your needs because it is simpler and easier to configure.

Extensive information on Qmail can be found at www.qmail.org.

The next section describes yet another Sendmail replacement: the Postfix MTA.

Postfix

Completing the MTA trilogy is Postfix, developed by Wietse Venema, who brought us other proven security packages (SATAN, TCP Wrappers). The Postfix project is at a much earlier stage than Sendmail and Qmail, and as of the writing of this book, Wietse still calls the shipping version *Beta*. In fact, releases are tagged with *snapshot* numbers (dates, really), rather than real (*major.minor*) version numbers.

Postfix is even more modular and simpler to configure than Qmail, and it appears to out-perform most other MTAs in use today in the number of messages that it can handle per unit of time. At the current growth rate in deployed installations, I expect that Postfix will be a strong challenger to both Sendmail and Qmail in the near future.

Postfix includes some critical security features:

Principle of Least Privilege   Most Postfix processes, including the SMTP client and the SMTP server, run at fixed low privilege in a chroot environment, which means that they are only aware of a limited section of the filesystem (a sandbox of sorts).

Process Insulation   Most Postfix processes are decoupled and insulated from one another, such that a vulnerability in one of them would be contained and not easily spread to the security-sensitive parts of the system, such as the local mail delivery daemon.

Process Ownership   None of the Postfix processes run under the ownership on the invoking user. Instead, they are owned by a daemon user with no parent-child relationship to the user process.

Setuid   No Postfix process runs with setuid permissions.

Large Inputs   Postfix developers have designed the system in order to be resilient to buffer overflows in the presence of unusually large SMTP input commands.

You can find more information on the Postfix project at www.postfix.org.

Up until now, this chapter has focused the discussion on MTA applications. The next section shifts the focus to the security issues associated with mail retrieval protocols, which are used by MUAs to fetch messages from a waiting queue in the mail server. Let's start by looking at the Post Office Protocol (POP), and continue by examining the Internet Mail Access Protocol (IMAP).

The Post Office Protocol (POP) V.3

When the Internet saw the transition away from time-sharing systems where all the mail was read online, to the PC-on-every-desktop model, it became evident that most PCs were not going to be up and running all the time. This made it necessary to devise a protocol by which users could send mail and request their incoming mail from a dedicated server. While the existing SMTP protocol was a good fit to handle outgoing mail, a new protocol had to be created to address the incoming mail. Enter the POP protocol. In 1984, the IETF drafted the first RFC document outlining the standard (RFC918) only to be enhanced in 1988 (RFC1081) into version 3 of the protocol (POP3), which is still in use today.

POP3 became the de facto standard for mail-retrieval clients throughout the late 1980s and early 1990s, until it began losing steam in favor of the IMAP protocol (discussed in the next section). There are still, however, millions of POP3 clients in operation today, with thousands of POP3 servers to which they connect, many of them hosted by Linux servers.

Of all the POP3 server packages, the one that has enjoyed the most popularity in the Linux community is the Qualcomm, Inc.'s Qpopper. Originally developed as a companion to the (also wildly successful) Eudora mail client, Qpopper was positioned as a full-featured, open-source POP3 server, whose development continues today. This section focuses on Qpopper because it's the best representative of this class of servers and discusses the security issues involved with its installation and use.

APOP

The APOP functionality extends the standard POP3 authentication sequence by adding the ability to send authentication information without exposing the password in the clear. The basic operation of the POP3 protocol is as follows:

1. The client connects to the appropriate port (TCP 110) of the POP3 server.

2. The client supplies a username and password that authenticates them to some mailbox on the server.

3. The client queries mailbox statistics (for example, number of new messages, total messages, etc.).

4. The client retrieves a number of messages.

5. The client deletes a number of messages.

6. The client closes connection.

For example, consider the client/server conversation in Listing 6.4.

Listing 6.4 POP3 session: conventional (USER/PASS) authentication

```
[ramon]$ telnet pop3.example.com 110
Trying 209.1.78.12...
Connected to pop3.example.com.
Escape character is '^]'.
+OK QPOP (version 3.1b6) at pop3 starting.  <3606.975375600@redhat>
USER ramon
+OK Password required for ramon.
PASS mysecret
+OK ramon has 1 visible messages (0 hidden) in 890 octets.
```

The main security flaw with the implementation in Listing 6.4 is the fact that the user must supply a password as part of the authentication sequence. This exposes a piece of secret material to eavesdropping over the public Internet, especially considering that some POP3 clients can be configured to automatically contact the server periodically to check for newly arrived e-mail.

In order to alleviate this risk, the POP3 protocol developers amended the original standard with a challenge/response mechanism by which the POP3 server presents the client with a challenge (the current decimal value of the system clock). It is then up to the client to generate an MD5 one-way hash of the challenge, appended to the authentication password that the POP3 administrator has assigned to the user. The client then returns the result of the hash in the APOP line. If the server successfully replicates the response at its end and it matches the one returned by the client, then the authentication is successful, and the user is allowed to retrieve messages from their mailbox.

In the example in Listing 6.5, username ramon is attempting to log on to pop3.example .com to read his mail.

Listing 6.5 POP3 session: APOP authentication

```
[ramon]$ telnet pop3.example.com 110
Trying 209.1.78.12...
Connected to pop3.example.com.
Escape character is '^]'.
+OK QPOP (version 3.1b6) at pop3 starting.  <3606.975375600@pop3>
APOP ramon s9df67s9df798s7d9fs7d9f7sd9f7s8g
+OK ramon has 1 visible messages (0 hidden) in 890 octets.
```

The POP3 server in Listing 6.5 presents the user with the challenge (a string of characters that they must use in their reply)

```
<3606.975375600@pop3>
```

which the client appends to the password to form the following string:

```
<3606.975375600@pop3>mysecret
```

It then proceeds to feed this string to the MD5 algorithm, which produces a hash value of

```
s9df67s9df798s7d9fs7d9f7sd9f7s8g
```

Note that the robustness of this approach comes from the fact that it is mathematically infeasible to obtain the original *seed* from the MD5 hash. Therefore, even if the eavesdropper knows the challenge that the POP3 server sent to the client, the risk of having them reverse the MD5 function to obtain the seed is minimal.

The next section walks you through the process of installing the Qualcomm Qpopper package, including how to configure the APOP authentication method.

Installing the Qpopper Software

The Qpopper package is not typically installed by default on most Linux distributions, but it can be easily obtained in RPM format and installed using the Linux rpm utility, as follows:

```
[ramon]$ sudo rpm -i qpopper-3.1b6-3k.i586.rpm
```

This command installs the server binary and the man pages, as well as a limited set of documentation. The next section shows you how to set up the POP3 server, as well as its extended authentication feature.

Configuring the Qpopper Software

The latest version of Qpopper at the writing of this book (3.1) does not automatically create an xinetd entry in order to spawn itself automatically. To make sure this happens, simply create the file /etc/xinetd.d/qpopper with the contents in Listing 6.6.

Listing 6.6   Contents of the */etc/xinetd.d/qpopper* file

```
service pop3
{
        socket_type             = stream
        wait                    = no
        user                    = root
        server                  = /usr/sbin/in.qpopper
        log_on_success          += USERID
        log_on_failure          += USERID
}
```

The directives in Listing 6.6 ensure that your server listens to requests for the POP3 service (TCP port 110) with the `/usr/sbin/in.qpopper` as the daemon.

If you are using `inetd` instead of `xinetd`, simply enter the following in your `inetd.conf` file:

```
pop3 stream  tcp nowait root     /usr/sbin/in.qpopper in.qpopper
```

The next step in the configuration is creating a username (e.g., pop) to own the authentication database (user/password associations) for APOP (see Figure 6.1). In this figure, `linuxconf` is being used on Red Hat to create a POP3 administrative account.

Figure 6.1   Creating a POP3 administrative account

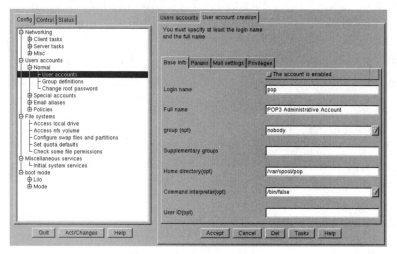

You should change the owner of the POP3-supplied `popauth` utility to be pop, and make it `suid` pop using the following commands:

[ramon]$ **cd /usr/sbin**

[ramon]$ **sudo chown pop popauth**

[ramon]$ **sudo chmod u+s popauth**

The very first time you run the `popauth` utility, you use it to create the authentication database, as follows:

[ramon]$ **sudo popauth -init**

You must make sure that the newly created authentication database file is only readable by the pop user:

[ramon]$ **ls -l /etc/pop.auth**

```
-rw-------   1 pop      popusers     1544 Nov 27 22:08 /etc/pop.auth
```

At this point, you have a fresh installation of Qpopper that is ready to be populated with new POP3 users. The next section explains how to do just that.

Using the Qpopper Software

As you add new users to your server, you also need to allow them to use APOP authentication to your POP3 server. This requires an entry in /etc/pop.auth for each new user. To add these entries, simply issue a popauth command like

```
[ramon]$ sudo popauth -user ramon
Changing only APOP password for ramon.
New password: mysecret
Retype new password: mysecret
```

Note that this example used the sudo command to run popauth as root, but in fact, the command could have been executed by user pop as well. If you need to revoke a user's POP3 access, simply delete that user from the database using the following command:

```
[ramon]$ sudo popauth -delete ramon
```

Once users have been added to /etc/pop.auth, they can change their own passwords, invoking the popauth utility as their own user, with no command-line options, as follows:

```
[ramon]$ popauth
Changing only APOP password for ramon.
Old password: mysecret
New password: newsecret
Retype new password: newsecret
```

This section discussed the POP3 protocol, its security shortcomings, and how you can get around them. The next section discusses the implementation of the IMAP protocol, an alternative to POP3 that is gaining a great deal of popularity in the Linux server community.

IMAP

While POP3 is still the most popular mail-retrieval protocol, one of its fundamental shortcomings is the fact that messages have to be downloaded to the user's computer (the client) in order to have access to them. This makes it difficult for the user to select which messages they want to see before actually downloading them. It also makes it a challenge to read mail from multiple clients, while still keeping the mailbox in synch. The Internet Mail Access Protocol (IMAP) was developed in Stanford University circa 1986 to address

Application Security

PART 3

this shortcoming, as well as to add a host of other improvements to the ubiquitous POP3 protocol.

IMAP is a true client/server protocol that is independent of the transport used to access the mail server. It also allows you to access different mail folders on the remote server, regardless of your identity and the user that owns the remote mailbox. While this offers unprecedented flexibility, it also introduces some concern and increases the risk of malicious eavesdropping of the mail traffic as it is being received from the IMAP server. More importantly, in the absence of any encryption between the client and the server, the username/password exchange will be in the clear as well.

If your needs are such that you can benefit from offering IMAP services to your mail users, the next section guides you through the process of installing the IMAP server software without jeopardizing the security of your server or the privacy of the mail contents and the user authentication exchange.

Installing the IMAP Server Software

The University of Washington's IMAP server is the most popular and most actively supported IMAP package available for Linux. While it's not typically installed by default on most Linux distributions, it can be easily obtained in RPM format and installed using the Linux rpm utility:

```
[ramon]$ sudo rpm -i imap-2000-3.i386.rpm
```

This command installs the server binary and the man pages, as well as a limited set of documentation. The next section shows you how to set up the secure IMAP server, and how to enable it on xinetd and inetd.

Configuring the Secure IMAP Server

The imapd-2000 package uses OpenSSL for its secure transport options (imaps). In order to configure the SSL service, simply create a self-signed certificate using the following commands:

```
[ramon]$ cd /usr/share/ssl/certs
[ramon]$ sudo make imapd.pem
```

This results in the creation of the file /usr/share/ssl/certs/imapd.pem, which contains both the key and the certificate that imap-2000 will use to add SSL protection to the IMAP exchanges. Note that IMAP inserts two files in the /etc/xinetd.d directory, as shown in the steps in Listing 6.7.

Listing 6.7   Xinetd IMAP definitions

```
[ramon]$ cd /etc/xinetd.d
[ramon]$ more imap
# default: off
# description: The IMAP service allows remote users to access their mail using
\
#               an IMAP client such as Mutt, Pine, fetchmail, or Netscape \
#               Communicator.
service imap
{
        socket_type             = stream
        wait                    = no
        user                    = root
        server                  = /usr/sbin/imapd
        log_on_success          += DURATION USERID
        log_on_failure          += USERID
        disable                 = yes
}
[ramon]$ more imaps
# default: off
# description: The SIMAP service allows remote users to access
# their mail using an IMAP client with SSL support
# such as Netscape Communicator or fetchmail.
  service imaps
{
        socket_type             = stream
        wait                    = no
        user                    = root
        server                  = /usr/sbin/stunnel
        server_args             = -l /usr/sbin/imapd -- imapd
        log_on_success          += DURATION USERID
        log_on_failure          += USERID
        disable                 = yes
}
```

The first file (imap) instructs your Linux server to look for connections on
TCP port 143 (imap service). The second file (imaps) instructs your server to handle
connections to TCP port 993, which is the port that has been reserved for the
imaps service (IMAP over SSL).

I recommend that you never enable IMAP in the clear (/etc/xinetd.d/imap). Instead, only enable /etc/xinetd.d/imaps, which is SSL protected. You can do this by simply deleting the line

```
disable                 = yes
```

from the /etc/xinetd.d/imaps file, and restarting the xinetd daemon.

If you are using inetd instead of xinetd, you can enable imaps by simply entering the following line in your inetd.conf file:

```
imaps stream tcp nowait root /usr/sbin/stunnel stunnel -l ⤶
/usr/sbin/imapd -- imapd
```

Using the Secure IMAP Server

Netscape Communicator, as well as Fetchmail and other mail clients, include built-in support for IMAP over SSL. This section will use Netscape Communicator as an example.

Start by importing your CA's root X.509 certificate into your user's Communicator application. This is necessary in order to kick-start the authentication process. Unless your mail server(s) use certificates that have been signed by a third party whose root certificates come preloaded in Communicator (VeriSign, Thawte, etc.), you need to load your CA's root certificate into your mail application so that you can strongly authenticate the LDAP server. Since Netscape Communicator only accepts certificates in the PKCS#12 format, you need to force OpenSSL to export a copy of the root certificate as a .p12 file using the following command:

```
[ramon]$ sudo openssl pkcs12 -export -in newcert.pem -inkey ⤶
newreq.pem -certfile cacert.pem -name "MY CERTIFICATE" -out ⤶
mycert.p12
```

You will be prompted for an *export* password that will protect the certificate. Enter the password twice for verification.

You should then distribute this file to all your users who wish to use SSL-enhanced LDAP. Alternatively, you can include this certificate standard with Communicator before your users are even assigned a workstation.

To import the certificate into Netscape Communicator, follow these simple steps:

1. Press Ctrl+Shift+I to bring up the Security window.

2. Select Certificates ➤ Yours from the menu on the left-hand side. The Your Certificates window appears (see Figure 6.2).

Figure 6.2   Netscape Communicator's Security window, Your Certificates

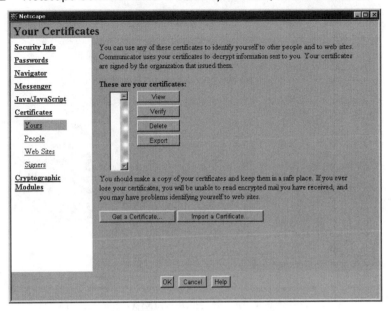

3. Click the Import a Certificate button.

4. Set a password for the Certificate DB. Remember this password because you have to enter it every time you add or delete certificates.

5. Locate the certificate on the local disk (if distributed by floppy) or on a remote network share.

6. Enter the password that you set to protect the certificate.

At this point, you have successfully loaded a CA certificate that Communicator will use to verify the identity of other certificates signed by it. You now need to inform Communicator that you trust this CA certificate. Take the following steps:

1. Select Certificates ➤ Signers and scroll until you find the certificate that you just imported.

2. Click the Edit button.

3. Enable acceptance of the certificate by clicking all four checkboxes in the lower part of the screen, as shown in Figure 6.3.

Figure 6.3   Enabling an imported CA certificate

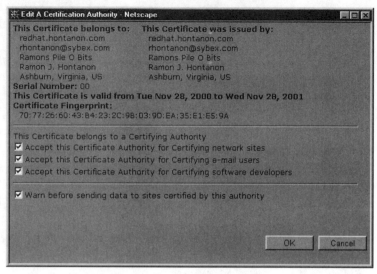

You are now ready to contact your SSL-enabled IMAP server. Figure 6.4 shows how your users can configure their Netscape Communicator mail clients to always use SSL when getting their mail from your IMAP server.

Figure 6.4   Configuring Netscape Communicator mail for SSL IMAP

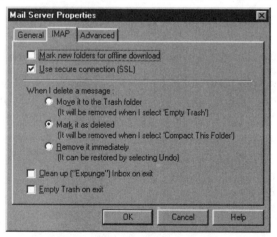

While POP and IMAP can both be updated and modified to provide a reasonable amount of privacy and authentication, a more comprehensive solution to the securing of your e-mail application can be found in end-to-end encryption. A pioneer in the use of public

key technology in a mass scale, Pretty Good Privacy (PGP) has been providing this end-to-end service for the last ten years. The next section is devoted to PGP and its open-source variants.

PGP and GnuPG

In 1991, Phil Zimmermann recognized the need to provide confidentiality at the application level, so he set off to build a tool that would allow users to add confidentiality to their e-mail applications. The package was named Pretty Good Privacy (PGP) and it made use of public-key technology to encrypt and digitally sign any document before sending it on the public Internet. PGP quickly became the most widely used mail encryption tool in the world.

Unlike the current public key infrastructure schemes, which rely on a hierarchical trust structure, PGP is based on a *trust-chain* model, where users securely store other user's public keys, and make (transitive) decisions of trust based on signatures from those keys.

Although the package was initially open source, later PGP versions were developed under the auspices of MIT, ViaCrypt, PGP, Inc. and, more recently, Network Associates, Inc. There are currently at least three different distributions of PGP:

PGP (Commercial)   This is the original product that was developed by PGP, Inc. (Phil Zimmermann's company). In 1997, Network Associates, Inc. (NAI) acquired PGP, Inc., and NAI still supports and distributes both a commercial and a freeware version of PGP that's based on the MIT work. Phil Zimmermann serves as a Senior Fellow at NAI.

PGPi   This is the international version of PGP that was first created by exporting the PGP source code in printed format and scanning it using optical character recognition (OCR) into electronic source files. This was done to circumvent U.S. trade laws regulating the exporting of cryptographic material. In September of 1999, the U.S. government lifted a number of these restrictions, making it possible for NAI to export the product in electronic form. Development of PGPi continues today, but their focus has changed from OCR scanning to "development, porting, translation, and localization," according to its supporters. While personal use of PGPi is unrestricted and the source code is available, commercial use of the latest version of PGPi requires a license agreement from NAI.

GnuPG   The GNU Privacy Guard (GnuPG) is an open-source PGP implementation. It has no relation at all to the original PGP or PGPi, but it is generally interoperable with both versions. Unlike PGP and PGPi, GnuPG is made available under the standard Gnu General Public License (GPL), so it's freely usable and distributable.

In keeping with the Linux tradition of open-source software and unrestricted licensing, this chapter will concentrate on GnuPG for the remainder of the discussion.

Installing GnuPG

While the latest Red Hat Linux distribution includes GnuPG as part of the standard installation, most Linux distributions do not. The package is readily available in RPM format from your favorite repository. To install GnuPG, simply issue a command like the following:

```
[ramon]$ sudo rpm -i gnupg-1.0.4-5.i386.rpm
```

This command installs the main GnuPG executable in /usr/bin/gpg. The next section shows you how to get started with GnuPG and how to use it to encrypt and sign files and e-mail messages.

TIP By default, the gpg executable is not suid root. While this is generally safer, it does prevent the application from "locking" its memory pages into RAM to prevent them from being swapped out to disk. This introduces a security risk because it makes it trivial for any local user to scan the swap partitions for private keys. I recommend that you make the gpg application suid root using the command sudo chmod u+s /usr/bin/gpg. This is safe because the application only uses its root privileges for the page-locking operation.

Configuring GnuPG

As with any public key–driven system, the first step after installing GnuPG is to create the public/private key pair that you will use to encrypt and digitally sign files and messages. To generate your first key pair, enter the following command:

```
[ramon]$ gpg --gen-key
public and secret key created and signed
```

You are prompted for a passphrase that will be used by GnuPG to protect the newly created secret key on your disk. This command automatically creates your secret *keyring*, which is a file where your secret key material is stored (~/.gnupg/secring.gpg, by default). In addition, it creates a public keyring (~/.gnupg/pubring.gpg) where you can manually add keys that are given to you by other users. It's imperative that you sign other users' public keys as you receive them, and only after you verify that they key is indeed valid for that individual. To do this, follow these simple steps, staring with the actual importing of the key:

```
[ramon]$ gpg --import werner.pgp
gpg: key 57548DCD: public key imported
```

```
gpg: /home/ramon/.gnupg/trustdb.gpg: trustdb created
gpg: Total number processed: 1
gpg:                 imported: 1
```

Note that when you import this key, GnuPG reports the key ID as 57548DCD. Use this or the key holder's e-mail address in all subsequent operations on this public key, or you can use the key holder's e-mail address also. Next, display the key fingerprint as in the next example, and verify it with the owner out of band (e.g., in person or by phone):

```
[ramon]$ gpg --fingerprint 57548DCD

pub  1024D/57548DCD 1998-07-07 Werner Koch (gnupg sig)
<dd9jn@gnu.~CAorg>

Key fingerprint = 6BD9 050F D8FC 941B 4341  2DCC 68B7 AB89 5754 8DCD
```

If the fingerprint matches, you should sign the key on your public keyring:

```
[ramon]$ gpg --edit-key 57548DCD

gpg (GnuPG) 1.0.2; Copyright (C) 2000 Free Software Foundation, Inc.
This program comes with ABSOLUTELY NO WARRANTY.
This is free software, and you are welcome to redistribute it
under certain conditions. See the file COPYING for details.


pub  1024D/57548DCD  created: 1998-07-07 expires: 2002-12-29
trust: -/q
(1)  Werner Koch (gnupg sig) <dd9jn@gnu.org>


Command> sign


pub  1024D/57548DCD  created: 1998-07-07 expires: 2002-12-29
trust: -/q
        Fingerprint: 6BD9 050F D8FC 941B 4341  2DCC 68B7
AB89 5754 8DCD


    Werner Koch (gnupg sig) <dd9jn@gnu.org>


Are you really sure that you want to sign this key
with your key: "Ramon J. Hontanon (Linux Student)
```

Application
Security

PART 3

```
<rhontanon@sybex.com>"

Really sign? y

You need a passphrase to unlock the secret key for
user: "Ramon J. Hontanon (Linux Student)
<rhontanon@sybex.com>"
1024-bit DSA key, ID 3C9EA164, created 2000-11-29
```

You now have a public/private key pair of your own, as well as the (verified and signed) public signature of one of your peers. These are the basic ingredients for the operation of GnuPG.

Using GnuPG

While there are a number of Linux MUAs that include transparent GnuPG support (Mutt, Pine, and VM, for example), this section will discuss the command-line use of the gpg utility. This is important because most MUAs support GnuPG by piping messages in and out to gpg using the command-line options that discussed in this section. Table 6.2 lists the most commonly used gpg command-line options.

Table 6.2   gpg Command-Line Options

Option	Meaning
--encrypt	Encrypt the message.
--armor	Use ASCII for the encryption output.
--clearsign	Sign the message to a cleartext file.
--sign	Sign the message (use in conjunction with the --encrypt option).
--decrypt	Decrypt the message.
--verify	Verify a signature.
--list-keys	Show keys in your public keyring.
--list-secret-keys	Show keys in your private keyring.

Examples

Consider as an example an e-mail message whose text is in the file `message.txt`. You want to digitally sign the message before sending it so that the recipient can be assured that it came from you. Enter the following commands to sign your message:

```
[ramon]$ gpg --clearsign message.txt
You need a passphrase to unlock the secret key for user: "Ramon J.
Hontanon (Linux Student) <rhontanon@sybex.com>"
1024-bit DSA key, ID 3C9EA164, created 2000-11-29
[ramon]$ cat message.txt.asc
-----BEGIN PGP SIGNED MESSAGE-----
Hash: SHA1


This is just a test message. We would like to ensure the integrity
of this message by attaching a digital signature to it.


Regards,


-- ramon
-----BEGIN PGP SIGNATURE-----
Version: GnuPG v1.0.2 (GNU/Linux)
Comment: For info see http://www.gnupg.org


iD8DBQE6JbeHnwa9rjyeoWQRAhnSAJ9WtkILSphi22rSWHoDpIG2bB8wOgCgh+uB
I/aU/+ZbCRDdhVpoxSwGJWo=
=peFJ
-----END PGP SIGNATURE-----
```

Note that GnuPG prompts you for the passphrase to unlock your secret key. This is because the signing algorithm needs to use the private key to generate a signature. Conversely, the recipient of the message needs your public key to verify that your message is really signed with your private signature:

```
[stacia]$ gpg --verify message.txt.asc
gpg: Signature made Wed Nov 29 21:12:23 2000 EST using DSA key
ID 3C9EA164
```

```
gpg: Good signature from "Ramon J. Hontanon (Linux Student)
<rhontanon@sybex.com>"
```

Consider the case where you want to ensure both the privacy and the integrity of a message. The following command signs and encrypts the message contained in the file message.txt:

```
[ramon]$ gpg --encrypt --sign --armor message.txt


You need a passphrase to unlock the secret key for
user: "Ramon J. Hontanon (Linux Student)
<rhontanon@sybex.com>"
1024-bit DSA key, ID 3C9EA164, created 2000-11-29


You did not specify a user ID. (you may use "-r")


Enter the user ID: stacia@example.com
```

When Stacia receives the message, she then uses her gpg utility to decrypt and verify the signature of the resulting message.txt.asc document:

```
[stacia]$ gpg --decrypt message.txt.asc


You need a passphrase to unlock the secret key for
user: "Stacia S. Hontanon (Linux Master)
<stacia@example.com>
1024-bit ELG-E key, ID A0626845, created 2000-11-29 (main key
ID 3C9EA034)


This is just a test message. We would like to ensure the integrity
of this message by attaching a digital signature to it.


Regards,


-- ramon
gpg: Signature made Wed Nov 29 21:21:54 2000 EST using DSA key
```

```
ID 3C9EA164

gpg: Good signature from "Ramon J. Hontanon (Linux Student)
<rhontanon@sybex.com>"
```

In this example, the output of the decryption/verification simply goes out to the screen. If you would like for the output to be directed to the file message.txt, simply use the following command (note the --output directive):

```
[stacia]$ gpg --output message.txt --decrypt message.txt.asc
```

As you can see, GnuPG is a comprehensive package that includes utilities to encrypt, decrypt, sign, and verify any type of document (including e-mail messages), as well as the tools to manage the private and public keys required to provide this service.

A tool like GnuPG is not only useful for securing e-mail exchanges, but it's also an additional privacy measure for protecting critical files that you need to store on your Linux server. I recommend that you use GnuPG to encrypt sensitive network topology diagrams, notes containing authentication passwords, and reports of network audits that reveal any vulnerabilities, at least until you've had a chance to address them.

In Sum

A layered approach to application security calls for mechanisms to ensure the privacy and authentication of the application transport (e.g., SSL) and the content of the packets themselves by applying encryption and digital signatures to the data before the traffic even hits the wire (e.g., GnuPG).

This is especially relevant in the case of electronic mail applications, due to the sheer volume of traffic that they handle and the increasingly sensitive content for which companies rely on electronic mail. Regardless of your choice of MTAs, you need to make sure that your mail user agents (clients) support the same type of privacy and authentication mechanisms as your transport agent. It's also imperative to make sure that your users receive the training they need to use the application in accordance with your security policy.

Electronic mail and Web browsing make up the bulk of the traffic traversing the Internet today. Chapter 7, "HTTP Services," continues the discussion on application layer security by examining the security issues surrounding the three types of open-source HTTP servers available for Linux servers.

7

HTTP Services

This chapter continues the discussion of Part 3, "Application Security," by taking an in-depth look at the Apache HTTP server, the dominant force behind the Web server explosion of the last five years. This chapter describes the overall security features of the base Apache package, as well as the standard authentication and access control configuration.

While system and network layer security can contribute to sealing most of the low-level threats to your Linux server, the harsh reality is that a service like HTTP requires you to open up a number of ports (TCP 80 and sometimes TCP 443) to the Internet population at large. This forces you to implement a complete set of security measures at the application layer, including authentication, access control, and the protection of the HTTP application server itself.

In addition, if your company conducts electronic commerce using your HTTP server, you'll need to ensure the privacy of the transactions, as well as provide strong authentication to your prospective customers and business partners. This can be addressed using SSL (Secure Sockets Layer) extensions to the base Apache HTTP distribution. This chapter describes two different packages that you can deploy to ensure the privacy and authentication of your HTTP transactions:

- mod_ssl (part of the OpenSSL initiative)
- Apache-SSL, on which mod_ssl was originally based

Let's kick off the discussion by describing the security-specific issues at play when you install, configure, and maintain the Apache HTTP server.

The Apache HTTP Server

Developed by the Apache Software Foundation, the Apache HTTP Web server is arguably the most successful piece of publicly available software since the advent of the Linux operating system itself. The Apache group is a collection of geographically dispersed developers who volunteer their time to enhance and maintain the HTTP server and other projects, such as XML-Apache (and an XML development environment) and TomCat (a Java Server reference implementation). Approximately six out of ten Web servers are currently running on Apache's HTTP software. That number is three times larger than the one for Microsoft's Internet Information Service (IIS), Apache's closest competitor.

Originally born out of the HTTP implementation developed by the National Center for Supercomputing Applications (NCSA), Apache owes its name to the fact that it got its start as a "patchy" version of the original NCSA HTTP server. When NCSA temporarily stopped development of their HTTP project, a group of programmers established a forum that would eventually lead to the first version of the Apache HTTP server (version 0.6.2) in April of 1995. Eight months later, this group released Apache 1.0, their first production-quality server with multi-platform support.

Thanks to the constant scrutiny of six million users worldwide, and to the efforts of a growing team of developers, the current Apache distribution is a robust, powerful, scalable, and modular server. It rivals commercial Web server offerings in performance and often exceeds them in security. To find out more about the Apache project, visit the Apache HTTP Server Project home page at `www.apache.org/httpd` (Figure 7.1).

The following section describes how to configure an existing Apache installation with security in mind. For a complete reference on the basic installation, configuration, and administration of Apache on a Linux server, please refer to *Linux Apache Web Server* by Charles Aulds (Sybex, 2001), part of the Craig Hunt Linux Library series.

Figure 7.1   The Apache HTTP Server Project home page

Application
Security

PART 3

Configuring Apache Security

Traditionally, there have been three distinct configuration files for the Apache server:

httpd.conf   httpd.conf is the main configuration file. It contains directives that control the operation of the server as a whole, such as logging and management of the server pool.

srm.conf   The srm.conf file contains directives that control the management of the namespace and resources in the filesystem, including file typing, directory indexes, and aliases.

access.conf   The access.conf file contains directives for access control in various directories.

These three files are located in the same directory (usually /etc/httpd/conf) and are processed by the daemon upon startup in the order listed previously. It is easier, however, to place all your directives in a single file; I suggest that you use httpd.conf for this purpose.

The next few sections discuss specific directives to control the security of your Apache server. All these directives should be included in the httpd.conf file.

Authentication

User authentication is often a necessary feature in an otherwise public service. The Apache HTTP server has the ability to enforce certain rules before the user is granted their HTTP request. The user is granted their HTTP request based on one of two criteria:

- A username/password provided by the HTTP requester
- The IP address of the host that generated the request

While most Web servers contain truly public content and run with no authentication, there are certain applications that force you to implement authentication controls. For example, your company may offer a subscription-based service that requires paying users to authenticate before obtaining the service. Or perhaps you have set up a Web server where your remote users can obtain proprietary software or confidential information. In these situations, you should use Apache authentication to ensure that only authorized users are being granted HTTP access to private parts of the *content tree* (the directory within your server that contains the HTML documents to be offered via HTTP).

At the most basic level, Apache supports four modules that allow the Webmaster to define and authenticate a list of users with their corresponding passwords. These modules are independent pieces of code that plug into the standard Apache functionality that provides specific authentication methods. While third-party developers can integrate any module into Apache, the following four authentication modules come standard with the distribution: mod_auth, mod_auth_dbm, mod_auth_db, and mod_auth_digest. The following sections describe each of these modules in detail.

mod_auth   The mod_auth module provides simple username/password authentication using plain-text files. To use this type of authentication, the administrator must add each user to the Apache password file using the htpasswd command. When mod_auth is in use, Apache prompts the user for a password every time they want to access a directory that contains an .htaccess file. If the user provides a username and password that match an entry in the Apache password file, access is granted.

The .htaccess file is used to include authentication directives for each subdirectory. To force users to authenticate using usernames and passwords, simply create an .htaccess file containing the following text:

```
AuthName "Restricted Files"
AuthType Basic
AuthUserFile /usr/local/etc/httpd/users
Require valid-user
```

Let's take a look at the meaning at each of these directives:

- Authname defines the authentication domain "Restricted Files." This allows users who have already authenticated to a given domain access to other directories with no username/password, provided that they are protected by the same domain.

- AuthType defines the authentication protocol. The keyword Basic instructs Apache to use the mod_auth module to receive the user-specified password in the clear.

- AuthUserFile points to the password file containing mod_auth user information.

- Require directs the server to apply this type of authentication to a portion of the password file, or to the entire password file. The previous example uses the valid-user value, which in fact applies Basic authentication to all the users in the file. You can use this directive to restrict directory access to a number of users (even though the password file may contain hundreds of usernames). For example, to restrict access to only usernames alice and bob, you would use the following .htaccess syntax:

```
AuthName "Restricted Files"
AuthType Basic
AuthUserFile /etc/httpd/conf/user-list
Require user alice bob
```

Due to the limitations of sequential searches of text files, this module is only suitable for installations where fewer than 500 users are required. The mod_auth module supports both a group file and a password file.

The group file follows the format

```
group : user-1 user-2 user-3 … user-n
```

where *group* is the name for the group, and *user-1* through *user-n* are the users to be included in the group. Listing 7.1 contains an example of an Apache group file.

Listing 7.1 Sample Apache group file

```
administrators: alice bob charlie
operators: david ernie
dba: fred george harry
```

The htpasswd utility is supplied with Apache and is used to create and update the user and group files. The command-line usage for this utility is as follows:

```
htpasswd [-c] passwd_file user
```

The -c option directs the utility to create a new password file (named *passwd_file*) and *user* is the username to add to the file.

NOTE Be careful not to create the *passwd_file* in the same directory that you're trying to protect because any authorized Web users will be able to examine the contents of the *passwd_file*.

To create a password file, issue a sequence of commands similar to those shown in Listing 7.2.

Listing 7.2 Using the *htpasswd* utility

```
[ramon]$ sudo htpasswd -c /etc/httpd/conf/user-list alice
New password:
Re-type new password:
Adding password for user alice
[ramon]$ sudo htpasswd /etc/httpd/conf/user-list bob
New password:
Re-type new password:
Adding password for user bob
[ramon]$ sudo htpasswd /etc/httpd/conf/user-list charlie
New password:
Re-type new password:
Adding password for user charlie
```

The format of each line in the password file is

```
user:password-hash
```

where *user* is the cleartext username and *password-hash* is the result of the cryptographic hash operation applied on the cleartext password.

Listing 7.3 contains the password file that results from executing the commands in Listing 7.2.

Listing 7.3   Sample Apache password file

```
[ramon]$ more /etc/httpd/conf/user-list
alice:9ti/4wVGB3Yug
bob:vsh73lcf4phh2
charlie:WqBos8Vas8XJg
```

Earlier in this section, you learned about the `.htaccess` file and the directives that you can add to make use of `mod_auth` module authentication. Table 7.1 includes the complete list of available directives, including their syntax and their meaning.

Table 7.1   *mod_auth* Directives

Directive	Meaning
AuthName *auth-domain*	Specifies the authentication domain to send the HTTP client.
AuthType *type*	Specifies the type of password transmission: Basic (in the clear) or Digest (MD5).
AuthGroupFile *filename*	Specifies the name of the file containing the group authentication information.
AuthUserFile *filename*	Specifies the name of the file containing the user authentication information.
AuthAuthoritative [on | off]	Avoid falling back to a lower form of authentication if user is not available. Defaults to on.

Application Security

PART 3

For example, consider the entry in Listing 7.4 from the `/var/www/html/.htaccess` file.

Listing 7.4   Using the *mod_auth* directives

```
AuthName "Private Information"
AuthType Basic
AuthUserFile /etc/httpd/conf/user-list
AuthGroupFile /etc/httpd/conf/group-list
AuthAuthoritative on
Require valid-user
```

The directives in Listing 7.4 have the following meanings:

- `AuthName "Private Information"` specifies a *domain*, a concept used by the Apache authentication modules to refer to the resource (directory) in question. A domain translates to the directory structure below the one in question. Once the browser has successfully authenticated, it can access any resources within the realm.

- `AuthType Basic` defines standard, *in-the-clear* transmission of the password.

- The `AuthUserFile` directive defines the path to the password file as `/etc/httpd/conf/user-list`.

- The `AuthGroupFile` directive defines the path to the group file `/etc/httpd/conf/group-list`.

- The `AuthAuthoritative` directive ensures that access is simply denied if the user does not exist. (Apache has the ability to cascade this request to other authentication methods if the first request fails).

- The `Require valid-user` directive instructs Apache to only grant access to a user that is present in the `AuthUserFile`. Alternatively, you could have specified the following:

  ```
  Require user alice
  Require user bob
  ```

  These two directives limit access to just the two users alice and bob. Username charlie, who also happens to be present in the `AuthUserFile`, is denied access. This is useful for restricting certain subdirectories within the Apache content tree to specific users, while relying on one central `AuthUserFile`. Furthermore, you can limit access to users within a certain group, using the following directive:

  ```
  Require group administrators
  ```

  This directive restricts access to those users who successfully authenticate as an authorized user in the password file and are also members of the `administrators` group.

WARNING While it is possible to use the standard Linux /etc/passwd to perform Apache server authentication, I strongly recommend against this practice. If the username/password pair exchanged for Apache authentication is captured (it typically travels in the clear), the intruder could then penetrate the user's shell account as well. In addition, Apache imposes no limit on unsuccessful logins, so an attacker could use a brute-force approach to guess system passwords by attempting repeated HTTP requests.

mod_auth_dbm   The mod_auth_dbm module provides simple username/password authentication using Linux DBM format for the user database. User lookups are much faster than those of mod_auth are, and the mod_auth_dbm module can support a very large user population (typically thousands of users). As with mod_auth, the use of mod_auth_ dbm is controlled by directives that can be included in the .htaccess directory within the Apache content tree. Table 7.2 lists the directives available for the mod_auth_dbm module.

Table 7.2   *mod_auth_dbm* Directives

Directive	Meaning
AuthName *auth-domain*	Specifies the authentication domain to send the HTTP client.
AuthType *type*	Specifies the type of password transmission: Basic (in the clear) or Digest (MD5).
AuthDBMGroupFile *filename*	Specifies the name of the DBM file containing the group authentication information.
AuthDBMUserFile *filename*	Specifies the name of the DBM file containing the user authentication information.
AuthDBMAuthoritative [on | off]	Avoid falling back to a lower form of authentication if user is not available. Defaults to on.

As an example, consider the entry in Listing 7.5 from the /var/www/html/.htaccess file.

Listing 7.5   Using the *mod_auth_dbm* directives

```
AuthName "Private Information"
AuthType Basic
AuthDBMUserFile /etc/httpd/conf/user-list-DBM
AuthDBMGroupFile /etc/httpd/conf/group-list-DBM
AuthDBMAuthoritative on
Require valid-user
```

The example in Listing 7.5 is similar to the example in Listing 7.4, except for the third and fourth lines. In Listing 7.5, the AuthDBMUserFile and AuthDBMGroupFile directives specify that the authentication lookup take place on DBM-format files called /etc/httpd/ conf/user-list-DBM and /etc/httpd/conf/group-list-DBM instead of on the flat files used in the example in Listing 7.4.

Application Security

PART 3

Apache includes a Perl utility called dbmmanage (usually installed in /usr/sbin) that you can use to create the DBM database initially and to populate the database with new users and groups. The command-line usage of dbmmanage is as follows:

```
dbmmanage filename [ command ] [ username [pw [group1[,group2] [
encpasswd ] ]
```

In the dbmmanage command line, *command* can be one of the following:

- add: This command adds an entry for *username* to *filename* using the encrypted password *encpassword* or the group(s) in the list of *group1* [,*group2*].
- adduser: This command prompts for a password and adds an entry for *username* to *filename*.
- check: This command prompts for a password and then checks if *username* is in *filename* and if its password matches the one specified.
- delete: This command deletes the *username* entry from *filename*.
- import: This command reads the *username:password* entries (one per line) from the standard Linux input and appends them to *filename*. The password must already be encrypted.
- update: This command is equivalent to the adduser command, except that it ensures that *username* already exists in *filename*.
- view: This command displays the complete contents of the DBM database file.

For example, to create the DBM user database file /etc/httpd/conf/user-list-DBM and add a new user named alice, enter the following command:

```
[ramon]$ sudo dbmmanage /etc/httpd/conf/user-list-DBM adduser alice
New password:
Re-type new password:
User alice added with password encrypted to vqQ/XX7ZhYLXQ using crypt
```

To view your newly created entry, enter the following command:

```
[ramon]$ sudo dbmmanage /etc/httpd/conf/user-list-DBM view
alice:vqQ/XX7ZhYLXQ
```

To delete the database entry for alice, enter the following command:

```
[ramon]$ sudo dbmmanage /etc/httpd/conf/user-list-DBM delete alice
`alice' deleted
```

In addition, you can create a new group database, keyed by the username, where the value field is a comma-separated list of groups to which the user belongs, using the following command:

```
[ramon]$ sudo dbmmanage /etc/httpd/conf/group-list-DBM add alice
staff,operators,admin
```

```
User alice added with password encrypted to staff,operators,admin
using crypt
```

```
[ramon]$ sudo dbmmanage /etc/httpd/conf/group-list-DBM view alice
```

```
alice:staff,operators,admin
```

mod_auth_db   Starting with Apache 1.1, the mod_auth_db module provides an alternative to mod_auth_dbm using the Berkeley Database (known as the Berkeley DB) format instead of the standard Linux DBM. The mod_auth_db directives, listed in Table 7.3, are similar to the ones for mod_auth_dbm.

Table 7.3   *mod_auth_db* Directives

Directive	Meaning
AuthName *auth-domain*	Specifies the authentication domain to send the HTTP client.
AuthType *type*	Specifies the type of password transmission: Basic (in the clear) or Digest (MD5).
AuthDBGroupFile *filename*	Specifies the name of the DB file containing the group authentication information.
AuthDBUserFile *filename*	Specifies the name of the DB file containing the user authentication information.
AuthDBAuthoritative [on | off]	Avoid falling back to a lower form of authentication if user is not available. Defaults to on.

You use the makedb utility to create a Berkeley DB file for both your password and your group lists. Two items are needed for makedb in order to create the proper database format:

- Password: a username, a colon, and an encrypted password
- Group: a group name, a colon, and a comma-separated list of groups

Application Security

PART 3

Note that the password you enter must have the same format as the output of the htpasswd utility. So, in order to add a new user to the Apache Berkeley DB database, simply do the following:

```
[ramon]$ sudo htpasswd /etc/httpd/conf/user-list bob
New password:
Re-type new password:
Adding password for user bob
[ramon]$ sudo makedb /etc/httpd/conf/user-list -o httpd/conf/user-
list-DB
```

The format of the group name you enter is not the same as the standard Apache group name, so you'll have to maintain a separate file to use as makedb input. Consider the following example:

```
[ramon]$ cat /etc/httpd/conf/group-list-for-db
staff: alice, bob, charlie
admin: alice, bob
operators: alice, bob, charlie, david
```

Once you make a modification to this list, simply use the makedb command to create a Berkeley DB database file for use by mod_auth_db using the following command:

```
[ramon]$ sudo makedb /etc/httpd/conf/group-list-for-db -o /etc/httpd/
conf/group-list-DB
```

mod_auth_digest   Available starting with Apache 1.3.8, the mod_auth_digest module provides MD5 digest authentication, which prevents the transmission of the username and password information in the clear between the client and the Apache server. The mod_auth_digest module does not come loaded by default on most standard distributions; to install it, you need to insert (or uncomment, in the case of Red Hat 7.0) the following lines in your httpd.conf file:

```
LoadModule digest_module      /etc/modules/mod_digest.so
AddModule mod_digest.c
```

These two lines make use of Apache's Dynamic Shared Objects (DSO) feature to incorporate an external shared module whose *handle* is digest_module, and that resides in the file /etc/modules/mod_digest.so. The AddModule directive makes reference to the mod_digest.c, which is the main source file of the mod_auth_digest module.

Table 7.4 lists the directives that apply to the mod_auth_digest module.

Table 7.4   *mod_auth_digest* Directives

Directive	Meaning
AuthName auth-domain	Specifies the authentication domain to send the HTTP client.
AuthType type	Specifies the type of password transmission: Basic (in the clear) or Digest (MD5).
AuthDigestDomain domain	One or more URLs that are in the same protection space.
AuthDigestGroupFile filename	Specifies the name of the DB file containing the group authentication information.
AuthDigestFile filename	Specifies the name of the file containing the MD5 digest authentication information.
AuthDBAuthoritative [on | off]	Avoid falling back to a lower form of authentication if user is not available. Defaults to on.

Note that this module uses a digest authentication file (AuthDigestFile) instead of a password file. The digest authentication file is maintained with the htdigest command, and its format is

   user:*password-hash*

where *user* is the cleartext username, and *password-hash* is the result of the cryptographic hash operation applied on the cleartext password.

An entry in the digest authentication file can also take the form

   user:*realm*:*MD5-password-hash*

where *user* is the cleartext username, *realm* is the realm name specified in the AuthName directive, and *MD5-password-hash* is the result of the MD5 hashing operation applied on the cleartext password. An example of the AuthDigestFile might be:

```
[ramon]$ more .htdigest
alice:private:sd7f90s8dfh0s89df70shdf0sd87f0sd
bob:private:a8839d9bc0d14b768a14423e1836fec4
charlie:private:sd907fsd09f780sd7f0sdy7f90sydf89
```

In order to facilitate the creation of the `AuthDigestFile`, Apache provides a utility called `htdigest`, with the following command-line usage:

```
htdigest [-c] digest_file realm user
```

In the `htdigest` command line, `-c` directs the utility to create a new digest file (*digest_file*), *user* denotes the username to add to the file, and *realm* specifies the authentication scope for the password.

In order to set up MD5 authentication on a directory, simply enter the directives listed in Listing 7.6 in your `.htaccess` file.

Listing 7.6 Using the *mod_auth_digest* directives

```
AuthType Digest
AuthName "private area"
AuthDigestDomain http://www.example.com/private/
AuthDigestFile /etc/httpd/conf/digest-file
require valid-user
```

This realm is called `private area`, and the file containing the digest authentication is located in `/etc/httpd/conf/digest-file`. Note that clients that authenticate successfully will have access to the entire `http://www.example.com/private/` URL.

Digest authentication is a feature with a distinct advantage, the protection of the username/password exchange for resource authentication. Digest authentication does, however, limit the number of users in the flat digest file. In addition, older Web browsers may not support this authentication method.

I recommend that you use digest authentication for critical resources that are only going to be accessed by a few users (the Web site administrators, perhaps), where you have complete control on the type of browsers that will be used.

Access Control

The Apache HTTP server supports two access control methods:

- Discretionary (username and password based)
- Mandatory (based on IP address of the client machine)

Discretionary access control requires that the HTTP client user provide something they know (a username/password combination). The choice of credentials is at the discretion of the user, who may elect to use different usernames according to the role they're playing at the moment. Mandatory access control methods, on the other hand, rely on credentials that are beyond the control of the user. The IP address of the HTTP client is the most popular mandatory access control credential.

The previous section described the details of discretionary authentication for access to Apache's content tree. This section examines the configuration steps necessary to enforce mandatory access control rules on your server's Web content, based on the IP address of the host requesting the content.

I recommend that you adopt a default security configuration that denies all access to the root tree, which forces you to grant access on an as-needed basis. This is accomplished with the following syntax in the `httpd.conf` file:

```
<Directory / >
Deny from all
AllowOverride None
</Directory>
```

The `Deny from all` directive effectively denies all HTTP requests for the directory tree starting at /, which includes all of its associated subdirectories.

The `AllowOverride` directive deserves special discussion. Its general format is as follows:

```
AllowOverride option_1 option_2 … option_n
```

As discussed earlier, when Apache encounters an `.htaccess` file in a content directory, it applies the access control directives found in the file to the current directory. However, when some of these directives are in conflict with those included in the `httpd.conf` file, the `AllowOverride` directive is consulted to determine which option Apache can override.

For example, if your `httpd.conf` specifies the directive

```
AuthType Digest
```

and you would like to have access to certain directories granted using Basic authentication by adding the following to the local `.htaccess` file:

```
AuthType Basic
```

then you need to add the directive

```
AllowOverride AuthType
```

to the `httpd.conf` file in order to allow an `.htaccess` file somewhere in the content tree to use Basic authentication instead of the Digest authentication declared in `httpd.conf`.

Application
Security

PART 3

Table 7.5 lists the options that can be overridden from .htaccess using AllowOverride.

Table 7.5   AllowOverride options

Option	Meaning	Examples
AuthConfig	Override authorization directives	AuthGroupFile, AuthName, AuthType, AuthUserFile, require
FileInfo	Override directives controlling document types	AddEncoding, AddLanguage, AddType, DefaultType, ErrorDocument, LanguagePriority
Indexes	Override directives controlling file indexing	AddDescription, AddIcon, AddIconByEncoding, AddIconByType, DefaultIcon
Limit	Override directives controlling host access	Allow, Deny
Options	Override directives controlling specific directory features	Options, XBitHack

If you would like to allow individual users to alter their default options individually, I recommend that you restrict this ability to the AuthConfig and Limit options using the following directive:

```
UserDir public_html
<Directory /export/homes/*/public_html>
Allow from all
AllowOverride AuthConfig Limit
</Directory>
```

Assuming that you are not concerned about the privacy of the content that your users can make available on their home directories, allowing the override of the AuthConfig and Limit options permits individual users to use authentication and access control to protect content that they consider sensitive.

Note that the first line defines the directory ~*user*/public_html as the place where individual users can place their HTML content, which will be available as the URL www.example.com/~*user*. In this case, you are allowing wide open access to the entire tree, unless the users specify otherwise in their local .htaccess files.

You may need to restrict part of your content tree to those clients whose host names and/or IP addresses meet a certain set of criteria. For instance, to restrict access of the URL www.example.com/intranet/ to hosts in the 10.10.10.0/24 subnet, use the following directives:

```
DocumentRoot "/var/www/html"

<Directory /var/www/html/intranet/>

    Allow from 10.10.10.0/24

</Directory>
```

In the following example, you are restricting access to the same URL to hosts whose reverse DNS lookups (PRT records) are in the example.com domain:

```
DocumentRoot "/var/www/html"

<Directory /var/www/html/intranet/>

    Allow from .example.com

</Directory>
```

In addition to the Allow from directive, Apache also supports a Deny from directive, as well as the ability to control the order in which both of these directives (Deny and Allow) are evaluated. Consider the following example. The Apache server evaluates the Deny from directives before the Allow from directives, and access is allowed by default. The result is that all hosts are allowed except the 10.10.10.0/24 block. The 10.10.10.1 host is allowed, however.

```
<Directory /var/www/html/intranet/>

Order deny,allow

Deny from 10.10.10.0/24

Allow from 10.10.10.1

</Directory>
```

Now consider the next example. In this case, you are evaluating the allow from directives before the deny from directives, and you are adopting a deny all stance. This results in the denial of all client connections except those coming from 10.10.10.0/24. The 10.10.10.1 block will be allowed in the following example:

```
<Directory /var/www/html/intranet/>
```

```
Order allow,deny
Allow from 10.10.10.0/24
Deny from 10.10.10.1
</Directory>
```

Finally, you need to add code to your `httpd.conf` file in order to prevent Web users from viewing the `.htaccess` file on any directory within the content tree, since it contains authorization information. The following directive instructs Apache to look for any filenames starting with the characters `.ht` anywhere within the content tree and denies their access to all users. This directive not only protects the `.htaccess` files, but it also protects any occurrences of the `.htpasswd` file, a common filename that is sometimes used to store password information.

```
<Files ~ "^\.ht">
    Order allow,deny
    Deny from all
</Files>
```

Hardening the Apache Server

As with any other application running on your Linux server, you need to ensure that the server's operation cannot be compromised by an intruder trying to gain unauthorized access to your system. Besides keeping up with the latest security advisories and patches on `www.apache.org` and `www.cert.org`, there are a number of areas where careful planning during the installation process can go a long way toward improving security.

The Apache User   While the Apache daemon must be started by root, it is imperative that the Apache daemon not be run under a username with privileged rights. The `httpd.conf` file supports two directives:

```
user apache-user
group apache-group
```

apache-user and *apache-group* are the user ID and group ID under which the server runs. The Apache user should be added to `/etc/passwd` and given a secure password, and its home directory should be the content tree. All content administration should be made using this user.

Content-Tree Ownership and Permissions   Only *apache-user* and *apache-group* should be able to write to the content tree, and the tree should be owned by this username/group combination. The following command is an example of how to assign this ownership:

```
[ramon]$ sudo chown -Rh apache:apache /var/www/html
```

Hiding Directory Contents   By default, when the browser requests a directory listing in the URL, Apache returns the contents of one of the files listed under the DirectoryIndex directive, for example:

```
DirectoryIndex index.html index.htm index.shtml index.php
index.php4 index.php3 index.cgi
```

However, if one of these files is temporarily unavailable, the user may actually get a listing of all the files on the directory, including script and header files that you may not want the user to be able to list. To prevent this, make sure that all content directories have their read bit turned off for group and other by executing the following commands:

```
[ramon]$ cd /var/www

[ramon]$ ls -ld html

drwxr-xr-x    2 apache      apache         1024 Dec   4 20:44⏎
html

[ramon]$ sudo -u apache chmod go-r html

[ramon]$ ls -ld html

drwx--x--x    2 apache      apache         1024 Dec   4 20:44⏎
html
```

CGI Scripts   Common Gateway Interface (CGI) scripts allow your users to execute code in response to HTTP input and return something meaningful to the remote browser. As with any executable, make sure that your users are writing safe scripts and that the ownership and permissions of these scripts are correct. To accomplish this, Apache allows you to restrict all CGI scripts to a single directory using an httpd.conf directive like the following:

```
ScriptAlias /cgi-bin/ "/var/www/cgi-bin/"
```

This directive ensures that all CGI scripts live on the /var/www/cgi-bin directory, where you can easily track and monitor them. You should examine this directory periodically to ensure that there are no world-writable script files on it.

Server Side Includes   Server side includes (SSIs) are extensions to the static HTML content that allow for conditional execution of external programs, as well as "just-in-time" content modification. SSIs represent a potential security problem, since it is difficult to put bounds on the programs that an HTML file is allowed to execute.

Disable SSIs that execute external programs (this function is known as exec) using the following directive:

```
Options IncludesNOEXEC
```

Once you have installed and configured Apache in a security-responsible manner, monitor the application logs for suspicious activity. The next section of this book describes Apache's logging facility and the contents of its log files.

Application Logs

Apache's standard logging facility offers a comprehensive array of diagnostics and allows system and security administrators to audit both routine events (such as successful HTTP requests), as well as suspicious and potentially malicious events. There are two log files that you check periodically:

access_log   The access_log file contains a line for each successful request made to the HTTP server. Its general format is as follows:

remote_host remote_user time_stamp request_type request_status

For example, the following two entries show a remote user whose client IP address is 209.1.78.12 attempting to access two files that are not available to the Apache server (/etc/shadow and /etc/passwd):

```
209.1.78.12- - [04/Dec/2000:21:03:45 -0500] "GET /etc/passwd↵
HTTP/1.1" 404 139

209.1.78.12- - [04/Dec/2000:21:03:47 -0500] "GET /etc/shadow↵
HTTP/1.1" 404 139
```

Note that a *request_status* of 404 139 refers to a "File not found" condition. A periodic search for this status code could yield important clues on would-be intruders looking around for unsecured content.

error_log   The error_log file records Apache server administration events, including server starts, stops, and failed attempts at executing privileged CGI scripts. It also reports execution errors within the scripts themselves. Its general format is as follows:

time_stamp error_type client_id error_description

For example, consider the following set of error_log entries. This example shows an ungraceful shutdown of the Apache application, followed by an immediate restart. This is one of the log entries that should be monitored with the help of an automated log-scanning package such as logcheck and swatch, as discussed in Chapter 3, "System Monitoring and Logging."

```
[Mon Dec 4 02:20:50 2000] [notice] httpd: caught SIGTERM, ⤶
shutting down

[Mon Dec 4 02:20:57 2000] [notice] Apache/1.3.14 (Unix)⤶
configured -- resuming normal operations

[Mon Dec 4 02:20:00 2000] [warn] pid file⤶
/usr/local/apache/var/run/httpd.pid overwritten - Unclean⤶
shutdown of previous apache run?
```

mod_ssl

Originally developed by Ralf S. Engelschall in early 1998, mod_ssl is the Web interface to the popular OpenSSL implementation by Eric Young and Tim Hudson. This implementation takes advantage of Apache's modular architecture and implements the Secure Sockets Layer extension as an external module in the standard Apache source tree.

The Secure Sockets Layer (SSL) allows for data privacy. Both endpoints of the communication conduct a preliminary handshake and define a secret key to be used for data encryption with a symmetric key algorithm such as DES or RC4. SSL also ensures the integrity of the data being exchanged using a message-digest algorithm such as SHA or MD5. Prior to communicating, SSL endpoints must authenticate each other using public key cryptography, where each end of the connection must present a digital certificate (typically in X.509 format) signed by a certificate authority (CA) that is commonly trusted.

Netscape developed the original SSL specification. Based on its widespread success, the IETF drafted a similar standard called Transport Layer Security (TLS) in RFC2246. TLS 1.0 is based on SSL v.3, and although it provides a way by which TLS peers can back down to SSL v.3, TLS is largely incompatible with SSL. OpenSSL supports both SSL and TLS.

By interposing OpenSSL between the TCP layer and the HTTP application layer, mod_ssl adds strong authentication, data integrity, and privacy to the transfers between the Web client and the Apache HTTP server using both SSL and TLS. Note that mod_ssl can coexist with the non-secure version of Apache. In fact, while plain HTTP uses TCP port 80 for control and data exchanges, all HTTPS (secure HTTP or HTTP over SSL) traffic goes to TCP port 443 on the Linux server.

mod_ssl is protected by the standard BSD license, which makes it freely distributable for both commercial and non-commercial use. At the writing of this book, mod_ssl makes up over 10% of the total Apache installations on the Internet, and that number has grown steadily during the last two years. The mod_ssl project Web page is very informative and up to date. It can be found at www.modssl.org (see Figure 7.2).

Figure 7.2   The mod_ssl Project home page

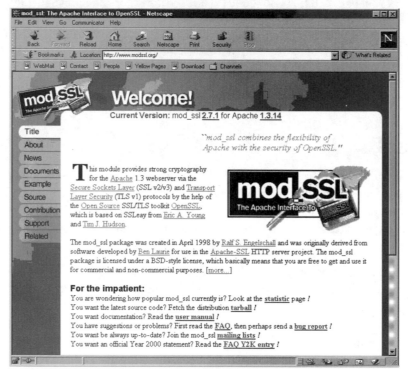

Installing mod_ssl

While most Linux distributions some standard with Apache, very few include mod_ssl by default. The package is readily available in RPM format, however. To install it, start by making sure that Apache and OpenSSL are installed also using this rpm command:

```
[ramon]$ rpm -q apache openssl
apache-1.3.14-3
openssl-0.9.5a-14
```

Then simply execute the following commands to install mod_ssl, if it is not installed already:

```
[ramon]$ rpm -q mod_ssl
package mod_ssl is not installed
[ramon]$ sudo rpm -i mod_ssl-2.7.1-3.i386.rpm
```

You have just added SSL support to your existing Apache installation. For this change to take effect, make sure to restart the Apache daemon:

```
[ramon]$ sudo /etc/rc.d/init.d/httpd restart
```

Your Apache server will now answer requests on both TCP ports 80 (HTTP) and 443 (HTTPS).

The following section describes how to configure mod_ssl.

Configuring mod_ssl

There is a fundamental choice to be made before configuring mod_ssl, which has to do with the way you will use digital certificates and authentication. You need to do one of the following:

- Seek the services of a well-known CA (Verisign, Thawte, Entrust, Xcert, etc.) whose root certificate comes preloaded with many of today's network applications (Web browsers, mail clients, etc.).
- Create your own CA using OpenSSL, create the Apache server's digital certificate, and sign it with the CA's private key (the one you've just created).
- Create a simple self-signed Apache server certificate.

The first approach, seeking the services of a well-known CA, has one important advantage: You don't have to preload your self-signed certificate in all your customer's applications since presumably, your Apache server certificate will be signed by one of these CAs, which will allow you to complete the "trust chain" with no intervention. The disadvantage to the first approach is that there is a cost associated with this, as well as a recurring fee when the certificate expires and needs to be reissued by the CA.

The second approach, creating your own CA using OpenSSL, involves more work but allows you to control the entire trust-verification process, including other applications besides the Apache server (e.g., mail clients, as described in Chapter 6, "Electronic Mail"). Since OpenSSL gives you the tools you need to create and maintain your own CA, this approach is discussed in this section.

The third approach, creating a simple self-signed Apache server certificate, is the most straightforward approach, and it's the easiest to implement, although it requires that the Web browser user verify a key fingerprint manually the first time they connect to the Apache server. This approach will also be described in this section.

Creating a Certificate Authority

Before you can establish an SSL session between your Apache server and your clients, both ends of the connection need to be issued certificates signed by a common CA. While there are a number of commercial CA services available today, you can set up your own CA by using the openssl utility to create the CA's private key, its certificate, and a CA-signed Apache server certificate. Let's start by creating a configuration file for the openssl utility using the following command:

```
[ramon]$ cp /usr/share/ssl/openssl.cnf /etc/httpd/conf/
```

The openssl.cnf file is the main configuration file for OpenSSL, where all the directories and environment variables are defined. The standard openssl.cnf is mostly correct for your purposes. Simply edit it to make sure that the [CA_default] section contains the correct directory paths:

```
[ CA_default ]
dir            = /etc/httpd/conf       # Where everything is kept
certs          = $dir/ssl.crt          # Where the issued certs are
                                         kept
crl_dir        = $dir/ssl.crl          # Where the issued crl are kept
database       = $dir/index.txt        # database index file
new_certs_dir  = $dir/ssl.crt          # default place for new certs
certificate    = $certs/cacert.crt     # The CA certificate
serial         = $dir/serial           # The current serial number
crl            = $dir/crl.crt          # The current CRL
private_key    = $dir/ssl.key/cakey.key# The private key
RANDFILE       = $dir/ssl.key/.rand     # private random number file
```

The [CA_default] section defines the location of all of the important CA files and directories. As you can see, in the previous example, the CA files are in the /etc/httpd/conf directory (the $dir variable).

At this point, you're ready to create the CA's private key in the file

```
/etc/httpd/conf/ssl.key/cakey.crt
```

as well as a new CA certificate in the file

```
/etc/httpd/conf/ssl.crt/cacert.crt
```

by issuing the following commands:

```
[ramon]$ cd /etc/httpd/conf
[ramon]$ sudo echo "01" > serial
[ramon]$ sudo cp /dev/null index.txt
[ramon]$ sudo openssl req -new -x509 -keyout ssl.key/cakey.key -out↵
ssl.crt/cacert.crt
```

Each certificate issued by this CA carries a serial number. By adding the text 01 to the file /etc/httpd/conf/serial, you are seeding the file that the CA will use for assigning serial numbers. The index.txt file is used by the CA to maintain the database of certificates, and it must be created empty. You then issue an openssl command to generate the CA's private key (cakey.key) and its X.509 certificate (cacert.crt).

Then, generate a certificate-signing request for the Apache server's certificate and sign it with the private key of the CA using these steps:

```
[ramon]$ sudo openssl req -nodes -new -x509 -keyout⤶
ssl.key/server.key -out newreq.crt -days 365

 [ramon]$ sudo openssl x509 -x509toreq -in newreq.crt -signkey⤶
newreq.crt -out tmp.crt

[ramon]$ sudo openssl ca -config openssl.cnf -policy policy_anything⤶
-out ssl.crt/server.crt -infiles tmp.crt
```

The first command creates a private key for the Apache server (server.key) as well as a certificate-signing request (newreq.crt). The second and third commands take the certificate-signing request and use the CA's private key to sign the certificate. The resulting Apache certificate file is saved as server.crt.

For these changes to take effect, you need to restart the Apache daemon:

```
[ramon]$ sudo /etc/rc.d/init.d/httpd restart
```

At this point, the Apache/mod_ssl server is ready to present the browser with a digital certificate that is signed by your CA's private key. Since your CA's certificate is not loaded onto commercial Web browsers by default, you have to do this by hand.

As you learned in the previous chapter, Netscape Communicator only accepts certificates in the PKCS#12 format, so in order to use SSL between your clients and your Apache servers, you need to force OpenSSL to export a copy of the root certificate as a .p12 file (the standard PKCS#12 file extension), using the following command:

```
[ramon]$ sudo openssl pkcs12 -export -in ssl.crt/cacert.crt -inkey⤶
ssl.key/cakey.key -name "MY CERTIFICATE" -out cacert.p12
```

This openssl command takes the server's ssl.crt/cacert.crt certificate and the server's ssl.key/cakey.key private key and exports a PKCS#12-formatted certificate (cacert.p12) suitable to import into Netscape clients.

You are then prompted for an *export password* to protect the certificate. Enter the export password twice for verification. Next, you have to distribute the cacert.p12 file to all your users' Web browsers. For example, to load this certificate onto Microsoft's Internet Explorer v.5, take the following steps:

1. Select Tools ➣ Internet Options ➣ Content.

Application Security

PART 3

2. Click the Certificates button.

3. On the Certificates window shown in Figure 7.3, click the Import button.

4. Follow the Wizard's instructions and locate the certificate file (`cacert.p12`).

5. Enter the certificate's passphrase.

6. Finish the import procedure by confirming the addition of the certificate.

Figure 7.3 Certificates dialog box, Trusted Root Certification Authorities

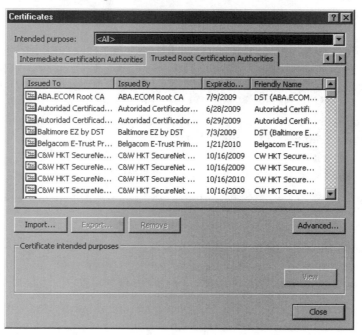

You have successfully loaded your CA's certificate onto your browser, so every certificate signed by your CA should now be accepted because they are digitally signed by your CA. To test this, point your browser to the main page of your Apache/mod_ssl Web server. Assuming that you're using Internet Explorer v.5, right-click anywhere on the page and select Properties. From the Properties window, click the Certificates button. Figure 7.4 shows how the browser reports a certificate issued by `ca.hontanon.com`, to our Apache server, `redhat.hontanon.com`, which is currently trusted.

Figure 7.4 Certificate window, General tab: Certificate Information

Using a Self-Signed Certificate

mod_ssl makes it extremely easy to jump-start the process of creating your own self-signed digital certificate to authenticate the Apache server to a Web browser. There are two files of interest:

- /etc/httpd/conf/ssl.key/server.key: This file is the secret half of the server's private/public pair.

- /etc/httpd/conf/ssl.cert/server.cert: This file is the server's digital self-signed certificate.

The mod_ssl installation comes with two dummy files in place of the files above, so start by deleting these two dummy files:

[ramon]$ **sudo rm /etc/httpd/conf/ssl.key/server.key**

[ramon]$ **sudo rm /etc/httpd/conf/ssl.cert/server.cert**

Next, use the Makefile provided in the /etc/httpd/conf directory to create a new server key and a new server certificate. Listings 7.7 and 7.8 show the steps involved.

Listing 7.7 Creating a new server key

```
[ramon]$ cd /etc/httpd/conf
[ramon]$ sudo make genkey
umask 77 ; \
/usr/bin/openssl genrsa -des3 1024 >⏎
/etc/httpd/conf/ssl.key/⏎
server.key
warning, not much extra random data, consider using the -rand option
Generating RSA private key, 1024 bit long modulus
...........................++++++
..............++++++
e is 65537 (0x10001)
Enter PEM pass phrase:
Verifying password - Enter PEM pass phrase:
```

The make genkey command invokes openssl to generate an RSA public/private key pair. This command prompts you for a passphrase, which will be used to protect the private key as it sits on the disk. This is done by PEM-encoding the key with the passphrase so you should use an actual phrase, with at least a half-dozen words; don't use just a single password.

Next, issue the commands in Listing 7.8 to create an X.509 certificate for your server.

Listing 7.8 Creating a new server certificate

```
[ramon]$ cd /etc/httpd/conf
[ramon]$ sudo make testcert
umask 77 ; \
/usr/bin/openssl req -new -key /etc/httpd/conf/ssl.key/server.key⏎
-x509 -days 365 -out /etc/httpd/conf/ssl.crt/server.crt
Using configuration from /usr/share/ssl/openssl.cnf
Enter PEM pass phrase:
You are about to be asked to enter information that will be⏎
incorporated into your certificate request.
What you are about to enter is what is called a Distinguished Name⏎
or a DN.
There are quite a few fields but you can leave some blank
For some fields there will be a default value,
If you enter '.', the field will be left blank.
-----
Country Name (2 letter code) [AU]:US
State or Province Name (full name) [Some-State]:Virginia
Locality Name (eg, city) []:Ashburn
```

```
Organization Name (eg, company) [Internet Widgits Pty Ltd]:Ramons↵
Pile O Bits
Organizational Unit Name (eg, section) []:
Common Name (eg, your name or your server's hostname) []:redhat.hontanon.com
Email Address []:rhontanon@sybex.com
```

Note that the make `testcert` command also invokes the `openssl` utility to create a new certificate and sign it with the private RSA key you created in Listing 7.7. The –days 365 option specifies that you want to create a certificate that will be valid for a year. You need to supply the passphrase that you supplied when the key was generated so you can decode it and use it to sign the newly created certificate. You also have to supply the following information to go into the X.509 certificate:

- Country name
- State or province name
- Locality name
- Organization name
- Common name
- E-mail address

These are the attributes that will be associated with your server's X.509 certificate and that will be visible from Web browsers when they connect to your site.

You have now successfully created a new server private key, along with a new certificate. Since Apache caches the certificate when it starts up, you need to restart the Apache daemon for the change to take effect, as shown in Listing 7.9.

Listing 7.9   Restarting the Apache server with the new certificate

```
[ramon]$ sudo /etc/rc.d/init.d/httpd restart
Shutting down http: [  OK  ]
Starting httpd: [  OK  ]
```

The first time a Web browser contacts the Apache HTTPS server, the user is prompted with a dialog box, asking them to verify the authenticity of the certificate, since it is self-signed and not signed by any well-known certification authority.

Figure 7.5 shows the dialog box displayed by Netscape Navigator whenever a site sends a digital certificate for the first time. Instruct your users to click the More Info button and verify that the fingerprint shown corresponds with the one from your certificate (Figure 7.6). A certificate's fingerprint is a unique summary of the certificate's contents, in a format that can be easily compared visually to a trusted reference. If your customers are concerned about the validity of the certificate, they can validate the fingerprint with you via out-of-band means (in person or over the phone). This is more convenient than verifying the entire contents of the certificate, and it's just as efficient.

Figure 7.5 A Web browser receiving a new digital certificate

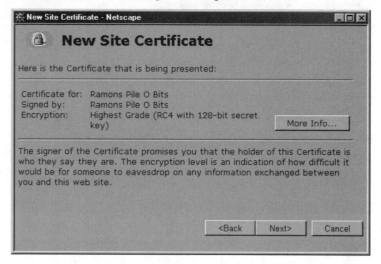

Figure 7.6 After clicking the More Info... button

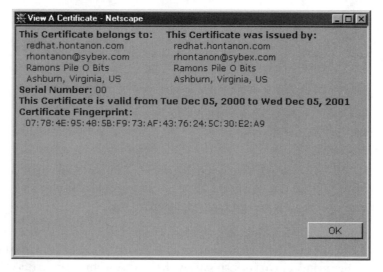

Note that you can obtain the fingerprint from your Apache server using the following commands:

```
[ramon]$ cd /etc/httpd/conf/ssl.crt/
```

```
[ramon]$ sudo openssl x509  -text -fingerprint -in server.crt |⏎
grep MD5
```

MD5 Fingerprint=80:46:26:AD:4D:9A:6D:63:5A:61:64:58:57:0E:8A:DA

The second command in this example invokes the openssl utility to import an X.509 server certificate (-in server.crt) and export a textual fingerprint (-text -fingerprint) corresponding to the input certificate. The result of this command is quite verbose, so I have piped it to a grep command to filter all lines except the one line of interest (the line containing the string MD5, a reference to the cryptographic hash algorithm used to extract the fingerprint from the whole certificate).

Once the user has verified the authenticity of the certificate, they can choose to accept it until it expires by selecting the right option on their Web browser (Figure 7.7).

Figure 7.7   Storing trust in a digital certificate

As you can see, setting up a small, purpose-built public-key infrastructure is not as challenging as you might think. Apache, OpenSSL, and mod_ssl are the only ingredients you need to build a certificate-driven authentication system to scale to thousands of users.

Apache-SSL

Developed by Apache core team member Ben Laurie in the United Kingdom, Apache-SSL was actually the precursor of mod_ssl. While they have followed different development paths over the last two years, both distributions provide equivalent functionality: the addition of SSL/TLS security to the base HTTP protocol.

Application Security

PART 3

One of the important differences between Apache-SSL and mod_ssl is their approach at integrating with the base Apache installation. While Apache-SSL is based on a comprehensive modification of the Apache source code, mod_ssl is a drop-in, or a modular addition, to Apache.

There is no overriding reason why I chose to describe mod_ssl instead of Apache-SSL in this chapter except, perhaps, the fact that a mod_ssl .rpm package is available for Red Hat 7.0, which is my primary home Linux server. Whichever flavor of Apache's SSL extension you choose, the concepts presented in the previous section are just as applicable.

The Apache-SSL Web page can be found at www.apache-ssl.org (see Figure 7.8).

Figure 7.8   The Apache_SSL Project home page

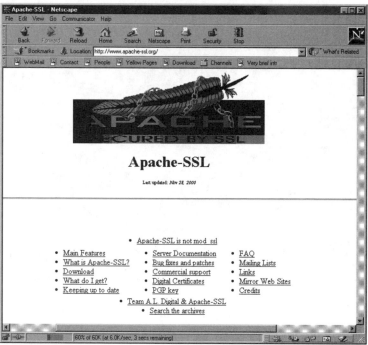

In Sum

Web content hosting is one of the most popular uses of a Linux server in a production environment. The Apache HTTP server is a complex software package, and ensuring its security is not a trivial pursuit. There are, however, a number of directives that can be used in its configuration file to ensure that your server provides the appropriate level of authentication, authorization, and access control.

In addition, mod_ssl is a mature complement to the base Apache installation that adds confidentiality, integrity, and authentication services by using OpenSSL extensions for SSL and TLS. Using OpenSSL to create a simple certification authority, you can build a complete public-key authentication system using freely available components that have been proven in the most mission-critical of environments, including e-commerce, intranet hosting, and large Web portals.

Chapter 8, "File Sharing and Printing," wraps up Part 3 of this book with a discussion on the security implications of sharing filesystems and local and network printers from your Linux server.

Application Security

PART 3

8

Samba Security

This is the third chapter that discusses security at the application layer. This chapter focuses on a well-known network application that makes files on Linux servers available to Windows clients: Samba. As the Linux operating system continues to make inroads in the Microsoft-dominated world of local area file servers, it's important to offer an alternative that can leverage the robustness and security of a Linux server, and at the same time offer file services to the ever-ubiquitous Windows desktop.

The Samba software addresses this need by providing a Linux-based server application capable of sharing files and printers transparently with Windows clients, using the Server Message Block (SMB) and NetBIOS protocols. Along with electronic mail and Web services, Samba is part of the essential suite of applications found in most Linux-based network installations.

Files are the most fundamental view of data stored on any server, and as such, they are the main targets of intruders looking for inside information. You need to ensure the availability and accessibility of these files to your users, while enforcing access controls via authentication and authorization. The good news is that Samba was first released in 1992, a year during which security was already a hot topic of discussion among designers of network applications. As such, Samba offers configuration parameters that allow the network administrator to easily control host and user authentication, access control, and the privacy of the file-sharing communication.

This chapter starts off by looking at the origins of the Samba server. It then goes on to describe a typical Samba installation procedure, including detailed information about the configuration parameters that directly affect the security of your server. Finally, this chapter explains how to add Secure Socket Layer (SSL) support to the standard Samba package, and it closes the discussion by looking at Samba's ability to operate as a primary domain controller (PDC) in a Windows NT environment.

The Samba Server

Samba is a full-featured implementation of a Server Message Block (SMB) server, which can offer transparent file services to Windows (95, 98, NT, 2000) clients, as well as to OS/2 clients. The brain child of LinuxCare's Andrew Tridgell back in 1992, Samba is now widely used and updated with help from programmers from all over the world.

Samba allows network administrators to use a Linux server's ability to store and manage a large number of files, while still preserving the use of Windows-based desktop clients. In addition to file services, Samba offers the following features:

- Print services, by making a Linux-controlled printer available from Windows desktops as a standard network printer
- Authentication and authorization services, where access to network shares is granted only after the appropriate username and password is provided
- Name resolution, by mapping network share (NetBIOS) names into standard IP addresses
- The ability to announce its existence in a "browse" list

Samba's popularity stems from the fact that Linux shares are viewed on a Windows client exactly as other Windows-based drives and printers are viewed, which makes the fact that Linux is being used totally transparent to the end user.

Another selling feature of Samba is its performance. Independent tests have shown that as of version 2, the Samba server is nearly twice as fast as an equivalent Windows NT 4.0 server using the same hardware.

Samba is an implementation of IBM's Network Basic Input Output System (NetBIOS) protocol, which runs over TCP in order to traverse IP routers and to extend the reach of NetBIOS beyond the LAN environment for which it was originally designed. The SMB blocks are transported inside NetBIOS data units, which make up the payload of the TCP packet Figure 8.1 illustrates the composition of a typical SMB packet, starting with the data link layer at the bottom (Ethernet), and going up the stack with the IP, TCP, and NetBIOS layers.

Figure 8.1   Samba's SMB transport over NetBIOS

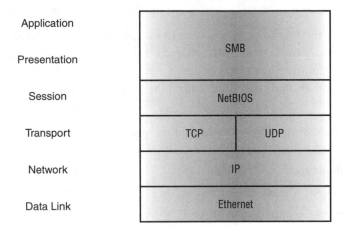

The original Microsoft LAN Manager implementation of file and printer sharing over a local area network did not use NetBIOS or TCP/IP as the underlying protocol. Instead, it used the special-purpose NetBEUI (NetBIOS Extended User Interface) protocol for this purpose (see Figure 8.2). The NetBEUI protocol makes up the network, transport, and session OSI layers. Due to NetBEUI's lack of WAN-routing abilities, the original LAN Manager implementation was not able to share files and printers over the Internet, just over the local network. This essentially eliminated security as a concern, but reduced its usefulness, since you couldn't share resources with remote offices connected via routed IP networks.

Figure 8.2   LAN Manager's SMB transport over NetBEUI

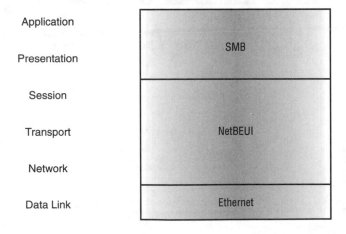

Application Security

PART 3

Samba is offered under Gnu's General Public License (GPL), which allows for the free use and distribution of the package, as long as the full source code is also made available.

This section of the book shows you how to install and configure the Samba server with security in mind. For a complete reference on the installation, configuration, and administration of the Samba server on a Linux server, please refer to *Linux Samba Server Administration,* by Roderick Smith (Sybex, 2000), part of the Craig Hunt Linux Library series.

The Samba home page (Figure 8.3) contains valuable information about the ongoing development of Samba. It includes the following information:

- News about the latest Samba release
- Resources for Samba developers
- Documentation, including the latest books on Samba
- Downloads of Samba source code for various operating system platforms
- Downloads of plug-ins for your Samba server
- Downloads and information about several graphical user interfaces (GUIs) that can simplify the configuration and management of your Samba server
- Information about Samba-related mailing lists

To get to the Samba home page, go to `www.samba.org` and choose the Web mirror site closest to your geographic location.

Figure 8.3   The Samba Project home page

Installing Samba

Most recent Linux distributions include the Samba server right out of the box. Here's how you can make sure Samba is installed on Red Hat 7.0:

```
[ramon]$ rpm -q samba samba-common
samba-2.0.7-21ssl
samba-common-2.0.7-21ssl
```

Two packages make up a complete Samba installation:

samba-2.0.7-21ssl   This is the base Samba server package and it includes the following files:

- Server executable
- Startup scripts
- Manual pages
- Text and HTML documentation
- Samba Web Administration Tool (SWAT)

samba-common-2.0.7-21ssl   This is the set of utilities and configuration files that are common to both the server and the client and that need to be installed to provide the service. This package includes the Samba *codepages*, the smb.conf configuration file, and several utilities to test the configuration before the server goes in production.

> **NOTE**   A Samba codepage definition file is a description that tells Samba how to map from uppercase to lowercase for characters greater than ASCII 127 in the specified DOS codepage.

If you are not running the latest version of these two packages, you can download them from your favorite repository. I recommend that you use a reputable, well-known archive such as www.rpmfind.net to minimize the risk that legitimate packages are replaced by Trojan horses.

Once you have obtained the RPM packages, install them using the following commands:

```
[ramon]$ sudo rpm -U samba-2.0.7-21ssl-i386.rpm
[ramon]$ sudo rpm -U samba-common-2.0.7-21ssl-i386.rpm
```

Application Security

PART 3

Samba Administration with SWAT

The Samba Web Administration Tool (SWAT) was included in the standard Samba server distribution starting with version 2.0. SWAT is a useful utility for managing the smbd and nmbd servers, as well as for managing the /etc/samba/smb.conf configuration file. As with other tools of this kind, SWAT is an HTTP server that listens on a special port (TCP 901, in this case) and can be used with any Web browser by just pointing to the URL http://my.samba.host:901 (see Figure 8.4), where my.samba.host is the name of your Linux server running Samba.

Figure 8.4   The Samba Web Administration Tool

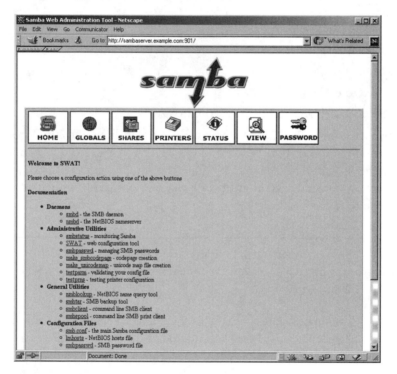

In order to start using SWAT, first make sure there is an entry in the /etc/services file for port TCP 901. You can do this with the following command:

```
[ramon]$ grep swat /etc/services
swat            901/tcp
```

Then simply modify inetd or xinetd so that it starts the listener daemon. If you're running inetd, add the following line to the /etc/inetd.conf file:

```
swat stream tcp nowait root /usr/sbin/tcpd /usr/sbin/swat
```

If you're running `xinetd`, edit the existing `/etc/xinetd.d/swat` file to enable the entry. Listing 8.1 shows a sample `/etc/xinetd.d/swat` file.

Listing 8.1   Sample *etc/xinetd.d/swat* file

```
# default: off
# description: SWAT is the Samba Web Admin Tool. Use swat \
#              to configure your Samba server. To use SWAT, \
#              connect to port 901 with your favorite web browser.
service swat
{
        port    = 901
        socket_type      = stream
        wait    = no
        only_from = 10.0.0.100
        user    = root
        server  = /usr/sbin/swat
        log_on_failure  += USERID
        disable = no
}
```

Note in Listing 8.1 that I have included the directive `only_from` to restrict connections to SWAT to my workstation (10.0.0.100). This is a very important security feature because you typically don't want people connecting to SWAT from just any host on your network, or on the Internet! If you're using `inetd`, make sure that only host 10.0.0.100 is able to connect to port 901 by adding the following line to `/etc/hosts.allow`:

```
swat: 10.0.0.100
```

In addition, add the following line to `/etc/hosts.deny`:

```
swat: ALL
```

> **WARNING**   In order to avoid exposure of the root password, restrict access to the SWAT server to the Linux server itself (ideally), or at least to hosts that are on a protected segment that includes the server. If you must access the SWAT service remotely, follow the SSL instructions described in the following section.

SWAT-SSL

Chapter 7, "HTTP Services," described the use of the Secure Sockets Layer implementation for Linux (OpenSSL) and its ability to protect the communication between Web clients and Apache HTTP servers. Like Apache, SWAT is an HTTP server, and as such, it can be integrated with OpenSSL to ensure the privacy of your Samba administration commands.

Application
Security

PART 3

First, make sure that OpenSSL is installed on your system:

```
[ramon]$ rpm -q openssl
openssl-0.9.5a-14
```

Next, download and install the stunnel package. The stunnel utility is a wrapper used to add SSL encryption to arbitrary network applications. The following command installs the /usr/sbin/stunnel daemon application:

```
[ramon]$ sudo rpm -i stunnel-3.8-4.i386.rpm
```

In order to successfully SSL-wrap SWAT, you need to create a server certificate as follows:

```
[ramon]$ cd /usr/share/ssl/certs
[ramon]$ sudo make stunnel.pem
```

The result is the creation of the necessary certificate in the file /usr/share/ssl/certs/ stunnel.pem. You are now ready to invoke the stunnel wrapper using this command:

```
[ramon]$ sudo stunnel -p /usr/share/ssl/certs/stunnel.pem -l /usr/
sbin/swat swat -d 901
```

Include this command as a startup file in the /etc/rc.d/init.d directory.

In addition, don't forget to disable the xinetd entry for SWAT (simply set disable = yes in /etc/xinetd.d/swat) and restart xinetd in order for the changes to take effect.

You can also start stunnel/SWAT from inetd by adding the following line to /etc/ inetd.conf:

```
swat stream tcp nowait root /usr/sbin/tcpd /usr/sbin/stunnel stunnel
-p /usr/share/ssl/certs/stunnel.pem -l /usr/sbin/swat
```

Or from xinetd, add the following commands to /etc/xinetd.d/swat:

```
# default: off
# description: SWAT is the Samba Web Admin Tool. Use swat \
#              to configure your Samba server. To use SWAT, \
#              connect to port 901 with your favorite web browser.
service swat
{
    port    = 901
    socket_type    = stream
    wait    = no
    only_from = 10.0.0.100
    user    = root
```

```
    server  = /usr/sbin/stunnel
    server_args = -p /usr/share/ssl/certs/stunnel.pem -l /usr/sbin/
swat
    log_on_failure  += USERID
    disable = no
}
```

You can now access the SWAT application via SSL using the URL https://
my.samba.host:901 from your favorite Web browser.

Note that you are prompted to accept the certificate since it is self-signed, and its trust
cannot be verified with any of the root certificates installed in your browser.

Securing Samba

This section discusses the security issues associated with running a production Samba
server, including user authentication, access control, and data privacy. Let's start by looking at Samba's options for user authentication using usernames and passwords.

User Authentication

Most remote SMB requests include some level of authentication credentials, including a
username and, optionally, a password. By default, Samba uses the existing Linux /etc/
passwd file to look up the username furnished with SMB requests. The client sends the
cleartext password, and Samba compares it to the hashed password found in /etc/
passwd. This procedure used to work just fine for older versions of Windows, but starting
with Windows 95 OSR2 (and including Windows 98, NT 4.0-SP3+, and 2000),
Microsoft clients only supply an encrypted password when authenticating to a remote
SMB server. Windows 9x uses an older style of encryption of LAN Manager legacy, while
Windows NT 4.0 and Windows 2000 use a newer, more robust encryption algorithm.

The framework for SMB password encryption is quite robust. Neither the client nor the
server keeps the passwords in the clear, and the client doesn't even send the encrypted
password when authenticating to the server. Instead, the server issues a challenge to the
client, which the client uses to hash the encrypted password. This hash is sent to the
server, which performs the same operation and compares the results.

Forcing the client to supply encrypted passwords is a very good idea, although it requires
a bit of work on the Samba server side. First, you must instruct Samba to accept encrypted
passwords by including the following directive in the smb.conf file:

```
[global]
    encrypt passwords = yes
```

NOTE The smb.conf file is where Samba stores all its runtime configuration information. This file is divided into *sections* (also called *stanzas*) that are delimited by a word inside square brackets (e.g., [*header*]). While most of these stanzas refer to a specific resource to be shared such as directories, files, and printers, the [global] header starts the stanza where you can place parameters that will be applied to all shares. Most security parameters will be placed in this stanza unless you need to define exceptions for a particular share.

Next, since Samba cannot verify an encrypted client password against the regular Linux /etc/passwd file, you need to create a parallel but separate Samba password file, which can be maintained using the Samba-supplied smbpasswd utility. By default, the Samba passwords are kept in the /etc/samba/smbpasswd file.

TIP Even though the passwords in smbpasswd are encrypted, make sure that file is not accessible (for either read or write) by anybody other than the root user.

To add a new user to the file, issue the following command:

```
[ramon]$ sudo smbpasswd -a stacia
New SMB password:
Retype new SMB password:
Added user stacia.
```

Or you can change your own password using the following command:

```
[ramon]$ smbpasswd
Old SMB password:
New SMB password:
Retype new SMB password:
Password changed for user ramon.
```

Note that both username stacia and ramon must already be present in the standard Linux /etc/passwd file. However, the password supplied to smbpasswd does not have to be the same one already present in /etc/passwd.

TIP Although there is a well-known procedure to force newer Windows clients to send cleartext passwords (by modifying the registry), I strongly discourage this. Passwords should always be encrypted to avoid trivial eavesdropping attacks over public networks.

Entries in the smbpasswd file follow this general format:

User:*UID*:*LAN-Manager-password*:*NT-password*:*account-flags*:*update-time*

Each of these fields has the following meaning:

User   *User* is the textual username supplied by the client. This field must match a username in the local /etc/passwd file.

UID   *UID* is the numeric user ID. This field must also match an /etc/passwd entry.

LAN-Manager-password   *LAN-Manager-password* is the encrypted representation of the old-style (Windows 9*x*) password. The actual entry is computed by DES-encrypting a well-known character sequence using the repeated password (in all capitals) as the key.

NT-password   *NT-password* is the encrypted representation of the new-style (Windows NT and 2000) password. This field results from the MD4 hashing of the password in Unicode format.

account-flags   The *account-flags* field is a combination of the following four types of flags:

- U: This flag indicates a standard user account.
- D: This flag indicates a disabled account (no logins allowed).
- N: This flag indicates an account with no password.
- W: This flag indicates a workstation account, which is used to configure Samba as an NT PDC.

update-time   The *update-time* field is the seconds since the epoch (1 January 1970) when the entry was last updated.

Access Control

Whenever the Samba server receives an SMB request from a client, the server tells the client which authentication setting it should conform to. Samba supports four fundamental modes of authentication, reflected as the four options to the following smb.conf directive:

    security = [share|user|server|domain]

Let's take a closer look at each of these four access-control choices.

***share* mode**   By setting up one or more passwords for general access to a file, directory, or printer, you can allow all your users access by providing the same password(s). This is generally not recommended, except for allowing access to guest shares, as well as giving general access to print servers.

Even though SMB clients are not required to provide a username for share mode resources, Samba still needs to operate within the Linux paradigm, which requires user ownership for all its resources. So Samba tries to come up with a good default username to use on the client's behalf. Here are the options that Samba uses as username defaults (in decreasing order of precedence):

- If smb.conf includes the configuration lines guest only = yes and guest account = guest, then the username guest is always chosen.

- If the client includes a user with the request anyway, the username supplied is chosen.

- If the client has previously connected to the Samba server, the username that was supplied at that time is chosen.

- If none of the above, then the name of the requested service is chosen.

- If the name of the requested service is not available, the NetBIOS name of the requesting client is chosen.

- As a last resort, the user descriptions present in the smb.conf file under the username= user1, user2,… directive are chosen.

It's important to note that if smb.conf includes the configuration lines guest only = yes and guest account = guest, then the username guest is always chosen. However, if guest only = no, and the password supplied by the client does not match one of the users included in the username= directive, access to the share is denied.

While all this seems overly elaborate, the point is simple: Samba must find a Linux username that can be authenticated with the password supplied by the requesting client. The easiest way to ensure this is to assign the same usernames for Windows clients and for interactive logins to the Linux server (/etc/passwd or /etc/shadow). This makes your users and shares easier to manage across both platforms.

For example, consider the following smb.conf configuration. The [Sales] stanza defines a resource to be shared, in this case, the /homes/marketing directory. This resource is writable and can be browsed using the standard Microsoft Network Neighborhood browsing facility. Note that the directive security = share is included in the [global] stanza, but you have qualified it with the guest only = no and username = ramon, stacia directives in the [Sales] stanza. This combination of directives allows share mode access to the Sales share, but only if the password supplied by the client matches the password for either ramon or stacia, or it matches the password for a user that has previously connected to the Samba server.

```
[global]
    security = share
[Sales]
    Comment = Sales Share
```

```
Path = /homes/marketing
writable = yes
browseable = no
guest only = no
username = ramon, stacia
```

***user* mode**   user mode goes a step beyond share mode by forcing each user to provide a unique username and password combination before granting access to a share. This is clearly recommended over share mode because it allows the administrator to grant or deny access to a share on a per-user basis, and eliminates the complex login used by share mode to assign a default user. user mode is the default authentication mode as of Samba 2.0.

NOTE If the guest only = yes directive is present in smb.conf, the Linux username will be changed to the one specified by the guest account = directive, but only after the supplied password has been verified to belong to the supplied username.

For example, consider the following smb.conf configuration. The security = user directive is included in the [global] stanza, but it is qualified with the valid users = ramon, stacia directive in the [Marketing] stanza (where the sharing of the /homes/marketing directory is defined). This combination of directives allows only users ramon and stacia access to the Marketing share, only after they have supplied a valid username and password combination.

```
[global]
    security = user
[Marketing]
    Comment = Marketing Share
    Path = /homes/marketing
    writable = yes
    browseable = no
    valid users = ramon, stacia
```

***server* mode**   When the server mode type of access control is specified, the supplied username and password combination is not checked locally, but instead, is sent to a remote SMB server for verification. The remote server then returns the outcome of the authentication request to the local server. If the remote server cannot authenticate the client, then the local server reverts to user mode access control. The remote server can be

Application Security

PART 3

a Windows NT machine or another Samba server configured to run in user mode. The name of the remote server must be specified with the password server = directive in the smb.conf file.

The server mode of authentication is useful when you're operating several Samba servers but only want to have a single authentication point for the majority of your user population. You still have to have the users present in the local /etc/passwd file, but their accounts can (and should) be disabled.

As an example, consider the following smb.conf configuration. This server consults with SMB server LINUX_SAMBA_1 for username/password authentication. If LINUX_SAMBA_1 is unavailable, it next consults with SMB server LINUX_SAMBA_2. Note however, that if LINUX_SAMBA_1 returns an authentication denial, the client is denied access before even consulting the next server on the list.

```
[global]
    security = server
    password server = LINUX_SAMBA_1 LINUX_SAMBA_2
```

***domain* mode**   domain mode is a special case of server mode, where the remote SMB server is an NT domain controller with which the local Samba server has previously established a trust relationship using the command

```
smbpasswd -j NT-Domain -r NT-Domain-Controller
```

In this command, *NT-Domain* is the name of the domain you wish to be part of and *NT-Domain-Controller* is the NetBIOS name of the primary domain controller (PDC) for the given domain. By establishing a trust relationship between the local Samba server and the remote Windows NT domain controller, you are allowing the local Samba server to validate the username/password supplied by a requesting client by passing it to a the Windows NT domain controller. This is the same way a Windows NT server that is a member of a given domain passes user authentication requests on to a domain controller for approval. This is a useful access control option for integrating a few Samba servers into an existing NT domain network.

To use domain mode access control, simply include the appropriate directive in the smb.conf file. In the following example, the NT domain controllers ENG_SAMBA_1 and ENG_SAMBA_2 are used (in that order) to authenticate clients' requests:

```
[global]
    security = domain
    workgroup = ENGINEERING
    domain logins = yes
    password server = ENG_SAMBA_1 ENG_SAMBA_2
```

> **NOTE** If your remote SMB server is a Windows NT server, domain mode access control is always preferable to server mode because server mode consumes a license on the Windows NT server for the duration of the client-server connection. domain mode authentication, on the other hand, releases the connection (and the Windows NT license instance) as soon as the authentication is performed. This is important because Microsoft's licensing strategy revolves around concurrent server connections.

Other Access Control Features In addition to these four access control methods, you may choose to take advantage of a trust relationship between your local NT domain and a second, trusted NT domain. As of Samba 2.0.4, the smb.conf directive allow trusted domain = yes can be used to gain authentication from an NT domain controller that, although it is not primary to your domain, is trusted by your PDC.

Another recent addition to the access control feature set of Samba is the add user script = *script* directive. This can be used in both user and domain access control modes to automatically add a user in the event that the user/password is authenticated by the password server but the user is not present locally. For example, you may want Samba to automatically add a user locally using the following smb.conf directive:

```
add user script = sudo /usr/sbin/useradd %u
```

Conversely, a delete user script = *script* directive can be specified to delete a user that exists locally but is no longer valid on the PDC. An example of this usage is as follows:

```
delete user script = sudo /usr/sbin/userdel %u
```

While adding and deleting local users in this fashion may be convenient, I urge you to implement it carefully because you are allowing the unattended creation and deletion of users in the same /etc/passwd or /etc/shadow files that you use for regular Linux server authentication.

The *[homes]* Directive A common approach to allowing all Linux server users access to their home directories is the special [homes] directive in the smb.conf file. Consider the following example:

```
[homes]
    comment = Home Directories
    browseable = no
    writable = yes
```

This directive specifies that any user in /etc/passwd can gain access to their home directory by pointing their SMB client to \\server\username. This is not always desirable because this file includes system-related accounts such as root, operator, uucp, and bin. To ensure that these users are not granted access, use the `invalid users =` directive to exclude these usernames, as in the following example:

```
[global]
invalid users = root, operator, uucp, bin
```

Privacy of Samba Communications

Samba uses the TCP/IP layer to carry NetBIOS traffic from client to server. This allows you to share drives over the Internet, a convenient but often insecure practice because the contents of your files are exposed to potential eavesdroppers. If you are going to be exchanging SMB traffic over a public (untrusted) network like the Internet, your security policy needs to include a provision to ensure the privacy and authentication of this type of traffic.

There is a way to secure the contents of the SMB traffic by using the ever-popular OpenSSL implementation you used to tunnel SWAT traffic that was described in the previous section. Since Windows SMB clients don't support SSL directly, you have to set up a proxying SSL station at the edge of your local (trusted) network, which encrypts traffic and forwards it to the destination SSL-enabled Samba server on the client's behalf. This process is illustrated in Figure 8.5.

Figure 8.5   Using SSL protection with Samba

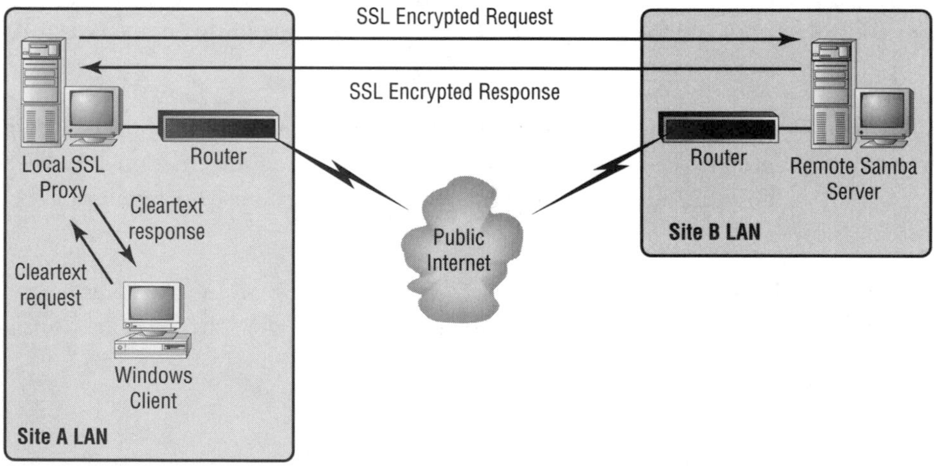

The figure shows two corporate sites (Site A and Site B) connected to the Internet by an access router. Behind Site A's access router, a Linux server has been set up as an SSL proxy. A typical Windows SMB client in Site A's LAN directs its SMB request to the local

SSL proxy, which then relays the connection to Site B's Samba server inside an OpenSSL tunnel. While Site B's server also replies with an encrypted response, Site A's SSL proxy relays it in the clear back to the Windows client. This ensures that the SMB traffic is protected, at least while traveling over the public Internet. Be aware, however, that the SMB traffic travels in the clear within Site A's local network.

Creating a Certificate Authority for Samba-SSL   The first step in setting up any SSL application is to create a certificate authority (CA) to issue the necessary digital certificates for the mutual authentication of the two endpoints. Start by making sure that OpenSSL is installed on your system:

```
[ramon]$ rpm -q openssl
openssl-0.9.5a-14
```

Then you need to create a new directory for the CA using the following commands. Start by creating the directory that will hold Samba's CA:

```
[ramon]$ sudo mkdir /etc/samba/CA
[ramon]$ cd /etc/samba/CA
```

Each certificate issued by this CA will carry a serial number. By adding the text "01" to the file /etc/samba/CA/serial, you are seeding the file that the CA will use for assigning serial numbers:

```
[ramon]$ sudo echo "01" > serial
```

The index.txt file is used by the CA to maintain the database of certificates and must simply be created empty:

```
[ramon]$ sudo cp /dev/null index.txt
```

Next, you need to create an appropriate OpenSSL configuration file that will suit your needs. Start by copying the original /usr/share/ssl/openssl.cnf file to the /etc/samba /CA directory:

```
[ramon]$ sudo cp /usr/share/ssl/openssl.cnf openssl.cnf
```

Now edit the newly created openssl.cnf file to include these new settings:

```
dir           = /etc/samba/CA      # Where everything is kept
new_certs_dir = $dir               # default place for new certs.
certificate   = $dir/ca-cert.pem   # The CA certificate
private_key   = $dir/ca-key.pem    # The private key
```

Note that you're simply changing the default base CA directory to be the one you created for Samba previously (/etc/samba/CA). You're also defining the CA's certificate and key to reside in /etc/samba/CA/ca-cert.pem and /etc/samba/CA/ca-key.pem, respectively.

Next, issue an `openssl` command to generate the CA's private key (`ca-key.pem`) and its X.509 certificate (`ca-cert.pem`):

```
[ramon]$ sudo openssl req -new -x509 -keyout ca-key.pem -out↵
ca-cert.pem -days 365 -config openssl.cnf
```

Now you're ready to create a new certificate for the Samba server itself and sign it with the CA's secret key. Enter the following commands:

```
[ramon]$ sudo openssl req -nodes -new -x509 -keyout server-key.pem↵
-out newreq.pem -days 365 -config openssl.cnf

[ramon]$ sudo openssl x509 -x509toreq -in newreq.pem -signkey↵
server-key.pem -out tmp.pem

[ramon]$ sudo openssl ca -config openssl.cnf -policy policy_anything↵
-out server-cert.pem -infiles tmp.pem
```

The first command creates a private key for the Samba server (`server-key.pem`) and a certificate-signing request (`newreq.pem`). The second and third commands take the certificate-signing request and use the CA's private key to sign the certificate. The resulting Samba certificate file is saved as the file `server-cert.pem`.

You also need to create a certificate for the client (the SSL proxy) because both the client and the server will need to authenticate each other. Create this certificate using the following commands:

```
[ramon]$ sudo openssl req -nodes -new -x509 -keyout proxy-key.pem↵
-out newreq.pem -days 365 -config openssl.cnf

[ramon]$ sudo openssl x509 -x509toreq -in newreq.pem -signkey↵
proxy-key.pem -out tmp.pem

[ramon]$ sudo openssl ca -config openssl.cnf -policy policy_anything↵
-out proxy-cert.pem -infiles tmp.pem
```

You now have client and server certificates called `proxy-cert.pem` and `server-cert.pem` respectively, as well as corresponding private key files `proxy-key.pem` and `server-key.pem`. Note that you need to copy the `proxy-cert.pem` and `proxy-key.pem` files to the proxy machine. You'll learn more about the placement of these files in the section "Downloading and Installing SSL Proxy" later in this chapter.

Congratulations! You have now completed the OpenSSL configuration necessary to tunnel SMB requests over SSL. Next, you need to inform Samba of the existence of this configuration, by entering the appropriate directives in the `/etc/samba/smb.conf` file. This is the topic of the next section.

Configuring Samba for SSL support   Table 8.1 lists the syntax of the directives necessary to make Samba SSL-aware, along with their meaning.

Table 8.1   Samba-SSL Configuration Directives

Directive	Meaning
`ssl = [yes|no]`	Add SSL support.
`ssl hosts = host1 host2 ..`	Hosts that must always use SSL to connect to this server
`ssl hosts resign = host1 host2 ..`	Hosts that do not use SSL to connect to this server
`ssl CA certDir`	Directory location of the certificates
`ssl CA certFile`	File containing all certificates
`ssl server cert`	Location of the server's certificate
`ssl server key`	Location of the server's private key
`ssl cyphers`	Cypher suite used during protocol negotiation

Using the directories in which the CA key and certificates were created in the previous section, the following `smb.conf` syntax configures SSL support into your Samba server:

```
[global]
ssl = yes
ssl hosts = 209.1.78.
ssl hosts resign = 209.1.78.1
ssl CA certFile = /etc/samba/CA/ca-cert.pem
ssl server cert = /etc/samba/CA/server-cert.pem
ssl server key  = /etc/samba/CA/server-key.pem
```

In this example, you're forcing all SSL proxies on the 209.1.78.0/24 network to use SSL, except for 209.1.78.1. Note that while `ssl CA certDir` allows you to have a number of CA certificates in the specified directory, `ssl CA certFile` is used when all your CA certificates are in the same physical file. This suits you better because you only have one CA certificate (your own). The same applies to `ssl server cert` and `ssl server key`.

Application Security

PART 3

Downloading and Installing SSL Proxy   Object Development's SSL Proxy package, the Web page for which is shown in Figure 8.6, can be installed on a Linux server on your network that will proxy SMB requests to all your remote Samba servers. You can download the SSL Proxy package from `http://www.obdev.at/Products/sslproxy.html`.

Figure 8.6   Object Development's SSL Proxy Web page

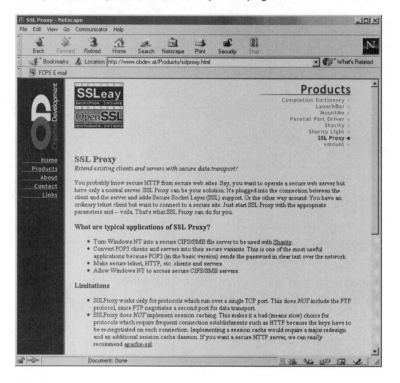

Simply scroll down to the bottom of the page and click the name of the source package. Once you have transferred the file to your home directory, enter the following commands:

```
[ramon]$ ls sslproxy.2000_Jan_29.tar
sslproxy.2000_Jan_29.tar
[ramon]$ gunzip sslproxy.2000_Jan_29.tar.gz
[ramon]$ tar xvf sslproxy.2000_Jan_29.tar
sslproxy.2000_Jan_29/
sslproxy.2000_Jan_29/Makefile
sslproxy.2000_Jan_29/README.txt
sslproxy.2000_Jan_29/dummyCert.pem
```

```
sslproxy.2000_Jan_29/sslproxy.c
```

```
sslproxy.2000_Jan_29/stdheaders.h
```

Since SSL Proxy comes in source format, you have to compile it using the included Makefile. Before you do that, however, make sure you have the openssl-devel RPM package, which is required by SSL Proxy. This package contains the OpenSSL header files and a library to compile applications against. Most distributions do not include openssl-devel in their standard installations, but you should be able to get the latest version from your favorite RPM archive. Once you have the RPM package, install it on your server using the following command:

```
[ramon]$ sudo rpm -i openssl-devel-0.9.5a-14.i386.rpm
```

Now you're ready to build your SSL Proxy executable. Enter the following commands:

```
[ramon]$ cd sslproxy.2000_Jan_29
[ramon]$ make
gcc -Wall -I/usr/local/openssl/include -O -c sslproxy.c -o sslproxy.o
gcc -Wall -I/usr/local/openssl/include -O -o sslproxy sslproxy.o \
    -L/usr/local/openssl/lib -lssl -lcrypto
[ramon]$ sudo mv sslproxy /usr/sbin/
[ramon]$ sudo chown root:root /usr/sbin/sslproxy
[ramon]$ ls -l /usr/sbin/sslproxy
-rwxr-xr-x   1 root    root    28016 Dec 19 21:35 /usr/sbin/sslproxy
```

You have now created the executable /usr/sbin/sslproxy to accept SMB requests from your private network's Windows clients and to forward them over an SSL tunnel to a remote SMB server across the public network. The sslproxy executable takes the command-line options listed in Table 8.2.

Table 8.2   sslproxy Command-Line Options

Option	Meaning
-h	Display help information.
-L local-address	Address where proxy should bind (0.0.0.0 is default)
-l port	Port where proxy should bind

Application Security

PART 3

Table 8.2   `sslproxy` Command-Line Options *(continued)*

Option	Meaning
`-R address`	Remote IP address to connect to
`-r port`	Remote port number to connect to
`-s`	Run as server proxy
`-n`	Support NetBIOS
`-p protocol`	Protocol to use: ssl23, ssl1, ssl3, or tls1 (ssl23 is default)
`-c certificate`	Use the following certificate
`-k keyfile`	Use the following private key
`-v file`	Location of the CA certificate

To start the SSL Proxy service, enter the following command:

```
[ramon]$ sudo sslproxy -l 139 -R tippecanoe -r 139 -s -n -c /etc↵
proxy-cert.pem -k /etc/proxy-key.pem
```

This command listens for SMB requests on port 139 and forwards them to the host name `tippecanoe` (the remote SMB server) over an SSL tunnel. Note that the files /etc /proxy-cert.pem and /etc/proxy-key.pem are the ones that you created in the previous section. Simply copy them into the /etc directory of the proxy.

Thus far, this chapter has discussed the ins and outs of authenticating SMB clients, applying access control to SMB requests, and has even shown how you can protect the SMB traffic as it traverses a public network. To finish up the topic of Samba security, let's examine one of Samba's most recent features: its ability to act as a primary domain controller of a Windows NT domain.

Using Samba as a Windows NT Primary Domain Controller

The previous section on user authentication and access control discussed the feature that allows Samba to pass a set of client credentials to a domain controller for authentication. In the Windows NT authentication model, a user can log on to any NT workstation using "domain" authentication, where the local workstation relies on a set of domain controllers to hold the authentication, access control, and policy for the entire domain. The NT host designated to be the main authenticator is called the *primary domain controller (PDC),* while its subordinates are called *backup domain controllers (BDCs).*

Samba cannot only act as a client to an existing NT PDC; it can actually be configured to act as the PDC and handle authorization and access control requests from Windows NT hosts and other Samba servers in the network. While the current version as of the writing of this book (2.0.7) offers experimental PDC support, version 2.1 (which may be out by the time you read this book) is scheduled to incorporate this as a standard feature.

> **NOTE** Samba 2.0.7 does not support Windows 2000 logins. Only Windows NT 3.51 SP5+ and 4.0 SP4+ machines can authenticate to Samba's PDC.

Samba PDC support includes adding new Windows NT client machines to the domain and providing domain authentication for users on those machines. These accounts can be viewed on the Windows NT host using the Server Manager and User Manager utilities, respectively. Samba allows for remote updates of both machine and user passwords. Absent from the list of supported features is the ability to establish a trust relationship between the Samba PDC and another domain controller, as well as the ability to act as a BDC.

The next section explains in detail how to configure a standard Samba installation to act as a PDC.

Setting Up the Samba PDC

First, make sure to modify the [global] stanza of your smb.conf file so that you are using password encryption. You also want to enable domain logons using the Samba PDC. These two capabilities are enabled in the following example:

```
[global]
    encrypt passwords = yes
    workgroup = ACCOUNTING
    domain logons = yes
```

Next, create machine accounts on the Samba server so that it knows how to interact with the Windows NT client hosts. Create an /etc/password entry using the NetBIOS name of the NT client, with a $ at the end. For example, the following entry is a machine account for an NT client named acct_server1:

```
acct_server1$:*:305:100:Accounting NT Server 1:/dev/null:/bin/false
```

Next, you need to add an entry to the separate Samba password file (typically named /etc/samba/smbpasswd), using the following command:

```
[ramon]$ sudo smbpasswd -a -m acct_server1
Added user acct_server1$.
```

On the NT host's acct_server1, run the User Manager for Domains and allow all users to log on locally. Also, run the Network Settings Control Panel utility and change your domain to ACCOUNTING (or whatever you set up in your smb.conf file). The NT host will welcome you to the new domain and ask you to reboot your PC.

When the NT machine comes back to life, press Ctrl+Alt+Del and watch the login dialog pop up. You should have two entries under Domain: the NetBIOS name of the NT host and the Samba Domain that you just created (ACCOUNTING). Enter a username and password combination that exists in the /etc/samba/smbpasswd file. If everything worked right the first time, you should be given access to the desktop after the authentication succeeds. If login is not successful, make sure that

- The username/password combination exists in the Samba server's standard Linux /etc/passwd file (and /etc/shadow if you have shadow password support enabled).
- You have successfully created an entry in /etc/samba/smbpasswd for the NT host that is requesting authentication on behalf of the user.

NOTE As you populate /etc/passwd with domain users with no need to log on to the Linux server, be sure to disable their accounts by inserting an asterisk (*) in their password field and use /bin/false as their shell.

Samba's PDC feature even allows you to assign domain administrator users, who can be given full privileges when they log on to the local NT system and authenticate using the Samba domain. Simply add the following line to the [global] stanza of smb.conf:

```
domain Admin Group = @admins
```

Then create a group called admins in the Linux /etc/group file that contains the list of users to whom you want to grant administrator privileges. In addition, Samba's PDC feature supports the use of NT logon scripts, which are small pieces of MS-DOS batch-style executable scripts that run every time a user logs on to the local NT host. By adding the following line to the [global] stanza of smb.conf

```
logon script = scripts\%U.bat
```

and a [netlogin] stanza as follows

```
[netlogin]
```

```
comment = Domain login service
path = /home/samba/login
public = no
writeable = no
browsable = no
```

you're specifying that there is a file in the scripts directory (relative to the directory specified in the [netlogin] stanza), named after the username in question (%U variable substitution) with the .bat extension. For example, the following example shows that the /home/samba/login/scripts directory contains three logon scripts for usernames alice, bob, and charlie:

```
[ramon]$ ls -l /home/samba/login/scripts
total 3
-rw-r--r--    1 root      root          152 Dec 20 23:14 alice.bat
-rw-r--r--    1 root      root          130 Dec 20 23:14 bob.bat
-rw-r--r--    1 root      root          122 Dec 20 23:14 charlie.bat
```

Even though you're making a general statement about the availability of these scripts for all users, no error is generated if a script does not exist for any particular user.

NT user profiles containing parameters like custom wallpaper, desktop arrangements, and shortcuts are stored in the user's Linux home directory every time they log off the domain, ready to be restored next time they log back in.

WARNING It's important to make sure that logon scripts are owned by root and not writeable by anybody other than root. A world-writeable script can be exploited by an attacker to execute random commands on all your Windows users' desktops. This could have catastrophic consequences.

This concludes our discussion of the security features of the Samba file-sharing server. While the package offers a stunning array of configurations and available features, the centralized smb.conf file makes it easy to administer the security features. Samba affords companies that have invested in Linux training the opportunity to address their Windows file-sharing needs without introducing a new flavor of server operating system into their data center. As with any other complex server package, special care must be taken when configuring the service, and the system administrator should stay abreast of any newly discovered vulnerability that may put the security of the system in jeopardy.

In Sum

Samba provides a number of configuration parameters that allow you to run a tight installation, but, as always, the devil is in the details. You should start by protecting the SWAT management tool with SSL in order to avoid unnecessary exposure of your configuration to eavesdropping attack.

Next, you need to decide what type of authentication you are going to use, based on the nature of shares that you'll be offering and the identity of your user population. If you need to make shares available to guest users, share mode authentication is the only feasible alternative. If your user population is known and trusted and you know their user names a priori, user mode authentication is a better option.

Access control can play a fundamental role in the security of your Samba server. Make use of the valid users directive to restrict shares to only those users who should be granted access to specific files within your Linux server. If you are integrating a Samba server into an existing Windows NT domain, you may want to consider server or domain mode authentication to leverage the user databases that already exist on your domain controller. Alternatively, Samba itself can be configured to be your primary domain controller.

Finally, if your users will be accessing remote Samba servers, you should be concerned about the privacy of your SMB traffic because it traverses the Internet backbone. OpenSSL can be used in conjunction with the SSL Proxy package to protect Samba communications using the Secure Sockets Layer.

This chapter wraps up the discussion of security for applications. The next chapter, "Network Layer Firewalls," kicks off Part 4 of this book, "Perimeter Security," dedicated to firewalls and other perimeter defense applications.

Part 4

Perimeter Security

Featuring:

- Understanding Perimeter Defense Concepts
- Choosing a Firewall Type
- Building a Network Layer Firewall with `ipchains` and `iptables`
- Using a Linux-Based Transport Layer Firewall
- Installing and Configuring the NEC SOCKS5 Proxy Server
- Understanding Application Layer Firewalls
- Protecting Your Perimeter with the TIS Firewall Toolkit

9

Network Layer
Firewalls

Part 4 of this book, "Perimeter Security," is devoted to the discussion of *firewalls,* software whose primary function is to enforce perimeter security rules by filtering, forwarding, redirecting, or logging connection requests that traverse a Linux server connected to both your private network and the public Internet.

Firewalls: An Overview

Firewalls can be implemented in a variety of ways, starting with three of the OSI layers: network, transport and application. Let's examine the advantages and disadvantages of deploying firewalls at each of these three layers:

> **Network Layer Firewalls**   Also referred to as *packet-filtering gateways,* these devices examine every IP packet that comes in any of the firewall's interfaces and they take appropriate action based on either its source or destination IP address, its TCP/UDP port number, or its IP payload type. The typical actions available are:
>
> - Drop (do not forward)
> - Allow (forward to next hop according to the server's routing table)
> - Log (note the fact that the packet was seen before dropping or allowing)

Packet-filtering firewalls are conceptually easy to understand and relatively easy to deploy, but they lack the ability to look deeper into the incoming packet to make a smarter decision based on the type of application that the packet contains. For example, you cannot deploy a network layer firewall to screen traffic based on user IDs of the incoming user or based on the Web URL that an internal user is trying to access.

Transport Layer Firewalls   By examining (and understanding) an actual TCP or UDP conversation, transport layer firewalls can make a more educated access decision and allow the security/network administrator to use user authentication as a criterion for granting or denying access. While it is virtually impossible to associate a user with a network layer conversation, transport layer firewalls can match up a username with a transport session, which not only allows you to know who is using what service but also allows you to log each transport request that traverses the firewall.

However, this advantage comes at a price: Transport layer firewalls often require users to modify their procedures or their client software in order to make them aware of the authentication needs of the firewall.

Application Layer Firewalls   Making access decisions at the application layer allows you to tailor your firewall to the needs of each server application that you would like to offer. An application layer firewall inserts itself into the conversation between a client and a server and must be able to fully understand the protocol at hand. This concept is called *proxying*. For example, a Web proxy must be able to handle HTTP requests as if it were the actual target server. This allows you to examine the actual URL requested by the Web client and to grant or deny access accordingly.

The disadvantage of application layer firewalls is that you need to configure, deploy, monitor, and maintain a firewall process for each application whose access you wish to control, instead of using a single firewall technology for all your connections (e.g., a packet-filtering firewall).

As with any other security mechanism, it is best to implement your security policy using a combination of firewalls at all three layers to avoid being exposed to a vulnerability that's particular to any one of these layers.

This chapter discusses the current state of the art in network layer firewalls. Chapter 10, "Transport Layer Firewalls," and Chapter 11, "Application Layer Firewalls," move up the OSI stack to examine the firewalls available at the transport and application layers.

The term *firewall* is perhaps the most commonly known concept in the information security arena. It evokes images of an insurmountable object whose mere presence in your network ensures that you will never be the victim of any of the Internet mischief that other, less-fortunate network administrators must suffer. The reality, however, is that firewalls do not ensure instant protection from an ever-changing array of threats. Furthermore, even the simplest of firewalls can be complicated to configure. Because of this, many firewalls in use today are misconfigured, and the overwhelming majority of them are underconfigured.

Unlike the bricks-and-mortar version, a network firewall must not only protect the inside network from intrusion, but it must also allow users to reach outside resources while allowing certain connections back to those users. This sounds like a simple concept, but its implementation is often challenging.

The good news, however, is that Linux itself easily serves as an efficient firewall device. The Linux kernel has the native ability to inspect the headers of packets received by the system. The `iptables` tool provides full control of packet filtering, network address translation, and even *stateful inspection*, where the decision of whether to accept or reject a packet is made in the context of a previously established flow (like an outgoing `telnet` request).

The classic example of the stateful inspection capability is what allows a firewall to permit an incoming `ftp-data` connection (TCP port 20) only when a local host has initiated an `ftp-control` connection (TCP port 21). By remembering the *state* of the outgoing connection from a given internal IP address, the firewall allows the incoming `ftp-data` connection only while the outgoing `ftp-control` connection is still in the ESTABLISHED state.

The combination of `iptables/ipnatctl` and kernel support makes Linux a very solid platform on which to protect your network perimeter.

Linux as a Firewall Platform

So why should you choose the Linux platform over the competing offerings, both open source and commercial? Ultimately, you are seeking the best protection for your network perimeter. So, before jumping into the discussion of *how* you go about setting up a Linux firewall, let's talk briefly about the reason *why* you would want to do this. These are the major advantages of a Linux platform over its competition:

Uniform Administration   There is nothing magical about using a Linux server to act as a firewall device, except for the fact that you'll be running a number of commands that affect kernel packet filtering and perhaps network address translation (NAT). Your training and experience as a Linux administrator can be applied toward the administration of your firewall. You know Linux and you understand it, which is your best protection when something goes wrong.

Commodity Hardware   Unlike some of the commercial firewall appliances that employ proprietary (i.e., expensive) and sometimes obscure hardware, the Linux firewall can be built with an existing off-the-shelf PC-compatible system, a PowerPC, or a Sparc/Ultra machine. This makes maintaining spare parts and repairing the system much easier in the event of an outage.

Robust Kernel-Based Filtering   While Linux makes use of user-level tools for configuring its firewall feature, the heart of its packet-filtering capability is implemented in the kernel, where it's safer and more efficient.

Tested Platform   Both the kernel and the user tools are widely deployed around the world, where they enjoy the constant enhancement and support of thousands of dedicated developers. Vulnerabilities are discovered and divulged in a timely fashion, with patches often available within hours.

Performance   With native support for fast Ethernet and even some WAN technologies (ISDN, T1), the Linux operating system can keep up with just about any type of connection that your company uses to reach the Internet. The bottleneck is likely to be that connection, even when you take into account the time it takes the firewall to inspect every packet that reaches its interfaces.

Cost   Using an open-source operating system as well as commodity hardware, a Linux firewall is the overall cost winner, often outperforming much larger commercial offerings. Not surprisingly, the more cost effective of these commercial firewalls are typically the ones based on the Linux operating system, like the Watchguard Firebox (`http://www.watchguard.com`) and the Xsentry Internet Firewall package (`http://www.trustix.com`).

There are, however, a few disadvantages of choosing Linux firewall support; here are two of them:

Support   I'm not going to enter into the age-old argument of open source vs. commercial, but the fact remains that many enterprises still feel uneasy about relying on an open-source system for protection. While there are plenty of support offerings for the Linux operating system, the firewall application support offered by most commercial vendors is bound to be more enticing to your CIO.

Application Bundling   Although there are some open-source packages that offer graphical user interface (GUI) interfaces to the command-line tools used to control packet filtering, the commercial sector is further ahead in offering an all-encompassing firewall application. These applications often include an installation and deinstallation script, a GUI, and a set of monitoring, logging, and reporting tools. This is of relative value, however, unless your company lacks the expertise necessary to install the more laborious "build-your-own" Linux alternative.

If you have analyzed these pros and cons, and are still ready to use Linux to protect your network, then read on! The next section introduces the concept of packet filtering, which is central to the way a Linux firewall goes about protecting your perimeter at the network layer.

Packet Filtering

The basic steps of packet filtering are as follows:

1. A packet arrives in one of the interfaces.

2. After the interface strips out its data link layer header, it passes the network layer payload to the kernel.

3. The kernel inspects the packet's header (IP address, port) and decides to drop it or forward it based on a set of rules that it knows about. This operation can take place in near real time and is totally transparent to the end user.

Packet filtering is not exclusive to firewalls since any Linux host can be configured to perform it, but it is most useful for building a perimeter control device (i.e., a firewall). A Linux server can be configured to act as a cost-effective firewall using the latest kernel's packet-filtering support. In fact, even an average machine (an entry-level Pentium with 48MB of RAM and a very small disk) has been shown to be more than adequate to keep up with Ethernet speeds while performing packet filtering and address translation.

The main advantage of packet filtering is that it is an efficient and non-intrusive way of adding security to your network. Unlike proxy-level firewalls (discussed in Chapter 10), and application layer firewalls (discussed in Chapter 11), users don't need to be aware of the packet-filtering firewall, and they don't need to authenticate themselves to use any outgoing services.

One important drawback of packet filtering is its inability to provide secure access to remote users that receive their addresses dynamically (using dial-up accounts via bootp or DHCP). A second drawback is the lack of user-level authentication authorization, especially when a remote host houses a number of users.

However, the most successful approach to security is a multi-layered one, and packet filtering should play a critical role in the overall defense of your network. The next section explains the concept of network address translation (NAT), which is often used in conjunction with packet filtering in most Linux firewalls.

The Legacy: *ipfwadm* and *ipchains*

Starting with kernel version 1.2.1, Linux has offered a number of utilities to configure the rules used by the kernel to accept or discard IP packets. The first incarnation of this utility was Alan Cox and Jos Vos' ipfwadm utility, which was based on BSD's ipfw utility and worked with kernel versions 1.2 through 2.1. The last version of ipfwadm was released in July 1996. Starting with kernel version 2.1.102 and later, ipfwadm has been replaced by Paul "Rusty" Russell and Michael Neuling's ipchains, which addresses some of ipfwadm's limitations, namely:

- 32-bit counters, which were previously unable to keep track of packets coming into high-speed network interfaces

- Inability to deal adequately with IP fragmentation

- No support for transport layer protocols other than UDP and TCP

- No support for inverse rules, where you look for the opposite of a condition (e.g., -i !eth0).

If your Linux distribution only supports ipfwadm, you are running an old system and you should upgrade to a newer version. Most recent Linux vendors include the ipchains utility in their standard distribution. The next section explains how to use the ipchains command and includes some real-life examples of how you can use it to build a network layer firewall.

Using *ipchains*

The name ipchains refers to the fact that the Linux kernel consults three separate *chains*, or sequence of rules, when it receives a network layer packet. There are three chains that come built-in with the Linux kernel:

Input Chain   The input chain handles packets that arrive at one of the server's interfaces and are bound for the local host.

Output Chain   The output chain handles packets that are originated by the local system and are bound for a remote host.

Forward Chain   The forward chain handles packets that arrive at one of the server's interfaces and are bound for a remote host.

Each of these three chains can contain a set of rules that define access controls based on the source/destination address, the TCP/UDP port, or the protocol ID. By specifying a set of rules that enforce the provisions of your security policy, you can build a firewall device using the Linux kernel as the underlying system and ipchains as your configuration tool. Let's take a look at the syntax of the ipchains command.

The ipchains utility uses the following syntax:

```
ipchains command chain rule-specifications [options] -j action
```

The *command* field is used to maintain the list of rules for a given chain and defines, for example, whether you're adding a rule, deleting a rule, or simply listing the rules that have already been defined for that chain. Table 9.1 contains a list of valid commands supported in ipchains.

Table 9.1   *ipchains* Commands

Switch	Meaning
-A	Add a rule to a chain (append to end of the chain).
-D	Delete a rule from a chain.
-C	Create a new chain.
-R	Replace an existing rule in the chain.
-L	List all rules in the chain.
-I	Insert numbered rules in the chain.
-F	Flush all rules from the chain (empty the chain).
-Z	Zero (reset) the packet and byte counters on all chains.
-N	Create a new chain.
-X	Delete the user-defined chain.
-P	Set policy for the chain to the given target.
-E	Rename the chain.
-M	View currently masqueraded connections.
-C	Check a given packet against a selected chain.
-S	Change the timeout values used for masquerading.

The *chain* field can be one of INPUT, OUTPUT, or FORWARD, or it can be a user-created chain (in the case of the -C command). You'll learn more about user-created chains later in this section.

The *rule-specifications* field is where you can specify one or more rules to be applied to each packet. Each incoming packet is compared to the parameters included in each rule, and, if a match is found, the appropriate *action* is taken for that packet. Table 9.2 lists the set of available constructors for the ipchains rules.

Table 9.2 *ipchains* Rule Specification Parameters

Parameter	Meaning
-p [!]*protocol*	Protocol ID to match. This can be tcp, udp, icmp, or any numeric or alphabetic representation of a service in /etc/services.
-s [!]*address*[/*mask*]	Source address to match. This can be a host name, an IP address, or a network name in network/mask format.
--sport [*port*:[*port*]]	Specification of source port or source port range.
-d [!]*address*[/*mask*]	Destination address to match. Same rules as the -s parameter apply here.
--dport [*port*:[*port*]]	Specification of destination port or destination port range.
-j *target*	Action to take when the rule finds a match (e.g., accept, drop). Note that in addition to being the name of an action, *target* can also be a user-specified chain or a built-in chain.
-i [!]*interface*	Interface through which the packet was received, such as eth0.
-o [!]*interface*	Interface through which the packet is to be sent, such as eth0.
[!] -f	Packet is a second or subsequent fragment of a larger fragmented packet.
-y	Only match TCP packets with the SYN bit set.

The parameters listed in Table 9.2 allow you to define any combination of source/destination IP address, port, protocol ID, and interface, along with the inverse of each of these conditions, by simply preceding the parameter with the exclamation mark [!].

Finally, the ipchains command needs to be told what action to take with each packet that matches the given rule. The action field is preceded by the -j option (which literally stands for *jump*), and can be one of the following:

- *chain*: This can be a user-defined chain. This allows you to "call" a chain within another chain, similar to the case where a subroutine calls another to perform a defined operation.
- accept: Let the packet through.
- deny: Quietly drop the packet on the floor.
- reject: Drop the packet and inform the sender via an ICMP message.
- masq: Modify (*masquerade*) the packet's source IP address as if it had originated from the local host. This action only applies to the forward chain and to any user-defined chains.
- redirect: Forward the packet to a local socket even if its destination is a remote host. This action only applies to the input chain and to any user-defined chains.
- return: Exit the present chain and return to the calling chain.

Ipchains Examples

Let's take a look at some examples of the ipchains command. Consider a Linux server called watchtower.example.com with the following interfaces:

- eth0: 63.54.66.1 (public interface)
- eth1: 38.110.200.1 (private interface)

Let's start by flushing the three built-in chains from all previously specified rules using the following commands:

```
ipchains -F input
ipchains -F output
ipchains -F forward
```

To set up a policy whereby all packets that are not matched by a specific rule within the chain will be rejected, use the following commands:

```
ipchains -P input REJECT
```

```
ipchains -P output REJET
ipchains -P forward REJECT
```

The previous three commands set up a restrictive policy where you have to explicitly define the kinds of traffic that you want to allow through your firewall. Suppose that your security policy allows incoming mail, HTTP, and telnet connections from any public host. You enforce by adding the appropriate rule to the forward chain:

```
ipchains -A forward -s 0.0.0.0/0 -d 38.110.200.0/24 -dport smtp -j↵
ACCEPT

ipchains -A forward -s 0.0.0.0/0 -d 38.110.200.0/24 -dport http -j↵
ACCEPT

ipchains -A forward -s 0.0.0.0/0 -d 38.110.200.0/24 -dport telnet -j↵
ACCEPT


ipchains -A forward -s 38.110.200.0/24  -d 0.0.0.0/0 -sport smtp -j↵
ACCEPT

ipchains -A forward -s 38.110.200.0/24  -d 0.0.0.0/0 -sport http -j↵
ACCEPT

ipchains -A forward -s 38.110.200.0/24  -d 0.0.0.0/0 -sport telnet -j↵
ACCEPT
```

Note that the first three rules will match incoming connections, while the last three rules will match outgoing responses to those connections. Since you have only added rules to the forward chain, you're not yet allowing any connections to the Linux firewall itself. Perhaps you want to be able to telnet to the server for maintenance, but only from a known internal host of IP address 38.110.200.10 (ideally, the system administrator's workstation). The following two rules will allow this:

```
ipchains -A input -s 38.110.200.10 -dport telnet -j ACCEPT

ipchains -A output -d 38.110.200.10 -sport telnet -j ACCEPT
```

As with the previous example, you need to allow both incoming access for the telnet traffic, but also outgoing access for the responses.

Finally, let's say that you want to guard against packet spoofing by ensuring that all traffic that leaves the internal network has the proper source address:

```
ipchains -A forward -i eth1 -s !38.110.200.0/24 -j REJECT
```

This command uses an inverse rule by stating that all traffic that enters the server at interface eth1 (the private interface) and does not contain a source IP address in the 38.110.200.0 class-C network should be rejected.

As of Linux kernel 2.4 (the latest stable version at the writing of this book), the functionality once provided by ipwfadm and ipchains is now being provided by Netfilter and its iptables user space tool. I recommend that you deploy your Linux firewall on a 2.4 kernel machine and that you use the Netfilter package for packet filtering. This is the topic of discussion of the next section.

The Present: Netfilter

Linux kernel 2.4 includes a number of features and stability enhancements that make it a very robust platform to use for your firewall. One of the most noticeable improvements of this kernel version is the packet-filtering subsystem, which is now named *Netfilter*. The development of Netfilter has been largely funded by Watchguard Technologies. This U.S.-based company develops and markets commercial firewalls appliances based on Linux platforms, as well as security services based on their firewall platforms. Figure 9.1 shows the Netfilter Project home page, located at `http://netfilter.kernelnotes.org`. This Web site features

- Information about the Netfilter Project team members and their contributions
- iptables downloads
- Documentation on Linux networking, packet filtering, network address translation, and the Netfilter architecture in English and several other languages
- Netfilter FAQs
- Information on Netfilter-related mailing lists

Perimeter Security

PART 4

Figure 9.1 The Netfilter Project home page

The next section explains how to configure your Linux kernel making use of the new Netfilter support to build a network layer firewall using a Linux server.

Configuring Netfilter

In order to configure Netfilter support into the kernel, install the 2.4 kernel sources and enter **Y** to the CONFIG_NETFILTER question during the make config stage of the kernel configuration.

NOTE The details of kernel configuration are beyond the scope of a Linux security book. See *Linux System Administration,* by Vicki Stanfield and Roderick W. Smith (Sybex, 2001) to find out more about Linux kernel configuration.

By default, a Linux system is configured as a network host—not as a router. The RFCs that define Internet standards require that hosts do *not* forward packets. However, for a Linux system to act as a firewall, it must forward packets. In effect, for a Linux system to act as a firewall, it must first act as a router. Therefore, once the kernel is configured to support filtering, you enable IP forwarding by setting the ip_forward switch to true. This can be done by setting the variable to 1. One way to do this is to set the value of the `ip_forward` switch through the `/proc` filesystem, as in the following example:

```
echo 1 > /proc/sys/net/ipv4/ip_forward
```

Every time the system restarts, the `ip_forward` switch is cleared to 0 and must be explicitly reset to 1. Add the `echo` line to a startup script such as `/etc/rc.d/rc.local` to set the switch back to 1. Some Linux distributions, for example, Red Hat and Caldera, attempt to simplify this process by providing an argument to the `network` startup script that explicitly sets the `ip_forward` switch. For example, on a Red Hat 7 system, setting `net.ipv4.ip_forward` in the `/etc/sysctl.conf` file sets the `ip_forward` switch to a corresponding value. The following example sets `ip_forward` to 1:

```
[ramon]$ head -2 /etc/sysctl.conf
# Enables packet forwarding
net.ipv4.ip_forward = 1
```

On a Caldera system, the `ip_forward` value can be set through the `/etc/sysconfig/network` file by setting a value for `IPFORWARDING`. If `IPFORWARDING` is set to `true` or `yes`, `ip_forward` is set to 1. If it is set to `false` or `no`, `ip_forward` is set to 0. The following example sets `ip_forward` to 1 to enable forwarding:

```
[ramon]$ cat /etc/sysconfig/network
NETWORKING=yes
IPFORWARDING=yes
HOSTNAME=ibis.foobirds.org
```

Personally, I recommend that you use the `echo` command to directly set `/proc/sys/net/ipv4/ip_forward`. The extensions that various vendors add to simplify setting this switch often increase the complexity of the task because the extensions are different. The `echo` command works the same on all Linux distributions.

> **NOTE**   The Netfilter kernel feature provides backward compatibility by allowing you to create packet-filtering rules with both `ipfwadm` and `ipchains`.

iptables

An integral part of Rusty Russell's Netfilter package, `iptables` is the user space utility that you use to affect changes in the three built-in network layer kernel-filtering chains (input, output, and forward). An evolution of the `ipchains` utility, `iptables` only runs on the 2.3 and 2.4 Linux kernels, and differs from `ipchains` in a number of important areas:

- The names of the built-in parameters (INPUT, OUTPUT, and FORWARD) have changed from lowercase to uppercase.

- The -i (interface descriptor) flag now designates the *incoming* interface and only works in the input and forward chains. If you need an interface descriptor for a rule in the forward or output chains, use the -o flag instead.
- The ipchains' -y flag (to match IP packets with the SYN bit set) is now --syn.
- You can now zero a single chain (with the -Z option) while listing it. (This capability did not work in ipchains.)
- Zeroing built-in chains clears policy counters (also a bug fix).
- REJECT and LOG chain actions are now extended targets (separate kernel modules).
- Chain names can now be up to 31 characters.
- The ipchains's MASQ chain is now called MASQUERADE and uses a different syntax (see the section "Network Address Translation").

Figure 9.2 shows the flow of packets as they move around the kernel and shows where the three chains fit within the overall process flow.

Figure 9.2   Linux kernel packet-filtering built-in chains

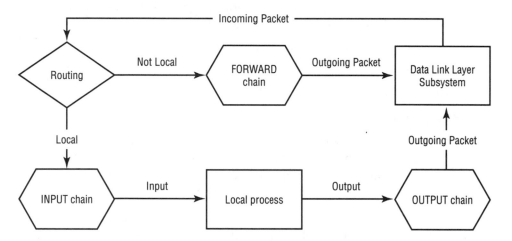

As discussed in the "Using ipchains" section, a *chain* is the term used to describe a set of rules that are checked in sequence. These rules determine what is done with the packets. Consider the following example:

```
[ramon]$ sudo iptables -A INPUT -p tcp --dport smtp -j ACCEPT
[ramon]$ sudo iptables -A INPUT -j DROP
```

This simple example adds two rules to the input built-in chain. The first rule matches all packets whose transport layer protocol is TCP and whose destination TCP port is 25 (Internet mail or SMTP). If a packet matches this rule, Netfilter is to accept this packet.

The second rule is a *catchall rule* (sometimes called the *stealth rule* because it hides the server from all external systems not explicitly allowed to talk directly to it). The catchall rule instructs Netfilter to drop all other input chain traffic. The two rules in the preceding example might be used to ensure that your mail server is only accepting connections destined for the SMTP port.

> **NOTE** One of the most important enhancements of the Netfilter framework over the legacy packet-filtering support in pre-2.4 Linux kernels is the handling of both the input and output chains. Before Netfilter, the kernel consulted the input chain for all packets received from the network driver, regardless of whether the packet would eventually be bound for another system (routing) or for the local system (local processing). The same applied to the output chain, with both forwarded and locally originated packets. This forced network administrators to apply non-intuitive rules to the input chain to account for both types of packets. With Netfilter, only packets bound for local processing are subject to the input chain, and only packets originated at the local host and bound for another host are subject to the output chain.

Both `iptables` and its ancestors (`ipfwadm`, `ipchains`) fulfill the same need: to reinstate a number of packet-filtering rules to the kernel every time the system reboots. Since the kernel does not have any non-volatile storage, you need to reinitialize your packet-filtering policy using the `iptables` scripts every time your system comes up. Since these rules do not survive system reboots, you must place your `iptables` commands in a script file and place the script inside `/etc/rc.d/init.d` directory.

Using *iptables*

Not all Linux distributions ship with `iptables` standard. Simply browse on over to your favorite RPM depot (my favorite is `www.rpmfind.net`) and install the latest version as follows:

```
[ramon]$ sudo rpm -i iptables-1.1.1-2.i386.rpm
```

This command installs a number of shared libraries in `/usr/lib`, a man page for `iptables`, and `/sbin/iptables`, the main executable.

You must operate with root privileges at all times when invoking the `iptables` command because it is actually writing the chain rules to the running kernel.

The general command-line syntax of the `iptables` command is as follows:

```
iptables -[ADC] chain rule-specifications [options]
iptables -[RI] chain rulenum rule-specifications [options]
iptables -D chain rulenum [options]
```

Perimeter Security

PART 4

```
iptables -[LFZ] [chain] [options]
iptables -[NX] chain
iptables -P chain target [options]
iptables -E old-chain-name new-chain-name
```

The command-line switches and their meanings are listed in Table 9.3.

Table 9.3   *iptables* Command-Line Switches

Switch	Meaning
-t *table*	Select the table to act upon. There are currently three of them: filter (the default), nat (network address translation, and mangle (specialized packet translation).
-A	Add a rule to a chain (append to end of the chain).
-D	Delete a rule from a chain.
-C	Create a new chain.
-R	Replace an existing rule in the chain.
-L	List all rules in the chain.
-I	Insert numbered rules in the chain.
-F	Flush all rules from the chain (empty the chain).
-Z	Zero (reset) the packet and byte counters on all chains.
-N	Create a new chain.
-X	Delete the user-defined chain.
-P	Set policy for the chain to the given target.
-E	Rename the chain.

The [*options*] field for the iptables command can take one of values listed in Table 9.4.

Table 9.4   *iptables* Command-Line Options

Option	Meaning
--verbose	Display rich (verbose) output.
--numeric	Output IP addresses in numeric format (no DNS lookup).
--exact	Expand numbers in the output.
--line-numbers	Show line numbers when listing the rules.

iptables Rule Specifications

The real power in the iptables command is its ability to match a specific type of traffic using its rich ruleset. Every packet that is forwarded from the server arrives at the server, or is originated by the server, and is compared to the ruleset for the appropriate chain (forward, input, and output). If the packet matches the rule, the specified action (defined by the -j *action* option) is taken. Table 9.5 lists the parameters to be used in the rule-specifications portion of the iptables command.

Table 9.5   *iptables* Rule Specification Parameters

Parameter	Meaning
-p [!]*protocol*	Protocol ID to match. This can be tcp, udp, icmp, or any numeric or alphabetic representation of a service in /etc/services.
-s [!]*address*[/*mask*]	Source address to match. This can be a host name, an IP address, or a network name in network/mask format.
--sport [*port*:[*port*]]	Specification of source port or source port range.

Perimeter Security

PART 4

Table 9.5 *iptables* Rule Specification Parameters *(continued)*

Parameter	Meaning
-d [!]*address*[/*mask*]	Destination address to match. The same rules as the -s parameter apply here.
--dport [*port*:[*port*]]	Specification of destination port or destination port range.
-i [!]*interface*	Interface through which the packet was received, such as eth0, ppp0, etc.
-o [!]*interface*	Interface through which the packet is to be sent, such as eth0, ppp0, etc.
[!] -f	The packet is a second or subsequent fragment of a larger fragmented packet.

Note that for each of the parameters listed in Table 9.5, a leading exclamation mark [!] instructs iptables to look for packets that do not meet that criterion. The rule specification parameters for iptables are very similar to the parameters available to ipchains, and they include options to match the protocol ID of the incoming packet (-p), the source and destination address (-s and -d) as well as the source and destination port number (-sport and -dport).

In addition to these basic parameters, you can specify extended matching parameters for packets of certain types (e.g., tcp, udp, and icmp), by using protocol-specific rules. For example, the following iptables line will match and accept all ICMP packets that carry the echo-request type (the type of packets used by the ping application).

```
iptables -A INPUT -p icmp --icmp-type echo-request -j ACCEPT
```

The converse of the previous command is

```
iptables -A OUTPUT -p icmp --icmp-type echo-reply -j ACCEPT
```

where you allow the local system to reply to the echo-request with an echo-reply, so that your system responds to ping requests properly.

Table 9.6 lists the protocol-specific parameters corresponding to the TCP, UDP, and ICMP traffic types included in iptables.

Table 9.6   *iptables* Protocol-Specific Packet-Matching Parameters

Parameter	Meaning	protocol type
--sport [!] [*port*[:*port*]]	Matches packets with a given source port, or from a given *port*:*port* range.	
--dport [!] [*port*[:*port*]]	Matches packets with a given destination port, or from a given *port*:*port* range.	tcp, udp
--port [!] *port*	Matches packets with an equal source and destination port.	
--tcp-flags [!] *mask comp*	Matches packets with TCP flags as specified. Flags are SYN, ACK, FIN, RST, URG, PSH, ALL, and NONE.	
[!] --syn	Matches TCP packets with the SYN bit set and the ACK and FIN bits cleared.	tcp
--tcp-option [!] *number*	Matches if the packet has the TCP option set.	
--icmp-type [!] *type-name*	Matches if the packet has the give ICMP type.	icmp

In addition, iptables allows you to load so-called *extended packet-matching modules*. These are similar to external plug-ins that can be added to the basic iptables package to dynamically extend its ability to match packets. In order to extend the syntax of an iptables command with one of these modules, simply use the -m *module* option.

The following extended packet-matching modules are included in the standard iptables distribution:

- owner: The owner module is used to match packets on the characteristics of the local packet creator. As such, it only applies to the output chain.

Perimeter Security

PART 4

- state: The state module allows access to the connection-tracking state for this packet.
- tos: The tos module matches the eight bits of the type-of-service field in the IP header.
- limit: The limit module regulates the rate at which the rule should match incoming packets. It is most often used in order to reduce the rate at which packets are accepted into an interface to avoid denial-of-service attacks.

Table 9.7 lists the parameters that are available for building rules when preceded by the -m *module* switch. The leftmost column includes the module to which the parameter applies.

Table 9.7 *iptables* Extended Packet-Matching Parameters

Parameter	Meaning	Extended Module
--uid-owner *userid*	Matches if the packet was created by a process with the given user ID.	
--gid-owner *groupid*	Matches if the packet was created by a process with the given group ID.	-m owner
--pid-owner *processid*	Matches if the packet was created by a process with the given process ID.	
--sid-owner *sessionid*	Matches if the packet was created by a process with the given session group.	
--state *state*	Matches one of the following states: INVALID, ESTABLISHED, NEW, or RELATED.	-m state
--tos *tos*	Matches the eight-bit type-of-service (TOS) field in the standard IPv4 packet.	-m tos

Table 9.7 *iptables* Extended Packet-Matching Parameters *(continued)*

Parameter	Meaning	Extended Module
`--limit` *rate*	Maximum average packet rate. Used to restrict a certain kind of packets to a maximum frequency. The rate must have one of the following suffixes: `/second`, `/minute`, `/hour`, or `/day`. Default is 5/hour.	`-m limit`
`--limit-burst` *number*	Maximum initial number of packets. Used to restrict the maximum burst of packets of a given type. Default is 5.	

For example, let's say that your firewall is protecting a private server whose primary mission is to serve Web content but also runs an FTP server for a few of your customers. You would like to allow unrestricted HTTP traffic to this server:

```
iptables -A FORWARD -p tcp -dport 80 -j ACCEPT
```

but you want to limit FTP connections to one every 30 seconds (or two per minute):

```
iptables -A FORWARD -p tcp --syn -dport 21 -m limit --limit 2/minute↵
-j ACCEPT
iptables -A FORWARD -p tcp -dport 21 -j ACCEPT
```

Note that in addition to the `-m limit` extended match, you're also matching `--syn` type connections in the first command in the preceding example. This ensures that you only rate-limit connection requests. The rest of FTP traffic is accepted by the second command.

As you can see, the `iptables` command has a very complex syntax. The next section presents some examples about how you can use `iptables`, describes a number of real-world network architecture scenarios, and offers suggested `iptables` commands that would be used in each case.

Perimeter Security

PART 4

Sample Firewall Scenarios

The following example scenarios should capture the most popular network architectures in place today, from the simple dial-on-demand connection to a complex scenario featuring a dedicated router and a demilitarized zone where you can offer public services without compromising the security of your private network.

Single-Homed Dial-up Server

Most small enterprises or branch offices have a single, non-dedicated connection to the Internet, and they don't want anyone coming back into their network or their firewall. Furthermore, many of these temporary connections are broadband (Internet over cable) connections, where the medium is shared by all the subscribers who are currently connected. This is breeding ground for intrusion and eavesdropping, and firewall protection should always be included in such a scenario.

In addition, most home users that use DSL or cable connections typically have more than one host on their network from which they want to access the public Internet. Linux offers NPAT network address translation through Netfilter's masquerading feature.

Consider the example (illustrated in Figure 9.3) where your dial-up server has two interfaces:

- ppp0, a dial-on-demand point-to-point protocol connection to your ISP
- eth0, a fast Ethernet connection to your private LAN

Figure 9.3 Single-homed dial-up server architecture

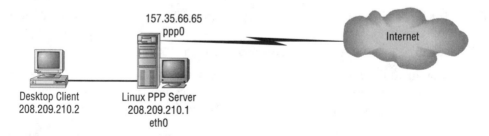

Let's create an iptables configuration for this scenario. Take a look at Listing 9.1.

Listing 9.1 Single-homed dial-up server

```
iptables -N protect
iptables -A protect -m state --state ESTABLISHED,RELATED -j ACCEPT
iptables -A protect -m state --state NEW -i ! ppp0 -j ACCEPT
```

```
iptables -A protect -j DROP
iptables -A INPUT -j protect
iptables -A FORWARD -j protect
```

The first line defines a new chain called protect, which is where you'll do all your filtering. (This is done for convenience, so that you don't have to enter the same filter rules in multiple built-in chains.) The second line instructs iptables to allow any incoming packets to the dial-up server as long as they are in response to a previously open connection (ESTABLISHED, RELATED). The third line allows new connections to be forwarded through the firewall, but only if the connection is not coming from interface ppp0; thus, it must be coming from eth0, the only other interface on the server. This ensures that it is an outgoing connection. The fourth line finishes the protect chain with a stealth rule, ensuring that any traffic that does not match a previous rule is dropped by the firewall.

The last two lines in Listing 9.1 are not part of the newly created protect chain, as the -A options of those lines clearly indicate. These two lines are the rules that send packets to the new chain by forwarding packets that arrive in the input, forward chains to the protect chain. Note that you are not restricting the output chain at all, so you are allowing any outbound connections that originate from the dial-up server itself.

Dual-Homed Firewall: Public and Private Addresses

At a company's central location and at some of its larger branch offices, you'll typically find a dedicated router supporting a full-time connection to the Internet. The most straightforward perimeter security architecture calls for a firewall device *in series* with the LAN connection to the router. Such a device ensures that all traffic coming in and out of the Internet is inspected by the packet-filtering firewall. Consider the sample architecture depicted in Figure 9.4, where the local network is 208.209.210.0/24 and the router's public interface is 157.35.66.65.

Figure 9.4   Dual-homed firewall architecture

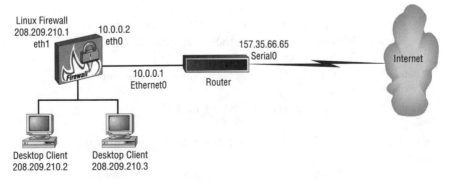

Perimeter Security

PART 4

> **NOTE** The firewall's public interface and the router's private interface do not need routable addresses because their connection is in essence point-to-point. You use the 10.0.0.0/24 network for this connection.

Let's consider a policy (in Listing 9.2) that allows for SSH inbound access, while blocking all other type of requests. All types of outbound TCP connections are still permitted. ICMP inbound traffic is restricted to echo requests (service 0).

Listing 9.2 Dual-homed firewall architecture: SSH incoming services

```
# Flush all the rules out of the the chains
iptables -F INPUT
iptables -F OUTPUT
iptables -F FORWARD

# Set the default policy for the FORWARD chain to deny all
iptables -P FORWARD deny

# Block all incoming traffic coming from public interface (eth0)
iptables -A INPUT -i eth0 -j DROP

# Block all outgoing traffic going out the public interface (eth0)
iptables -A OUTPUT -o eth0 -j DROP

# Instruct Netfilter to accept fragmented packets (-f)
iptables -A FORWARD -f -j ACCEPT

# Accept incoming TCP packets from established connections
# (--state ESTABLISHED,RELATED)
iptables -A FORWARD -m state -p tcp --state ESTABLISHED,RELATED -j ACCEPT

# Accept incoming TCP connections to SSH arriving at eth0
iptables -A FORWARD  -p tcp -i eth0 -d 208.209.210.0/24 --dport ssh -j ACCEPT

# Accept all outgoing TCP connections entering the private
# interface (eth1)
iptables -A FORWARD -p tcp -i eth1 -j ACCEPT

# Accept all outgoing UDP connections entering the private
# interface (eth1)
iptables -A FORWARD -p udp -i eth1 -j ACCEPT
```

```
# Accept incoming ICMP packet of "echo reply (=0)" type (ping replies)
iptables -A FORWARD  -p icmp -i eth0 -d 208.209.210.0/24
    --icmp-type 0 -j ACCEPT


# Accept all outgoing ICMP connections entering the private
# interface (eth1)
iptables -A FORWARD -p icmp -i eth1 -j ACCEPT


# Drop all other traffic in the FORWARD chain
iptables -A FORWARD -j DROP
```

Note that the last line is not really needed because you have established a deny policy (where everything is denied by default unless specifically allowed) for the forward chain at the top of the script. However, it's always a good idea to err on the side of caution.

Next, let's restrict the previous policy by only allowing SSH, WWW, SMTP, and DNS outbound services (see Listing 9.3).The lines in **boldface** are the changes from the previous scenario in Listing 9.2.

Listing 9.3 Dual-homed firewall architecture: SSH incoming services, SSH, WWW, SMTP, and DNS outgoing services only

```
# Flush all the rules out of the chains
iptables -F INPUT
iptables -F OUTPUT
iptables -F FORWARD


# Set the default policy for the FORWARD chain to deny all
iptables -P FORWARD deny


# Block all incoming traffic coming from public interface (eth0)
iptables -A INPUT -i eth0 -j DROP


# Block all outgoing traffic going out the public interface (etho)
iptables -A OUTPUT -o eth0 -j DROP


# Instruct Netfilter to accept fragmented packets (-f)
iptables -A FORWARD -f -j ACCEPT


# Accept incoming TCP packets from established connections
# (--state ESTABLISHED,RELATED)iptables -A FORWARD -m state -p tcp --state↵
ESTABLISHED,RELATED -j ACCEPT
```

```
# Accept incoming TCP connections to SSH arriving at eth0
iptables -A FORWARD  -p tcp -i eth0 -d 208.209.210.0/24 --dport ssh -j ACCEPT

# Accept outgoing TCP connections to SSH, WWW, SMTP only
iptables -A FORWARD  -p tcp -i eth1 --dport ssh,www,smtp -j ACCEPT

# Accept incoming UDP packets as response from DNS service (port 53)
iptables -A FORWARD -p udp -i eth0 --sport domain -j ACCEPT

# Accept outgoing UDP connections to port 53 (DNS) only
iptables -A FORWARD -p udp -i eth1 --dport domain -j ACCEPT

# Accept incoming ICMP packet of "echo reply (=0)" type (ping replies)
iptables -A FORWARD  -p icmp -i eth0 -d 208.209.210.0/24
    --icmp-type 0 -j ACCEPT

# Accept all outgoing ICMP connections entering the private
# interface (eth1)
iptables -A FORWARD -p icmp -i eth1 -j ACCEPT

# Drop all other traffic in the FORWARD chain
iptables -A FORWARD -j DROP
```

Note that, unlike TCP services like SSH and `telnet`, you cannot effectively restrict return UDP traffic to packets that reflect an established outgoing connection. This means that you need to allow your firewall to accept all UDP traffic whose source port is 53 (DNS—domain lookup service).

Triple-Homed Firewall with a Demilitarized Zone

A more elaborate network architecture features a triple-homed firewall, including a public interface, a private interface, and a third interface that services a demilitarized zone (DMZ). The DMZ allows you to offer public services with some degree of control, and without allowing anonymous users entry in your private network space. Figure 9.5 illustrates the triple-homed firewall, which adds a new network 64.65.66.0/24 that serves the DMZ with two servers (Web and Mail) to the architecture depicted in Figure 9.4.

Figure 9.5   Triple-homed firewall architecture with DMZ

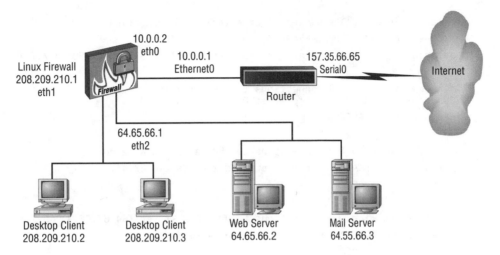

To extend the dual-homed firewall example (SSH and telnet inbound, all outbound), you add a policy (see Listing 9.4) that allows only your remote branch users (from network 128.129.130/24) access to the DMZ Web server, while granting unrestricted Internet access to the DMZ Mail server. The lines in **boldface** are the changes from the previous scenario (Listing 9.3).

Listing 9.4   Sample *iptables* script for triple-homed firewall architecture
with DMZ

```
# Flush all the rules out of all three default chains
iptables -F INPUT
iptables -F OUTPUT
iptables -F FORWARD

# Set the default policy for the FORWARD chain to deny all
iptables -P FORWARD deny

# Block all incoming traffic coming from public interface (eth0)
iptables -A INPUT -i eth0 -j DROP

# Block all outgoing traffic going out the public interface (eth0)
iptables -A OUTPUT -o eth0 -j DROP

# Instruct Netfilter to accept fragmented packets (-f)
```

```
iptables -A FORWARD -f -j ACCEPT

# Accept incoming TCP packets from established connections
# (--state ESTABLISHED,RELATED)
iptables -A FORWARD -m state -p tcp --state ESTABLISHED,RELATED -j ACCEPT

# Accept incoming TCP connections to SSH  arriving at eth0
iptables -A FORWARD  -p tcp -i eth0 -d 208.209.210.0/24
--dport ssh -j ACCEPT

# Accept incoming TCP connections to SSH  arriving at eth0
iptables -A FORWARD  -p tcp -i eth0 -d 208.209.210.0/24
--dport ssh -j ACCEPT
```

```
# Accept incoming TCP connections to DMZ SMTP server (64.65.66.3)
iptables -A FORWARD  -p tcp -i eth0 -d 64.65.66.3
--dport smtp -j ACCEPT

# Accept incoming TCP connections to Web server from remote branch only
iptables -A FORWARD  -p tcp -i eth0 -s 128.129.130.0/24 -d 64.65.66.2 --dport↵
www -j ACCEPT
```

```
# Accept all outgoing TCP connections received via both eth1 and eth2
# (the private and the DMZ interfaces respectively)
iptables -A FORWARD -p tcp -i eth1,eth2 -j ACCEPT

# Accept all outgoing UDP connections received via both eth1 and eth2
# (the private and the DMZ interfaces respectively)
iptables -A FORWARD -p udp -i eth1,eth2 -j ACCEPT

# Accept incoming ICMP packet of "echo reply (=0)" type (ping replies)
iptables -A FORWARD  -p icmp -i eth0 -d 208.209.210.0/24
    --icmp-type 0 -j ACCEPT
```

```
iptables -A FORWARD  -p icmp -i eth0 -d 64.65.66.0/24
    --icmp-type 0 -j ACCEPT
```

```
# Accept all outoing ICMP connections received from either the
# private interface (eth1) or the DMZ interface (eth2)
iptables -A FORWARD -p icmp -i eth1, eth2 -j ACCEPT

# Drop all other traffic in the FORWARD chain
iptables -A FORWARD -j DROP
```

In Listing 9.4, you have simply added two rules to the forward chain, one to allow all SMTP traffic to the mail server (64.65.66.3) and another to allow traffic source from 128.129.130.0/24 to connect to port 80 of the DMZ Web server (64.65.66.3). Note that you must also allow ICMP responses to enter eth0 bound for the DMZ, and to exit through the DMZ interface, eth2.

Protecting Against Well-Known Attacks

Aside from the capability to enforce access control to your internal hosts, Netfilter and iptables can be used to protect against specific types of Internet attacks by filtering traffic that matches the fingerprint of the attack. This section describes sample iptables statements that you can use to address a number of these well-known vulnerabilities.

Address Spoofing

Many firewall configurations allow the packet to be forwarded after verifying that it has an address from the private network in the source field of the header. The problem is that it's trivial for an attacker to synthetically create a "spoofed" packet generated from their network but with your source address. Protect your site from address spoofing by requiring that packets with the local network's source address be received on the interface connected to the local network using an iptables command like the following:

```
iptables -A FORWARD -s internal_network -i public_interface -j DROP
```

This command is adding a rule to the forward chain that matches traffic sourced from the internal network, but that enters the system at the public interface. By adding this command, you are forcing Netfilter to drop spoofed packets arriving at the public interface of your firewall.

For example, consider the dual-homed firewall architecture depicted back in Figure 9.4, where the local network is 208.209.210.0/24 and the router's public interface is 157.35.66.65. An address-spoofing rule for this firewall would look like the following:

```
iptables -A FORWARD -s 208.209.210.0/24 -i eth0 -j DROP
```

This rule examines packets that arrive in the public interface (eth0) and drops them quietly if they carry a source address in the (private) 208.209.210.0/24 network.

Smurf Attack

A *smurf* attack is staged by sending an ICMP echo request (ping) packet to the broadcast address of your internal network. The packet's source is forged with the address of the target of the smurf attack, which gets flooded by ICMP echo responses from all your internal hosts.

The following `iptables` command should guard against smurf attacks by preventing the forged ICMP echo-request from entering your network:

```
iptables -A FORWARD -p icmp -d internal_network_broadcast_address -j↵
DENY
```

This command adds a rule to the forward chain that matches any ICMP packets coming into any of the interfaces of the firewall whose destination is the broadcast address of your internal LAN. When this rule is matched, the packet takes the DROP action. For example, in the network depicted back in Figure 9.4, you would use the following command:

```
iptables -A FORWARD -p icmp -d 208.209.210.255 -j DENY
```

In this case, you're looking for ICMP traffic whose destination is 208.209.210.255, the broadcast address of the 208.209.210.0/24 network.

Syn-Flood Attack

A *syn-flood* attack is staged by sending a large number of TCP connection requests (with the SYN flag set) to a host while suppressing the normal SYN-ACK responses, thereby attempting to consume all its available data structures, which are busy keeping track of these half-open connections.

Using the `limit` external matching module, you can throttle the acceptance of TCP SYN requests to one per second using the following `iptables` command:

```
iptables -A FORWARD -p tcp --syn -m limit --limit 1/s -j ACCEPT
```

A rate of one TCP SYN request per second should be acceptable for most Internet servers, but it restricts just enough occurrences of incoming SYN requests to ensure that your systems always have enough available resources to handle legitimate connections.

Port-Scanner Attack

Many port-scanner applications try to identify every open TCP and UDP port in your system by sending a SYN or FIN signal to a given port range and expecting a RST signal for those ports not active. You can limit this activity to one incidence per second with the following `iptables` command:

```
iptables -A FORWARD -p tcp --tcp-flags SYN,ACK,FIN,RST RST -m limit -↵
-limit 1/s -j ACCEPT
```

This command adds a rule to the forward chain that matches TCP traffic that arrives at the firewall with the SYN, ACK, and FIN flags unset, and the RST flag set. When a packet matches this description, it is only accepted at a rate of one per second.

Ping-of-Death Attack

It is possible to kill certain operating systems by sending unusually large and unusually frequent ICMP echo (ping) requests. This is called a *ping-of-death* attack. The following iptables command limits the acceptance of such pings to one per second:

```
iptables -A FORWARD -p icmp --icmp-type echo-request -m limit↵
--limit 1/s -j ACCEPT
```

In fact, I recommend that you block ICMP requests at your firewall altogether using the command

```
iptables -A FORWARD -p icmp --icmp-type echo-request -j DROP
```

unless you have a legitimate need to have your host be reached via ping from the outside.

Network Address Translation

One of the problems facing the current installed base of Internet-connected hosts is the scarcity of network addresses. IP version 4 is limited to 2^{32} unique addresses. While four billion IP addresses may seem like more than enough addresses to go around, a good number of those are actually not usable because of subnetting and non-contiguous allocation. In addition, many enterprises never felt the need to connect their networks to the public Internet, so they used addresses from the non-routable blocks (RFC1819), a number of addresses set aside for use in non-Internet-connected networks.

When faced with the task of integrating a privately numbered network with the Internet, you have to make an important choice: renumber or translate. On the one hand, you can request a routable IP block from your Internet service provider and go through the pain of renumbering (and often re-subnetting) your entire network, or, if your connectivity needs are modest, you could use network address translation (NAT).

The advantages of NAT are twofold: On one hand, you are free to use whatever numbering scheme you choose while still allowing your users to connect to the public Internet. On the other hand, if you use non-routable internal addresses, intruders can't access your internal hosts as easily as if they were naturally routable, especially when they're hidden behind NAPT, a many-to-one NAT described shortly.

NAT involves modifying the source address of the packet before sending the packet to its destination. This requires the NAT device to keep track of this modification so that the step can be reversed when a response is received. There are three types of network address translation that vary depending on how the NAT device keeps track of the translation: NAPT, Static NAT, and LSNAT.

Perimeter Security

PART 4

Network Address Port Translation (NAPT)   Also known as *many-to-one NAT*, NAPT is best suited for network gateways that can only use a single public address. The NAT device accepts outbound connection requests from private clients and keeps track of each connection with two pieces of information:

- the private IP address of the internal host
- the source port that the NAT device used as the transport layer port number for the request

This allows the NAT device to route return traffic properly, even when there are two internal clients connecting to the same external server. Deploying NPAT hides your entire private network behind a single public address, thereby reducing your exposure to the Internet and drastically reducing your needs for routable address space. The principal disadvantage of NPAT is the fact that you cannot host any services on your internal network because the NPAT device is unable to accept incoming requests from the Internet. Use Static NAT if hosting services on your internal network is a requirement.

Static NAT   Also known as *one-to-one NAT*, Static NAT is the simplest case, where a single public address is mapped to a single private address. The NAT device must be configured to perform this mapping beforehand. Unlike NAPT, for example, where you can have a whole network hiding behind a single address, you have to know beforehand which addresses you will be protecting because you need to assign them a public equivalent.

Load-Sharing Network Address Translation (LSNAT)   An extension to plain, static network address translation, LSNAT allows you to advertise a single address to the public Internet while requests made to that address are serviced by a number of internal hosts. Consecutive requests are handed to the pool of internal addresses in a round-robin fashion, which achieves a load-sharing effect for incoming connections. This is useful when deploying a Web server farm in your DMZ, where all servers can contain exact replicas of your Web content. As the demand increases, simply add additional servers and register the new private address with the binding tables in your NAT device. To the outside world it still appears as if there is only one Web server.

Configuring NAT using *iptables*

Consider the network architecture depicted in Figure 9.3. If your internal network does not contain routable addresses, and you still want to connect to the Internet from your private hosts, you need to perform NAT. The most popular approach for a small network with a single routable address is NPAT, which is also referred to as *masquerading* or *hiding*. Simply add the line in Listing 9.5 to your iptables configuration.

Listing 9.5 Sample *iptables* NPAT configuration

```
iptables -t nat -A POSTROUTING -o ppp0 -j MASQUERADE
```

Notice that the command in Listing 9.5 uses the option -t nat. The majority of iptables commands operate on the *filtering* table (which contains the built-in chains input, output, and forward). NAT relies on a different Netfilter table, appropriately named nat, which contains the built-in chains prerouting, postrouting, and output. These chains have the following characteristics:

- The prerouting chain is the chain that attempts to match the packet as soon as it enters the system.

- The postrouting chain is the chain that attempts to match the packet once the routing decision has been made based on its destination.

- The output chain is the chain that matches locally generated traffic before a routing decision has been made based on its destination.

The -o ppp0 option directs iptables to apply the MASQUERADE rule to the packet just before it goes out the ppp0 interface so that any other processes on the server itself will see the packet with its original source address. This is an important point because it implies that packet-filtering rules applied to that packet will also see the packet with its original source address. Keep this in mind as you write your iptables rules.

The example in Listing 9.5 performs NPAT on the outgoing packet, using the address assigned to ppp0 as the *masquerade-as address*. What if you want to statically bind a specific routable address (e.g., 208.209.210.1) to a non-routable, private address (e.g., 10.10.10.1)? You could use Static NAT by specifying the syntax in Listing 9.6.

Listing 9.6 Sample *iptables* Static NAT configuration

```
iptables -t nat -A POSTROUTING -s 10.10.10.1 -o eth0 -j SNAT --to↵
208.209.210.1
iptables -t nat -A PREROUTING -s 208.209.210.1 -i eth0 -j DNAT --to↵
10.10.10.1
```

The first command in Listing 9.6 makes sure that the source field of packets originating from 192.168.1.1 is changed to 208.209.210.1 just before it leaves interface eth0. The second command performs the opposite destination translation just as the packet arrives in eth0 and before routing takes place.

Load-sharing NAT (LSNAT) can be accomplished by simply specifying a -j DNAT rule where you perform destination NAT from one incoming address to several destination addresses. For example, consider the case where you are hosting a popular Web server on public address 208.209.210.1, but would like to share the incoming load to that server among identical servers 10.10.10.1, 10.10.10.2, and 10.10.10.3. Just modify the commands in the previous example, as shown in Listing 9.7.

Listing 9.7   Sample *iptables* LSNAT configuration

```
iptables -t nat -A POSTROUTING -s 10.10.10.1 -o eth0 -j SNAT --to↩
208.209.210.1
iptables -t nat -A PREROUTING -s 208.209.210.1 -i eth0 -j DNAT --to↩
10.10.10.1-10.10.10.3
```

The only difference between Listing 9.7 and Listing 9.6 is that the second rule is translating the incoming 208.209.201.1 destination into the range 10.10.10.1–10.10.10.3, rather than the single 10.10.10.1 address.

In Sum

Building a Linux firewall is conceptually easy, but the devil is in the details. This chapter has walked you through the general concept of packet filtering and its implementation in the Linux kernel. You've learned about two user space tools that you can use to define the necessary filtering rules: ipchains (introduced with kernel 2.1), and the newer iptables (introduced with kernel 2.3). You got a chance to look at a number of detailed network scenarios, and you've seen several sample iptables configurations that reflecting several different security policies.

Although the initial cost of deploying a Linux firewall will be lower than many commercial alternatives, crafting a configuration to reflect your security policy takes some serious attention to detail. Packet filtering is your first level of perimeter defense, but a comprehensive security stance will make use of protection at the transport and application layer as well. In the next chapter of this book, we shift our focus to transport-layer firewalls, when you'll get a close look at the SOCKS proxying protocol.

10

Transport Layer
Firewalls

While filtering at the network layer is fairly straightforward and easy to implement, there are cases where a finer grain of authentication and authorization is required. For example, you may want to allow all users SMTP access to the Internet, while allowing only your Marketing group to access Web hosts. In such instances, network access may be awarded or denied based on the identity of the user that requests it. Transport layer firewalls make it possible to control Internet access by *proxying* outgoing connections on behalf of the internal user.

Transport layer firewalls offer two distinct advantages over packet filters: They control access to public network resources at a user level while reducing your enterprise's Internet exposure to the single public IP address of the proxy server. By having a single point of entry in and out of your network, you can centrally log all your users' activity for each specific service (Web, Mail, FTP, etc.). On the other hand, proxy firewalls typically require you to use custom network client software on users' workstations that has been modified to be "proxy-aware." In addition, proxy firewalls are usually more difficult to set up and maintain than a simple packet-filter firewall, since you need to keep track of both users and services.

If your security policy defines different groups of users with different privileges, or you are responsible for providing details of network usage on a per-application basis, I strongly recommend that you consider deploying a proxy firewall. Packet filtering is simply not going to allow you enough control to enforce this type of policy, and the logging that you get will not allow you to drill down into the types of applications being used.

This chapter defines the concept of a proxy server and describes the SOCKS framework for building standards–based proxy firewalls. It also describes the installation and configuration of NEC's SOCKS5, a freely available implementation of the SOCKS protocol for Linux distributions.

Proxy Servers

Proxy devices examine the requester's authentication credentials and consult a list of access control rules before granting or denying the network access request. This ruleset should have a default-deny stance, such that it denies access *unless* there is a rule that specifically grants it. If the access is granted, the proxy device establishes the desired connection to the outside host on the requester's behalf. The outside host then responds to the proxy device's address, so it's the proxy's responsibility to keep track of all outstanding network requests, and of the internal hosts to which these responses should be directed. Figure 10.1 illustrates the operation of a proxy server device handling an HTTP access request.

Figure 10.1   Protocol detail of a proxied HTTP request

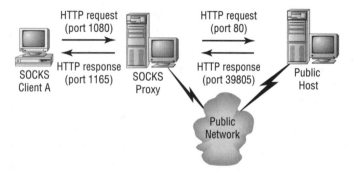

There are two distinct types of proxy servers:

Transport Layer Proxy Servers   Proxy servers operate just above the network layer in the ISO stack, and they accept all connection requests on a common TCP/ UDP port, regardless of the type of application traffic being received. Transport layer proxy servers are also known as *circuit layer proxy servers* because they serve to establish a *virtual circuit* between the user application and the target host, without inspecting the payload of the packets being proxied. In Figure 10.1, the SOCKS proxy server is required to maintain enough state information in order to identify which internal host requested a particular external connection. In Figure 10.1, the server maps the incoming HTTP response bound for source port 39805 into port 1165 of SOCKS client A, which made the request in the first place.

Application Layer Proxy Servers   Proxy servers are customized to handle specific application traffic only, and they are typically accessed via a TCP/UDP port number that is particular to each application. These proxy servers are often "smarter" than their transport layer counterparts, but the fact that they are application-dependent makes them considerably less flexible and much less comprehensive.

NOTE   Chapter 11, "Application Layer Firewalls," focuses on the TIS Firewall Toolkit, a popular implementation that relies on application layer–proxying technology.

The SOCKS Protocol

The Internet Engineering Task Force (IETF) standard *SOCKS* (SOCK-et-S) protocol defines a common framework for the design and operation of proxy firewall systems. This is a generic specification for the interaction between proxy-aware clients in a private network and a proxy server that acts as a firewall by relaying client requests to the public Internet.

The major driving force behind the SOCKS protocol is its popularity; most networked applications available today have built-in support for SOCKS proxying, eliminating the need to distribute special client software or to modify the procedures that your users currently employ to access the Internet. In addition, SOCKS proxy servers allow network administrators to protect and log a wide array of network applications using a standard management infrastructure. In fact, the SOCKS specification allows the client application to authenticate the user and establish the communication using the same transport-layer port number (e.g., TCP 1080).

There are two versions of the SOCKS protocol in use today. The next section of this chapter discusses the differences between them.

SOCKS4 vs. SOCKS5

The current SOCKS implementation, SOCKS5, was based on a previous version (SOCKS4) of the protocol, originally published by David Koblas and extended by Ying-Da Lee at NEC USA, Inc.'s Networking Systems Laboratory (NSL). While SOCKS4 was a fully functional protocol definition, it lacked support for strong authentication, an essential feature for the secure operation of a proxy system. This limitation prompted the IETF to undertake the

Perimeter Security

PART 4

SOCKS5 standardization (RFC1928), which added a host of new features to the original work by Koblas and Lee, including the following:

- Strong authentication with multiple authentication methods
- Transparent proxying of DNS queries
- Message integrity and privacy using GSS-API (RFC1961)
- Limited UDP traffic support

In addition, SOCKS5 removed the requirement that client applications recompile with the SOCKS libraries in order to be proxy-aware. SOCKS5 implementations now ship with a dynamic library that Linux client applications can load at runtime, thereby eliminating any need to modify client code.

Do You Need SOCKS?

There are a number of situations where a SOCKS-based proxy server is the most appropriate choice of firewall. In general, if you need to control network access based on the users' credentials instead of on the client's IP addresses, a proxy firewall is the obvious choice. The following situations are just a sample of the types of situations that require access controls based on user credentials that can be easily met with a SOCKS proxy:

- You have application users that need `telnet` and `ftp` access all day but Web browser access only after business hours.
- You have network clients whose IP addresses should never be allowed to traverse the firewall.
- You have a number of application users but only a single Internet-routable IP address.
- You need to track which URLs your employees are accessing, and you need to block a number of them.
- You are restricted to the use of a single-homed firewall (only one network interface).

The NEC SOCKS5 Proxy Server

The NEC NSL SOCKS reference implementation was a pioneer in the field of application layer security, offering a full-featured proxy server application based on version 5 of the popular SOCKS protocol. This chapter walks you through the process of compiling, installing, and configuring the Linux version of NEC's SOCKS5 implementation. It also describes how to use SOCKSCap, which is a WinSock-based library that provides seamless SOCKS support for Microsoft Windows applications that are not natively SOCKS-aware.

At the heart of the SOCKS firewall implementation is the SOCKS5 daemon that runs on the Linux server. This daemon needs to run on a host that has a clear IP network path to both your internal network and to the public Internet. This is accomplished by setting up your firewall host in one of two modes:

Single-Homed   A single-homed system has a single interface on a network segment from which both private and public networks are reachable.

Dual-Homed   A dual-homed system has two interfaces, one for the public network and one for the private, trusted network.

SOCKS5 can be used in either of these two configurations, although a dual-homed firewall is typically more straightforward to set up and maintain and consequently is more secure.

Linux distributions do not include the SOCKS5 package by default, so you have to obtain it in either RPM format or as a `tar` archive of the sources. I picked mine up from `www.rpmfind.net`.

Installing SOCKS5 with RPM

Use the `rpm` command with the `-q` (or `--query`) option to see if SOCKS5 is already installed on your system:

```
[ramon]$ rpm -q socks5
socks5-1.0r08-1
```

If SOCKS5 is already installed, but you would like to upgrade the installed package to a more recent version, use the `-U` (or `--upgrade`) with the new version of the package:

```
[ramon]$ sudo rpm -U socks5-1.0r11-1.i386.rpm
[ramon]$ rpm -q socks5
socks5-1.0r11-1
```

In addition to the base server package (SOCKS5), I recommend that you also install three additional RPM packages:

- The SOCKS5 Linux clients (`socks5-clients`)
- The SOCKS5 share library wrapper (`runsocks`)
- The SOCKS5 development environment (`socks5-devel`)

Use the following commands to install these three packages:

```
[ramon]$ sudo rpm -i socks5-clients-1.0r11-1.i386.rpm
[ramon]$ sudo rpm -i runsocks-1.0r11-1.i386.rpm
[ramon]$ sudo rpm -i socks5-devel-1.0r11-1.i386.rpm
```

The SOCKS5 RPM modules depend on both the `libc.so.X` and the `libpthread.so.X` libraries, so make sure that your `glibc` package (where both libraries reside) is up-to-date.

If you prefer to compile the SOCKS5 software yourself, the next section describes how to configure and compile SOCKS5 from the source distribution.

Compiling the Latest SOCKS5 Release

The SOCKS5 Linux distribution can be downloaded in source format from NEC's Web site at `http://www.socks.nec.com/cgi-bin/download.pl` (see Figure 10.2).

Figure 10.2   Downloading the SOCKS5 source distribution from the NEC Web site

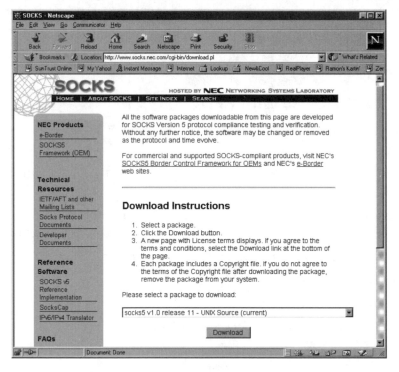

In addition to the freely available reference implementation, NEC's NSL offers a fully supported commercial SOCKS5 product named e-Border. More information on e-Border, including how to download it, is available at `http://www.socks5.nec.com` (see Figure 10.3).

Figure 10.3 NEC's e-Border: a commercial SOCKS5 implementation

Once you have downloaded the gnu-zipped distribution file, proceed to unzipping and expanding the archive using the steps in Listing 10.1.

Listing 10.1 Creating the SOCKS5 source code directories

```
[ramon]$ ls
socks5-v1.0r11.tar.gz
[ramon]$ gunzip socks5-v1.0r11.tar.gz
[ramon]$ ls
```

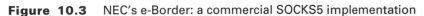

```
socks5-v1.0r11.tar
[ramon]$ tar xf socks5-v1.0r11.tar
[ramon]$ cd socks5-v1.0r11
[ramon]$ ls -l
total 234
-rw-r--r--    1 ramon     users         22907 Aug 16 11:38 ChangeLog
-rw-r--r--    1 ramon     users          3495 Feb  3  1999 Copyright
-rw-r--r--    1 ramon     users          4753 Jul 16  1998 INSTALL
-rw-r--r--    1 ramon     users          3439 Oct 20  1999 Makefile.in
-rw-r--r--    1 ramon     users         10883 Feb  4  1999 README
-rw-r--r--    1 ramon     users          2454 May 27  1999 acconfig.h
-rw-r--r--    1 ramon     users         10692 May 27  1999 aclocal.m4
drwxr-xr-x    7 ramon     users          1024 Aug 16 11:38 clients
-rwxr-xr-x    1 ramon     users        148397 Aug  2  1999 configure
-rw-r--r--    1 ramon     users          9885 Aug  2  1999 configure.in
drwxr-xr-x    2 ramon     users          1024 Aug 16 11:38 doc
drwxr-xr-x    2 ramon     users          1024 Aug 16 11:38 examples
drwxr-xr-x    2 ramon     users          1024 Aug 16 11:38 include
-rwxr-xr-x    1 ramon     users          4772 Jan 25  1999 install-sh
drwxr-xr-x    2 ramon     users          1024 Aug 16 11:38 lib
drwxr-xr-x    4 ramon     users          1024 Aug 16 11:38 man
drwxr-xr-x    2 ramon     users          1024 Aug 16 11:38 patches
drwxr-xr-x    2 ramon     users          1024 Aug 16 11:38 server
drwxr-xr-x    2 ramon     users          1024 Aug 16 11:38 shlib
-rw-r--r--    1 ramon     users            29 Nov 15  1996 stamp-h.in
drwxr-xr-x    2 ramon     users          1024 Aug 16 11:38 test
```

In this version of SOCKS5 (v1.0, release 11) there are ten subdirectories:

- clients: Sample Linux SOCKS5 clients
- doc: General product documentation
- examples: Sample configuration files
- include: Header files
- lib: Source code for the SOCKS5 static libraries
- man: Manual pages
- patches: Separate (and optional) patches to the source
- server: Source code for the SOCKS5 server
- shlib: Source code for the shared SOCKS5 libraries
- test: Utilities to verify and exercise the software

In addition, there are a number of release information files (for example, Changelog and Copyright), a README document, and a shell script file named configure, which is the topic of the next section of this book.

Once the files have been successfully extracted in the new socks5-v1.0r11 directory, you're ready to build the SOCKS5 daemon.

> **NOTE** You need an ANSI-compatible C compiler to compile and install the SOCKS5 distribution. The GNU gcc compiler provided with your Linux distribution should work fine.

Most source distributions of software packages offer users a number of options that allow you to customize the package to your environment. The following section describes the options available for configuring the SOCKS5 source before compilation.

Linux Compilation Parameters

Look for the configure shell script in the main source directory:

```
[ramon]$ ls -l configure
-rwxr-xr-x   1 ramon     users      148397 Aug  2  1999 configure
```

Run the configure script with no command-line options to create a default set of compilation files, as shown in Listing 10.2.

Listing 10.2   Executing the SOCKS5 *configure* script

```
[ramon]$ ./configure
loading cache ./config.cache
checking for gcc2... (cached) gcc
checking for gcc... (cached) gcc
checking whether the C compiler (gcc  ) works... yes
checking whether the C compiler (gcc  ) is a cross-compiler... no
checking whether we are using GNU C... (cached) yes
checking whether gcc accepts -g... (cached) yes
checking how to run the C preprocessor... (cached) gcc -E
checking whether gcc needs -traditional... (cached) no
checking for working const... (cached) yes
checking for inline... (cached) inline
checking for ranlib... (cached) ranlib
checking for a BSD compatible install... (cached) /usr/bin/install -c
checking for makedepend... (cached) true
checking for autoconf... (cached) autoconf
```

```
checking for autoheader... (cached) autoheader
checking for fcntl.h... (cached) yes
checking for memory.h... (cached) yes
checking for unistd.h... (cached) yes
checking for string.h... (cached) yes
checking for strings.h... (cached) yes
checking for bstring.h... (cached) no
checking for varargs.h... (cached) yes
checking for stdarg.h... (cached) yes
checking for stdlib.h... (cached) yes
checking for time.h... (cached) yes
checking for syslog.h... (cached) yes
checking for ifaddrs.h... (cached) no
checking for crypt.h... (cached) yes
checking for sys/stat.h... (cached) yes
checking for sys/param.h... (cached) yes
checking for sys/signal.h... (cached) yes
checking for sys/resource.h... (cached) yes
checking for sys/socket.h... (cached) yes
checking for sys/uio.h... (cached) yes
checking for sys/time.h... (cached) yes
checking for sys/wait.h... (cached) yes
checking for sys/ttychars.h... (cached) yes
checking for sys/ipc.h... (cached) yes
checking for sys/bitypes.h... (cached) yes
checking for sys/mbuf.h... (cached) no
checking for sys/sem.h... (cached) yes
checking for sys/select.h... (cached) yes
checking for sys/file.h... (cached) yes
checking for sys/ioctl.h... (cached) yes
checking for sys/fcntl.h... (cached) yes
checking for sys/filio.h... (cached) no
checking for sys/sockio.h... (cached) no
checking for sys/termios.h... (cached) yes
checking for sys/termio.h... (cached) no
checking for termios.h... (cached) yes
checking for termio.h... (cached) yes
checking for sys/un.h... (cached) yes
checking for netinet/in_systm.h... (cached) yes
checking for net/route.h... (cached) yes
checking for machine/endian.h... (cached) no
checking for paths.h... (cached) yes
```

```
checking for nl_types.h... (cached) yes
checking whether time.h and sys/time.h may both be included...(cached) yes
checking for ANSI C header files... (cached) yes
checking for dirent.h that defines DIR... (cached) yes
checking for opendir in -ldir... (cached) no
checking for main in -lsocket... (cached) no
checking for main in -ldl... (cached) yes
checking for main in -ldld... (cached) no
checking for main in -lsvld... (cached) no
checking for setupterm in -ltermcap... (cached) no
checking for setupterm in -lcurses... (cached) yes
checking for gethostbyname in -lc... (cached) yes
checking if we can use -lnsl... (cached) no
checking for shared libc... (cached) libc.so.6
checking for shared libnsl... (cached) libnsl.so.1
checking for shared libsocket... no
checking for shared libresolv... (cached) libresolv.so.2
checking for shared libdgc... no
checking for pid_t... (cached) yes
checking for size_t... (cached) yes
checking return type of signal handlers... (cached) void
checking whether sockaddr_un has sun_len... (cached) no
checking for sig_atomic_t... (cached) yes
checking for cc_t... (cached) yes
checking for sig_t... (cached) yes
checking for getpassphrase... (cached) no
checking for sys_errlist... (cached) yes
checking for dlopen... (cached) yes
checking for shl_load... (cached) no
checking for setupterm... (cached) yes
checking for tgetent... (cached) yes
checking for gethostbyname2... (cached) yes
checking for gethostbyname_r... (cached) yes
checking for gethostbyaddr_r... (cached) yes
checking for getpwuid_r... (cached) yes
checking for getservbyname_r... (cached) yes
checking for memset... (cached) yes
checking for memcmp... (cached) yes
checking for memmove... (cached) yes
checking for strchr... (cached) yes
checking for strrchr... (cached) yes
checking for strdup... (cached) yes
```

```
checking for strerror... (cached) yes
checking for bcopy... (cached) yes
checking for bcmp... (cached) yes
checking for bzero... (cached) yes
checking for index... (cached) yes
checking for rindex... (cached) yes
checking for setenv... (cached) yes
checking for putenv... (cached) yes
checking for unsetenv... (cached) yes
checking for getenv... (cached) yes
checking for getdomainname... (cached) yes
checking for rresvport... (cached) yes
checking for sendmsg... (cached) yes
checking for setsid... (cached) yes
checking for setpgid... (cached) yes
checking for setpgrp... (cached) yes
checking for getifaddrs... (cached) no
checking for waitpid... (cached) yes
checking for flock... (cached) yes
checking for dgettext... (cached) yes
checking for sigaction... (cached) yes
checking for sigprocmask... (cached) yes
checking for re_comp... (cached) yes
checking for strspn... (cached) yes
checking for getcwd... (cached) yes
checking for vfork... (cached) yes
checking for herror... (cached) yes
checking for genget... (cached) no
checking for getopt... (cached) yes
checking for vprintf... (cached) yes
checking whether setpgrp takes no argument... (cached) yes
checking for finger... (cached) /usr/bin/finger
checking for traceroute... (cached) /usr/sbin/traceroute
checking for ping... (cached) /bin/ping
checking shared library support... lflags: -shared cflags: -fpic
creating ./config.status
creating Makefile
creating lib/Makefile
creating test/Makefile
creating shlib/Makefile
creating shlib/runsocks
```

```
creating server/Makefile
creating server/stopsocks
creating include/Makefile
creating clients/Makefile
creating clients/pt/Makefile
creating clients/ftp/Makefile
creating clients/finger/Makefile
creating clients/archie/Makefile
creating clients/telnet/Makefile
creating clients/telnet/libtelnet/Makefile
creating stamp-h
creating include/config.h
include/config.h is unchanged
```

At this point, you may want to consider specifying some command-line switches to customize the software for your needs. Table 10.1 lists all the configuration options, what they do, and the Linux default value of each option.

Table 10.1   SOCKS5 Configuration Options

Configure Option	Description	Default
--prefix=*PREFIX*	Specifies the installation root directory.	/usr/local
--with-krb5[=*path*]	Specifies Kerberos5 authentication support and instructs SOCKS5 to look in *path* for the Kerberos libraries.	N/A
--with-ident[=*path*]	Specifies Ident authentication support and instruct SOCKS5 to look in *path* for the Ident library.	N/A
--with-debug	Activates debug mode. Useful for troubleshooting compilation problems.	N/A
--with-srvpidfile=*filename*	Specifies the file where SOCKS5 keeps its process ID.	/tmp/socks5.pid

Table 10.1   SOCKS5 Configuration Options *(continued)*

Configure Option	Description	Default
--with-srvpwdfile=*filename*	Specifies the server username/password authentication file.	/etc/socks5.passwd
--with-srvidtfile=*filename*	Specifies the server Ident file.	/tmp/socks5.ident
-- with-srvconffile=*filename*	Specifies a custom server configuration file.	/etc/socks5.conf
-- with-libconffile=*filename*	Specifies a custom client configuration file. This file determines the default settings for SOCKS-ified client applications that run natively on the Linux server.	/etc/libsocks5.conf
--with-default-port=*number*	Specifies the SOCKS port number.	1080
--with-default-server=*hostname*	Specifies the default SOCKS5 server.	localhost
--with-syslog-facility=*facility*	Specifies the default syslog facility.	LOG_DAEMON

I recommend that you accept the default options as indicated in Table 10.1 unless your directory structure keeps all locally built packages in separate directories. For example, if you want all SOCKS5 files to be rooted in /usr/local/socks5, use the command:

```
[ramon]$ ./configure --prefix=/usr/local/socks5
```

WARNING   The configure option --with-passwd can be used to allow SOCKS5 to use the standard Linux /etc/passwd file for user authentication. I strongly discourage this, however, because the username/password exchange between network clients and the SOCKS5 server travels over the network in the clear. This is risky and should be avoided.

Software Not Supplied with SOCKS5

Two of the SOCKS5 configuration options shown in Table 10.1 require you to pre-install additional software:

Kerberos5 Authentication (`--with-krb5[=path]`)   The default client authentication in SOCKS5 is simply username and password. If you want your server to use extended Kerberos5 GSS-API authentication (see RFC1961), you must supply your own Kerberos5 libraries. If you're running a Linux distribution that supports RPM, simply verify that the Kerberos5 library package has been installed as follows:

```
[ramon]$ rpm -q krb5-devel
krb5-devel-1.1.1-9
```

Ident (`--with-ident[=path]`)   Certain network services are only accessible when the client can provide its identity, even after traversing the SOCKS5 firewall. The Ident standard (RFC1413) provides a framework for passing extended client identity information to public network services. In order to add Ident support to NEC SOCKS5, the Ident library and server source should be downloaded from `ftp://ftp.lysator.liu.se/pub/ident`. Alternatively, RPM users can verify that Ident support files are installed as follows:

```
[ramon]$ rpm -q pidentd
pidentd-2.8.5-3
[ramon]$ rpm -q libident
libident-0.22-1
```

Building the SOCKS5 Server Binary

Once the `configure` script has been executed, you are ready to start compiling the source. Enter the following command:

```
[ramon]$ make all
```

This command builds all the components of the SOCKS5 distribution:

- SOCKS5 server
- SOCKS5 static and shared libraries
- Client applications

Perimeter Security

PART 4

WARNING   Red Hat Linux 5.0 uses a version of `glibc` (2.0.5) that has a bug in the `getservbyport` module. This causes the SOCKS5 daemon to crash on a segmentation fault. You can get around this problem by setting the environment variable $SOCKS5_NOSERVICENAME before starting the daemon.

If the compilation is successful and you don't see any errors or warnings, go on to the installation phase. This has to be done as the root user, so don't forget to prefix the command with sudo (Chapter 2, "System Installation and Setup," explains the sudo utility):

```
[ramon]$ sudo make install
```

This command installs all the SOCKS5 binaries, libraries, clients, and configuration files in the /usr/local directory, unless you specify otherwise with the --prefix option of the configure command.

WARNING   The modified telnet client included in the SOCKS5 distribution requires the development library of termcap, curses, or ncurses that has tgetent or setupterm. To compile the telnet client, install the ncurses or termcap development library (e.g., ncurses-devel-4.2-18.i386.rpm).

Configuring the SOCKS5 Server

Once you have successfully installed the distribution, it's time to start configuring the server. The default master configuration file for the SOCKS5 server is /etc/socks5.conf. The user is responsible for creating this text file from scratch, although a number of sample files are provided under the examples directory of the distribution. The socks5.conf file is consulted by the SOCKS5 daemon every time it is started, or during execution whenever it receives a SIGHUP signal.

Start by taking a close look at the man page for this file:

```
[ramon]$ man socks5.conf
```

The /etc/socks5.conf file contains the directives described in the following sections.

The *ban* Directive

The SOCKS5 server can be instructed to ignore connection requests from a certain client address, and furthermore, from a specific source port from that address using the ban directive.

Syntax   ban *source-host source-port*

The arguments to the ban directive are as follows:

- *source-host* is the IP address or host name from which connections should be disallowed.
- *source-port* is the port number from which connections should be disallowed.

Examples Here are some examples of use of the ban directive:

- To ignore requests from source port 555 on host 192.168.32.11:

      ban 192.168.32.11 555

- To ignore all requests from source port 555 on all hosts:

      ban - 555

- To ignore all requests from host 192.168.32.11:

      ban 192.168.32.11 -

The ban directive is especially useful when you need to allow access to all of your network clients with the exception of a few addresses.

The *auth* Directive

Since SOCKS5 supports several authentication methods, you need to specify which method you want to use. Notice that you can only use the Kerberos authentication method if you configure your source with Kerberos support (using the --with-krb5 option as described in Table 10.1). By default, SOCKS5 only supports username/password authentication. You can choose a different authentication method for each source-host and source-port combination in your network.

Syntax auth *source-host source-port auth-methods*

The arguments to the auth directive are as follows:

- *source-host* is the IP address or host name for which the specified authentication method should be used.

- *source-port* is the port number of the request for which the specified authentication method should be used.

- *auth-methods* is a comma-separated list of one or more of the following:

  - k (=Kerberos)

  - u (=username/password)

  - n (=none)

  - - (=any)

Examples Here are some examples of use of the auth directive:

- To use any authentication method available on all hosts:

      auth - - -

- To use user/password authentication on all hosts and Kerberos on host 192.168.32.11:

  ```
  auth - - u
  auth 192.168.32.11 - k
  ```

- To try user/password authentication and fall back to no authentication:

  ```
  auth - - n,u
  ```

If you omit the `auth` directive, the server accepts any authentication method. I recommend that you always take advantage of SOCKS authentication support by using at least username/password authentication for all your internal clients. You can never be too safe when you are securing your network.

The *interface* Directive

Use the `interface` directive to define the interface(s) available on your server and to inform SOCKS5 which interfaces are public and which are private. If your server is single-homed (single network interface), you do not need to specify this directive at all. On each `interface` line, you are informing the proxy server to only listen to requests from clients that fit the specified host and/or port specification.

Syntax   `interface` *net port interface-address*

The arguments to the `interface` directive are as follows:

- *net* is the IP address of the network that is allowed to send requests to the interface in question.

- *port* is the port number from which clients are allowed to send requests to the interface in question.

- *interface-address* can be either an IP address or a Linux interface descriptor (e.g., eth0).

Examples   For a multi-homed server (with interfaces `eth0` and `eth1`) where the local subnet (192.168.32.0/24) is proxied via the server's public interface (`eth1`), which has an address of 198.41.0.6, use the following example:

```
interface 192.168.32. - eth0
interface - - eth1
```

Or, use its equivalent:

```
interface 192.168.32. - 192.168.32.1
interface - - 198.41.0.6
```

Don't forget to include an `interface` directive for each of your network interfaces on the server because this tells the SOCKS5 server which addresses it should expect to see on which interfaces. This prevents outside attackers from spoofing, or from impersonating an internal address to gain access to the SOCKS5 server. If no `interface` directive is present, SOCKS5 assumes that the server is single-homed.

The *proxy-type* Directives

Some network architectures are such that a SOCKS5 proxy request must traverse another proxy in order to reach the public network. Such a situation is illustrated in Figure 10.4, where the SOCK5 proxy request is traversing a SOCKS4 proxy to the Internet. In those cases, the first server must act as a SOCKS5 client to the second server. The *proxy-type* directive determines which SOCKS protocol the first server uses to contact the second.

Figure 10.4   A SOCKS5 request traversing a SOCKS4 server on its way to an external Web server

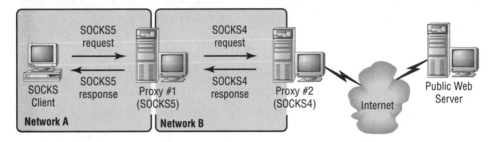

Syntax `proxy-type dest-host dest-port proxy-server-address`

In this syntax, *proxy-type* can be one of the following:

- Socks4 (= SOCKS version 4)
- Socks5 (= SOCKS version 5)
- Noproxy (= direct connection, no proxying)

The arguments to the *proxy-type* directives are as follows:

- *dest-host* is the IP address for the host or network to be proxied.
- *dest-port* is the port number for the request to be proxied.
- *proxy-server-address* is the IP address for the proxy host to which to send the request.

Examples   Consider the configuration in Figure 10.4. Proxy #1 is dual-homed, with addresses 192.168.32.1 and 192.168.64.1. It is protecting Network A (192.168.32.0/24) and must proxy through Proxy #2 (192.168.64.1, a SOCKS4 server) in order to reach the public network. Proxy #1 would be configured as follows:

```
noproxy 192.168.32. - -
```

```
noproxy 192.168.64. - -
socks4 - - 192.168.32.254
```

Note that you must instruct Proxy #1 not to contact Proxy #2 when the destination address of the request falls within either of its local segments (192.168.32.0/24 and 192.168.64.0/24). This is a common configuration where hosts from Network A have to be firewalled from Network B, but the hosts from Network A need to go through it in order to reach the Internet.

The *permit/deny* Directive

Once the SOCKS5 server has authenticated the client attempting the connection, it must consult its access control configuration before granting the proxying request. You use the permit directive or the deny directive to instruct the server to permit or deny a connection request, based on both the source and the destination of the request.

Syntax   permit *auth cmd src-host dest-host src-port dest-port* [*user-list*]

deny *auth cmd src-host dest-host src-port dest-port* [*user-list*]

In this syntax, the arguments are as follows:

- *auth* is an authentication type (u for username/password, k for Kerberos, or n for none).
- *cmd* is the command that the authenticated user is allowed to execute.
- *src-host* is the IP address or host name to match as the source of the request.
- *dest-host* is the IP address or host name to match as the destination of the request.
- *src-port* is the port number to match as the source of the request.
- *dest-port* is the port number to match as the destination of the request.
- *user-list* is the list of users allowed to traverse the server. (This field is optional.)

Examples   Here are some examples of use of the permit/deny directive:

- To grant use of your proxy server to users in the 192.168.32.0/24 network only:

  ```
  permit - - 192.168.32. - - - -
  ```

- To further restrict the use of your proxy server to HTTP traffic only:

  ```
  permit - - 192.168.32. - - 80 -
  ```

- To extend your policy to allow only Kerberos-authenticated use of your proxy:

  ```
  permit k - 192.168.32. - - 80 -
  ```

- To only accept proxy use to alice, bob, and charles:

  ```
  permit k - 192.168.32. - - 80 alice, bob, charles
  ```
- To add a rule where every other proxy request is denied (recommended):

  ```
  deny - - - - - - -
  ```

WARNING   Although it may be useful for debugging your initial configuration, never leave your server configured with a wide-open permit directive (all dashes). Such configuration poses a serious security risk because it leaves your server wide open for a malicious intruder to "hide" behind your server to attack a third site.

The *set* Directive

The SOCKS5 server uses a number of environment variables to control its execution, primarily to determine the level of debugging information that it should write to log files. You can use the set directive to initialize any SOCKS5 environment variable when the daemon is started.

Syntax   set *environment-variable value*

The arguments to the set directive are as follows:

- *environment-variable* is the name of the SOCKS5 environment variable you want to set. Table 10.2 contains a list of all SOCKS5 environment variables.
- *value* is the value you want assigned to the specified environment variable.

Examples   To change the SOCKS5 password file from the Linux default of /etc/socks5.passwd to /usr/local/etc/socks5.passwd, use the following set directive:

```
set SOCKS5_PWDFILE /usr/local/etc/socks5.passwd
```

Understanding *socks5.conf* Pattern Matching

The SOCKS5 configuration file syntax supports a number of regular expressions to allow flexibility when specifying host names, port numbers, authentication schemes, proxy commands, and user definitions. This section describes the general conventions for specifying command-line arguments inside the socks5.conf configuration file.

Host Patterns   Most entries in the SOCKS5 configuration file refer to a host name or an IP address. You can use either a host name or an IP address interchangeably. The advantage of using host names is that you don't have to modify the configuration file when you renumber a host. The disadvantage of using host names is that name lookups may be momentarily unavailable, which would affect the SOCKS5 service. The advantage of using IP addresses is that you don't have to worry about DNS resolution. But if you rely too much on IP addresses, you'll have to modify the SOCKS5 configuration file every time you move the server to a new network, or renumber any of your network clients.

Table 10.2   SOCKS5 Server Environment Variables

Variable name	Value	Value default	Description
SOCKS5_BINDINTFC	Host:port	0.0.0.0	Host and port number on which the SOCKS5 server runs.
SOCKS5_CONFFILE	Filename	/etc/ socks5.conf	Server configuration file.
SOCKS5_DEMAND_ IDENT	N/A	N/A	Force a client's response to server's Ident authentication request.
SOCKS5_ENCRYPT	N/A	N/A	Use encryption when GSS-API is in use.
SOCKS5_FORCE_ ENCRYPT	N/A	N/A	Force client to encrypt data.
SOCKS5_IDENTFILE	Filename	/tmp/ socks5.ident	Indent information file.
SOCKS5_MAXCHILD	Value	64	Maximum number of server children processes that can exist at once.
SOCKS5_NOIDENT	N/A	N/A	Omit Ident requests.
SOCKS5_NOINTCHK	N/A	N/A	Omit integrity checking.
SOCKS5_ NONETMASKCHECK	N/A	N/A	Disregard server's host mask check.
SOCKS5_REVERSEMAP	N/A	N/A	Map addresses to host names.
SOCKS5_SERVICENAME	N/A	N/A	Map port numbers to server names.

Table 10.2   SOCKS5 Server Environment Variables *(continued)*

Variable name	Value	Value default	Description
SOCKS5_PASSWD	Pass-word	N/A	Password for server-to-server authentication.
SOCKS5_USER	User-name	N/A	Username for server-to-server authentication.
SOCKS5_PIDFILE	Filename	/tmp/socks5.pid	File to store the running server's process ID.
SOCKS5_PWDFILE	Filename	/etc/socks5.passwd	Location of server password file.
SOCKS5_TIMEOUT	Minutes	15	Maximum duration of idle connections.
SOCKS5_UDPPORTRANGE	Port1-Port2	N/A	Source port range for proxying UDP requests.
SOCKS5_V4SUPPORT	N/A	N/A	Accept SOCKS4 protocol requests.

Table 10.3 lists the host patterns that SOCKS5 recognizes.

Table 10.3   *socks5.conf* Host Patterns

Pattern	Description
IP-address/mask	IP address with four-octet mask.
-	Wildcard (all addresses match).
a.b.c.d	IP address must match exactly.
a.b.c	Matches the first three octets of an IP address.
.domain.com	Host name must end in *.domain*.com.
host.domain.com	Host name must match exactly.

Port Patterns SOCKS5 allows you to select appropriate actions based on both the source and destination ports in the connection request. You will use the destination most often. I recommend that you enter a port name in /etc/services for all the ports you use in the configuration file. This makes the configuration file more readable and guards against the typing mistakes common in port numbers. Table 10.4 lists the port patterns that SOCKS5 recognizes.

Table 10.4 *socks5.conf* Port Patterns

Pattern	Description
Port-name	Service name as per /etc/services
Port-number	Port number (must match exactly)
-	Wildcard (all port numbers match)
[x,y]	Port number range from *x* to *y*

Auth Patterns A single letter is used to instruct SOCKS5 to use one of the available types of authentication (listed in Table 10.5). Username and password is the simplest form of authentication and works with very little additional configuration. Kerberos 5 support must be compiled in the SOCKS5 server executable. Always use either username/password or Kerberos authentication.

Table 10.5 *socks5.conf* Auth Patterns

Pattern	Description
u	Username/password
k	Kerberos 5 (when GSSI-API support is compiled in)
n	No authentication
n, k, u	Multiple authentication methods (last one used first)
-	Wildcard (all authentication methods match)

Command Patterns   Along with user-based and host-based authentication, SOCKS5 allows you to selectively specify which commands the client is allowed to execute through the server. Table 10.6 shows the patterns for these commands. Note that, as with authentication methods, you can specify a comma-separated list containing any combination of commands.

Table 10.6   *socks5.conf* Command Patterns

Pattern	Description
c	Connect
b	Bind
u	UDP
p	Ping
t	Traceroute
c, b, p	Multiple commands (any combination)
–	Wildcard (all commands match)

The SOCKS5 Password File

It's always a good idea to have your SOCKS5 clients authenticate themselves using usernames and passwords when traversing the proxy server. To enable this feature, you need to create and maintain a password file on the server. The format of this file is straightforward, with one line of plain text for each user. Each line starts with the username, followed by one or more empty spaces, followed by the password assigned to that user. The following excerpt includes three sample lines in a SOCKS5 password file:

```
alice     myKat_4
bob       $shOtS
charlie   MandMs
```

Note that, unlike in the standard Linux password files, the SOCKS5 password appears in cleartext; that is, unencrypted and unhashed. In order to minimize the exposure of this password file, no user logins should be allowed on the SOCKS5 server host, and its access should be closely monitored. It's also important to make sure that this file has the minimum amount of permissions necessary. It only needs to be accessible by the root user for read/write access, with no other access to any other groups and users. When you first create the file, set the permissions with the following command:

[ramon]$ **sudo chmod 600 /etc/socks5.passwd**

Keep in mind that in order for the server to recognize a newly added (or modified) username/password combination, you need to either restart the SOCKS5 daemon or send a SIGHUP signal to the SOCKS5 process ID.

Starting and Stopping the SOCKS5 Server

The main SOCKS5 daemon application (located, by default in /usr/local/bin/socks5) must be running at all times in order for your server to proxy incoming connections. The process listens on a pre-specified port (1080, by default), where internal clients can contact it to request proxy service. The SOCKS5 daemon can be started in one of four different modes:

Stand-alone   Stand-alone mode is the default for most Linux network servers. The system starts a single socks5 process from the usual startup directory (e.g., /etc/rc.d/init.d for Red Hat). When the daemon receives a connection request, it spawns a separate process to handle it, which frees up the original listener to accept subsequent connection requests. Children processes are cleaned up when no longer needed. Stand-alone mode is not optimal, but I recommend that you select this mode initially, because tracking a single instance of the server simplifies the process of debugging your initial configuration.

Preforking   The process of spawning a separate SOCKS5 instance for each connection is an expensive one, and it should be avoided when possible. Preforking mode allows you to start a number of copies of the socks5 process. In Linux, the default number of preforked processes is 64. This is a good initial setting. If your system is not going to be dedicated to running SOCKS5 and will be running other network services, decrease this number to 32. (See the -n option listed in Table 10.7.) Preforking is the preferred mode of running the server for non-Linux systems that do not support threads.

inetd   SOCKS5 can be added to /etc/inetd.conf to be executed by the main inetd daemon whenever it receives a request on the SOCKS5 port. This is perhaps the least effective way to configure the daemon because it's the mode that incurs the most overhead.

Threaded   Threaded mode is the optimal mode for starting the SOCKS5 daemon on a Linux system. Taking advantage of Linux support of POSIX threads, the daemon can be started as a threaded application.

As with any other Linux executable, you can specify a variety of switches on the command line when you invoke the SOCKS5 server. Table 10.7 lists the command-line options that are accepted in conjunction with the socks5 executable:

Table 10.7 *socks5* Command-Line Options

Option	Description
-I	Run daemon from inetd.
-f	Run in the foreground (useful for debugging).
-p	Run a preforking daemon.
-n	Fork a maximum of n processes.
-t	Run a threaded daemon.
-d	Run in debug mode.
-s	Send all output to stderr rather than syslog. This option is also useful for debugging.

For example, to start the server in the foreground with debugging enabled, use the following command:

> [ramon]$ **sudo /usr/local/bin/socks5 -f -d**

To start the server in preforking mode with an initial set of 32 children, use the following command:

> [ramon]$ **sudo /usr/local/bin/socks5 -p -n 32**

To stop the server, simply execute the script /usr/local/bin/stopsocks (see Listing 10.3) with one of the standard command-line options described in Table 10.8.

Listing 10.3 The *stopsocks* script

```
#!/bin/sh

KILL=kill
PORT=
PIDFILE=${SOCKS5_PIDFILE-/tmp/socks5.pid}
```

```
if [ "$#" != "0" ] ; then
      if [ "$1" = "-p" ] ; then
              if [ "$#" != "1" ] ; then
                       shift
                       PORT=$1
                       shift
              fi
      fi
fi


if [ -z "$PORT" ] ; then
      FILE=${PIDFILE}-1080
else
      FILE=${PIDFILE}-$PORT
fi

if [ ! -f "$FILE" -a "$#" != "2" ] ; then
      echo "PID file $FILE does not exist"
      exit
fi

case $# in
0)
      SIGNAL=-HUP
      PID=`cat $FILE`
      ;;
1)    SIGNAL=$1
      PID=`cat $FILE`
      ;;
2)    SIGNAL=$1
      PID=$2
      ;;
*)
      echo "usage: $0 [-p port] [signal] [pid]"
      exit 1;
      ;;
esac

case "$SIGNAL" in
'-HUP')
```

```
            ${KILL} -HUP ${PID}
            ;;
    '-1')
            ${KILL} -1 ${PID}
            ;;
    *)
            ${KILL} ${SIGNAL} -${PID}
            rm $FILE
            ;;
    esac
```

Note that the Linux utility killall generally works the same way as stopsocks, but it lacks the ability to stop a specific SOCKS5 server in cases where you're running multiple servers on different TCP ports. This can only be easily accomplished with the -p option of the stopsocks command.

Table 10.8   *stopsocks* Script Command-Line Options

Option	Description
-INT	Gracefully stops the SOCKS5 daemon.
-KILL	Abruptly stops operation of the SOCKS5 daemon.
-HUP	Forces the SOCKS5 daemon to re-read its configuration file.
[-p=*port*]	Stops a server running on the specified port.
[*pid*]	Process ID of server.

To stop the server on PID 1245, use the following command:

    [ramon]$ **sudo /usr/local/bin/socks5 -INT 1245**

To force the server on port 1080 to read its configuration, use the following command:

    [ramon]$ **sudo /usr/local/bin/socks5 -HUP -p 1080**

The *runsocks* Script

The SOCKS5 distribution comes with a compile option to build a dynamically linked library (/usr/local/lib/libsocks5_sh.so) that can be used by native Linux client applications in conjunction with a SOCKS5 server. The script /usr/local/bin/

runsocks works by adding the location of the SOCKS5 dynamic library to the front of the standard Linux $LD_LIBRARY_PATH, and effectively SOCKS-ifies any standard Linux network clients by replacing references to the commonly used Berkeley Sockets systems calls with their SOCKS5 equivalents.

Notice that the runsocks script is only effective for clients that have been compiled with support for dynamic loading of shared libraries. Applications that have been built to include static libraries cannot be executed by runsocks. Listing 10.4 shows how to use runsocks with the standard Linux ftp client to contact a remote FTP server (public.example.com) through a Proxy server (proxy.example.com). Note that there are three environment variables that need to be set prior to runsocks execution: $SOCKS5_SERVER, $SOCKS5_USER, and $SOCKS5_PASSWD. These variables specify which proxy server to use and the username and password to use for authenticating to the proxy server. These variables can also be defined in the libsocks5.conf file, which is explained in detail in the next section.

Listing 10.4   Using the *runsocks* script

```
[ramon]$ export SOCKS5_SERVER=proxy.example.com
[ramon]$ export SOCKS5_USER=ramon
[ramon]$ export SOCKS5_PASSWD=mypassword
[ramon]$ runsocks ftp public.example.com
220 public FTP server (Version wu-2.4.2-VR17(1)
Mon Apr 19 09:21:53 EDT 1999) ready.
Name (public.example.com:ramon):
331 Password required for ramon.
Password:
230 User ramon logged in.
Remote system type is UNIX.
Using binary mode to transfer files.
ftp>
```

SOCKS5 Shared Library Configuration

In order to control the execution of the SOCKS5 library and the operation of the SOCKS-ified clients, you must first create a configuration file, typically named /etc/libsocks5.conf. The contents of this file are analogous to the *proxy-type* directives in /etc/socks5.conf, discussed earlier in this chapter. The primary purpose of this file is to define which target hosts should be reached via the proxy and which target hosts should be addressed directly. Consider the following lines from a libsocks5.conf file:

```
socks5 - - - - 192.168.32.1
noproxy - - 192.168.32. -
```

This example specifies that clients use SOCKS5 proxying to server 192.168.32.1 in all instances, except when the destination falls within the 192.168.32.0 network (the local LAN), in which case a direct connection should be established.

In addition to the configuration that controls the shared library itself, there are a number of environment variables that can be set by each user in order to tailor the execution of the library to their environment. Table 10.9 includes the most commonly used of these environment variables.

Table 10.9   *libsocks5.conf* Environment Variables

Variable name	Value	Value default	Description
SOCKS5_USER	User-name	N/A	Username for server authentication.
SOCKS5_PASSWD	Password	N/A	Password for server-to-server authentication.
SOCKS5_SERVER	host:port	per libsocks5.conf	Overwrites the SOCKS5 server to use.
SOCKS5_ENCRYPT	N/A	N/A	Specifies to use encryption when GSS-API is in use.

So far, this chapter has described the SOCKS5 server and the ability to configure Linux clients to connect to the server. However, most Linux servers are also expected to provide services to other platforms. The following section explains how Windows clients can take advantage of a Linux-based proxy firewall.

Configuring Windows SOCKS5 Clients

While it's fairly trivial to modify the Linux environment for SOCKS5 clients, there is typically also a strong need for Windows-based clients to use the proxy server to connect to the public Internet. You clearly cannot modify each Windows application to use the SOCKS5 libraries, so you need a *shim*, a network driver that will insert itself in the WinSock TCP/IP stack and intercept all connection requests. The SOCKS5 developers augmented the capability of the Linux server with SOCKSCap, a Windows-based application that effectively SOCKS-ifies any WinSock-compliant Windows application.

Perimeter Security

PART 4

Available from NEC USA's Web site in ready-to-install format, SOCKSCap can be executed in the background whenever a Windows user needs to access a host outside the SOCKS5 server. To install and configure SOCKSCap, just follow these simple steps:

1. Download the self-extracting SOCKSCap binary from www.socks.nec.com.

2. Double-click the binary and follow the directions of the Install wizard.

3. Once the installation is complete with no errors, start the application. On its first execution, it prompts you to enter the initial configuration (see Figure 10.5). While SOCKSCap supports both the SOCKS4 and SOCKS5 protocol, I strongly suggest that you use SOCKS5 for all your clients when possible. Don't forget to click the Username/Password checkbox at the bottom of the Settings window.

Figure 10.5   Setting the SOCKSCap initial configuration options

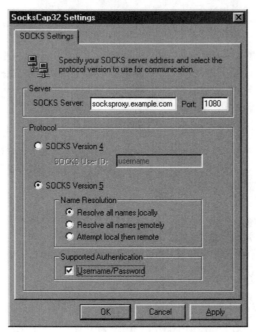

4. From this point forward, simply invoke the SOCKSCap application from the Start menu. When configured for SOCKS5, SOCKSCap prompts you for your SOCKS5 username/password (as shown in Figure 10.6). This is the authentication information that SOCKSCap uses on behalf of all your SOCKS-ified applications.

Figure 10.6   The SOCKSCap user authentication dialog

5. Once you have entered your authentication information, the standard SOCKSCap panel appears, on which you can add new applications that you want to launch using SOCKS5. For example, you may want to SOCKS-ify your Secure Shell (SSH) client. Simply click the New button and specify the path and working directory of the SSH application (see Figure 10.7). This adds `ssh32` to the list of SOCKS-ified applications that SOCKSCap controls.

Figure 10.7   Adding a new application to be launched by SOCKSCap

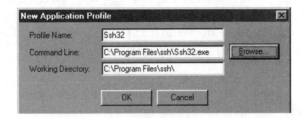

6. At this point you're ready to launch the new application under SOCKSCap. Simply click the application's icon inside SOCKSCap, right-click and select Run Socksified, as shown in Figure 10. 8. From this point on, your user will authenticate to the Linux proxy as Stacia and the password will be the one entered in the authentication box. To stop execution of the SOCKS-ified application, simply exit from it as you normally would. SOCKSCap can control any number of network applications, as long as they're Winsock-compliant.

Perimeter Security

PART 4

Figure 10.8   Launching an application from SOCKSCap

The SOCKS5 IPv4-to-IPv6 Translator

A little-known bonus that you get with the SOCKS5 reference implementation is the ability to bridge the gap between IPv4 and IPv6 hosts in your network. This is currently accomplished via a patch to the standard SOCKS5 server distribution, although NEC plans to eventually roll IPv6-to-IPv4 translation support in the standard SOCKS5 distribution.

The translator, named *Socks-Trans*, functions by accepting both IPv4 and IPv6 requests, either on separate interfaces (as a multi-homed server) or on the same physical interface (in a single-home configuration). This effectively allows you to gradually roll IPv6 onto your network, while taking advantage of the security features that SOCKS5 provides.

Once you have downloaded and expanded the standard SOCKS5 package, you need to download the separate software patch that provides the translation service; at the writing of this book, this file is called `socks5-trans-v1.3-patch.gz`. Place the patch file in the main source directory of the package and proceed to unzip it and apply it as follows:

```
[ramon]$ ls *patch*
socks5-trans-v1.3-patch.gz
[ramon]$ gunzip socks5-trans-v1.3-patch.gz
[ramon]$ ls *patch*
socks5-trans-v1.3-patch
[ramon]$ patch -p < ./socks5-trans-v1.3-patch
```

This results in the modification of all the source code files necessary for IPv6 support and IPv4-to-IPv6 translation.

There are some extra `configure` script options to consider when Socks-Trans is present. Table 10.10 lists the most important options.

Table 10.10   Socks-Trans Configuration Options

Configure Option	Description	Default
--enable-ipv6	Enables IPv6 protocol support.	Support is enabled by default if detected in the Linux installation.
--disable-ipv6	Disables IPv6 protocol support.	Support is enabled by default if detected in the Linux installation.
--enabled-mapped-addresses	Enables support for IPv4-mapped IPv6 addresses. (See RFC2133 for details.)	N/A
--disable-mapped-addresses	Disables support for IPv4-mapped and IPv6-mapped addresses.	N/A
--with-ipv6-ping=PATH	Specifies the IPv6-specific ping command.	ping6
--with-ipv6-traceroute=PATH	Specifies the IPv6-specific traceroute command.	traceroute6

Perimeter Security

PART 4

In addition, there is an IPv6-specific configuration line for the /etc/socks5.conf file:

    filter *name auth cmd src-host dest-host src-port dest-port user-list*

The arguments on this line are as follows:

- *name* is the type of custom filter. (Only ftv6 is supported in version 1.3 of the Socks-Trans). These filters provide the translation rules necessary for certain applications that differ drastically from IPv4 and IPv6. For example, ftv6 allows IPv4 (RFC959) implementations of the FTP protocol to interoperate with their IPv6 counterparts (RFC1639).

- *auth* is a list of authentication methods (n, k, u, -).

- *cmd* is the command to be applied by the filter.

- *src-host* is the IP address of the source machine.
- *dest-host* is the IP address of the destination machine.
- *src-port* is the port number of the source machine.
- *dest-port* is the port number of the destination machine.
- *user-list* is the list of users to which the filter should apply.

For example, to allow any of your internal IPv4 clients to connect to any external IPv6 FTP server, use the following configuration line:

```
filter ftpv6 k c - - - ftp
```

Socks-Trans is a great transition tool that you can use to bridge the gap between the hosts that have been already modified to use IPv6 and those that still remain on IPv4.

In Sum

Transport layer proxying is a convenient way to control public network access using a single public address and a central point of administration, including user authentication and connection logging. SOCKS5 is straightforward to build, configure, and maintain, and it can adapt to varying network topologies and configurations, including environments where clients based on IPv4 and IPv6 must coexist.

The network administrator can choose to recompile network clients with SOCKS5 support, use the existing Linux clients with a dynamically linked library, or simply use the existing Windows clients by installing the provided SOCKSCap launcher. You also have the option to proxy network applications by changing user procedures rather than the clients themselves. This is the topic of Chapter 11, "Application Layer Firewalls."

11

Application Layer Firewalls

Chapter 10, "Transport Layer Firewalls," discussed proxying at the transport layer, where a number of TCP and UDP services share a common transport layer port on the proxy device using the SOCKS protocol. This type of appliance is considered a *circuit-level firewall,* where several applications share a common proxying framework, defined by the SOCKS protocol.

An alternate approach to transport layer firewalls is one where each application type on the internal network connects to a separate proxying process on a firewall that's dedicated to forwarding connections for that specific type of application traffic. These types of firewalls are referred to as *application layer firewalls,* and they are the topic of discussion in this chapter.

Application layer proxying allows the firewall to tailor each of the proxy processes for the application that it is designed to handle. It can then support special types of caching, authentication, or access control, as the application requires it. An application layer firewall protects the private network from the untrusted public Internet by not allowing any connections on its public interface. In fact, the only connections that are allowed, even from the internal network, are the ones for which the firewall is running an application proxy process. As with any firewall device, the basic *deny-all stance* should be used, where all services are denied by default and specific services must be allowed explicitly.

In addition, all connections should be blocked through the firewall, with the exception of those allowed in writing by your security policy.

This chapter explains the TIS Firewall Toolkit, which is perhaps the most popular example of a freely available application layer proxying firewall, or, more accurately stated, a set of tools and configuration practices that you can use to build a firewall that suits your specific application layer security needs.

FWTK: The TIS Firewall Toolkit

The Firewall ToolKit (FWTK) is a complete application layer firewall package freely available on the Internet. FTWK can be compiled to run on a Linux server without any source code modifications. First released to the public back in 1993, FWTK was written by Trusted Information Systems (TIS), now part of Network Associates International, with funding from the U.S. government through the Advanced Research Projects Agency (ARPA). Marcus Ranum, who is now a legendary figure in Internet security, spearheaded the FTWK development project. FWTK would eventually be the seed for the TIS Gauntlet, the first commercially available application layer proxy firewall product.

The goal of the FWTK project was to provide an integrated collection of proxy processes that would accept internal connections for popular services such as SMTP, Telnet, FTP, and HTTP and would then request the connection to the Internet host on behalf of the internal host. The basic framework was scalable and easily extensible, allowing for the simple addition of new proxies as new Internet services and applications became popular. The FWTK has been extremely popular during the last eight years; over 50,000 downloads from six continents have been registered.

Although the FWTK software is available in source code and is free, you are not permitted to distribute it or make it available to anyone else without written permission from TIS. However, you are allowed to use it and even modify it to suit your own needs, as long as you use it for non-commercial purposes and only internally in your company.

There are some valuable Web resources for FWTK, including the `http://www.fwtk.org` Web site (see Figure 11.1), which features Keith Young's informative (and up-to-date) FAQ. There is also a mailing list for FTWK discussion. To subscribe to this mailing list, send a message to `majordomo@lists.nai.com` containing the text "subscribe fwtk-users" in the body of the message. After subscribing, you can send list messages to `fwtk-users@lists.nai.com`.

Figure 11.1   FWTK information clearinghouse on the Web

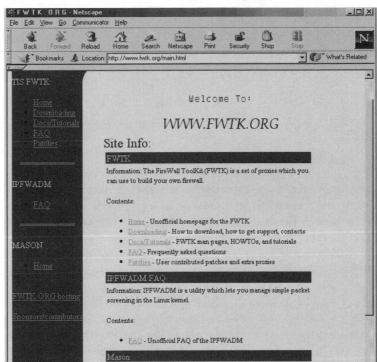

Installing the FWTK Firewall Toolkit

Due to the special terms and conditions in the licensing agreement, FWTK is only available for download via FTP from the TIS FTP site. You have to read the license, agree to it, and register your identity on their site before actually downloading the software. Start this process by reading the text file located at `ftp://ftp.tislabs.com/pub/firewalls/toolkit/LICENSE`.

After you've reviewed this license agreement and found it acceptable, send an e-mail to the address `fwtk-request@tislabs.com` that contains the word "accepted" as the only content in the body of the message. This message is processed automatically by TIS's mailer, which sends you a reply that contains the exact location from which to download the software; the directory location is arbitrary and will only exist for about 12 hours. Listing 11.1 contains an example of the e-mail you'll receive from TIS acknowledging your request.

Listing 11.1   TIS e-mail acknowledgment of license agreement

```
From: fwtk-req@tislabs.com
Date: Wed, 24 Jan 2001 08:18:08 -0500 (EST)
To: rhontanon@sybex.com
Subject: Response to your fwtk-request request

Thank you for your interest in our Firewall Toolkit. You will find
the current source in the following "hidden" directory on
ftp.tislabs.com:

/pub/firewalls/toolkit/dist/fwtk-02d13d

Please change directory directly to the entire path provided. This
Directory will exist for at least 12 hours. If you are unable to
download before this time period expires, you can send another
request to fwtk-request@tislabs.com to receive a new path.

If you are unable to establish a connection on ftp.tislabs.com,
your IP address may not have the appropriate reverse mapping of
address to hostname in the Domain Name System.

As a security precaution, we do not allow connections to our ftp
server that do not have this DNS information properly configured. Please
contact your System Administrator in regard to correcting
this.

-NAI Labs
```

NOTE   Note that in order for you to download the FWTK software, your host must have a valid reverse DNS (PTR) record. The TIS FTP server will not allow you to access it if it can't match your IP address to a known host name.

Once you receive the e-mail (it should only take 5–10 minutes), log on to the TIS FTP site (see Listing 11.2) and go to the directory specified in the body of the message. You need to download (in binary form) two files:

- The main FWTK distribution (`fwtk.tar.Z`)
- The documentation archive (`fwtk-doc-only.tar.Z`)

Listing 11.2   Downloading FWTK from the TIS FTP site

```
[ramon]$ ftp ftp.tislabs.com
Connected to portal.gw.tislabs.com.
```

```
220 portal FTP server (Version 5.60auth/mjr) ready.
500 'AUTH GSSAPI': command not understood.
Name (ftp.tislabs.com:hontanon): anonymous
Password:
230 Guest login ok, access restrictions apply.
Remote system type is UNIX.
Using binary mode to transfer files.
ftp> cd /pub/firewalls/toolkit/dist/fwtk-02d13d
ftp> dir fw*
227 Entering Passive Mode (192,94,214,101,194,195)
150 Opening ASCII mode data connection for /bin/ls.
-rw-r--r--   1 179 10   423991 Sep 13  1996 fwtk-doc-only.tar.Z
lrwxrwxrwx   1 0    1       13 Feb 27  1998 fwtk.tar.Z -> ⏎
fwtk2.1.tar.Z
-rw-r--r--   1 179 10   481055 Mar  2  1998 fwtk2.1.tar.Z
226 Transfer complete.
ftp> get fwtk-doc-only.tar.Z
local: fwtk-doc-only.tar.Z remote: fwtk-doc-only.tar.Z
227 Entering Passive Mode (192,94,214,101,194,190)
150 Opening BINARY mode data connection for fwtk-doc-only.tar.Z⏎
   (423991 bytes).
226 Transfer complete.
423991 bytes received in 3.2 seconds (1.3e+02 Kbytes/s)
ftp> get fwtk.tar.Z
local: fwtk.tar.Z remote: fwtk.tar.Z
227 Entering Passive Mode (192,94,214,101,194,194)
150 Opening BINARY mode data connection for fwtk.tar.Z (481055⏎
   bytes).
226 Transfer complete.
481055 bytes received in 3.1 seconds (1.5e+02 Kbytes/s)
ftp> quit
```

NOTE As of the writing of this book, the most current version of FTWK is 2.1, which dates back to early 1998. FTWK development is a volunteer effort, and although no resources have been available to work on it for the last three years, it's still surprisingly robust, even by today's security standards.

Once you have downloaded both files, simply decompress them and extract their contents. Both the source and document archives write files to an fwtk directory:

```
[ramon]$ uncompress fwtk-doc-only.tar.Z fwtk.tar.Z
[ramon]$ tar xf fwtk-doc-only.tar
```

```
[ramon]$ tar xf fwtk.tar
[ramon]$ cd fwtk
[ramon]$ ls -l
total 88
-rw-r-----    1 ramon    users    15984 Feb  5  1998 CHANGES
-rw-r-----    1 ramon    users     1465 Nov  4  1994 DISCLAIMER
-rw-r-----    1 ramon    users     5846 Mar 12  1997 LICENSE
-rw-r-----    1 ramon    users      989 Nov  4  1994 Makefile
-rw-r-----    1 ramon    users     2591 Mar  4  1997⏎
Makefile.config
-rw-r--r--    1 ramon    users     2660 Feb  5  1998⏎
Makefile.config.aix3
-rw-r-----    1 ramon    users     2626 Mar  4  1997⏎
Makefile.config.decosf
-rw-r--r--    1 ramon    users     2571 Mar  4  1997⏎
Makefile.config.hpux
-r--r--r--    1 ramon    users     3014 Jan 13  1998⏎
Makefile.config.linux
-rw-r-----    1 ramon    users     2696 Mar  4  1997⏎
Makefile.config.sco5
-rw-r--r--    1 ramon    users     2928 Mar  4  1997⏎
Makefile.config.solaris
-rw-r--r--    1 ramon    users     2600 Jul 15  1997⏎
Makefile.config.sunos
-rw-r-----    1 ramon    users     6969 Feb 26  1998 README
drwxr-x---    2 ramon    users     1024 Mar  1  1998 auth
-rw-r-----    1 ramon    users     3219 Nov  4  1994 auth.h
drwxr-x---    2 ramon    users     1024 Mar  1  1998 config
drwxr-xr-x    3 ramon    users     1024 Sep 12  1996 doc
-r--r-----    1 ramon    users     5389 Mar  1  1998 firewall.h
-rwxr-x---    1 ramon    users      791 Sep  5  1996 fixmake
drwxr-x---    2 ramon    users     1024 Mar  1  1998 ftp-gw
drwxr-x---    2 ramon    users     1024 Mar  1  1998 http-gw
drwxr-x---    2 ramon    users     1024 Mar  1  1998 lib
drwxr-x---    2 ramon    users     1024 Mar  1  1998 netacl
```

```
drwxr-x---    2 ramon    users     1024 Mar  1 1998 plug-gw
drwxr-x---    2 ramon    users     1024 Mar  1 1998 rlogin-gw
drwxr-x---    2 ramon    users     1024 Mar  1 1998 smap
drwxr-x---    2 ramon    users     1024 Mar  1 1998 smapd
-rw-r--r--    1 ramon    users     5526 Mar 26 1996 sysexits.h
drwxr-x---    2 ramon    users     1024 Mar  1 1998 tn-gw
drwxr-x---    5 ramon    users     1024 Jan 18 1997 tools
drwxr-x---    2 ramon    users     1024 Mar  1 1998 x-gw
```

As you can see, the FTWK distribution includes a number of preconfigured Makefile.config examples for several popular operating systems, including Linux. Note also that the source code for each of the proxies (ftp-gw, http-gw, etc.) is housed in a different subdirectory. Start by preserving the original Makefile.config file and moving the supplied Makefile.config.linux file in its place using the following commands:

[ramon]$ **mv Makefile.config Makefile.config.ORIG**

[ramon]$ **cp Makefile.config.linux Makefile.config**

TIP If you're building FWTK on Red Hat 7.0, you'll have to edit the resulting Makefile.config file and change the value of the XLIBDIR variable from /usr/X11/lib to /usr/X11R6/lib. In addition, you'll have to set the value of AUXLIB to -lcrypt and the value of DBMLIB to -lndbm.

You're now ready to compile, link, and install the package using the following two commands:

[ramon]$ **make**

[ramon]$ **sudo make install**

I found that the man pages do not get installed by default, so I copied them in place by hand:

[ramon]$ **cd doc/man**

[ramon]$ **sudo cp *.8 /usr/share/man/man8/**

[ramon]$ **sudo cp *.5 /usr/share/man/man5/**

[ramon]$ **sudo cp *.3 /usr/share/man/man3/**

The FWTK package installs both its executables and configuration files in the /usr/local/etc directory tree. Here's what this directory should look like once the FWTK package is completely installed:

[ramon]$ **ls -l /usr/local/etc**

```
total 14960
-rwxr-xr-x    1 root    root        1954587 Jan 28 14:28 ftp-gw
-rwxr-xr-x    1 root    root        2073268 Jan 28 14:28 http-gw
-rwxr-x---    1 root    root            362 Jan 28 14:28 mqueue
-rwxr-xr-x    1 root    root        1777157 Jan 28 14:28 netacl
-rw-r--r--    1 root    root           3101 Jan 28 14:28 netperm-table
-rwxr-xr-x    1 root    root        1866661 Jan 28 14:28 plug-gw
-rwxr-xr-x    1 root    root        1912963 Jan 28 14:28 rlogin-gw
-rwxr-xr-x    1 root    root        1794972 Jan 28 14:28 smap
-rwxr-xr-x    1 root    root        1697757 Jan 28 14:28 smapd
-rwxr-xr-x    1 root    root        1944219 Jan 28 14:28 tn-gw
-rwxr-xr-x    1 root    root         217794 Jan 28 14:28 x-gw
```

The FTWK developers subscribed to the *divide-and-conquer* approach to security software design. Instead of creating a single monolithic tool, they developed separate packages that work independently and provide separate services (e.g., FTP, Telnet, and HTTP). The advantage of this is that a vulnerability is only likely to affect one of the packages, and therefore will only compromise a single service running on your Linux system. This makes each FWTK component straightforward enough to be understood completely by the system administrator, and it even makes it possible for you to read the component's source code to verify its integrity and correctness, if necessary. Each of these applications will be discussed later in this chapter. For now, simply make sure that these files are present in the /usr/local/etc directory.

The next section of this chapter guides you through the process of preparing your system to act as an application layer firewall, and configuring the FTWK environment to provide the proxy service through your Linux server. The first step in that process is to understand the FWTK architectures.

FWTK Architectures

Deploying a successful application level proxy firewall starts by designing the overall architecture of your network and deciding where to place the firewall. This is just as important as placing a network layer firewall at the appropriate location of your network. Let's examine two popular options for deploying FTWK on a Linux server: single-homed proxy firewalls and dual-homed proxy firewalls.

Single-Homed Proxy Firewalls

If you are deploying an application layer firewall in addition to a network layer firewall device (for example, a Netfilter Linux firewall or a router with access control lists), use the FWTK proxy server as a bastion host on the DMZ segment of your network firewall, as illustrated in Figure 11.2.

Figure 11.2   Single-homed FWTK architecture

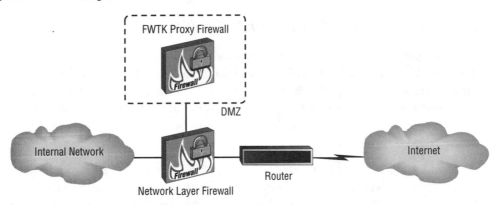

To use this architecture, make sure that your proxies are configured to accept internal proxy requests on the same Ethernet interface that you'll be using to forward them on to the Internet. Don't worry that using a single interface might make your server vulnerable to address spoofing; the network layer firewall handles the address filtering.

Dual-Homed Proxy Firewall

If the application layer firewall will be your only method of controlling access to your network, I recommend that you make the FTWK proxy server the only point of entry to your internal network from the public Internet. This can be accomplished by deploying a dual-homed proxy firewall, with one interface on your internal network and another interface on the same segment as the downstream interface of your Internet access router, as illustrated in Figure 11.3.

Figure 11.3   Dual-homed FWTK architecture

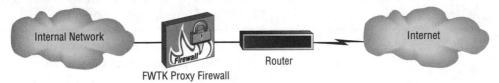

Perimeter Security

PART 4

The dual-homed proxy firewall configuration has the advantage that the hosts on your internal network do not have to use legal IP addresses as long as you don't plan to do any network layer routing between the two interfaces of your firewall (which I strongly discourage).

After selecting the architecture of the FWTK, it's time to configure the components that enforce your security policy and protect the resources of your internal network. This is the topic of the next section.

Configuring the FWTK Firewall Toolkit

The fundamental difference between a network layer firewall (as discussed in Chapter 9, "Network Layer Firewalls") and an application layer firewall is the method used to forward packets between the internal and the external interfaces. While a network layer firewall relies on the kernel to make forwarding decisions at the IP layer, an application layer firewall relies on proxies at the application stack to bridge two networks that are often not even directly routable.

To enhance the overall security stance of your proxy server, make sure you disable all IP forwarding on its kernel. This will keep any traffic from *leaking* through the proxy server at the network layer. To make sure of this, you need to issue the following command to disable IP forwarding by setting the `ip_forward` switch to `false`:

```
echo 0 > /proc/sys/net/ipv4/ip_forward
```

This command needs to be executed every time the system comes up. To make sure of this, I recommend that you add the preceding line to `/etc/rc.d/rc.local`.

In addition, make sure that your server is not listening for any connections other than the ones allowed by your security policy. Use your application layer firewall exclusively to proxy internal connections to the public network (e.g., the Internet). Once you have disabled all extraneous services on this server, issue the `netstat` command to see what services it is still listening for:

```
[ramon]$ netstat --inet -a | grep LISTEN
tcp        0      0 *:ssh                  *:*                      LISTEN
```

This sample output (I used `grep` to filter it to only show connections in the `LISTEN` state) shows that only Secure Shell (SSH) connections are being allowed into the proxy server. (SSH is discussed in the next Chapter 12, "Virtual Private Networking.")

NOTE I strongly discourage you from maintaining user accounts on the FTWK firewall server. The smaller your password file, the less vulnerable you are to intruders.

With forwarding disabled and listening services cut to the bare minimum, it is time to configure FTWK. The FTWK configuration is located in a central file named /usr/local/etc/netperm-table. This file contains two distinct types of rules:

- NetACL rules, which control which clients have access to which proxy services
- Gateway rules, which specify a variety of configuration parameters particular to each of the proxy services provided in FTWK

NetACL Rules

Rather than a proxy per se, NetACL is a supporting tool for other FWTK services. Similar in function to TCP Wrappers (discussed in Chapter 4, "Network Services Configuration"), NetACL provides access control and logging to TCP services based on the characteristics of the client requesting the connection. But the real power of NetACL is its ability to select different responding applications according to the identity of the requesting client. For example, you may want to configure your firewall such that whenever your workstation requests a service on port 23, you get the regular telnet daemon on the server (telnetd). However, whenever a regular user requests the same service, you want them to get the FWTK-provided telnet proxy application (tn-gw) instead. Start by inserting the lines in Listing 11.3 into the /etc/xinetd.d/telnet file.

Listing 11.3 *xinetd* configuration for *telnet*

```
service telnet
{
        flags          = REUSE
        socket_type    = stream
        wait           = no
        user           = root
        server         = /usr/local/etc/netacl
        server_args    = in.telnetd
        log_on_failure += USERID
        disable        = no
}
```

Insert the line in Listing 11.4 into the inetd configuration file, /etc/inetd.conf.

Listing 11.4 *inetd* configuration for *telnet*

```
telnet stream tcp nowait root /usr/local/etc/netacl netacl  in.telnetd
```

Perimeter Security

PART 4

Note that instead of invoking the daemon directly with the server directive, you invoke /usr/local/etc/netacl and pass the daemon name (in.telnetd) as a server argument. Don't forget to restart xinetd by issuing the command:

[ramon]$ **sudo /etc/rc.d/xinetd restart**

or its inetd equivalents:

```
[ramon]$ ps aux | grep inetd
root        466  0.0  0.0  1348    0 ?        SW   Mar17   0:00 [inetd]
[ramon]$ sudo kill -HUP 466
```

You then add the appropriate configuration to the /usr/local/etc/netperm-table file, according to the format

netacl-*daemon*: [permit-hosts|deny-hosts] *host-description* [-exec↵ *command*]

where *daemon* is the name of the server executable specified under server_args (see Listing 11.3), *host-description* is one or more IP addresses (or networks) and *command* is the full path to the server executable. Listing 11.5 contains an excerpt from the /usr/local/etc/netperm-table file that illustrates a sample NetACL configuraton for the telnet service.

Listing 11.5   Defining NetACL rules in the *netperm-table*

```
netacl-in.telnetd: permit-hosts 127.0.0.1 -exec /usr/sbin/in.telnetd
netacl-in.telnetd: permit-hosts 10.0.0.50 -exec /usr/sbin/in.telnetd
netacl-in.telnetd: permit-hosts 10.0.0.*  -exec /usr/local/etc/tn-gw
netacl-in.telnetd: deny-hosts *
```

The configuration in Listing 11.5 specifies that whenever the firewall receives a connection to port TCP 23 (telnet), it should examine the IP address of the connecting client. If the host trying to connect is the local host (127.0.0.1) or your workstation's IP address (10.0.0.50), you should see a regular telnet response (from the normal daemon). All other clients in your 10.0.0.* class-C network should be directed to the FWTK telnet proxy instead (tn-gw). Any other hosts (the ones matching the *host-description* *) will be denied service. tn-gw and other gateway proxies are discussed in the next section.

Gateway Rules

In addition to the NetACL utility, the FWTK includes a number of specialized application layer proxies that are installed as separate executables in the /usr/local/etc directory. These include the following proxies:

- tn-gw: the Telnet proxy for handling interactive terminal connections

- ftp-gw: the FTP proxy for handling File Transfer Protocol connections
- http-gw: the HTTP proxy for handling HTTP connections to a Web server
- plug-gw: a generic proxy that can be configured to handle any type of transport layer connection
- smap: an SMTP proxy for handling Internet mail server connections

Let's take a closer look at the rules that are available for each of these application layer proxies.

tn-gw: Telnet Proxy

The previous section described the NetACL rules and used telnet as an example to illustrate its operation. The FWTK telnet proxy is located by default in /usr/local/etc/tn-gw.

You'll need to configure your xinetd or inetd service to use the tn-gw proxy instead of the native telnet service. If your server uses xinetd, create a file called /etc/xinetd.d/telnet with the contents shown in Listing 11.6.

Listing 11.6 *xinetd* configuration for *telnet*

```
service telnet
{
        flags           = REUSE
        socket_type     = stream
        wait            = no
        user            = root
        server          = /usr/local/etc/tn-gw
        log_on_failure  += USERID
        disable         = no
}
```

If you use inetd, add the line shown in Listing 11.7 to the /etc/inetd.conf file.

Listing 11.7 *inetd* configuration for *telnet*

```
telnet stream tcp nowait root /usr/local/etc/tn-gw tn-gw
```

The basic operation of the telnet proxy is as follows:

1. The user is instructed, perhaps in your security policy, to connect via telnet to the private interface (or the only interface) of the proxy firewall instead of the target system.

Perimeter Security

PART 4

2. The user gets the following prompt (subject to access control and authentication):

   ```
   [ramon]$ telnet fwtk-internal.example.com
   Trying 10.0.0.2...
   Connected to fwtk-internal.
   Escape character is '^]'.
   Welcome to the TIS Firewall Toolkit TELNET Proxy!
   tn-gw->
   ```

3. The user types the external `telnet` command at the prompt:

   ```
   tn-gw-> connect anyhost.anydomain.com
   Trying 203.204.205.206 port 23...
   Connected to anyhost.anydomain.com.
   Escape character is '^]'.
   Red Hat Linux release 7.0 (Guinness)
   Kernel 2.2.16-22 on an i686
   login:
   ```

4. The user continues with the proxied connection until the remote escape command is entered. At that point, the connections to both the remote system and the proxy servers are torn down.

In addition to configuring NetACL, the `/usr/local/etc/netperm-table` file can also be used to control the behavior of the FWTK `telnet` proxy. There are several `/usr/local/etc/netperm-table` configuration arguments for the `telnet` proxy that you should be aware of. The general format for this proxy in the configuration file is

```
tn-gw: attribute-group
```

where *attribute-group* can have one of the following formats:

authserver *host port*   This format specifies a host and port running an authentication server. The configuration of the authentication server is covered in the "Using Strong Authentication with FWTK" section later in this chapter.

denial-msg *file*   This format specifies a file that contains a text message to be displayed when the user does not have the necessary permissions to use the proxy.

help-msg *file*   This format specifies a file that contains a text message to be displayed when the user requests help from the proxy.

welcome-msg *file*   This format specifies a file that contains a text message to be displayed when the user successfully logs on to the proxy.

denydest-msg *file*   This format specifies a file that contains a text message to be displayed when the user is not allowed to connect to the requested destination.

directory *directory*   This format specifies the directory to which to change the default root (chroot) before executing the proxy command.

userid *user*   This format specifies the user ID under which the proxy should run.

groupid *group*   This format specifies the group ID under which the proxy should run.

prompt *prompt*   This format specifies the prompt to be used by the proxy.

timeout *seconds*   This format specifies the idle time (in seconds) after which the proxy terminates the connection.

permit-hosts *host-description* [-dest *host-description*] [-auth][-passok]
This format specifies the hosts that are allowed to use the proxy (*host-description*), along with the destinations that they're allowed to proxy to (-dest *host-description*), whether they should provide authsrv authentication (-auth) to be granted use of the proxy, and whether they should be permitted to change their passwords (-passok). authsrv authentication is discussed in detail later in this chapter.   deny-hosts *host-description*   This format specifies the hosts that are not allowed to use the proxy.

For example, consider the portion of tn-gw configuration shown in Listing 11.8. This example performs several important steps:

- Specifies files containing text for denial, welcome, and help messages.
- Requests that the connections be terminated after 10 minutes of idle time.
- Allows proxy connections from clients in the 10.0.0.0/24 network, but only those destined for the 63.64.65.0/24 network.
- Disallows proxy requests coming from any other hosts.

Listing 11.8   Defining *tn-gw* rules in the *netperm-table*

```
tn-gw: denial-msg    /usr/local/etc/tn-deny.txt
tn-gw: welcome-msg   /usr/local/etc/tn-welcome.txt
tn-gw: help-msg      /usr/local/etc/tn-help.txt
tn-gw: timeout 600
tn-gw: permit-hosts 10.0.0.* -dest 63.64.65.*
tn-gw: deny-hosts *
```

Note that Listing 11.8 contains a specialized version of the deny-hosts attribute group:

```
tn-gw: deny-hosts unknown
```

This attribute forces the proxy to perform a reverse DNS lookup on the IP address of the client to look for a valid host name (a *PTR record*, in DNS lingo). If no such binding exists, the connection is denied.

ftp-gw: FTP Proxy

The ftp-gw FTP proxy works much the same way as tn-gw. Let's start by instructing your xinetd or inetd service to use ftp-gw instead of the native FTP service. If your server is using xinetd, do this by creating a file called /etc/xinetd.d/ftp with the contents shown in Listing 11.9.

Listing 11.9   *xinetd* configuration for FTP

```
service ftp
{
        flags           = REUSE
        socket_type     = stream
        wait            = no
        user            = root
        server          = /usr/local/etc/ftp-gw
        log_on_failure  += USERID
        disable         = no
}
```

If you use inetd, add the line shown in Listing 11.10 to the etc/inetd.conf file.

Listing 11.10   *inetd* configuration for FTP

```
ftp stream tcp nowait root /usr/local/etc/ftp-gw ftp-gw
```

Here is how the FTP proxy works:

1. The user is instructed, perhaps by your security policy, to point their FTP client to the private interface (or the only interface) of the proxy firewall, instead of the target system. In order to establish a connection to a public FTP server (such as ftp.sybex.com, for example), the user starts by entering the following (assuming that fwtk-internal.example.com is the host name corresponding to your proxy firewall's private interface):

   ```
   [ramon]$ ftp fwtk-internal.example.com
   Connected to fwtk-internal.
   220 fttk-internal.example.com FTP proxy (Version V2.1) ready.
   ```

```
Name (fwtk-internal:ramon):
```

2. The user provides the FTP proxy with the username and remote host name that they wish to FTP to. Note the *user@remote-hostname* format in the following response:

```
Name (fwtk-internal:ramon): anonymous@ftp.sybex.com

331-(----GATEWAY CONNECTED TO ftp.sybex.com----)

331-(220- kermit WAR-FTPD 1.67-04 Ready)

331-(220 Please enter your user name.)

331 User name okay. Give your full Email address as password.

Password:

230 User logged in, proceed.

ftp>
```

3. The user continues with the proxied connection until the remote escape command is entered (e.g., **bye** on FTP). At that point, the connections to both the remote system and the proxy servers are torn down.

The `/usr/local/etc/netperm-table` configuration arguments for the FTP proxy are very similar to their `telnet` equivalents:

```
ftp-gw: attribute-group
```

In this format, the *attribute-group* can be any of the constructs used for `tn-gw` (see the previous section), except for the following:

> permit-hosts *host-description* [-dest *host-description*] [-auth
> {*operation1 operation2…*}] [-authall] [-log {*operation1 operation2…*}]
> This format specifies the hosts that are allowed to use the proxy (*host-description*), along with the destinations that they're allowed to proxy to (-dest *host-description*), and whether they should provide authsrv authentication (-auth) for specific types of FTP operations, for example, retrieving a file (RETR) or uploading a file (STOR). The -authall attribute forces proxy users to authenticate themselves for *all* FTP operations.

> In addition, you can direct `ftp-gw` to log to `syslog` all attempts to perform any types of operations supported by the FTP protocol (e.g., RETR, STOR, etc.).

For example, consider the `/usr/local/etc/netperm-table` configuration in Listing 11.11. This example specifies a 10-minute idle timeout for proxied FTP connections and allows the 10.0.0.0/24 block to initiate FTP connections. You will log via the local `syslog` facility all attempts to retrieve and store a file on the remote FTP server.

Perimeter Security

PART 4

Listing 11.11 Defining *ftp-gw* rules in the *netperm-table*

```
ftp-gw:  timeout 600
ftp-gw:  permit-hosts 10.0.0.* -log { RETR STOR }
```

> **TIP** The RLOGIN proxy server (rlogin-gw) functions in a way that is virtually identical to the telnet gateway (tn-gw). However, I recommend that you avoid using the RLOGIN proxy server because fewer and fewer remote systems support this protocol and it is difficult to secure. For this reason, it is not covered in detail in this book.

http-gw: HTTP Proxy

The http-gw proxy can be used to relay HTTP requests from internal Web browsers to a Web server on the public network. You will need to modify your inetd (or xinetd) configuration to ensure that an http-gw session is started when a connection request is received on port 80 of the firewall . If your server is using xinetd, do this by creating a file called /etc/xinetd.d/http with the contents shown in Listing 11.12.

Listing 11.12 *xinetd* configuration for HTTP

```
service http
{
        flags            = REUSE
        socket_type      = stream
        wait             = no
        user             = root
        server           = /usr/local/etc/http-gw
        log_on_failure   += USERID
        disable          = no
}
```

If you use inetd, add the line shown in Listing 11.13 to the /etc/inetd.conf file.

Listing 11.13 *inetd* configuration for HTTP

```
http stream tcp nowait root /usr/local/etc/http-gw http-gw
```

Upon restarting inetd (or xinetd), your firewall will start accepting HTTP requests on behalf of your internal clients. Figure 11.4 shows the HTTP Proxy configuration on Netscape Communicator. Figure 11.5 shows how to configure an HTTP Proxy on Microsoft Internet Explorer.

In these two examples, you are instructing the browser to proxy incoming HTTP connections to port 80 of fwtk-internal.example.com, the host name that corresponds to the internal (private) interface of the FTWK proxy server. Note that you've entered the `internal.com` domain in the Exceptions box. This instructs the browser not to use this proxy for connections to hosts whose names end in `internal.com`. The assumption is that these are internal hosts that do not need to be scrutinized by the proxy server.

Figure 11.4   Netscape Communicator HTTP Proxy Configuration

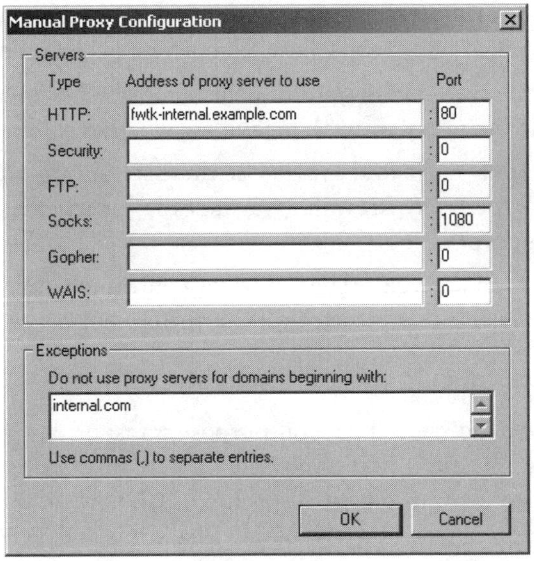

Figure 11.5   Microsoft Internet Explorer HTTP Proxy Configuration

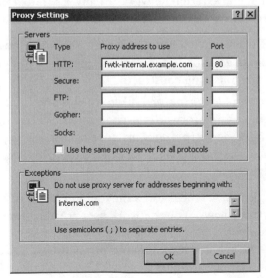

The /usr/local/etc/netperm-table configuration arguments for the HTTP proxy are similar to their telnet equivalents:

    http-gw: *attribute-group*

In this format, the *attribute-group* can be the same constructs used for tn-gw, with the following differences:

default-policy *option* [*options*]   This format specifies which filter rule to apply to active content. The *options* value can be one of the following:

-java, -nojava   These options determine whether to allow Java content to traverse the proxy firewall (-java) or whether to block it (-nojava).

-javascript, -nojavascript   Use these settings to allow JavaScript content to traverse the proxy firewall (-javascript) or whether to block it (-nojavascript).

-activex, -noactivex   These settings control whether you should allow ActiveX controls (-activex) or block them (-noactivex).

plug-gw: The General-Purpose TCP Proxy

The *plug* proxy, or plug-gw, is a general-purpose transport layer proxy mechanism that is used to tunnel applications that don't enjoy native support by an FWTK proxy. The plug works by accepting traffic from a specified TCP port on the private side and forwarding the request to a specified destination IP address and TCP port on the public side according to a set of access control rules. This is useful for situations where you don't need the fine control and logging provided by a real application layer proxy, but you want to keep your internal and external networks totally separate nonetheless (perhaps because your internal network does not use legal IP addresses).

As with any other FWTK proxies, plug-gw looks in the /usr/local/etc/netperm-table for its configuration. In addition to the standard constructs outlined for tn-gw, the plug-gw proxy supports the following construct:

port *port-id host-description* [-plug-to-host *host-name*]   This construct specifies the rule used to forward the connection. When the request comes in over *port-id*, the *host-description* is matched against the requesting IP address. If there is a match, the connection is forwarded to the host name specified in the -plug-to-host option.

For example, consider a case where you want your internal hosts to connect to your ISP's NNTP server to retrieve news. Your network uses private addresses, and you want to control NNTP access so that your ISP's news server only receives connections from a single public address (the public address of your proxy firewall). You can simply instruct your users to point their newsreaders to port TCP 119 (standard NNTP port) of your firewall, which then forwards the requests to port 119 of your ISP's NNTP server. The following /usr/local/etc/netperm-table entry accomplishes this:

```
plug-gw: port 119 10.0.0.* -plug-to nntp-server.example.com
```

This entry redirects all requests from network 10.0.0.0/24 to 119 of the firewall to the same port of server nttp-server.example.com.

> **NOTE** This is especially useful for dealing with ISPs that limit their customers' NNTP connections to only a small number of IP addresses. You will, in fact, always be connecting from the same address, the external address of the FWTK firewall.

smap: SMTP Mail Proxy

The FWTK includes an SMTP application proxy called smap that accepts incoming mail connections using the smap executable. Mail messages are cached on the firewall system until they are picked up by the periodically running smapd executable. smapd then hands off the incoming messages to the local mail transport agent (MTA), typically Sendmail.

This store-and-forward processing prevents would-be attackers from gaining real-time access to the local MTA, thereby reducing the risk of popular exploits like a buffer over-flow on the Sendmail daemon. The smapd application "wakes up" every 60 seconds (by default), and only forwards the spooled messages to the local MTA after performing an exhaustive inspection of the mail headers, failing to forward any message that is mal-formed or otherwise suspicious.

You will need to configure inetd (or xinetd) on your server to ensure that an smap session is started when a connection request is received on port 25 (SMTP) of the external interface of the proxy server. To accomplish this, simply substitute smap for tn-gw in Listing 11.6 or 11.7.

Next, make sure that you have configured the /usr/local/etc/netperm-table file with the appropriate smap/smapd configuration. The general entry for the smap proxy lines in the configuration file is of the type

```
smap: attribute-group
```

In addition to the standard attributes outlined for tn-gw, the *attribute-group* field can take the following construct:

directory *directory* This construct specifies the *directory* where smap should store incoming messages before smapd processes them.

You can also configure the operation of the smapd daemon by using lines of the type

```
smapd: attribute-group
```

There are five constructs that are specific to the smapd configuration:

directory *directory*   This construct specifies the directory where smapd should look for incoming messages spooled by smap.

sendmail *program*   This construct instructs smapd to use the mail transport agent in *program* (e.g., Sendmail) to deliver mail to its destination.

badadmin *user*   This construct specifies the user to which the smapd server should forward mail that it cannot deliver.

baddir *directory*   This construct specifies the directory to which the smapd server saves any spooled mail that it cannot deliver normally.

wakeup *seconds*   This construct instructs the smapd daemon to wake up and process the waiting mail queue at the interval specified by *seconds*. By default, smapd wakes up every 60 seconds.

Using Strong Authentication with FWTK

When configuring one of the FTWK proxies, the administrator has the option to force the user to authenticate to the proxy server itself before requesting a remote connection. For example, the netperm-table line

```
tn-gw: permit-hosts 204.205.206.* -dest safehost.example.com -auth
```

states that users on any host in the 204.205.206.0/24 network are allowed to connect to the telnet gateway and connect to host name safehost.example.com, but only if the users can authenticate themselves to the proxy first using a valid set of credentials (-auth option).

The authsrv subsystem is responsible for handling this type of authentication within FWTK.

authsrv

The authsrv daemon is an authentication facility for the use of any of the FTWK proxies. It maintains a database with a record for each known proxy user. The record consists of the following fields:

Username   The username field is the unique user description that characterizes each proxy user.

User Group   The user group field is the primary group to which the user belongs.

Full Name   The full name field represents the name of the user in first, middle initial, last format (e.g., Ramon J. Hontanon).

Last Successful Proxy Login   The last successful proxy login field contains a reference to the last date when the user was able to log on to the proxy successfully.

Authentication Mechanism to be Used for That User   The following authentication mechanisms are supported:

- RSA SecureID challenge/response and timed token authentication
- Digital Pathways' Secure Net Key (SNK), a challenge response system
- BellCore's S/Key one-time password system
- Reusable passwords

authsrv can be instructed to use one of these mechanisms for authenticating a particular user by specifying the proper value for the proto option in the authsrv utility command (see the proto command syntax in Table 11.1).

Regardless of the authentication mechanism defined for each user, the authsrv daemon can handle the creation, modification, disablement, or deletion of user entries through the use of the authsrv administrative utility, described later in this section.

Let's start the configuration of the authsrv daemon by entering the appropriate configuration in the /etc/xinetd.d/authsrv file (see Listing 11.14).

Listing 11.14   *xinetd* Configuration for *authsrv*

```
service authsrv
{
        flags           = REUSE
        socket_type     = stream
        wait            = no
        user            = root
        server          = /usr/local/etc/authsrv
        log_on_failure  += USERID
        disable         = no
}
```

If your system uses inetd, add the line in Listing 11.15 to the /etc/inetd.conf file.

Listing 11.15   *inetd* configuration for *authsrv*

```
authsrv stream tcp nowait root /usr/local/etc/authsrv authsrv
```

Note that in order for your server to recognize the authsrv keyword as a service, you have to create the following authsrv entry in /etc/services:

```
authsrv    7777/tcp
```

Upon restarting the xinetd service, you'll have a working authsrv daemon listening for connections on port TCP 7777. Define the authsrv options in your /usr/local/etc/ netperm-table file. The general entry in the configuration file is of the type

>   authsrv: *attribute-group*

In addition to the standard attributes outlined for tn-gw, the *attribute-group* field can take one of the following constructs:

directory *directory*   This construct specifies the directory to be used as the working directory before executing the proxy command.

badsleep *seconds*   This construct specifies the amount of time in seconds that a user who has failed authentication five times in a row should be blocked from authenticating again.

database *path*   This construct specifies the path to the authentication database file.

nobogus true   This construct specifies whether the authentication server should report when an attempt is made to log on with a non-existent user.

{permit | deny}-operation {user *users* **| group** *groups*} *service destination* **[options] [time** *start end* **]**   This construct specifies whether certain operations are permitted or denied for a particular user or group at a particular time of the day.

secureidhost *firewall*   This construct specifies the firewall name to be used for RSA SecureID authentication.

For example, consider the excerpt from /usr/local/etc/netperm-table in Listing 11.16. This configuration in this example

- Instructs authsrv to only allow connections from the local firewall host, which is a good idea.

- Shows that the database file is in the directory /usr/local/etc/fw-authdb.

- Shows that users who have failed authentication should be banned from the service for 20 minutes.

- Instructs authsrv to report attempts to log on with a non-existent user.

Listing 11.16   Defining *authsrv* rules in the *netperm-table*

```
authsrv: permit-hosts localhost
authsrv: database /usr/local/etc/fw-authdb
authsrv: badsleep 1200
authsrv: nobogus true
```

The next step is to enter the authsrv command by hand (as the root user) to create users in the database. Suppose you want to create a new username toro that will use password authentication. As you can see in Listing 11.17, you enter the authsrv interface and are immediately greeted by the authsrv# prompt. At that prompt, you start by adding the new username toro with its full name (Toro T. Bravo). By default, new users are disabled, so you need to explicitly enable the newly entered user (enable toro). You then specify the authentication protocol to be used by the toro username. Finally, you specify the initial password to be used. The list command allows you to view the users that are currently in the authsrv database.

Listing 11.17 Creating a new user in the *authsrv* authentication database

```
[ramon]$ sudo /usr/local/etc/authsrv
authsrv# list
Report for users in database
user       group      longname      status proto      last
----       -----      --------      ------ -----      ----
authsrv# adduser toro 'Toro T. Bravo'
ok - user added initially disabled
authsrv# enable toro
enabled
authsrv# proto toro password
changed
authsrv# pass toro 'sctPassW0rd'
Password for toro changed.
authsrv# list
Report for users in database
user       group      longname      status proto      last
----       -----      --------      ------ -----      ----
toro                  Toro T. Bravo   y    passw      never
authsrv# exit
```

Table 11.1 lists all the commands available in the authsrv interface.

Table 11.1 *authsrv* Commands

Command	Description
adduser *user* [*full-name*]	Adds *user* to the authentication database with an optional *full-name*.
deluser *user*	Removes *user* from the authentication database.

Table 11.1 *authsrv* Commands *(continued)*

Command	Description
disable *user*	Disable *user* from the authentication database.
enable *user* [onetime]	Enable a user (*user*) that has been previously disabled. It the onetime option is present, the user is only disabled for one more authentication.
display *user*	Display the status, the authentication protocol, and the last login for the specified user.
group *user group*	Assigns *user* to the specified *group*.
list *group*	Display all the users who are members of *group*.
passwd *user* [*passwd-text*]	Sets the password for user to the optional *passwd-text*. If *passwd-text* is not supplied, you will be prompted for it.
proto *user protocol*	Sets the authentication *protocol* for user to *user*. The *protocol* field must have one of the following values: "secureid" (RSA SecureID token authentication) "snk" (Digital Pathways Secure Net Key), "skey" (BellCore S/Key one-time password system), or "password" (traditional reusable password).
rename *user newuser* [*full-name*]	Change the username in *user* to *newuser* and change their *full-name* if supplied.
exit	Quit the authsrv utility.

You are now ready to configure your proxies with the auth option in /usr/local/etc/ netperm-table. For example, consider the configuration for the FTP proxy (ftp-gw) in Listing 11.18. The first line instructs the FTP proxy to authenticate users by contacting the local host on port TCP 7777. The second line allows the trusted network 10.0.0.0/24 to use the FTP proxy, but requires authentication to those users who choose to upload files (the FTP STOR operation). The last line requires all other (untrusted) users to authenticate themselves to the proxy.

Listing 11.18   Using *authsrv* authentication in *ftp-gw* rules

```
ftp-gw: authserver localhost 7777
ftp-gw: permit-hosts 10.0.0.* -auth {STOR}
ftp-gw: permit-hosts * -authall
```

In Sum

This chapter focused its attention of the FWTK firewall toolkit, a collection of processes and configuration files that can be used to build your own application layer firewall. By working a layer above the SOCKS proxy that was discussed in the last chapter, the FTWK toolkit can add some high-level access control mechanisms, allowing security administrators to apply different access rules to each of the applications that they need to support.

FWTK includes ready-made proxies for the most popular Linux network applications like Telnet, FTP, HTTP, and SMTP, along with a general-purpose proxy that can be used to forward arbitrary applications through the firewall. The smap/smapd proxy provides a true store-and-forward mail delivery mechanism, where mail can be spooled at the firewall and forwarded to the target system asynchronously.

This chapter closes out the discussion on perimeter security and firewall devices. The next and final part of this book focuses on a topic of increasing importance in today's global and roaming workplace: remote access and authentication.

Perimeter Security

PART 4

Part 5

Remote Access and Authentication

Featuring:

- Understanding VPN Technology and the IPsec Protocol
- Implementing IPsec VPNs with FreeS/WAN
- Using Linux as a PPTP Server with PoPToP
- Replacing Telnet with OpenSSH
- Configuring the Kerberos V5 Authentication System
- Implementing One-Time Passwords Using OPIE
- Understanding Linux Pluggable Authentication Modules (PAMs)

12

Virtual Private Networking

Just when you think you understand the basics of multi-layered security and your Linux network is protected by a good policy and set of mechanisms, along comes remote access to make security even more of a challenge. As the 20th century came to a close, so did the idea of local area networks (LANs). The traditional office expanded to include the *home* office, and now it has been replaced by the *virtual* office. Your users are no longer happy just dialing in to a pool of modems to get their mail; they now expect you to extend the boundaries of your network to their laptops, home PCs, and even personal digital assistants (PDAs), using both wired and wireless technologies.

The challenge is to embrace the global remote access model without compromising the security of your network. The emphasis should be on a comprehensive security policy that covers the cases where the users will not be physically at the corporate location, and that includes clear provisions for authentication, authorization, and access control.

Part 5 of this book, "Remote Access and Authentication," contains two chapters that look at this brave new world of roaming users and telecommuters and describes a number of packages and configurations that can be deployed to provide convenient remote access while ensuring the privacy and integrity of your data. This chapter is devoted to the discussion of virtual private networks (VPNs). This technology is universally expected to be the fastest growing area of IP networking in the next three to five years, due to its clear economic advantage over dedicated private network facilities and the ubiquitous nature of the VPN enabling technology. Chapter 13 covers the topic of "Strong User Authentication," a concept that goes hand in hand with both secure remote access and virtual private networking.

Let's dive right in by explaining the concept of VPNs and introducing the basic terminology you need to be aware of.

A VPN Primer

Consider a company named ACME Enterprises that has four separate geographical locations: Sales in Boston, Engineering in Washington, Human Resources in Denver, and Marketing in Los Angeles. In the traditional wide area network (WAN) model, ACME's IT organization would have to lease, maintain, and support six dedicated WAN links to have a full mesh network, with the associated distance-sensitive telephone company charges in order to ensure full connectivity among all four of its branches. (Figure 12.1 illustrates this situation.) Chances are that at least two of these locations (Sales and Marketing) are going to need access to the Internet, so ACME's IT department will also have to lease two dedicated circuits to the nearest ISP hub.

Figure 12.1   ACME's WAN connections

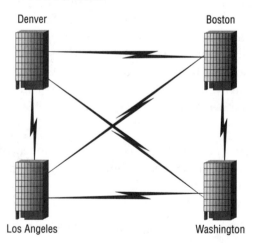

This setup is less than ideal. The Boston (Sales) and Los Angeles (Marketing) branches have two separate leased lines for private data and Internet access. And that is only the beginning. The real inefficiency of this approach is in evidence whenever ACME decides to branch out to a new location. Let's say that an ACME manufacturing facility is opened in Seattle. The IT department must now purchase dedicated lines from Seattle to all four existing branches. Furthermore, the more branches that ACME opens up, the more prohibitive it becomes to connect them to the existing locations via dedicated leased lines.

Virtual private networking capitalizes on the ubiquity of the Internet to offer a cost-effective, distance-insensitive alternative to private WAN links. There are two steps to building a VPN:

- Connect all branches to the Internet by purchasing a connection to an ISP with a local *point of presence (POP)*, also known as a *hub*.

- Once all branches can reach each other via the Internet, build *virtual* links over the existing Internet IP infrastructure to ensure the confidentiality and integrity of the data as it travels from branch to branch.

Figure 12.2 shows the ACME WAN network using a VPN design.

Figure 12.2   ACME's VPN connections

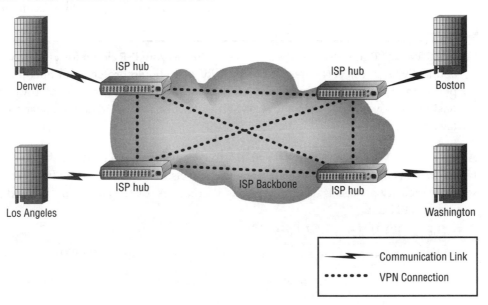

The advantages of VPNs over dedicated leased lines are three-fold:

Distance-Independent Connection Costs   The fact that each new corporate branch can connect to the other branches using an Internet connection, regardless of the location of the rest of the branches, reduces cost. The cost of the local loop is kept to a minimum and is often bundled into the monthly charges from the ISP. In addition, some ISPs offer discounts with quantity connection orders and now all of the offices have Internet access also, but this would not be a benefit in some cases.

Remote Access and Authentication

PART 5

Topology-Independent Connection Costs   Corporate WANs come in three flavors:

- *hub-and-spoke*, where all branches connect only to a central office
- *fully meshed*, where all branches are fully interconnected to one another.
- *partially meshed*, where branches are connected to one another according to business needs.

The fully meshed topology realizes the highest savings when deployed using VPN technology. Since each new branch is simply being connected to the Internet, the cost to incorporate the second branch is the same as connecting the 20th branch or the 200th branch.

Reuse of Existing Internet Connections   Connections to the Internet are now as necessary to conduct business as fax machines and package delivery. VPN technology allows your enterprise to use a single circuit for both private corporate communications and general Internet access, provided that you have configured the separation of both traffic types properly (more on that later in this chapter).

WARNING   Regardless of whether you'll be using your ISP circuit for VPN-only connectivity, or for VPN+Internet connectivity, you should protect your network perimeter by installing a firewall device. Chapters 9, 10, and 11 show you how to design, deploy and maintain a firewall at the network, transport, and application layers respectively.

At the heart of VPN technology is the ability to encapsulate VPN traffic inside normal IP traffic in order to protect the private data as it travels through the public Internet. Two separate security protocols have emerged as alternatives for the encapsulation and protection of VPN data:

- The IETF's *IP Security (IPsec)*
- Microsoft Corporation's *Point-to-Point Tunneling Protocol (PPTP)*

The following two sections are devoted to the discussion of these two specifications.

The IP Security Protocol (IPsec)

Defined in detail in RFCs 2401 through 2412, the IP Security framework (IPsec for short) is the IETF's response to an Internet community that has been shouting for such a standard for quite a long time. While only mandatory in IPv6 implementations, IPsec has seen its way to a good number of IPv4 stacks, and most network security software vendors have embraced the IPsec technology to some extent. Rather than mandating a specific type of encryption or hashing technology, IPsec is a framework used by both ends of the connection to select security parameters for that session. This makes the IPsec standard more durable because it can accommodate new algorithms for data privacy, integrity, and authentication as the existing ones become obsolete or are found to be vulnerable.

Before IPsec-formatted packets can be exchanged, both peers must agree on a security association (SA) that contains a set of parameters that include

- cryptographic algorithms
- key expiration time
- encapsulation type
- compression

While this negotiation can take place manually, yielding static SAs, a more secure and practical way to establish these parameters is to use the Internet Key Exchange (IKE) protocol. When two IPsec peers support IKE, they can negotiate the SAs on the fly just before the secure communication takes place, provided that they have a way to authenticate each other. This authentication is accomplished using either shared secrets (preloaded at each end), or using a public-key infrastructure that includes digital certificates. The actual agreement on session keys (which are ephemeral) is based on the famous Diffie-Hellman algorithm.

The session-key agreement process starts when both endpoints on the connection generate a private/public key pair and share their public keys with each other. Next, both endpoints perform a mathematical calculation using their own secret key and the remote public key as input. This is a critical part of the Diffie-Hellman algorithm because this calculation should yield the same result at both ends. While this shared value could be used to encrypt actual transmission data, it is more efficient for one of the endpoints to make up a symmetric key, encrypt it with the shared value from the previous calculation, and send it to the other endpoint, which decrypts it and stores it. This symmetric key can then be used as the session key for the symmetric algorithm negotiated during the SA agreement phase. Some examples of symmetric encryption algorithms are DES, Triple DES, IDEA, and Blowfish.

Once the SAs are in place and both endpoints have agreed to a session key, the actual secure data exchange can take place. The heart of IPsec is its ability to take a private IP packet and either encapsulate it completely into another IP packet or append to its header enough information to ensure its integrity. Let's take a closer look at both of these options.

IP Authentication Header

As your traffic travels though the Internet, it is subject to a number of vulnerabilities, including one where an attacker modifies the content of your IP packets. This is easy to do in the current Internet model, a store-and-forward architecture where your packet is guaranteed to traverse a number of intermediary systems over which you have no control. One way to ensure that the content of your IP packets is not altered along the way is to affix a header with a one-way hash value of the state of the original packet. This header is called an *authentication header (AH)*. If an attacker modifies the packet, the receiver is aware that this has happened because the hash value included in the header does not match the end state of the packet.

The IETF has created a formal protocol for this AH, which is inserted by the IPsec-aware sender between the IP and TCP headers before the packet is sent out (see Figure 12.3). This field contains a number of indexes and parameters for processing by the remote end, but at the heart of the AH is a hash value that is computed using the entire IP packet as its input. Although IPsec in general is built to accommodate new hashing algorithms, the RFC2402 specification mandates the support of MD5 and SHA-1 algorithms for the implementation to be standards compliant.

Figure 12.3   IPsec AH packet format

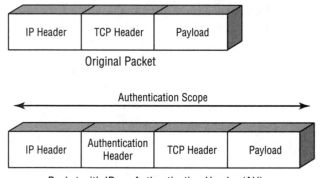

IP Encapsulating Security Payload (ESP)
==

IP Encapsulating Security Payload (ESP)

While the AH solves the problem of IP packet integrity and authentication, it does not address the issue of confidentiality. In many cases, you need to make sure that nobody is gaining unauthorized access to the payload of your IP packets as they travel over an untrusted network. The IP Encapsulated Security Payload (ESP) specification allows for a security gateway to completely encapsulate a private outgoing packet before it travels via the public Internet. This can be done in one of two ways: ESP transport mode and ESP tunnel mode.

ESP Transport Mode

You can use ESP transport mode to protect the payload of IP packets exchanged between two security gateways that are implementing IPsec security. When ESP transport mode is used, the security gateway inserts an ESP header between the original IP and TCP headers (see Figure 12.4). This header contains a pointer to the security association (SA) that was negotiated between the two security gateways, as well as to the pointers to the next ESP packet that the endpoint should expect.

Figure 12.4   IPsec ESP transport mode packet format

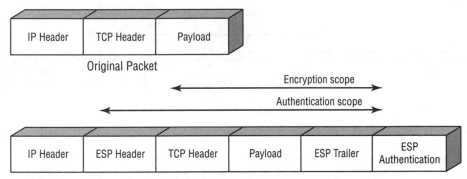

After the TCP header and TCP payload, the security gateway inserts an ESP trailer that contains a variable number of padding characters to make sure the packet to be protected is of a fixed length.

Finally, the security gateway appends an ESP authentication value consisting of a hash value calculated using the entire ESP packet (minus the authentication value) as the input. This works similarly to the AH protocol and ensures the integrity of the packet.

Note that ESP encrypts the contents of the original TCP header and payload and ensures the authentication of the entire ESP packet.

ESP Tunnel Mode

Note that ESP transport mode protects the TCP header and TCP payload of the original packet, but it does not protect the original IP header. If you need to ensure the confidentiality, integrity, and authentication of the entire original IP packet, you should opt for ESP tunnel mode. ESP tunnel mode effectively encapsulates the entire IP packet and inserts it into a brand new packet whose source IP address is typically the externally reachable address of the security gateway that is doing the IPsec encapsulation.

The ESP tunnel mode packet format, illustrated in Figure 12.5, is similar to the format used for ESP transport mode, except for the fact that the original IP header is also authenticated and encrypted.

Figure 12.5 IPsec ESP tunnel mode packet format

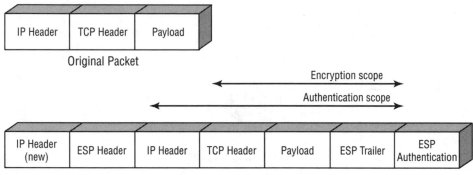

Another advantage of ESP tunnel mode is that packets originating from an IPsec-protected network need not use legal Internet addresses because those addresses will be effectively "hidden" while the packet is in transit over the Internet.

While the ESP specification (defined in RFC2406) allows for new encryption algorithms to be used, it also mandates that IPsec-conformant implementations include support for the DES encryption algorithm, as well as for the MD5 and SHA-1 authentication algorithms mentioned earlier in this chapter in the section "IP Authentication Headers." Since the strength of the DES algorithm has been brought into question recently, most IPsec software vendors typically support stronger encryption algorithms such as 3DES, IDEA, and Blowfish.

As is usually the case, the Linux open-source community has stepped up to develop a robust implementation of the IPsec standard. The FreeS/WAN Linux IPsec package is the topic of discussion in the next section of this chapter.

FreeS/WAN

Project leader John Gilmore started the FreeS/WAN development in 1996 as an attempt to "secure 5% of the Internet traffic against passive wiretapping." The Free Secure Wide Area Network (FreeS/WAN) thus aims to make every Linux server a VPN-capable host using the standard IETF IPsec protocol to ensure the confidentiality, integrity, and authentication of IP communications. Due to the once rigid U.S. restrictions governing the export of cryptographic material, most of the original FreeS/WAN development has taken place outside of the U.S. In fact, just to be on the safe side, the FreeS/WAN developers have also avoided any assistance from any U.S. citizens or residents.

Obtaining FreeS/WAN

The FreeS/WAN software is available in source code format under the GPL licensing agreement. While a limited number of Linux distributions (SuSE, Connectiva, and Polished, for example) offer the FreeS/WAN package as part of the standard installation, most distributions do not, especially the ones based in the U.S. There is quite a bit to learn in the process of installing FreeS/WAN so I recommend that you download the source distribution from the official site and build it yourself. FreeS/WAN is available from `http://www.freeswan.org` (see Figure 12.6).

Figure 12.6   The official FreeS/WAN Web site

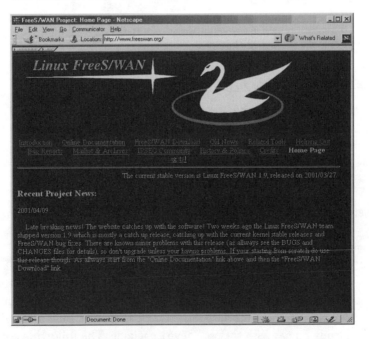

You can either download the distribution following the links on the FreeS/WAN Web site or obtain it right from the FTP site using the following commands:

```
[ramon]$ cd /usr/src
[ramon]$ sudo ftp ftp.xs4all.nl
Connected to reflectix.xs4all.nl.
```

```
220 reflectix.xs4all.nl FTP server (Version wu-2.6.1(12) Tue Oct 10
18:09:22 CEST 2000) ready.

Name (ftp.xs4all.nl:ramon): anonymous

331 Guest login ok, send your complete e-mail address as password.

Password:

230-Welkom op de FTP server van XS4ALL

230---------------------------------

230 Guest login ok, access restrictions apply.

Remote system type is UNIX.

Using binary mode to transfer files.

ftp> cd pub/crypto/freeswan

250 CWD command successful.


ftp> get freeswan-1.8.tar.gz

local: freeswan-1.8.tar.gz remote: freeswan-1.8.tar.gz

227 Entering Passive Mode (194,109,6,26,80,118)

150 Opening BINARY mode data connection for freeswan-1.8.tar.gz
(1447587 bytes).

226 Transfer complete.

1447587 bytes received in 96.2 secs (15 Kbytes/sec)

ftp> bye
```

The next step is to decompress and expand the archive file that you've just downloaded:

```
[ramon]$ sudo tar -xzf freeswan-1.8.tar.gz

[ramon]$ cd freeswan-1.8
```

Before proceeding to the FreeS/WAN installation, make sure that you have the gmp-devel RPM package installed on your system. This is the GNU Arbitrary Precision Math library. Most distributions come with the libgmp.so library, but you need the header file gmp.h, which only comes with the gmp-devel package. The following command installs the RPM version of the gmp-devel package on your system:

```
[ramon]$ sudo rpm -i gmp-devel-3.0.1-5.i386.rpm
```

Now you're ready to install the FreeS/WAN software itself. The first step in installing the FreeS/WAN software builds a modified Linux kernel.

Installing FreeS/WAN

There are four fundamental pieces to the FreeS/WAN software distribution:

- Kernel source patches and additions
- The IKE daemon, which is called pluto
- A set of scripts to manage the package
- Man pages and configuration files

Start by installing the kernel patches. Go to the /usr/src/freeswan directory and enter the make xgo command:

```
[ramon]$ cd /usr/src/freeswan-1.8
```

```
[ramon]$ sudo make xgo
```

To install the FreeS/WAN software, you need a valid source tree because the make xgo command rebuilds the kernel. I recommend that you download the kernel source, including the headers, for your distribution and build a standard kernel before running make xgo. Downloading the kernel source and headers allows you to become familiar with the kernel-building process before you modify the kernel to suit the needs of FreeS/WAN. This saves you from having to debug issues related to building your kernel. The make xgo command requires the same input as any kernel-building process. Make the kernel changes appropriate to your system's hardware and save the configuration changes.

WARNING Make sure to save the configuration changes, even if you have not modified any of the default kernel values.

As you exit the graphical interface of the make xgo command, the system starts the kernel recompilation with the new patches. This can take anywhere from a few minutes to several hours depending on your CPU speed, the amount of RAM on your system, and the types of disk drives. At the end of the compilation, you should see the following two lines:

```
make[1]: Leaving directory `/usr/src/linux-2.2.16'
utils/errcheck out.kbuild
```

If your results are different, the chances are that something went wrong in the kernel build. Check out the out.kbuild file for information on the problem. If all went well, finish up the kernel installation process from the same directory with the following command:

```
[ramon]$ sudo make kinstall
```

Remote Access and Authentication

PART 5

This is equivalent to issuing the following traditional kernel-building steps:

```
make
make install
make modules
make modules_install
```

As with the previous step, if all went well, you should see the following two lines at the bottom of the screen:

```
make[1]: Leaving directory `/usr/src/linux-2.2.16'
utils/errcheck out.kinstall
```

If you have already built and installed this version of the kernel before (which I strongly recommend), your /etc/lilo.conf file should not need to be modified. Simply rerun the lilo command:

```
[ramon]$ sudo /sbin/lilo
```

Then reboot your system. Upon startup, you should see messages of the type

```
klips_debug:ipsec_tunnel_init: initialisation of device: ipsec0
```

and you should verify that the IKE daemon (**pluto**) is active:

```
[ramon]$ ps -ef | grep pluto
root     490   1  0 20:43 ?  00:00:00 /usr/local/lib/ipsec/pluto --
deb
```

In addition, you may want to make sure that your system now has at least one virtual IPsec interface:

```
[ramon]$ ifconfig ipsec0
ipsec0    Link encap:IPIP Tunnel  HWaddr
          NOARP  MTU:0  Metric:1
          RX packets:0 errors:0 dropped:0 overruns:0 frame:0
          TX packets:0 errors:0 dropped:0 overruns:0 carrier:0
          collisions:0 txqueuelen:10
```

If everything looks to be in place, go on to the next section and begin configuring your IPsec connections!

Configuring FreeS/WAN

If you have made it this far, your system is currently IPsec enabled and is ready to be configured to establish secure connections with other Linux servers.

This section uses the WAN vs. IPsec scenario depicted in Figures 12.1 and 12.2 as an example. Consider that you have placed Linux servers as perimeter devices doing network layer filtering in both the Denver and the Boston locations. The conceptual diagram of this scenario is illustrated in Figure 12.7.

Figure 12.7   Using Linux FreeS/WAN to implement a dedicated VPN connection

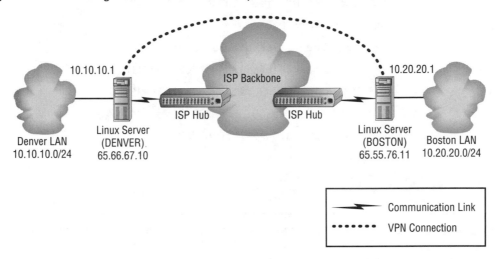

The challenge is to configure the Denver and Boston servers as security gateways that can act as IPsec tunnel endpoints to protect any traffic that travels from the Denver LAN to the Boston LAN and vice versa. Note that although both security gateways have Internet routable addresses on their public interfaces (65.66.67.10 for DENVER and 65.55.76.11 for BOSTON), their internal addresses are not routable (10.10.10.1 and 10.20.20.1 respectively). This does not present a problem for IPsec routing, as long as ESP tunnel mode is used and network address translation (NAT) is performed at the security gateways.

Let's start by ensuring that both DENVER and BOSTON are configured to forward IP packets. Insert the following line in the /etc/rc.local script of both gateways:

```
echo "1" > /proc/sys/net/ipv4/ip_forward
```

Editing the *ipsec.secrets* File

Next, edit the /etc/ipsec.secrets file to establish a set of secrets for the authentication of all your remote peers:

```
[ramon]$ sudo cat /etc/ipsec.secrets
# Pre-shared key
```

Remote Access and
Authentication

PART 5

```
65.66.67.10 65.55.76.11 : PSK "0x6c75ff4e_726ffd6f_08e0d143_3d31cd8e_
1279a10c_44f0eb1c_0398b736_↵
c50647f2"
```

```
# RSA private key
```

```
10.0.0.1 10.0.0.2: RSA {

        Modulus: xccec0dfafeb7b800d6d8ac7988f1831e...

        PublicExponent: 0x03

        PrivateExponent: x889d5ea7547a7aabef657698...

        Prime1: xe8fa28491068933b4b58902ffde71fdba...

        Prime2: xe12c294a7d3cfa110cacb332073e95166...

        Exponent1: x9b517030b59b0cd2323b0acaa944bf...

        Exponent2: x961d70dc537dfc0b5dc87776af7f0e...

        Coefficient: x261e965745e79966d4216ce281c7...

        }
```

NOTE In the preceding example, the lines ending in ... have been concatenated for brevity.

The format of an entry in the /etc/ipsec.secrets file is

> index1 index-2 ... index-n : [PSK|RSA] "secret-key"

where index1, index2, and so on, can be one of the following constructs:

- A numeric IP address (e.g., 65.66.67.10)
- A fully qualified domain name (e.g., peer6.example.com)
- username@domain (e.g., roaming5@example.com)
- The wildcard %any

To establish a Pluto IKE connection, two peers must either have a common shared-secret key or a valid RSA key in their configuration files.

The PSK literal stands for *pre-shared key* and signals the fact that a common secret is to be used for endpoint authentication. The secret then follows and it must be enclosed in double quotes; the secret can be any string of any length as long as it is identical on both ends of the IKE connection. However, I recommend that you make the secret at last 256 bits long. To generate an appropriate shared secret, you can use the FreeS/WAN-supplied ipsec utility in the following form:

```
[ramon]$ ipsec ranbits 256
```

```
0xf075a446_67aee060_c3abae12_f55ce414_4e24bb7a_08adc82d_695e0abb_ ⤶
09fb7d7f
```

You can then surround this string in double quotes and place it at both ends of the IKE connection by adding it to both of the /etc/ipsec.secrets files.

WARNING Be sure to use a secure remote terminal when creating or modifying the /etc/ipsec.secrets files at both peers in order to avoid exposing the secrets as you edit the file.

The RSA literal indicates that an RSA secret key is in use and will be used for IKE authentication. RSA keys can also be generated with the ipsec utility, in the following form:

```
[ramon]$ ipsec rsasigkey 2048

# RSA 2048 bits    ipsec-peer.example.com    Mon Apr 16 22:51:33 2001

# for signatures only, UNSAFE FOR ENCRYPTION

#pubkey=0x0103ccec0dfafeb7b800d…

#IN KEY 0x4200 4 1 QPM7A36/re4ANbYrHmI/
Wc2cYMeTJOfF61i5gKT9DYeBkX2zj~CAOEY

# (0x4200 = auth-only host-level, 4 = IPSec, 1 = RSA)

Modulus: xccec0dfafeb7b800d6d8ac7988fd673671831e4c939f17ad62e60293f4 ⤶
361

PublicExponent: 0x03

# everything after this point is secret

PrivateExponent: x889d5ea7547a7aab39e5c85105fe44cef6576988626a0fc8ec ⤶
995

Prime1: xe8fa28491068933b4b58902ffde71fdba70599117bf30d86c9dc7ac9666 ⤶
e88

Prime2: xe12c294a7d3cfa110cacb332073e95166c05714be93e0d7e40f788e388c ⤶
540

Exponent1: x9b517030b59b0cd2323b0acaa944bfe7c4ae660ba7f75e59dbe851db ⤶
999

Exponent2: x961d70dc537dfc0b5dc87776af7f0e0ef2ae4b87f0d408fed5fa5b42 ⤶
5b2

Coefficient: x261e965745e79966d4216ce281c7ed76d2753c3a5047be88739ad4 ⤶
f18
```

Note in the preceding example that 2048 is the length of the key in bits. I recommend that you use keys of at least 2048 bits. To configure your host with this RSA key, simply copy the result of the preceding command into your /etc/ipsec.secrets file by surrounding it with curly brackets:

```
# RSA private key
10.0.0.1 10.0.0.2: RSA {
        Modulus: xccec0dfafeb7b800d6d8ac7988f1831e...
        PublicExponent: 0x03
        PrivateExponent: x889d5ea7547a7aabef657698...
        Prime1: xe8fa28491068933b4b58902ffde71fdba...
        Prime2: xe12c294a7d3cfa110cacb332073e95166...
        Exponent1: x9b517030b59b0cd2323b0acaa944bf...
        Exponent2: x961d70dc537dfc0b5dc87776af7f0e...
        Coefficient: x261e965745e79966d4216ce281c7...
        }
```

The preceding example shows an RSA key to be used to authenticate the local host 10.0.0.1 to the remote peer 10.0.0.2.

NOTE   /etc/ipsec.secrets file syntax mandates that you indent the contents of any key that spans past the first line.

Pluto scans the /etc/ipsec.secrets file looking for the most specific indexes first, and then defaults to more general matches for the local host and the remote peer using the following general rules:

- If no index is specified, the entry will be used for any host and peer combination.
- If a single index is specified, the entry will be used if the host address matches the index (the peer addressed is not considered).
- If multiple indexes are specified, the entry will be used only if both the host and the peer find a match in the list of indexes, in any order.

For example, the /etc/ipsec.secrets file shown earlier in this section specifies the shared secret to be used between the local host 65.66.67.10 and the remote peer 65.55.76.11 (or vice versa).

WARNING   It is extremely important to protect the /etc/ipsec.secrets file from eavesdropping. If an intruder learns the shared secret for any given connection, they can easily impersonate the remote peer and steal your information. The /etc/ipsec.secrets file should only be readable by its owner (root).

Editing the *ipsec.conf* File

The /etc/ipsec.conf file is the main FreeS/WAN configuration file; all control and configuration information for all your IPsec peer connections is defined in this file. The ipsec.conf file has three separate sections:

- The basic configuration section, where you define the settings that apply to your FreeS/WAN installation as a whole. This section starts with the keyword config setup in a line by itself.

- The connection-defaults configuration section, where you can include parameters to be applied to all your IPsec connections (tunnels). This section is marked by the line conn %default.

- The connection-specific configuration section, where you can specify parameters to be applied only to the specified tunnel. Note that there is a connection-specific configuration section for every tunnel you want to define. You start a connection-specific configuration section by using the string conn *ipsec-tunnel*, where *ipsec-tunnel* refers to a pair of IPsec peers. The examples in this section make references to denver-boston. This is the name for the tunnel between the local host (DENVER) and the remote peer (BOSTON). You can use any string to refer to tunnels, but it helps to make them meaningful.

The first part of the ipsec.conf file defines the general configuration parameters that apply to the FreeS/WAN application. Listing 12.1 contains the first part of an ipsec.conf file using the configuration for the DENVER security gateway as an example.

Listing 12.1 Defining the basic configuration parameters in the */etc/ipsec.conf* file

```
# basic configuration
config setup
   # virtual and physical interfaces for IPSEC, normally a single
   # `virtual=physical' pair, or a (quoted!) list of pairs.  In the
   # simple case, where you only want to run IPSEC on one interface,
   # the virtual (ipsec0) shouldn't need changing but the physical
   # (eth999) will (to the interface connecting to the public network,
   # network, e.g. eth0 or ppp0 or something like that).
   # *This must be correct* or almost nothing will work.
   interfaces="ipsec0=eth0"
   # KLIPS debugging output.  "none" for none, "all" for lots
   klipsdebug=none
   # Pluto debugging output.  "none" for none, "all" for lots
   plutodebug=none
   # connections to load into Pluto's internal database at startup
   plutoload=denver-boston
```

```
# connections for Pluto to try to negotiate at startup
plutostart=denver-boston
# Close down old connection when new one using same ID shows up.
uniqueids=yes
```

The `klipsdebug` and `plutodebug` options instruct FreeS/WAN to log debug information. Set them to none unless you suspect that something is not working. By default, FreeS/WAN sends debug output to `syslog` via the `daemon.error` facility, and it sends lots of it. The `plutoload` and `plutostart` commands ask that the `denver-boston` connection be loaded and negotiated when the system comes up. The `plutoload and plutostart` settings prevent the system from incurring IKE overhead when the first connection is bound for the BOSTON system. Finally, the `uniqueids` variable is set to yes to make sure that you don't have two connections to the same remote subnet open at the same time.

The second section in the `ipsec.conf` file (see Listing 12.2) defines a set of defaults that apply to each subsequent connection that is defined in the rest of the file.

Listing 12.2 Defining the defaults for connections in the */etc/ipsec.conf* file

```
# defaults for subsequent connection descriptions
conn %default
    # How persistent to be in (re)keying negotiations (0 means very).
    keyingtries=0
    # How to authenticate gateways
    authby=secrets
```

As the comments suggest, the `keyingtries` parameter defines the number of times that the local end will try to re-establish a connection with the remote end. There is no reason why this shouldn't be set to 0 (a special value that signals "retry constantly") unless you're doing the initial configuration of your system and you're not sure that you've set things up correctly. Setting it to 1 (which means "attempt to reestablish the connection one time and give up if unsuccessful") would be a good idea in that case.

The `authby` parameter defines the method used to authenticate the remote IKE peer. The supported values are:

- `rsasig`: Use RSA digital signatures
- `secret`: Use pre-shared secrets

RSA keys is the preferred method of authentication for Pluto IKE, especially after the RSA patent on their public key technology expired in September of 2000.

Finally, let's look at the section of `ipsec.conf` that actually defines an IPsec connection. As you read the configuration of the tunnel itself, note that the `left` and `right` nomenclature is arbitrary. It's simply a convenience so you can easily visualize which addresses belong on which end of the connection. Using this left and right nomenclature allows you to go to the BOSTON gateway and define a mirror image ipsec.conf configuration. Ultimately, each gateway determines whether it is left or right according to the addresses specified in ipsec.conf and according to the addresses configured on its own interfaces. If neither right nor left match a local interface, Pluto reports the error "unable to orient connection."

Listing 12.3 contains an example of the conn section of ipsec.conf.

Listing 12.3   Defining an IPsec connection in the /etc/ipsec.conf file

```
# Tunnel from Denver to Boston
conn denver-boston
        # left security gateway (public-network address)
        left=65.66.67.10
        # next hop to reach right
        leftnexthop=65.66.67.11
        # subnet behind left
        leftsubnet=10.10.10.0/24
        # RSA key for left
        leftrsakey=0x0103ccec0dfafeb7b800d…
        # right security gateway (public-network address)
        right=65.55.76.10
        # next hop to reach left
        rightnexthop=65.55.76.11
        # subnet behind right
        rightsubnet=10.20.20.0/24
        # RSA key for left
        rightrsakey=0x0103b81976c76cb5e1e4…
        auto=start
```

The configuration in Listing 12.3 is simply an enumeration of the interfaces used in Figure 12.7 starting with the left security gateway, which is the public address of the DENVER Linux server. The leftnexthop is the address of the router to which the DENVER gateway must send packets in order to forward them toward the BOSTON gateway. Note that this is typically the internal address of the access router provided by your ISP. The leftsubnet is simply the address used by the internal hosts in the ACME LAN in Denver (behind the Linux server). The leftrsakey contains the public half of the RSA key used by the DENVER gateway for IKE authentication.

Remote Access and Authentication

PART 5

WARNING Although it is not necessary to protect the privacy of the public half of the RSA keys used in FreeS/WAN, you do want to verify the integrity of the keys that you use in `rightrsakey` and `leftrsaskey`, ideally via an out-of-band method (in person or over the phone). This is to protect yourself against a man-in-the-middle attack, where an intruder replaces the real public key with their own, with the intent to impersonate one of your peers and intercept the information destined for these peers.

Figure 12.8 shows each of the entities involved tagged with the appropriate definition in the `ipsec.conf` file.

Figure 12.8 Using Linux FreeS/WAN to implement a dedicated VPN connection: *ipsec.conf* nomenclature

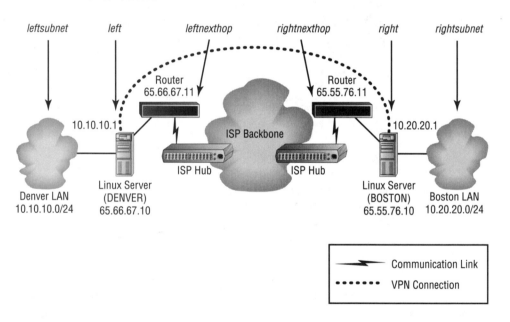

NOTE Although you have the option to use fully qualified domain names in the `ipsec.conf` file, I recommend that you use IP addresses exclusively. This eliminates any vulnerability related to the configuration and availability of DNS resolution.

Congratulations! You have just installed a VPN connection between two sites, and hopefully you'll save your company a large sum of money in dedicated WAN links. But before you move on, let's make sure that your VPN connection is working properly.

Testing the Configuration

To make sure that both ends of the tunnel are configured correctly and that hosts on leftsubnet are indeed using the Denver-Boston tunnel to communicate with hosts on rightsubnet, issue the following commands on the DENVER gateway (for example):

```
[ramon]$ sudo ipsec auto --up denver-boston

[ramon]$ sudo ipsec auto --down denver-boston

[ramon]$ sudo ipsec look
```

After restarting the connection, the output of this last command should be similar to the following:

```
athena.example.com Sun Feb 4 22:51:45 EST 2001

------------------------

10.10.10.0/24 -> 10.20.20.0/24 => tun0x200@65.55.76.10⤸
esp0x202@65.55.76.10

------------------------

tun0x200@65.55.76.10 IPv4_Encapsulation: dir=out   65.66.67.10 ->⤸
65.55.76.10

esp0x203@65.66.67.10 3DES-MD5-96_Encryption: dir=in⤸
iv=0xc2cbca5ba42ffbb6  seq=0  bit=0x00000000  win=0  flags=0x0<>

esp0x202@65.55.76.10 3DES-MD5-96_Encryption: dir=out⤸
iv=0xc2cbca5ba42ffbb6  seq=0  bit=0x00000000  win=0  flags=0x0<>

Destination  Gateway     Genmask      Flags  MSS Window  irtt Iface

10.10.10.0   0.0.0.0     255.255.255.0  U    1500 0        0  eth1

10.20.20.0   65.55.76.10 255.255.255.0  UG   1404 0        0  ipsec0
```

If you see a similar report, your FreeS/WAN installation has been correctly configured.

Point-to-Point Tunneling Protocol (PPTP)

The fact that IPsec is a standards-based framework developed under the auspices of the IETF has made it the most widely implemented VPN technology to date. In addition, since IPsec is a mandatory element of a standards-compliant IPv6 implementation, its popularity is only going to increase as the new IP version starts to gain momentum. But there are other competing protocols in the field of virtual private networking that have enjoyed some support from the Linux community. One of those is PPTP.

Developed under the auspices of the Microsoft Corporation, PPTP is an alternative to IPsec that was designed to provide a way to tunnel internal network packets out to remote office users using the Internet. PPTP uses the Point-to-Point Protocol (PPP) as the basis for tunneling, so all PPTP implementations rely on an existing (or bundled) PPP installation. While PPTP is primarily a packet encapsulation standard, it includes provisions to add connection security in two areas:

Authentication   PPTP uses the authentication methods typically supported by PPP devices, both Microsoft and third-party devices such as PAP (Password Authentication Protocol), which is actually not secure at all, and CHAP (Challenge Handshake Authentication Protocol), including its Microsoft and Shiva variants.

Privacy   Microsoft defined an optional encryption protocol to be used to protect the privacy of PPTP packet payload as it traverses an untrusted network. The Microsoft Point-to-Point Encryption (MPPE) protocol uses the RC4 encryption algorithm with the password as the seed to generate session keys for encryption.

A PPTP client (typically a Windows laptop or home user) works directly with the PPTP server at the edge of the corporate LAN, as illustrated in Figure 12.9.

Figure 12.9   A look at the protocols used in a PPTP session

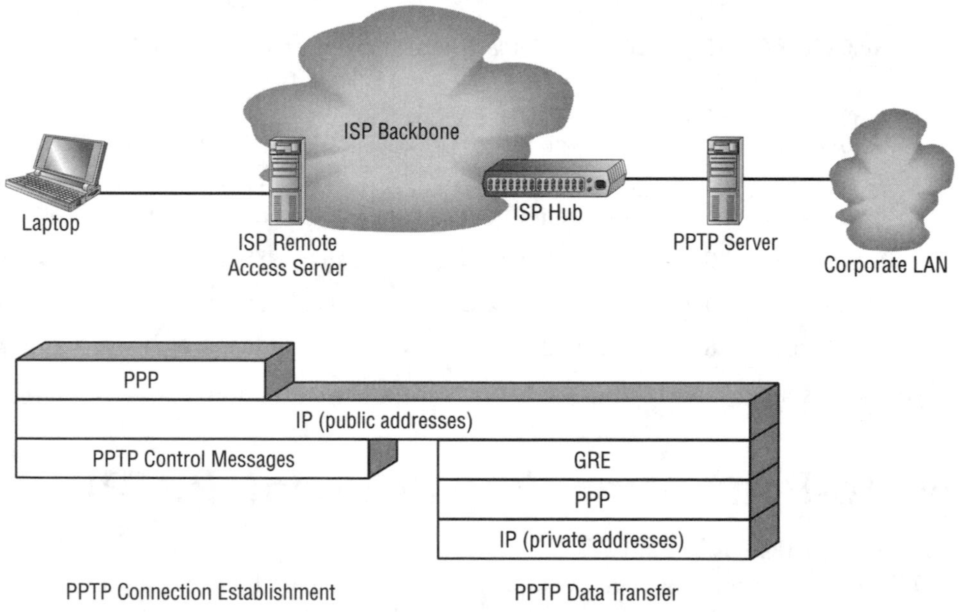

Once the PPTP client has established IP connectivity, typically over PPP to the ISP's nearest remote access server (RAS), it uses PPTP messages (which run on top of TCP) to establish a connection to the PPTP server and negotiate a set of tunnel addresses. The PPP process at the PPTP server assigns both a local and a remote address for the resulting PPP tunnel. After the user has authenticated successfully, a Generic Routing Encapsulation (GRE) session is built from end to end that sustains the PPP connection just negotiated. Only after these steps have taken place can both peers start exchanging IP packets. Note that the addresses of the PPP-encapsulated IP packets are negotiated by the two endpoints and do not have to be legal Internet addresses.

> **NOTE**   While the PPTP specification is solid overall, Microsoft's implementation has come under scrutiny over the last few years. Some improvements have been made, but I recommend that you take a quick look at http://www.counterpane. com/pptp-faq.html for more information on this controversy.

While Microsoft bundles both a client and a server implementation in its Windows platforms, there is an open-source PPTP server for Linux that can interoperate with the Windows-supplied clients. This implementation, called PopTop, is discussed in the next section.

PopTop

PopTop is an implementation of the PPTP protocol that includes a Linux port, as well as many other UNIX variants. It consists of

- A simple daemon (pptpd)
- A configuration file named /etc/pptpd.conf
- A set of man pages and supporting documentation.

PopTop is interoperable with Microsoft Windows 95, 98, NT, and 2000 clients. Its home page can be found at http://poptop.lineo.com, and a well-frequented mailing list can be accessed by subscribing at that Web site.

Downloading PopTop

PopTop is available on most repositories of RPM format packages. Simply download the latest distribution and install as follows:

```
[ramon]$ sudo rpm -i pptpd-1.1.1-1.i686.rpm
```

You'll see the main PPTP daemon executable in /usr/sbin/pptpd and a sample configuration file in /etc/pptpd.conf.

To make sure you have PPP installed (you'll need version 2.3.5 or later), execute the following command:

```
[ramon]$ rpm -q ppp
ppp-2.3.11-7
```

Remote Access and
Authentication

PART 5

Configuring PopTop

Let's start by configuring the PPP layer. Edit the `/etc/ppp/options` file and make sure that it contains the following options:

- `name athena`: This is the name of the local system.
- `auth`: This option requires the peer to authenticate itself.
- `require-chap`: This option specifies to only accept CHAP authentication.
- `proxyarp`: This option adds an entry to this system's ARP (Address Resolution Protocol) table with the IP address of the peer and the Ethernet address of this system.

The `require-chap` setting ensures that PPP requires the remote end to authenticate itself using the CHAP algorithm. Avoid using PAP because it sends the username and password in the clear (unencrypted or unhashed). In addition, the `proxyarp` setting specifies that the PPTP server listen for proxy requests for the remote user and forward packets to them accordingly.

You should also set up some basic authentication. Let's start by creating some entries in `/etc/ppp/chap-secrets` of the following form:

```
alice athena       "alicespassWorD"       10.20.20.100
bob athena         "bobspassWorD"         10.20.20.101
charlie athena     "charliespassWorD"     10.20.20.102
```

Using these settings, you will now accept CHAP authentication requests for `alice`, with password `alicespassWorD`. The second field is simply a reference to the local server (`redhat`). The fourth field contains the IP address that will be assigned to the user's end of the PPP connection.

Finally, create the `/etc/pptpd.conf` file and insert the following sample values:

```
localip 192.168.1.1
remoteip 10.20.20.100-254
```

The `localip` value can be the same for all connections; it is simply the local end of the PPP tunnel established to support all incoming PPTP connections. While the local end can be common, there is a requirement that the remote end be uniquely addressed. The `remoteip` line specifies the range of IP addresses that incoming clients will use for that purpose.

NOTE   If you do not allow a large enough `remoteip` range to accommodate enough concurrent users, connections that exceed the allocated number will be turned away.

Running PopTop

Once you have configured the PPP layer and the PPTP daemon, make sure that the process starts with every system start:

```
/usr/sbin/pptpd
```

Note that the pptpd daemon automatically sends itself to the background if invoked from a terminal. Don't forget to set the Linux server to forward packets:

```
echo 1 > /proc/sys/net/ipv4/ip_forward
```

PPTP uses destination port TCP 1723 on the Linux server and IP protocol ID 47 to exchange the data once the control connection has been established. If you are using IPtables to filter packets at the network layer, you need to allow these two ports through the filter.

Figure 12.10 illustrates a typical use of the PPTP protocol. One of ACME's remote users is in a hotel room, dialing into the local ISP. That user has established a PPP session to the hub's RAS that connects to ACME's Boston PPTP server via IP end to end. If authentication is successful, the remote user sees a virtual interface on the laptop with the address 10.20.20.100. This interface "appears" to the Boston LAN as if it were a local interface. This allows the remote user to access resources in the local network 10.20.20.0/24 as if the laptop is physically connected to it.

Figure 12.10 A typical PPTP remote access scenario

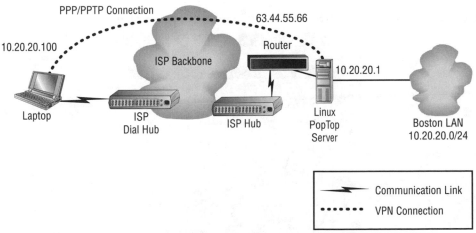

Configuring the PPTP Client on Windows 2000

Here is how to configure your users' Windows 2000 Professional systems to connect to the Linux PPTP server that you've just built.

Remote Access and Authentication

PART 5

Start by selecting Start ➣ Settings ➣ Network and Dialup Connections. Double-click the Make New Connection icon. Click Next and then select Connect to a Private Network Through the Internet (see Figure 12.11). Enter the IP address of the PPTP server.

Figure 12.11 Setting up PPTP on Windows 2000

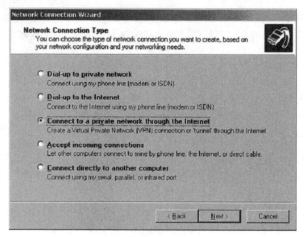

When prompted for connection availability, click Only for Myself and give the connection a name. Before connecting, click the Properties button and select the Security tab (see Figure 12.12).

Figure 12.12 Setting up PPTP security settings on Windows 2000

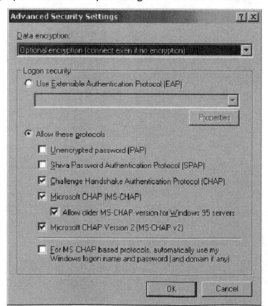

Select Optional Encryption from Data Encryption pull-down menu at the top of the dialog box. Click Allow these Protocols, and be sure to deselect PAP. Go back to the logon username and password dialog and click Connect. You should now be able to access other resources in the 10.20.20.0/24 as if you were physically on the network!

> **NOTE** Note that Windows' PPTP client implementation directs the default route of the laptop through the PPTP server once the connection is established. This means that the PPTP server should have a way to route internal packets to the Internet if the laptop user expects to access Internet resources as well as private ones.

Secure Shell (SSH)

Originally developed by Tatu Ylönen at Helsinki University of Technology, the secure shell (SSH) package and protocol specification provides a secure alternative to more traditional remote session and file transfer protocols like telnet and rlogin. The SSH protocol supports authentication of the remote host, thereby minimizing the threat of client impersonation via IP address spoofing or DNS manipulation. In addition, SSH supports several secret-key encryption protocols (DES, 3DES, IDEA, and Blowfish) to help ensure the privacy of the entire communication, starting with the initial username/password exchange.

SSH provides a virtual private connection at the application layer, including both an interactive login protocol (ssh and sshd) as well as a facility for the secure transfer of files (scp). I strongly recommend that you disable telnet and rlogin in favor of SSH. See Figure 12.13 for a requiem for telnet, rlogin, and rsh. (rsh is the insecure equivalent of SSH.)

Figure 12.13 Requiem for *telnet, rlogin,* and *rsh*

The Linux version of SSH is freely available and it includes both client and server software. There are also several excellent PC-based client implementations of SSH that are available free of charge.

How SSH Works

Consider an example where a client is attempting to access a Linux server via SSH. Both the SSH daemon running on the Linux server and the SSH client have a pre-computed public/private key pair that makes up their SSH "identity." Here are the basic connection steps:

1. The client binds to a high local port and connects to port 22 on the server.
2. The client and server agree on the SSH version to use. This is necessary because v.1 and v.2 are not compatible.
3. The client requests the server's public key and host key.
4. The client and server agree on the encryption algorithm to use such as 3DES or IDEA.
5. The client generates a session key and encrypts it using the server's public key.
6. The server decrypts the session key, re-encrypts it with client's public key, and sends it back to client for verification.
7. The user authenticates to the server inside a data stream encrypted with the session key.

At this point, the connection has been established, and the client may proceed to interactively work on the server or to transfer files to or from it. Note that step 7 (client authentication) can be done in a number of ways (username/password, Kerberos, RSA, etc.). Chapter 13, "Strong User Authentication," discusses the topic of strong authentication in more depth.

There is a plethora of SSH implementations out there, but a GPL-protected open-source variant stands out among them: OpenSSH.

OpenSSH

While the original implementation of SSH was freely available, starting with v.1.2.12, the licensing was made increasingly more restrictive until it eventually became a commercial product currently available from Data Fellows, Inc. The open-source community realized that the SSH concept was too valuable in the public domain and embarked on an organized effort to rewrite SSH into a free derivative. Starting in 1999, Björn Grönvall, and later the OpenBSD development team, took the original v.1.2.12 implementation and evolved it into what would be called *OpenSSH*. More than two years later, OpenSSH is now in version 2 and boasts support for an impressive array of platforms, including

Linux. OpenSSH version 2 no longer makes use of the once-patented RSA public-key algorithm for authentication and fixes a cyclic redundancy check (CRC) problem that compromised the integrity checks in version 1 of the standard.

WARNING There have been several vulnerabilities found in many of the older SSH v.1 implementations. I suggest that you only use SSH v.2 software.

Let's take a look at how to install and configure OpenSSH on your Linux server and on other Linux clients.

Obtaining OpenSSH

The OpenSSH RPM package should be readily available from your favorite Web repository, such as www.rpmfind.net. Look for the following three packages:

- openssh-2.5.2p2-1.7.2-i386.rpm contains
  - The man pages
  - The configuration files
  - The critical generation utilities
- openssh-server-2.5.2p2-1.7.2-i386.rpm contains
  - The sshd daemon
  - The startup files
  - The sftp server
- openssh-clients-2.5.2p2-1.7.2-i386.rpm contains
  - The ssh client
  - The sftp client

Once you've obtained these three packages, go ahead and install them (or upgrade them, depending on your situation) with the following commands:

```
[ramon]$ sudo rpm -i openssh-2.5.2p2-1.7.2-i386.rpm
[ramon]$ sudo rpm -i openssh-server-2.5.2p2-1.7.2-i386.rpm
[ramon]$ sudo rpm -i openssh-clients-2.5.2p2-1.7.2-i386.rpm
```

Configuring OpenSSH

The main OpenSSH daemon configuration file is located in /etc/ssh/sshd_config. Entries in this file are of the form:

variable value

Remote Access and Authentication

PART 5

Table 12.1 lists the most frequently used variables in the sshd_config file.

Table 12.1 /etc/ssh/sshd_config Variables

Option	Meaning	Default
AllowTcpForwarding	Specifies whether TCP forwarding is permitted.	Yes
AllowUsers user1 user2...	Specifies users to allow SSH access (exclusively).	All users allowed
DenyUsers user1 user2...	Specifies users to ban from SSH access (exclusively).	No users banned
Ciphers cipher1, cipher2...	Specifies encryption cipher to be used (SSH v.2).	3des-cbc, blowfish-cbc, arcfour, cast128-cbc
DSAAuthentication	Specifies whether DSA authentication is allowed (SSH v.2).	Allowed
IgnoreRhosts	Specifies whether .rhosts and .shosts should be ignored.	Yes
KerberosAuthentication	Specifies whether Kerberos authentication is allowed.	Yes
PasswordAuthentication	Specifies whether password authentication is allowed.	Yes
PermitEmptyPasswords	Specifies whether empty passwords should be allowed.	No
PermitRootLogin	Specifies whether root logins over SSH should be allowed.	Yes

Table 12.1   */etc/ssh/sshd_config* Variables *(continued)*

Option	Meaning	Default
Protocol 1 [,2]	Specifies whether the SSH daemon should support v.1 and/or v.2 of the SSH protocol.	v.1 only
RhostsAuthentication	Specifies whether .rhosts authentication should be sufficient to authenticate clients.	No
RSAAuthentication	Specifies whether RSA authentication is allowed.	Yes
SkeyAuthentication	Specifies whether S/Key authentication is allowed.	Yes
StrictModes	Specifies whether SSH should check file modes and ownership of the user's files and home directory before accepting login.	Yes

Choose the settings that best fit your environment and *always* include the following settings:

```
IgnoreRhosts yes
RhostsAuthentication no
StrictModes yes
```

The first two settings ensure that rhosts authentication is never used exclusively. This is the kind of authentication that relies on appropriate entries being present in the $HOME/.rhosts file or the /etc/hosts.equiv file of the server. This is very insecure. You should also enable StrictModes in order to guard against users' leaving their home directories world writeable, which presents a clear security vulnerability.

The following is an example of a complete sshd_config file that I often use on my Linux servers:

```
[ramon]$ more /etc/sshd_config
# This is ssh server systemwide configuration file.
IgnoreRhosts yes
RhostsAuthentication no
StrictModes yes
AllowTcpForwarding no
Protocol 2
PermitRootLogin no
RSAAuthentication yes
PasswordAuthentication no
```

Note that the first three lines were discussed previously. In addition, I have denied TCP connection forwarding because it makes it hard to track where users are tunneling connections within SSH, which could lead to a security vulnerability. I've also restricted the protocol versions used to v.2, even if my sshd daemon is compiled to also accept v.1; this is due to the fact that several vulnerabilities have been found in v.1. I then go on to restrict root logins via SSH, an extra step to guard against the potential of an attacker gaining remote root access; I can always log on as a regular user and use sudo. Finally, in the last two lines in the preceding example, I am defining my authentication method to be based on RSA keys only by disabling password authentication. RSA authentication is easy to administer and does not require that users expose their passwords at all.

In addition to the server configuration file, SSH also includes a client-side configuration file (/etc/ssh/ssh_config) that sets up the defaults for clients wanting to use the ssh application. Table 12.2 lists the most useful directives in the /etc/ssh/ssh_config file.

Table 12.2   */etc/ssh/ssh_config* Directives

Option	Meaning	Default
BatchMode	Disables user/password prompting for use of SSH in unattended scripts.	N/A
Cypers *cypher1, cyper2...*	Specifies encryption cypher to be used (SSH v.2).	3des-cbc, blowfish-cbc, arcfour, cast128-cbc

Table 12.2   */etc/ssh/ssh_config* Directives *(continued)*

Option	Meaning	Default
Compression	Specifies whether to use compression.	N/A
CompressionLevel level	Level of compression to use (1=fast to 9=best).	6
DSAAuthentication	Specifies whether DSA authentication should be attempted (SSH v.2).	N/A
FallBackToRsh	Specifies whether the connection should fall back to plan rsh if ssh is not successful.	N/A
KerberosAuthentication	Specifies whether Kerberos authentication should be attempted.	N/A
PasswordAuthentication	Specifies whether password authentication should be attempted.	N/A
Protocol 1 [,2]	Specifies whether the SSH client should attempt v.1 and/or v.2 of the SSH protocol.	1,2
RhostsAuthentication	Specifies whether .rhosts authentication should be attempted.	N/A
RSAAuthentication	Specifies whether RSA authentication should be attempted.	N/A

Remote Access and
Authentication

PART 5

Table 12.2 /etc/ssh/ssh_config Directives (continued)

Option	Meaning	Default
SkeyAuthentication	Specifies whether S/Key authentication should be attempted.	N/A
StrictHostKeyChecking	Never automatically add remote host key into $HOME/.ssh/known_ hosts. Rely on its existence for the connection to succeed.	N/A

Out of these client options, you should always specify the following settings:

```
RhostsAuthentication no

FallbackToRsh no

StrictHostKeyChecking yes
```

The first two settings disable the use of rhosts authentication and the use of the insecure rsh command. The third setting forces your client to know the public key of the remote host in advance. This makes it impossible for an intruder to stage a man-in-the-middle attack, impersonating the server to which you're trying to connect. The drawback is that you'll have to collect all the host keys of the servers to which you typically connect and store them in your $HOME/.ssh/known_hosts file.

A Word About RSA Authentication

As of September 2000, RSA Security, Inc. no longer holds the patent to the RSA algorithm for public-key authentication. This means that you can create a public/private RSA key pair on your client machine and distribute the public pair to the administrator of any Linux server to which you want to authenticate securely.

Start by running the ssh-keygen to generate the pair in your home directory. This command is run as a regular user. Each of your users should run ssh-keygen to create their own sets of keys. Here's an example of the ssh-keygen command in action:

```
[ramon]$ ssh-keygen
Generating RSA keys:  Key generation complete.
Enter file in which to save the key (/home/ramon/.ssh/identity):
Enter passphrase (empty for no passphrase):
```

Enter same passphrase again:

Your identification has been saved in /home/ramon/.ssh/identity.

Your public key has been saved in /home/ramon/.ssh/identity.pub.

The key fingerprint is:

b7:35:6b:f9:4a:7b:b4:40:f4:78:30:d2:4a:98:5c:25 ↵ ramon@redhat.example.com

The ssh-keygen command generates two identity files, as Listing 12.4 illustrates.

Listing 12.4   Identity files created by the *ssh-keygen* command

```
[ramon]$ cd $HOME/.ssh
[ramon]$ ls -l identity*
-rw-------    1 ramon      users          540 Feb  7 17:01 identity
-rw-r--r--    1 ramon      users          344 Feb  7 17:01 identity.pub
[ramon]$ more identity.pub
1024 35
2390480234952851043183643051819290900822440389577264580737235658973537083178043675381748121970375946993871941884887547481017847954020737163386241481285585501347130885236181266160465898811941993491027939235137895964935103899644024191711520404533990054508712560344118021095371662846509718109183189 ramon@redhat.example.com
```

The purpose of these two files is as follows:

- The $HOME/.ssh/identity file contains the secret half of your RSA key. You should never, under any circumstance, share this file with anybody.

- $HOME/.ssh/identity.pub is the file you should provide to the administrators of remote SSH systems that you need to access. When RSA authentication is allowed in the remote SSH server (with the RSAAuthentication directive from Table 12.1), you won't have to enter your password to log on to the system.

On the remote system, simply paste the complete contents from identity.pub into the $HOME/.ssh/authorized_keys file for the appropriate user. For example, suppose you want to use RSA authentication to log onto suse.example.com as ramon from both caldera.example.com and redhat.example.com. Simply take the contents of your identity.pub file from both caldera.example.com and redhat.example.com and insert them into suse.example.com's .ssh/authorized_keys as shown here:

```
[ramon]$ more .ssh/authorized_keys
1024 35 26176636242440780346519543108953529879251559446371894563887009604555778782718985791357113568998025123565846241198583673104293773
```

Remote Access and Authentication

PART 5

```
619374038515642525995896839408820873304551517270274007730290429786159
603224444666445293262921876776658946288815929526320347072304809238408
09214279923487927349792347011 hontanon@caldera.example.com
```

```
1024 35 2390480234952851043183643051819290900822440389577264580737235
658973537083178043675381748121970375946993871941884887547481017847954
020737163386241481285585501347130885236181266160465898811941993491027
939235137895964935103899644024191711520404533990054508712560344118021
095371662846509718109183189 ramon@redhat.example.com
```

Note that you use two different usernames on the remote machines (hontanon at caldera.example.com and ramon at redhat.example.com). This is just fine as long as you enter those keys correctly in suse.example.com's .ssh/authorized_keys file.

Using OpenSSH

The first time you start the sshd daemon, you'll see the following:

```
[ramon]$ sudo /etc/rc.d/init.d/sshd start
Generating RSA keys:  Key generation complete.
Your identification has been saved in /etc/ssh/ssh_host_key.
Your public key has been saved in /etc/ssh/ssh_host_key.pub.
The key fingerprint is:
96:26:e0:4b:4e:9b:28:6d:e7:b9:92:65:1b:7a:7c:09 root@redhat.example.
com
Generating DSA parameter and key.
Your identification has been saved in /etc/ssh/ssh_host_dsa_key.
Your public key has been saved in /etc/ssh/ssh_host_dsa_key.pub.
The key fingerprint is:
09:92:6c:84:28:54:8b:45:7d:a7:d6:76:80:1d:21:b2
root@redhat.example.com
Starting sshd: [  OK  ]
```

As you can see, the daemon knows that it is running for the first time and it creates two sets of keys, both RSA and DSA for backward compatibility. These are the keys that the sshd daemon will use to authenticate itself to remote hosts from now on, similarly to the way you use RSA to authenticate at the user level.

The RSA keys are stored in the following files:

- /etc/ssh/ssh_host_key (private half)
- /etc/ssh/ssh_host_key.pub (public half)

The DSA keys are located in the following files:

- /etc/ssh/ssh_host_dsa_key (private half)
- /etc/ssh/ssh_host_dsa_key.pub (public half)

You are now ready to accept SSH connections over port 22. Make sure that any perimeter security devices that may be in front of the OpenSSH server allow incoming connections to TCP port 22.

The SSH client takes a number of command-line options. Table 12.3 lists the most important ones.

Table 12.3   Table 12.3: *ssh* Client Command-line Options

Option	Meaning
-l *user*	Log on as username *user*.
-i *file*	Identity file for RSA authentication (other than $HOME/.ssh/identity).
-v	Display verbose output (useful for debugging).
-V	Display version number.
-q	Don't display any messages (quiet).
-c [3des | blowfish]	Select an encryption algorithm.
-C	Enable compression.
-o *option*	Specify an option (using the same format as /etc/ssh/ssh_config) for this session only.

Remote Access and
Authentication

PART 5

For example, to connect to remote SSH server `remote.example.com` as root using the Blowfish encryption algorithm, use the following command:

```
[ramon]$ ssh -l root -c 'blowfish' remote.example.com

root@remote.example.com's password:

Last login: Wed Feb  7 16:55:33 2001 from redhat.example.com

remote:~ #
```

Or, to connect to the same server with the `StrictHostKeyChecking` option (listed in Table 12.2) turned off, use the following command:

```
[ramon]$ ssh -l root -c 'blowfish' -o StrictHostKeyChecking=no↵
remote.example.com

Warning: Permanently added 'remote.example.com,209.207.155.67' (DSA)↵
to the list of known hosts.

root@remote.example.com's password:

Last login: Wed Feb  7 17:03:37 2001 from redhat.example.com

remote:~ #
```

Note that the local SSH client has warned you that you have received a DSA host key from the remote end. If you ever need to disable the `StrictHostKeyChecking` option, I encourage you to check the validity of the resulting host key with the server's administrator (ideally, offline).

In Sum

This chapter introduced the concept of virtual private networking and the increasingly prevalent role that this technology is going to play in your Linux network, especially if your company has several branch offices that need to be interconnected. The IPsec specification has been universally accepted as the leading candidate for implementing VPN endpoints, and the FreeS/WAN Linux implementation includes all the features necessary for you to roll it out as a production solution.

For remote access to protected internal resources, the PPTP protocol allows you to leverage a potentially large installed base of PPTP-compliant Windows remote users. This is a tremendous advantage over VPN technologies that would force you to roll out a proprietary client. Although Windows 2000 now ships with IPsec capabilities, the older Windows versions (95, 98, and NT) lack an established IPsec client. The PopTop Linux PPTP package is now in version 1.1 and offers a good alternative to a Windows NT or 2000-based PPTP server.

Secure Shell (SSH) is an essential addition to your Linux server, especially if you need to log on interactively using password authentication. Although SSH encrypts the username/password exchange, using RSA authentication further ensures that you do not expose password information on the wire.

The next chapter wraps up this book by visiting the issue of strong authentication using secret key technology, one-time passwords, and how Linux can provide seamless support for heterogeneous authentication mechanisms.

13

Strong User Authentication

A significant number of security breaches are due to the theft of authentication credentials (passwords or other secret keys) via both eavesdropping and brute-force guessing attacks. This chapter addresses both of these concerns by introducing two strong authentication facilities: the Kerberos secret-key authentication system and the S/Key one-time password system.

By definition, strong authentication differs from conventional username/password authentication in the types of credentials used and in the exposure of these credentials. The Kerberos system enhances the security of your Linux server by eliminating the exchange of passwords in the clear. Kerberos users obtain encrypted tickets locally and use the ticket to authenticate themselves to other network resources. This eliminates the need to provide cleartext passwords every time a network service is requested. The S/Key system still relies on regular username/password exchanges but it uses a different password with every access request, thereby eliminating the risk of eavesdropping.

In addition, this chapter introduces the Pluggable Authentication Modules (PAM) facility. PAM is a framework for providing a single point of configuration where system and security administrators can request authentication mechanisms from all network applications running on the Linux server.

Let's get started by taking a closer look at the Kerberos authentication system.

Kerberos

Originally designed by R.M. Needham and M.D. Schroeder at MIT, Kerberos gets its name from the three-headed dog that, according to Greek mythology, guarded the entrance to the underworld. In real life, Kerberos is a service based on secret keys that is used for strong authentication of users and services. Instead of providing separate authentication credentials to each server on your network, Kerberos allows users to request their credentials once in the form of a Kerberos *ticket* and then use this ticket to authenticate themselves to any Kerberos-enabled server on your network. Both users and servers rely on a central Key Distribution Center (KDC) to obtain and authenticate tickets.

The main advantage of Kerberos over standard username/password authentication is that passwords are never exposed on the network. This is accomplished using shared keys between Kerberos participants (including humans, servers, and the Kerberos central authority). Before authentication credentials are exchanged, they are always encrypted to ensure their privacy.

Figure 13.1 gives you an idea of what's available on the Kerberos home page at `http://web.mit.edu/kerberos/www/`.

Figure 13.1   Kerberos home page

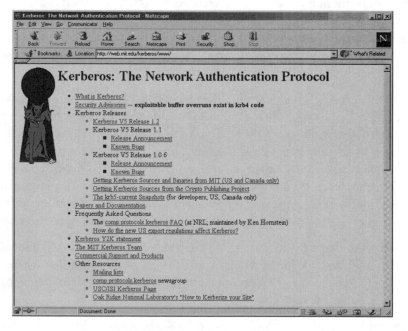

Kerberos, like many technical systems, has its own language for describing its components and functions. Before digging into the operation of the Kerberos protocol, let's define some key terminology that will be used throughout this chapter:

Principal   A *principal* is a user or server program (service) that will be using Kerberos authentication.

Key Distribution Center (KDC)   The *KDC* is a physically secure server that contains a database that includes all principals in the system as well as their master keys.

Master Key   The *master key* is a secret key that is shared between the KDC and each principal in the system.

Credentials   *Credentials* are encrypted authentication evidence presented by a principal to a service or to the KDC for authentication.

Ticket   A *ticket* is a special type of credential that allows a principal to log on to a specific service.

Ticket-Granting Ticket   A *ticket-granting ticket (TGT)* is a special type of credential used by a service on behalf of a user to request a service-specific ticket (e.g., to log on to a given server).

Realm   A *realm* is a set of Kerberos principals, servers, services, and KDCs under a common administrative domain. (A realm is similar in concept to a DNS domain.)

The Linux Kerberos system consist of three parts:

Key Distribution Center   The KDC is the centerpiece of the Kerberos authentication. As described earlier in this section, it contains the database of all Kerberos participants (principals). The KDC is typically also used to host the administration daemon (kadmin) that allows authorized principals to manage the Kerberos database remotely using Kerberos authentication.

Kerberized Services   Kerberized services are direct replacements for popular Linux server daemons such as Telnet, FTP, remote login, and remote shell. Kerberized services have been modified to use Kerberos authentication, but they provide all the other functionality that you are used to.

Kerberized Clients   Kerberized clients are the companion clients to the Kerberized services described in the previous paragraph. They too are equivalent in functionality to the traditional Telnet, FTP, and remote login clients and can be used to connect to non-Kerberized services.

Remote Access and Authentication

PART 5

A typical Kerberos interaction among a user (Alice), her local workstation (Atlantis), and a remote Telnet server (Challenger) works as follows (some of the steps have been simplified):

1. Alice logs onto her local workstation (Atlantis).
2. Alice supplies her Kerberos password to Atlantis.
3. Atlantis requests a TGT from the KDC on Alice's behalf.
4. KDC verifies Alice's master key and issues the TGT, if appropriate.
5. Alice requests a login to Challenger.
6. Atlantis presents the TGT to KDC and asks for a ticket to Challenger.
7. KDC replies with Alice's ticket to log onto Challenger.
8. Atlantis connects to Challenger with this ticket.
9. Challenger verifies the validity of the ticket.
10. Challenger allows Alice's connection, if appropriate.

Figure 13.2 illustrates these steps. Note that the numbers on the figure correspond with the steps listed.

Figure 13.2   Alice connects to Challenger using Kerberos authentication

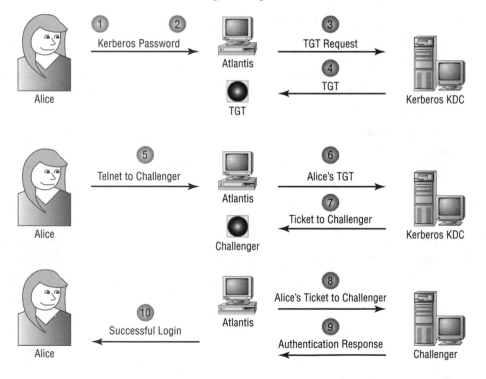

Before moving on, let's make some observations on this exchange:

- The KDC has previous knowledge of Alice's password.
- The KDC's master key for Alice is derived from this password.
- The KDC shares a secret key with Atlantis.
- All exchanges between Atlantis and the KDC are encrypted with this secret key.

One of the questions that often comes up when explaining the operation of the Kerberos protocol is, "What is the purpose of the TGT?" In essence, the TGT is granted to the Kerberos principal (Alice) so that the KDC does not have to remember anything about Alice's request. This is important because it frees the KDC from having to keep *state information,* such as a list of the principals who are currently authenticated to any given service. When the KDC sends the TGT to Alice, it includes in the TGT the expiration date, the session key, and other perishable data items necessary for Kerberos operation. By not keeping these items on the KDC itself, the Kerberos system could survive a sudden corruption or total failure of the KDC by simply diverting future ticket requests to a spare KDC equipped with a copy of the static authentication database.

The advantages of Kerberos over a standard username/password authentication service are twofold:

Privacy   When users authenticate to a service using Kerberos, they do not expose any cleartext passwords on the network. In addition, Kerberos uses secret shared keys for authentication, which greatly facilitates the encryption of the entire session, including data transfer.

Convenience   Once users obtain a Kerberos ticket, they can present it to more than one Kerberos-enabled service as many times as they wish until the ticket expires.

Kerberos has been made available in open-source format from its inception. The next section explains how to download the Linux version of Kerberos (including all its components) and how to install it and configure it to support secret-key authentication on your Linux server.

Configuring the Kerberos Domain Controller (KDC)

There are three distinct phases to configuring a Kerberos authentication environment:

1. First, you need to configure your Kerberos KDC, which listens for ticket requests from Kerberos clients.
2. Next, you have to populate the database on the KDC with the Kerberos principals for which you will be seeking authentication.
3. Finally, you have to configure your Kerberos-enabled servers to make use of Kerberos authentication for popular services such as Telnet and FTP.

All Kerberos systems need the correct software. If Kerberos is not installed on your system, you need to locate and download three packages before you can begin the configuration:

- `krb5-libs-1.2.1-8`: the libraries
- `krb5-workstation-1.2.1-8`: the workstation binaries
- `krb5-server-1.2.1-8`: the server binaries

These packages are readily available in RPM format from your favorite repository. Note that you must install `krb5-workstation-1.2.1-8.i386.rpm` before `krb5-server-1.2.1-8.i386.rpm` because it's one of its dependencies. Execute the following commands in this order to install these three packages:

```
[ramon]$ sudo rpm -i krb5-libs-1.2.1-8

[ramon]$ sudo rpm -i krb5-workstation-1.2.1-8.i386.rpm

[ramon]$ sudo rpm -i krb5-server-1.2.1-8.i386.rpm
```

Begin the Kerberos configuration by creating a primary KDC. First, check out the `/etc/krb5.conf` file. This is the general Kerberos configuration file, which is divided into several sections, or stanzas. Each of these section starts with a heading, followed by a number of variable assignments:

```
[stanza heading]
variable1 = value
variable2 = value

...
```

The sample `/etc/krb5.conf` file supplied with the server package is a good starting point for your configuration. Pay special attention to the `[logging]` and the `[realms]` sections.

The `[logging]` section instructs the KDC and the Kerberos administration server to send log events to a specific file or facility. The variables defined in the `[logging]` section are as follows:

- `admin_server` specifies a target file or device for the administrative server to perform its logging.
- `kdc` specifies a target file or device to which the KDC server should log its events.
- `default` specifies how to perform logging in the absence of an entry for `admin_server` or `kdc`.

The values to be used for these variables can be as follows:

- `FILE=filename` to specify a regular Linux file.
- `STDERR` to specify the standard error log.
- `CONSOLE` to specify the Linux console.

- DEVICE=*devicename* to specify a Linux device other than a file.
- SYSLOG[:<*severity*>[:<*facility*>]] to specify syslog logging to the named *facility* with the named *severity* level.

Listing 13.1 shows a sample [logging] section that is logging KDC, the administrative server, and other events to three separate files.

Listing 13.1   The *[logging]* section of *krb5.conf*

```
[logging]
 default = FILE:/var/log/krb5libs.log
 kdc = FILE:/var/log/krb5kdc.log
 admin_server = FILE:/var/log/kadmind.log
```

The [realms] section of krb5.conf contains one or more blocks of information delimited by the following syntax:

```
[realms]
REALM_NAME_1 = {
variable1 = value
variable2 = value
}
REALM_NAME_2 = {
variable1 = value
variable2 = value
}

...
```

Each *REALM_NAME_N* section uses similar variables to the [logging] section:

- admin_server specifies the name of the host running the administration server for the given realm.
- kdc specifies the name of the host running the KDC for the given realm.
- default_domain specifies the default domain to which hosts in this realm belong.

Listing 13.2 shows an example of a [realms] section containing a single realm definition (HONTANON.COM) where both the KDC and the administration server are running on the host kerberos.hontanon.com. Note that the port numbers are specified after the hosts to separate the KDC service (TCP port 80) from the administration service (TCP port 749).

Remote Access and Authentication

PART 5

Listing 13.2 The *[realms]* section of *krb5.conf*

```
[realms]
HONTANON.COM = {
 kdc = kerberos.hontanon.com:88
 admin_server = kerberos.hontanon.com:749
 default_domain = hontanon.com
}
```

The [domain_realm] section of krb5.conf defines a translation from any host name to a Kerberos realm name for the services provided by that host. For example, Listing 13.3 shows a [domain_realm] section that defines hosts ending in hontanon.com or *anyhostname*.hontanon.com to be in the HONTANON.COM realm.

Listing 13.3 The *[domain_realm]* section of *krb5.conf*

```
[domain_realm]
.hontanon.com = HONTANON.COM
hontanon.com = HONTANON.COM
```

The KDC Configuration File (*kdc.conf*)

Now let's take a look at the Kerberos KDC configuration file (/var/kerberos/krb5kdc/kdc.conf) that is supplied with the Kerberos server package. This is the file where the KDC looks for configuration information that is specific to any one realm. The default file is a good starting point, but there are two sections that you'll want to pay attention to:

The [kdcdefaults] section contains default information for all realms. The following variables are typical examples of these defaults:

- acl_file points to the file used to define the access control lists (ACLs) to the KDC. This file is described in detail later in this chapter.

- dict_file points to a file that contains a list of passwords that are not allowed for use because they are too weak.

- admin_keytab points to the location of the keytab file that the Kerberos administration server uses to authenticate to the database. This file is described in detail later in this chapter.

The [realms] section is similar to the equivalent section in the krb5.conf file described in the previous section and typically contains the following variable definitions:

- master_key_type is the type of encryption used to protect the communication of the KDC's master key.

- supported_enctypes is a reference to all the types of encryption supported by the KDC for this realm.

Listing 13.4 shows the complete contents of a typical kdc.conf file.

Listing 13.4 Contents of a typical *kdc.conf* file

```
[ramon]$ more /var/kerberos/krb5kdc/kdc.conf
[kdcdefaults]
 acl_file = /var/kerberos/krb5kdc/kadm5.acl
 dict_file = /usr/dict/words
 admin_keytab = /var/kerberos/krb5kdc/kadm5.keytab

[realms]
 HONTANON.COM = {
  master_key_type = des-cbc-crc
  supported_enctypes = des-cbc-crc:normal des3-cbc-raw:normal⤸
des3-cbc-sha1:normal des-cbc-crc:v4 des-cbc-crc:afs3
  }
```

You may want to create a similar configuration for your KDC. On my server, I also have a DNS alias kerberos.hontanon.com pointing to the IP address of my server, mostly for convenience. This allows me to change the IP address of the server platform, if needed, without having to change the configuration files. I simply make a DNS change for the host name to point to the new address.

The *kdb5_util* Utility

The kdb5_util utility comes bundled with the Kerberos server package and allows you to perform administrative procedures on the Kerberos authentication database. You can use kdb5_util to create the database, add new principals (humans and machines), and modify and delete those principals.

Let's start by creating the KDC database with the kdb5_util utility, as shown in Listing 13.5.

Listing 13.5 Creating the KDC database with *kdb5_util*

```
[ramon]$ sudo /usr/kerberos/sbin/kdb5_util create -r HONTANON.COM -s
Initializing database '/var/kerberos/krb5kdc/principal' for realm
'HONTANON.COM',
master key name 'K/M@HONTANON.COM'
You will be prompted for the database Master Password.
It is important that you NOT FORGET this password.
```

```
Enter KDC database master key:
Re-enter KDC database master key to verify:
```

The command in Listing 13.5 prompts you for the Kerberos master key (you should pick a word that is hard to guess, containing both mixed-case characters and numbers) and creates the following files:

- /var/kerberos/krb5kdc/principal: This is a Kerberos database file.

- /var/kerberos/krb5kdc/principal.kadm5: This is the Kerberos administrative database.

- /var/kerberos/krb5kdc/principal.kadm5.lock: This is the lock file associated with the Kerberos administrative database.

- /var/kerberos/krb5kdc/.k5.HONTANON.COM: This file is called the *stash*, a local copy of the master key that is used to authenticate the KDC to itself before starting the kadmind and krb5kdc daemons.

WARNING The stash file should be heavily guarded and should by owned and readable only by the root user. The stash file should not be part of your regular backup scheme because this would force you to protect the privacy of your backup media (which would contain the master key of the KDC).

The *kadm5.acl* File

Take a look at the kadm5.acl file, typically located in /var/kerberos/krb5kdc. This file defines which principals are allowed to use the kdb5_util to modify which parts of the database. You need to have at least one Kerberos principal in this file, along with a list of permissions for that principal. The format of entries in the kadm5.acl file is as follows:

principal permissions [*target-principal*]

These fields have the following meanings:

- *principal* is an entry that uses the syntax

  primary/*instance*@*REALM*

  where *primary* is a username (e.g., ramon in the following example), *instance* defines a specific role (e.g., admin in the following example) and *REALM* corresponds to a Kerberos realm (e.g., HONTANON.COM in the following example). For example, a complete principal specification would be

  ramon/admin@HONTANON.COM.

- The *permissions* field can be made up of one or more of the characters listed in Table 13.1.

Table 13.1   *kadm5.acl* Permissions Options

Option	Meaning
a	Allow the addition of principals.
A	Prohibit the addition of principals.
d	Allow the deletion of principals.
D	Prohibit the deletion of principals.
m	Allow the modification of principals.
M	Prohibit the modification of principals.
c	Allow the changing of passwords for principals.
C	Prohibit the changing of passwords for principals.
i	Allow inquiries to the database.
I	Prohibit inquiries to the database.
l	Allow the listing of principals or policies.
L	Prohibit the listing of principals or policies.
*	Allow all privileges.

- *target-principal* is an optional field that you can use to restrict certain actions to only apply to the specified principal.

  For example, if you have a principal alice/admin@HONTANON.COM who simply needs to list all principals in the Kerberos database and change their passwords, you could use the following entry:

  ```
  alice/admin@HONTANON.COM  cli
  ```

  To grant the principal bob/admin@HONTANON.COM all access to the principal */ root@HONTANON.COM only (any principal in the HONTANON.COM realm that has the instance root), you would add the following line:

  ```
  bob/admin@HONTANON.COM  *    */root@HONTANON.COM
  ```

To grant the principal ramon/admin@HONTANON.COM permission to change all of the database fields on any principal, add the following line:

```
ramon/admin@HONTANON.COM    *
```

The *kadmin.local* Utility

Next, you need to add an administrator to the Kerberos database using the kadmin.local utility. This utility is a command-line interface to the Kerberos administration server and it must be executed on the same host as the Kerberos KDC. The administrator principal that you choose to add must be present in the kadm5.acl file.

Once you enter the kadmin.local utility, a kadmin.local: prompt appears, where you can specify one of the following commands:

- addprinc *principal*: This command adds a new principal to the database.
- delprinc *principal*: This command deletes an existing principal from the database.
- modprinc *principal*: This command allows you to modify an existing principal.
- renprinc *new old*: This command renames a principal from *new* to *old*.
- cpw *principal*: This command allows you to change a principal's password.
- getprinc *principal*: This command displays a principal's record.
- listprincs: This command lists all principals in the database.
- ktadd -k *keytab principal* [*principal*]: This command adds one or more principal(s) to a keytab.
- ktremove -k *keytab principal* [*principal*]: This command removes one or more principal(s) from a keytab.

To create an administrator ramon/admin@HONTANON.COM, enter the following command. In this example, the addprinc command adds a new principal to the Kerberos database with administrator privileges.

```
[ramon]$ sudo /usr/kerberos/sbin/kadmin.local
Authenticating as principal root/admin@HONTANON.COM with password.
kadmin.local:  addprinc ramon/admin@HONTANON.COM
Enter password for principal "ramon/admin@HONTANON.COM":
Re-enter password for principal "ramon/admin@HONTANON.COM":
Principal "ramon/admin@HONTANON.COM" created.
```

Next, you need to create a kadmind *keytab*. A keytab is just a special key that will be used by the Kerberos administration daemon (kadmind) to decrypt the administrators' Kerberos tickets before granting them access to the Kerberos database. Note that there are two principals for whom you will be creating keytabs: kadmin/admin and kadmin/changepw. These two principals are automatically created by Kerberos when the database is first generated. You use the kadmin.local command, as before, to create the keytabs, as shown in Listing 13.6.

Listing 13.6   Creating the keytabs with *kadmin.local*

```
[ramon]$ sudo /usr/kerberos/sbin/kadmin.local
Authenticating as principal root/admin@HONTANON.COM with password.
kadmin.local:  ktadd -k /var/kerberos/krb5kdc/kadm5.keytab kadmin/admin
kadmin/changepw
Entry for principal kadmin/admin with kvno 4, encryption type DES↵
cbc mode with CRC-32 added to keytab WRFILE:/var/kerberos/krb5kdc/
kadm5.keytab.
Entry for principal kadmin/admin with kvno 4, encryption type Triple DES cbc
mode raw added to keytab WRFILE:/var/kerberos/krb5kdc/kadm5.keytab.
Entry for principal kadmin/changepw with kvno 4, encryption type DES cbc mode
with CRC-32 added to keytab WRFILE:/var/kerberos/krb5kdc/kadm5.keytab.
Entry for principal kadmin/changepw with kvno 4, encryption type↵
Triple DES cbc mode raw added to keytab WRFILE:/var/kerberos/krb5kdc/
kadm5.keytab.
```

The ktadd command is invoked with the -k switch, followed by the location of the keytab file. This file should match the value of the admin_keytab variable in the kdc.conf file (/var/kerberos/krb5kdc/kadm5.keytab in the example earlier in this section).

You are now ready to start both the main KDC daemon and the administration daemon with the following commands:

[ramon]$ **sudo /usr/kerberos/sbin/krb5kdc**

[ramon]$ **sudo /usr/kerberos/sbin/kadmind**

Once the commands have been entered, the processes will fork and move into the background, freeing up your terminal for other work. If you want these processes to start at system boot time, you can add symbolic links to the scripts

/etc/rc.d/init.d/krb5kdc

/etc/rc.d/init.d/kadmin

to the /etc/rc.d/rc5.d directory.

NOTE   If at all possible, dedicate a system to perform the KDC functions exclusively. Running other services (FTP, WWW, and SMTP) on the KDC increases the risk that the Kerberos database will be compromised via a vulnerability in these additional services.

Remote Access and Authentication

PART 5

Populating the KDC Database

Once the Kerberos server is up and running, you can start adding the principals that you wish to authenticate. You populate the Kerberos database using the `kadmin` utility. This is very similar to the `kadmin.local` utility. In fact, the only difference is that while the `kadmin.local` utility must be executed at the KDC, `kadmin` can be executed remotely and uses Kerberos authentication to grant remote access to the KDC database.

You can add a new principal using the command:

```
kadmin: addprinc principal
```

For example, to add username ramon and create an initial password, do the following:

```
[ramon]$ /usr/kerberos/sbin/kadmin
Authenticating as principal ramon/admin@HONTANON.COM with password.
Enter password:
kadmin:  addprinc alice
Enter password for principal "alice@HONTANON.COM":
Re-enter password for principal "alice@HONTANON.COM":
Principal "alice@HONTANON.COM" created.
```

Note that in order to use the `kadmin` command, you have to authenticate yourself as the principal ramon/admin@HONTANON.COM, who has been given administrative privileges to modify the Kerberos database.

Once a principal has been created for a given user, they can change their Kerberos password themselves by issuing the `kpasswd` command:

```
[alice]$ kpasswd
Password for alice@HONTANON.COM:
Enter new password:
Enter it again:
Password changed.
```

Configuring Kerberos-Enabled Servers

Once you have successfully configured a KDC and have populated its database with the information from the principals that you want to authenticate, it's time to enable your servers to use Kerberos authentication when a user requests access to a specific service.

The first step is making the KDC database aware of the servers and services that you wish to authenticate. You have to create a principal for each service/server combination.

For example, to allow the server caldera.hontanon.com to use Kerberos authentication for both the Telnet and FTP daemons, you need to create the following principals:

host/caldera.hontanon.com

ftp/caldera.hontanon.com

The host/caldera.hontanon.com principal is used for authentication of the telnet, rsh, and rlogin services. You can add these principals to the database using the addprinc command inside the kadmin utility, just as in the previous section. See Listing 13.7 for the details.

Listing 13.7   Using *kadmin* to add principals to the KDC database

```
[ramon]$ kadmin
Authenticating as principal ramon/admin@HONTANON.COM with password.
Enter password:
kadmin:   addprinc host/caldera.hontanon.com
Enter password for principal "host/caldera.hontanon.com@~CAHONTANON.COM":
Re-enter password for principal "host/caldera.hontanon.com@HONTANON.COM":
kadmin:   addprinc ftp/caldera.hontanon.com
Enter password for principal "ftp/caldera.hontanon.com@~CAHONTANON.COM":
Re-enter password for principal "ftp/caldera.hontanon.com@HONTANON.COM":
Principal "ftp/caldera.hontanon.com@HONTANON.COM" created.
```

You have created the appropriate host and ftp principals in the KDC's database, but you still have to enable the caldera.hontanon.com server to authenticate itself to the KDC for these two services. The authenticating server (caldera.hontanon.com) needs to have keytabs for the appropriate principals (host, ftp) stored in its local /etc/krb5.keytab. You use the ktadd command inside the kadmin utility to create the keytab file, as shown in Listing 13.8.

Listing 13.8   Using *kadmin* to create the keytab file (*/etc/krb5.keytab*)

```
[ramon]$ sudo /usr/kerberos/sbin/kadmin -p ramon/admin
Authenticating as principal ramon/admin with password.
Enter password:
kadmin:   ktadd host/caldera.hontanon.com
Entry for principal host/caldera.hontanon.com with kvno 8, ↵
encryption type DES cbc mode with CRC-32 added to keytab WRFILE:/etc/
krb5.keytab.
Entry for principal host/caldera.hontanon.com with kvno 8, ↵
encryption type Triple DES cbc mode raw added to keytab WRFILE:/etc/
krb5.keytab.
```

```
kadmin:  ktadd ftp/caldera.hontanon.com
```
Entry for principal ftp/caldera.hontanon.com with kvno 2, ↵
encryption type DES cbc mode with CRC-32 added to keytab WRFILE:/etc/
krb5.keytab.
Entry for principal ftp/caldera.hontanon.com with kvno 2, ↵
encryption type Triple DES cbc mode raw added to keytab WRFILE:/etc/
krb5.keytab.

Note that you are running the kadmin command on the target server (caldera
.hontanon.com), which must be configured to point to the kadmind daemon on
kerberos.hontanon.com. This is defined in the [realms] section of /etc/krb5.conf
file, as explained in the previous section, "Configuring the Kerberos Domain Controller
(KDC)." You must execute the command as root (using sudo), and you use the
-p ramon/admin option to specify which principal you want to use in order to gain
administrative permissions to the Kerberos database.

As you can see from its output, the ktadd command adds the appropriate keytab entry to
the /etc/krb5.conf file on the target server. In this case, caldera.hontanon.com should
be ready to use Kerberos authentication for ftp, telnet, rsh, and rlogin.

The next step is to modify the target server's network setup to use the *Kerberized* versions
of the network daemons. If your system is using /etc/inetd.conf to spawn off services,
add the following lines:

```
ftp      stream tcp nowait root /usr/kerberos/sbin/ftpd ftpd -a -l

telnet  stream tcp nowait root /usr/kerberos/sbin/telnetd telnetd↵
-a valid

kshell  stream tcp nowait root /usr/kerberos/sbin/kshd kshd -ec

eklogin stream tcp nowait root /usr/kerberos/sbin/klogind klogind↵
-ec
```

Note that you may have to add the following Kerberos-specific entry to your server's
/etc/services file, depending on your distribution (Red Hat 7.0 and Caldera eServer 2.3
include it, but SuSE 7.0 does not):

```
eklogin   2105/tcp                       # Kerberos encrypted rlogin
```

If you are using xinetd, use the following format (ftpd is shown as an example):

```
[ramon]$ more /etc/xinetd.d/ftp

service ftp

{
        flags          = REUSE

        socket_type    = stream
```

```
        wait            = no
        user            = root
        server          = /usr/kerberos/sbin/ftpd
        server_args     = -a -l
        log_on_failure  += USERID
        disable         = no
}
```

Note that you specified the -la arguments when invoking /usr/kerberos/sbin/ftpd. Let's take a closer look at the options available on each of these Kerberized services. For each of these services (ftp, telnet, kshell, and klogin) you will learn about the command-line options that are particular to the Kerberos version of the server.

ftpd The Kerberos FTP server allows you to make files on your server available for transfer over a TCP connection. Table 13.2 contains the Kerberos-specific command-line options when invoking the /usr/kerberos/sbin/ftpd daemon.

Table 13.2   Kerberos *ftpd* Daemon Command-line Options

Option	Meaning
-A	Only allow connections for users who can authenticate via the ftp AUTH mechanism. Prompt for password if they require one.
-a	Only allow connections for users who can authenticate via the ftp AUTH mechanism and who are authorized to connect to the FTP server without a password.
-C	Users should be prompted for a password unless they present Kerberos authentication credentials.
-r *realmfile*	Specify the Kerberos realm to use. (The default is the value of the default_realm variable in /etc/krb5.conf.)

I recommend that you invoke `ftpd` with the following options:

```
ftpd  -a -l
```

This command forces the user to use Kerberos authentication to access the FTP server rather than their username/password combination. In addition, the -l option (not Kerberos-specific) instructs the `ftp` daemon to write an event to `syslog` every time a user fails authentication.

telnetd   The Kerberos version of the Telnet server uses the command-line options listed in Table 13.3.

Table 13.3   Kerberos *telnet* Daemon Command-line Options

Option	Meaning
-a debug	Turn on authentication debugging code.
-a user	Only allow connections when the remote user can provide valid authentication information to identify the remote user and is allowed access to the specified account without providing a password.
-a valid	Only allow connections when the remote user can provide valid authentication information to identify the remote user. The login(1) command will provide any additional user verification needed if the remote user is not allowed automatic access to the specified account.
-a none	No authentication information required (default).
-a off	Disable authentication altogether.

I recommend that you invoke `telnetd` with the following options:

    telnet -a valid

This command forces the remote user to provide proper Kerberos authentication before being handed over to the `login` program for interactive access.

kshd The `kshd` daemon is the Kerberized version of the `rshd` remote shell server that comes standard with Linux. Table 13.4 lists the options available when invoking the `kshd` command.

Table 13.4   Kerberos *kshd* Daemon Command-line Options

Option	Meaning
`-A`	Don't allocate a reserved port for the `stderr` connection.
`-c`	Require clients to present a cryptographic checksum of initial connection informa-tion such as the name of the user that the client is trying to access in the initial authenticator.
`-e`	Require client to support encryption.
`-M realm`	Specify the Kerberos realm to use. (The default is the value of the `default_realm` variable in `/etc/krb5.conf`.)

I recommend that you invoke `kshd` with the following options:

    kshd -e -c

This command ensures the privacy of the connection by encrypting all the packets exchanged. In addition, the `-c` option prevents an attacker from changing the initial connection information.

Remote Access and
Authentication

PART 5

klogind   Table 13.5 lists the options that are unique to the Kerberos implementation of rlogind (klogind).

Table 13.5   Kerberos *klogind* Daemon Command-line Options

Option	Meaning
-A	Don't allocate a reserved port for the stderr connection.
-c	Require clients to present a crypto-graphic checksum of initial connection information such as the name of the user that the client is trying to access in the initial authenticator.
-e	Require client to support encryption.
-P	Always prompt users for a password.
-p	Prompt for a password if Kerberos authentication does not succeed.
-M *realm*	Specify the Kerberos realm to use. (The default is the value of the default_realm variable in /etc/krb5.conf.)

I recommend that you invoke klogind with the same options as kshd:

```
klogind -e -c
```

Do not use either the -P or the -p options. Kerberos authentication should be the only mode of authentication for this service.

Managing Kerberos Credentials

The non-privileged user interacts with the Kerberos system to manage the Kerberos tickets that are used to request network services. There are four commands used for this purpose:

     klist   The klist command displays a list of the Kerberos tickets that you are currently holding. The ticket information is kept in the file /tmp/krb5cc_*XXX*, where *XXX* is your UID on the Linux server.

kinit The kinit command requests a ticket-granting ticket from the KDC and holds it in the /tmp/krb5cc_*XXX* file for inspection by the klist command.

kdestroy The kdestroy command removes any Kerberos tickets that you are currently holding.

kpasswd The kpasswd command changes your current Kerberos password (which protects your master secret associated with your principal).

Listing 13.9 contains an example of a user acquiring and displaying a Kerberos ticket-granting ticket.

Listing 13.9 Acquiring and displaying a TGT using *klist*

```
[ramon]$ klist
klist: No credentials cache file found (ticket cache FILE:/tmp/krb5cc_500)


Kerberos 4 ticket cache: /tmp/tkt500
klist: You have no tickets cached
[ramon]$ kinit
Password for ramon@HONTANON.COM:
[ramon]$ klist
Ticket cache: FILE:/tmp/krb5cc_500
Default principal: ramon@HONTANON.COM

Valid starting      Expires             Service principal
02/24/01 17:50:05   02/25/01 03:49:52   krbtgt/HONTANON.COM@~CAHONTANON.COM


Kerberos 4 ticket cache: /tmp/tkt500
klist: You have no tickets cached
```

User ramon uses the klist command to display his credentials, and he doesn't yet have any. He then runs kinit and obtains a TGT, but only after he provides the password that protects his principal's master secret. A new invocation of the klist commands reveals that the username ramon now has a TGT in his credentials cache.

NOTE Note that the klist command reports both version 5 and version 4 tickets. This is because the standard RPM Kerberos packet includes support for the older Kerberos v.4 protocol.

By default, the kinit command attempts to obtain a TGT for the principal *user@REALM*, where *user* is the username that requests the ticket, and *REALM* is the value of the default_realm variable in the /etc/krb5.conf file. To obtain a ticket for a different principal, specify the principal name on the command line, as in the following example:

```
[ramon]$ kinit alice@SYBEX.COM
```

The klist commands shows that the ticket you've just acquired is valid until 2/25/01 at 3:39 A.M. (10 hours from now). If you want to discard this ticket, use the kdestroy command to delete it from the cache (see Listing 13.10).

Listing 13.10 Deleting a ticket from the cache using *kdestroy*

```
[ramon]$ kdestroy
[ramon]$ klist
klist: No credentials cache file found (ticket cache FILE:/tmp/krb5cc_500)

Kerberos 4 ticket cache: /tmp/tkt500
klist: You have no tickets cached
```

Finally, the kpasswd command should be used by non-privileged members on a regular basis to change their Kerberos password to minimize its exposure. The use of the kpasswd utility is virtually identical to the use of the standard Linux passwd command, as you can see in Listing 13.11.

Listing 13.11 Changing a Kerberos password with *kpasswd*

```
[ramon]$ kpasswd
kpasswd: No credentials cache file found getting principal from⤶ cache
[ramon]$ kinit
Password for ramon@HONTANON.COM:
[ramon]$ kpasswd
Password for ramon@HONTANON.COM:
Enter new password:
Enter it again:
Password changed.
```

Note that in order to issue the kpasswd command, you need to be in possession of an unexpired TGT. This makes sense because you'll need this TGT to prove to the KDC that it really is you issuing the kpasswd command, and you'll need the TGT to encrypt the new password while in transit.

WARNING It is extremely important that you choose a good password and that you change it on a regular basis. Unlike your standard Linux password, the Kerberos password can be used to obtain tickets to access other services on your behalf, so the potential damage from an intrusion is much greater.

Using Kerberos to Allow Others to Access Your Account

The ability to grant temporary access rights to your account is one of the most useful features of Kerberos authentication on a Linux server. By creating a .k5login file in your home directory, you can grant temporary access to other users without having to give them your password. Instead, simply add their principal names (one per line) to the .k5login files to allow them access, as in the following example:

```
[ramon]$ more .k5login
alice@HONTANON.COM
bob@SYBEX.COM
```

If Alice or Bob can successfully obtain a ticket for their principal, they will be allowed to log in to your account. This feature can also be used to grant non-privileged users temporary root access by simply entering their principal name in /.k5login (assuming that your root user's home directory is /). This saves you from both giving out the root password and from exposing the password on the network.

Using Kerberos-Enabled Applications

Once a user has a TGT, they can use a number of Kerberized applications to access remote services without having to identify themselves to each of them. The Linux Kerberos distribution ships with modified versions of the most popular network clients: telnet, ftp, rlogin, rsh, and rcp. Let's take a look at the Kerberos use of these applications.

telnet

Kerberos extends the standard Linux command with the command-line options listed in Table 13.6.

Table 13.6 Kerberos *telnet* Client Command-line Options

Option	Meaning
-k *realm*	Request tickets for a realm other than the one specified in the default_realm variable in the /etc/krb5.conf file.
-K	Authenticate but do not log in.
-a	Perform automatic login with your credentials and your local username (the client will not prompt for it).
-x	Enable encryption.

For example, consider the sequence of commands in Listing 13.12.

Listing 13.12   Obtaining a Kerberos ticket for use with the Kerberized *telnet* client

```
[ramon]$ hostname
atlantis.hontanon.com
[ramon]$ kinit ramon@HONTANON.COM
Password for ramon@HONTANON.COM:
[ramon]$ klist
Ticket cache: FILE:/tmp/krb5cc_501
Default principal: ramon@HONTANON.COM


Valid starting     Expires            Service principal
02/24/01 20:59:12  02/25/01 06:59:12  krbtgt/HONTANON.COM@~CAHONTANON.COM


Kerberos 4 ticket cache: /tmp/tkt501
klist: You have no tickets cached
[ramon]$ telnet -x -a -k HONTANON.COM challenger
Trying 163.109.21.167...
Connected to challenger (163.109.21.167).
Escape character is '^]'.
Waiting for encryption to be negotiated...
[ Kerberos V5 accepts you as ``ramon@HONTANON.COM'' ]
done.
Last login: Sat Feb 24 20:58:07 from atlantis
You have mail.
[ramon]$ exit
logout
Connection closed by foreign host.
[ramon]$ klist
Ticket cache: FILE:/tmp/krb5cc_501
Default principal: ramon@HONTANON.COM


Valid starting     Expires            Service principal
02/24/01 20:59:12  02/25/01 06:59:12  krbtgt/HONTANON.COM@HONTANON.COM
02/24/01 20:59:29  02/25/01 06:59:12  host/challenger@HONTANON.COM


Kerberos 4 ticket cache: /tmp/tkt501
klist: You have no tickets cached
```

This sequence begins on the host `atlantis.hontanon.com`, where user ramon starts out with no Kerberos tickets. ramon then requests a TGT for the principal `ramon@HONTANON.COM` using the `kinit` command. ramon then logs in to the machine `challenger.hontanon.com` using a Kerberized `telnet` client. An encrypted connection is then established because ramon has included the `-x` option in the `telnet` command.

Upon exiting from the `challenger` session, user ramon now has an additional Kerberos ticket:

```
02/24/01 20:59:29 02/25/01 06:59:12 host/challenger@HONTANON.COM
```

This is the ticket that his local host (`atlantis`) requested from the KDC in order to gain `telnet` access to `challenger`. Note that you will be able to use this ticket to access `challenger` until 6:59 A.M. on 2/25/01. At that point, you will be asked to run `kinit` again (to obtain a new ticket) when attempting the `telnet` operation.

ftp

Much like the `telnet` command, the Kerberized `ftp` client has two command-line options that are different from its standard Linux equivalent. They are listed in Table 13.7.

Table 13.7   Kerberos *ftp* Client Command-line Options

Option	Meaning
-k *realm*	Request tickets for a realm other than the one specified in the default_realm variable in the /etc/krb5.conf file.
-x	Enable encryption.

Just like the normal `ftp` client, the file `.netrc` is used to automate the connection-establishment process:

```
[ramon]$ cat .netrc
machine ftp.uu.net login anonymous password rhontanon@sybex.com
machine ftp.netscape.com login anonymous password rhontanon@aol.com
default login ramon
```

The first two lines of the `.netrc` file in the preceding example define the default username/passwords for specific remote FTP servers. The last line in this example defines a default username to use for all other hosts. Take a look at a typical sequence of commands involving a Kerberized `ftp` client in Listing 13.13.

Listing 13.13 Obtaining a Kerberos ticket for use with the Kerberized *ftp* client

```
[ramon]$ hostname
atlantis.hontanon.com
[ramon]$ kinit ramon@HONTANON.COM
Password for ramon@HONTANON.COM:
[ramon]$ klist
Ticket cache: FILE:/tmp/krb5cc_501
Default principal: ramon@HONTANON.COM


Valid starting     Expires            Service principal
02/24/01 21:20:59  02/25/01 07:20:59  krbtgt/HONTANON.COM@↵
HONTANON.COM


Kerberos 4 ticket cache: /tmp/tkt501
klist: You have no tickets cached
[ramon]$ ftp -x challenger
Connected to challenger.
220 challenger.hontanon.com FTP server (Version 5.60) ready.
334 Using authentication type GSSAPI; ADAT must follow
GSSAPI accepted as authentication type
GSSAPI authentication succeeded
200 Data channel protection level set to private.
232 GSSAPI user ramon@HONTANON.COM is authorized as ramon
Remote system type is UNIX.
Using binary mode to transfer files.
ftp> pwd
257 "/home/ramon" is current directory.
ftp> bye
221 Goodbye.
[ramon]$ klist
Ticket cache: FILE:/tmp/krb5cc_501
Default principal: ramon@HONTANON.COM


Valid starting     Expires            Service principal
02/24/01 21:20:59  02/25/01 07:20:59  krbtgt/HONTANON.COM@↵
HONTANON.COM
```

```
02/24/01 21:21:10  02/25/01 07:20:59  ftp/challenger@HONTANON.COM

Kerberos 4 ticket cache: /tmp/tkt501
klist: You have no tickets cached
```

As in the telnet example, the ftp session is encrypted. Also, note that after exiting the session and looking at your Kerberos credentials, you now have a ticket of the form:

```
02/24/01 21:21:10  02/25/01 07:20:59  ftp/challenger@HONTANON.COM
```

This is the ticket that atlantis requested from the KDC to access challenger's FTP service.

rlogin, rsh, and rcp

Table 13.8 lists the Kerberos-specific command-line options found in the Kerberized rlogin, rsh, and rcp clients.

Table 13.8 Kerberos *rlogin*, *rsh*, and *rcp* Client Command-Line Options

Option	Meaning
-k *realm*	Request tickets for a realm other than the one specified in the default_realm variable in the /etc/krb5.conf file.
-x	Enable encryption.

The use of these three types of clients is best illustrated with an example. Let's start by establishing an encrypted rlogin session to host name challenger, as shown in Listing 13.14.

Listing 13.14 Obtaining a Kerberos ticket for use with the Kerberized (and encrypted) *rlogin* client

```
[ramon]$ hostname
atlantis.hontanon.com
[ramon]$ kinit ramon@HONTANON.COM
Password for ramon@HONTANON.COM:
[ramon]$ klist
Ticket cache: FILE:/tmp/krb5cc_501
Default principal: ramon@HONTANON.COM
```

```
Valid starting      Expires            Service principal
02/24/01 21:29:54   02/25/01 07:29:54  krbtgt/HONTANON.COM@↵
HONTANON.COM


Kerberos 4 ticket cache: /tmp/tkt501
klist: You have no tickets cached
[ramon]$ rlogin -x challenger
This rlogin session is using DES encryption for all data↵
transmissions.
Last login: Sat Feb 24 21:29:33 from atlantis.hontanon.com
You have mail.
[ramon]$ exit
logout
Connection closed.
[ramon]$ klist
Ticket cache: FILE:/tmp/krb5cc_501
Default principal: ramon@HONTANON.COM


Valid starting      Expires            Service principal
02/24/01 21:29:54   02/25/01 07:29:54  krbtgt/HONTANON.COM@↵
HONTANON.COM
02/24/01 21:30:06   02/25/01 07:29:54  host/challenger@HONTANON.COM


Kerberos 4 ticket cache: /tmp/tkt501
klist: You have no tickets cached
```

It's important to note that the rlogin, rsh, and rcp applications use the same type of host/host name ticket as telnet:

```
02/24/01 21:30:06   02/25/01 07:29:54   host/challenger@HONTANON.COM
```

Next, you use the Kerberized rsh application to obtain a file listing from the remote host using Kerberos authentication (see Listing 13.15).

Listing 13.15 Using Kerberos authentication to obtain a file listing from a remote host

```
[ramon]$ rsh -x challenger.hontanon.com ls -l /usr/local/etc/*-gw
This rsh session is using DES encryption for all data transmissions.
-rwxr-xr-x 1 root root   1954587 Jan 30 21:22 /usr/local/etc/ftp-gw
-rwxr-xr-x 1 root root   2073268 Jan 30 21:22 /usr/local/etc/http-gw
-rwxr-xr-x 1 root root   1866661 Jan 30 21:22 /usr/local/etc/plug-gw
-rwxr-xr-x 1 root root   1912963 Jan 30 21:22 /usr/local/etc/↵
rlogin-gw
```

```
-rwxr-xr-x 1 root root    1944219 Jan 30 21:22 /usr/local/etc/tn-gw
-rwxr-xr-x 1 root root     217794 Jan 30 21:22 /usr/local/etc/x-gw
```

And finally, you copy a number of files from the remote host, using the Kerberized rcp client supplied with the distribution. In the following example, the first command copies the files in an encrypted channel, while the second command issues a remote shell request (also encrypted) to verify that the files have been transferred successfully (see Listing 13.16).

Listing 13.16   Using a Kerberized *rcp* client to copy files from a remote host

```
[ramon]$ rcp -x file* ramon@challenger.hontanon.com:/tmp/
[ramon]$ rsh  challenger.hontanon.com ls -l /tmp/file*
-rw-r--r--   1 ramon    users         4522 Feb 24 21:37 /tmp/file1
-rw-r--r--   1 ramon    users         4522 Feb 24 21:37 /tmp/file2
-rw-r--r--   1 ramon    users         4522 Feb 24 21:37 /tmp/file3
```

This wraps up the discussion of the Kerberos authentication system. The next section introduces the S/Key and OPIE systems for one-time passwords.

S/Key and OPIE

One of the major drawbacks of using conventional authentication is that if an attacker gains access to a password, they would be able to impersonate the user in question. But what if the password was different every time? The concept of *one-time passwords* is what inspired Bellcore engineers to design the S/Key system. By using a hash algorithm seeded by a small secret key (e.g., a password), the S/Key system allows you to use a pre-defined sequence of passwords to log onto a Linux server, using each password only once.

The success of this scheme hinges on the fact that it is extremely hard to predict the next password if the current one is learned. This is accomplished with a strong hash function (based on the MD4 algorithm) that uses a password as a seed value. A sequence of eight-byte passwords is then produced and translated into six English words. Every time the user wants to log on to the server, they have to use this six-word sequence as the password.

The server expects the last password of the sequence first and then expects the rest of the passwords in reverse order. This means that if an attacker gets hold of the current password, they would have to guess the previous password in the sequence, which would mean reversing the hash function. This is extremely difficult, given the strength of the MD4 algorithm.

In 1994, the U.S. Naval Research Laboratory (NRL) took the S/Key concept and re-implemented it using the stronger MD5 hashing algorithm. The so-called OPIE system

Remote Access and Authentication

PART 5

(One-time Passwords In Everything) also introduces a number of bug fixes and includes an installation system much easier than the original Bellcore S/Key installation system.

Installing OPIE

RPM distributions of the OPIE system should be readily available from your favorite Linux repository. Simply download the latest package and install it using the following command:

```
[ramon]$ sudo rpm -i opie-2.32-5.i686.rpm
```

Configuring OPIE

You need to perform three tasks to get OPIE running on your Linux server. First, create a file named /etc/opieaccess to define which network clients are allowed to use regular passwords and which network clients are allowed to use one-time passwords. By default, OPIE allows the use of both regular and one-time passwords, and you may want to have at least one host from which to log on using regular passwords in case you experience problems generating one-time passwords. This should be the local host (i.e., the console).

The general format of the /etc/opieaccess file is:

```
action network mask
```

The value of the *action* field can be either permit or deny. The *network* and *mask* fields denote the network to which the action pertains. Consider the following example where you allow the local host (127.0.0.1) as well as the entire 163.179.251.0 class-C network to use regular passwords, except for host 163.179.251.1, which, along with all other non-specified hosts, needs to provide an OPIE response to a challenge in order to successfully log on:

```
[ramon]$ more /etc/opieaccess
permit 127.0.0.1 255.255.255.255
permit 163.179.251.0 255.255.255.0
deny 163.179.251.1 255.255.255.255
```

Second, you need to replace the standard Linux /bin/login program with the OPIE login program (/usr/sbin/opielogin). Simply enter the following commands:

```
[ramon]$ cd /bin
[ramon]$ sudo mv login login.ORIG
[ramon]$ sudo cp /usr/sbin/opielogin /bin/login
[ramon]$ ls -l /bin/login
-rwxr-xr-x    1 root      root           16508 Feb 26 22:34 /bin/login
```

Third and finally, you need to create an initial secret for each of the users that you want to authenticate via OPIE using the opiepasswd utility. You can set an initial password for them as root. In the following example, you use the -c option to signal that you are in a secure terminal (you should only set passwords on the system console). You also specify the -n 15 option to force opiepasswd to generate 15 one-time passwords for username alice:

[ramon]$ **sudo opiepasswd -c -n 15 alice**

Adding alice:

Only use this method from the console; NEVER from remote. If you are using telnet, xterm, or a dial-in, type ^C now or exit with no password.

Then run opiepasswd without the -c parameter.

Using MD5 to compute responses.

Enter new secret pass phrase:

Again new secret pass phrase:

ID alice OTP key is 15 re6667

BEER HANG ONTO DEAD WEAR DANE

Alternatively, you may want to rely on your users to set their own passwords:

[alice]$ **opiepasswd -c -n 15**

Adding alice:

Only use this method from the console; NEVER from remote. If you are using telnet, xterm, or a dial-in, type ^C now or exit with no password.

Then run opiepasswd without the -c parameter.

Using MD5 to compute responses.

Enter new secret pass phrase:

Again new secret pass phrase:

ID alice OTP key is 15 re6667

BEER HANG ONTO DEAD WEAR DANE

This is the same command as the one from the previous example, but since user alice executes it herself, she does not need root privileges.

Remote Access and Authentication

PART 5

WARNING Only use the opiepasswd command when logged in using a secure terminal, one that is physically connected to the target system, typically the system console. If exposed in the clear, the secret passphrase is subject to eavesdropping, which defeats the whole purpose of using one-time password authentication.

As you can see, there are three arguments to the opiepasswd command:

```
opiepasswd -c -n sequence username
```

These fields have the following meanings:

- The -c argument informs the utility that you are using a secure terminal, and it is okay to set the passphrase over this connection.

- The -n *sequence* argument sets the number of one-time passwords on the sequence (more on that in the next section).

- The *username* informs opiepasswd of the username for which it is initializing a secret passphrase.

Using OPIE

Now that you have initialized the OPIE login for Alice, she is ready to log on to the target system and authenticate using a challenge/response one-time password. Since you have installed the OPIE-specific /bin/login program, any interactive-access daemon such as telnet or rlogin forces Alice to authenticate using an OPIE response to a challenge, unless the network that she's attempting to log in from has been included in the /etc/opieaccess file. In that case, she can either issue a response or use her regular Linux password.

If Alice is on host atlantis and wishes to log on to the remote host challenger using OPIE, she is presented with the prompt in Listing 13.17.

Listing 13.17 Logging on to a remote host using OPIE

```
[alice]$ hostname
atlantis
[alice]$ telnet challenger
Trying 192.168.1.2...
Connected to challenger (192.168.1.2).
Escape character is '^]'.
```

```
Red Hat Linux release 7.0 (Guinness)
Kernel 2.2.16-22 on an i686
login: alice
otp-md5 15 re6667 ext
Response:
```

At this point, alice has two options. The first option is to use the otp-md5 utility on her own system (atlantis) in another xterm window, as shown in Listing 13.18.

Listing 13.18   Using the *otp-md5* utility in an *xterm* window

```
[alice]$ hostname
atlantis
[alice]$ otp-md5 15 re6667 ext
Using the MD5 algorithm to compute response.
Reminder: Don't use opiekey from telnet or dial-in sessions.
Enter secret pass phrase:
BEER HANG ONTO DEAD WEAR DANE
```

The otp-md5 utility simply generates a one-time password using the MD5 hashing algorithm. It takes two arguments:

otp-md5 *sequence seed*

The *sequence* is the number of MD5 iterations that the otp-md5 utility uses to hash the seed into a one-time password (the response). Note that both the *sequence* (15) and the *seed* (re6667) are included in the challenge in the previous example. Once the response has been calculated, Alice can simply cut it from the atlantis window and paste it at the prompt in the challenger window, as follows:

login: **alice**

otp-md5 15 re6667 ext

Response: **BEER HANG ONTO DEAD WEAR DANE**

Last login: Tue Feb 27 15:38:47 from atlantis

You have mail.

Alice's second option is to pre-print a number of one-time passwords and keep the entire sequence with her. She can use the otp-md5 utility to do this by specifying the -n *sequence* option, as shown in Listing 13.19.

Listing 13.19   Using the *otp-md5* utility to pre-print one-time passwords

```
[alice]$ otp-md5 -n 15 15 re6667
Using the MD5 algorithm to compute response.
```

```
Reminder: Don't use opiekey from telnet or dial-in sessions.
Enter secret pass phrase:
1: SAP GRAD COT BOWL BOLD TASK
2: OLAF DATA JIVE COLD REIN IRE
3: GRID TAR FUNK FIND TWIG TOAD
4: HAP WILD KONG TWIT HYMN HERS
5: GAIL SUNK READ CLAW HALL DAR
6: EDIT RUDY SAN BAG HATH SUE
7: TOW LEO DUAL TINA HATE BUB
8: BEAN ROVE SALT BOSE RECK BOLT
9: TOE MITE GAM GINA REB RODE
10: HACK MARC JAY CEIL SUM DARE
11: SIRE AD IONS RUE RASH LOB
12: TROD BOGY CEIL GREW NIL LUND
13: TEN DUB SAD MORT FORE REB
14: YET MART VEND IOWA TOE MONK
15: BEER HANG ONTO DEAD WEAR DANE
```

Or, if Alice would like to print out the list so she can take it with her, she would enter the following command:

```
[alice]$ otp-md5 15 re6667 ext | lp
```

Note that every time Alice successfully logs on to challenger with her OPIE response, the sequence number is decremented by one. So the next time she will be prompted with the 14th challenge.

As you can see, these is a fair amount of up-front work to be done to set up OPIE, but once it is ready, the advantages over regular username/password authentication are obvious: There will never be a need to expose user passwords in the clear again.

Pluggable Authentication Modules (PAMs)

With the explosion of network-aware Linux applications, authentication has become an important issue. Traditionally, Linux application developers included their own authentication mechanisms in their programs, ranging anywhere from no authentication (e.g., TFTP) to strong Kerberos and S/Key authentication (e.g., telnet). Hard-coding authentication into each application has several drawbacks:

- The user is forced into a specific mode of authentication.
- Changing authentication mechanisms involves recompiling the application.

- Systems administrators must manage heterogeneous authentication mechanisms.

Originally developed by Sun Microsystems, the Pluggable Authentication Modules (PAM) framework allows administrators to control authentication parameters for network applications. Developers simply adhere to the PAM standard and call a set of dynamic libraries that come with PAM. PAM support is now included in all major Linux distributions, and a growing number of network applications are now using PAM for authentication.

There are two parts to the PAM system:

- A set of dynamically linked shared libraries (modules) that are typically installed in /lib/security or /usr/lib/security
- A set of configuration files that are typically installed in /etc/pam.d/

The developer of a networked application (for example, login) simply specifies that authentication is needed in the code before the user is granted a shell. You, as the system administrator, have complete control, using the /etc/pam.d/login configuration file, to specify what type of authentication you want your users to undergo before login gives them access to their shell.

The tasks that PAM takes care of fall into four categories or management groups:

- *Authentication management*, where PAM establishes whether the user is who they claim to be. This can be achieved using a simple method like standard username/ passwords, using a more complex method such as challenge-response authentication, or using a time-based hardware token card.
- *Account management*, where PAM provides verification services based on the account information. This management group concerns itself with questions like
  - Has the user password expired?
  - Does this user belong to the right group to be allowed access to a particular service?
- *Password management,* where PAM takes care of any necessary updates to the authentication token associated with the user. Once the user is authenticated, the password management group prompts a user for a new password if the previous has expired.
- *Session management*, where PAM does a number of things in preparation for granting the user access to the resources or right before the service is to be withdrawn. Session management tasks include logging events, mounting home directories, etc.

Installing PAM

Although PAM has become a standard package in most Linux distributions, it's always advisable to make sure you have the latest version. To update an existing PAM installation, enter the following commands:

```
[ramon]$ rpm -q pam
pam-0.72-26
[ramon]$ sudo rpm -U pam-0.72-37.i386.rpm
[ramon]$ rpm -q pam
pam-0.72-37
```

The preceding example shows you were running stock Red Hat 7.0, which came with PAM 0.72-26. This system has now been upgraded to version 0.72-37 using the RPM command.

Configuring PAM

PAM consults a configuration file for each type of network service to authenticate. All files are of the type /etc/pam.d/*service* where *service* is the name of the network service to authenticate.

NOTE The /etc/pam.d/other file has a special meaning because it is always consulted after the file specific to the service in question.

For example, the file that controls authentication for the ftp program is in /etc/pam.d/ftp.

Each line in one of these files is of the format:

```
module-type   control-flag   module-path   arguments
```

Let's take a closer look at each of these four fields:

    module-type   A PAM module can be of one of four types:

- auth
- account
- session
- password

Each of these module types corresponds to one of the four fundamental PAM management groups described in the previous section.

control-flag   Since modules are often stacked and executed in sequence, the *control-flag* field determines what effect the success or failure of a single module should have on the overall authentication result returned to the application. This field can be one of the following:

- required: Failure in this module results in overall authentication failure. Execution continues to the remaining modules.

- requisite: This value means the same as required, but the execution of the module sequence halts if the result is a failure.

- sufficient: Success in this module is enough to result in an overall authentication success. If no other required modules are in the sequence, execution stops.

- optional: Success of this module is not necessary for overall success.

module-path   This specifies the path name of the dynamically loadable object file itself, for example, /lib/security/pam_access.so.

arguments   This field is a list of command-line arguments passed to the loadable module when it is invoked by PAM. This is an optional field, since many loadable modules do not take any command-line arguments. The following arguments are common to all modules:

- debug: The debug argument sends debug information to syslog.

- no_warn: The no_warn argument forces the module to suppress warning messages to the application.

- use_first_pass: The use_first_pass argument instructs the module not to prompt the user for a password. Instead, the module should use the previously typed password (from the preceding module). If that does not work, the user is not authenticated.

- try_first_pass: The try_first_pass argument is similar to the use_first_pass argument, but the user is prompted for a password if the previous one fails.

PAM Examples

Let's start by taking a look at the /etc/pam.d/other file, which gets examined by all PAM authentication requests after the more specific configuration file. Consider the example in Listing 13.20.

Listing 13.20   A sample */etc/pam.d/other* file

```
[ramon]$ sudo more /etc/pam.d/other
#%PAM-1.0
auth       required      /lib/security/pam_deny.so
account    required      /lib/security/pam_deny.so
```

```
password required      /lib/security/pam_deny.so
session  required      /lib/security/pam_deny.so
```

The entries in Listing 13.20 ensure that attempts to access a given service are denied when there is not a more specific /etc/pam.d/ file for the service. The pam_deny.so module simply fails any authentication attempt levied against it.

Consider the more complicated example in Listing 13.21. This example illustrates the PAM configuration used to authenticate the sshd service on a Linux host.

Listing 13.21   PAM configuration for the *sshd* service

```
[ramon]$ sudo more /etc/pam.d/sshd
#%PAM-1.0
auth        required      /lib/security/pam_stack.so service=⤶
system-auth
auth        required      /lib/security/pam_nologin.so
account     required      /lib/security/pam_stack.so service=⤶
system-auth
password    required      /lib/security/pam_stack.so service=⤶
system-auth
session     required      /lib/security/pam_stack.so service=⤶
system-auth
session     required      /lib/security/pam_limits.so
session     optional      /lib/security/pam_console.so
```

The first module called is pam_stack. This is simply a way to include the stack from another service, in this case, /etc/pam.d/system-auth. This is the equivalent of including an entire header file inside a code listing by using an include directive. The pam_limits module is used to set limits on the system resources that can be obtained in a user session, such as the maximum number of open files, the maximum number of concurrent processes, etc. Finally, the pam_console module awards the user certain privileges only when they are physically logged onto the system console.

Since the previous example included the system-auth service (using the pam_stack module), let's look at the configuration of that service in the /etc/pam.d/system-auth file, shown in Listing 13.22.

Listing 13.22   PAM configuration for the *system-auth* service

```
[ramon]$ sudo more /etc/pam.d/system-auth
#%PAM-1.0
auth        sufficient    /lib/security/pam_unix.so likeauth nullok ⤶
md5 shadow
auth        required      /lib/security/pam_deny.so
account     sufficient    /lib/security/pam_unix.so
account     required      /lib/security/pam_deny.so
```

```
password    required    /lib/security/pam_cracklib.so retry=3
password    sufficient  /lib/security/pam_unix.so nullok ↵
use_authtok md5 shadow
password    required    /lib/security/pam_deny.so
session     required    /lib/security/pam_unix.so
```

This particular file is significant because it is *included* in from several other files in the /etc/pam.d directory. It includes the following PAM-loadable modules:

pam_unix   The pam_unix module verifies the identity of a Linux user and sets their credentials based on their entry in the /etc/passwd and /etc/shadow files (when appropriate). (This module is explained in more detail in Appendix B, "PAM Module Reference.") In the previous example, the pam_unix module is shown with the following optional arguments:

- nullok: The nullok argument permits the changing of a password from an empty one.

- md5: The md5 argument performs the encryption with the MD5 function as opposed to the conventional crypt call.

- use_authtok: The use_authtok argument forces this module to set the new password to the one provided by the previously stacked password module. For example, you may invoke pam_cracklib (a password-strength-checking module) before pam_unix and would like pam_unix to use the password set by pam_cracklib (see the example at the end of this section).

- shadow: The shadow argument enables the use of the /etc/shadow file for password authentication. (See Chapter 2, "System Installation and Setup," for an explanation of the advantages of shadow passwords.)

pam_cracklib   The pam_cracklib module relies on the cracklib routine to check the strength of a user password. Even if the cracklib routine likes the password, it goes on to perform some additional checks on the password to make sure that the new password is not:

- a palindrome of the old password
- the old password with only a change of case
- too much like the password
- too small
- a rotated version of the old password
- already used in the past (previously used passwords are kept in the /etc/security/opasswd file)

Remote Access and Authentication

PART 5

The `pam_craklib` module can be invoked with the following arguments:

- `retry=n` : This argument specifies the default number of times that this module will request a new password (for strength checking).

- `minlen=n`: This argument specifies the minimum acceptable size for the new password plus one.

- `difok=n`: This argument specifies the number of characters in the new password that must not be present in the old password.

For example, consider the following example from a `/etc/pam.d/passwd` file:

```
password    required    pam_cracklib.so retry=3 minlen=8 difok=3
password    required    pam_unix.so use_authtok nullok md5
```

This file shows how you can define an authentication policy for the Linux `passwd` utility by stacking two modules. The `pam_cracklib` module prompts the user for a new password (the user has to type it in twice to make sure it is typed correctly) and examines the new password to ensure that it is strong enough. Note that the user has three chances to type in a good password, which must be at least seven characters long and have at least three characters that are not in the old password.

The `pam_unix` module is then invoked, but by using the `use_authtok` argument, you make sure that the user is not prompted again for the password. Instead, the one that they just entered into `pam_cracklib` is used.

In Sum

This chapter described three important concepts in strong user and server authentication. The Kerberos system is a proven client-server facility for authentication using encrypted credentials. It provides an elegant solution to the problem of exposing secret keys and passwords over clear communication channels. Although configuring a Kerberos KDC can be time-consuming, the benefits are not only a more secure server infrastructure, but also a straightforward authentication scheme that is scalable and centrally manageable.

The S/Key and OPIE mechanisms for user authentication use a unique approach to password management—they use one-time passwords. This essentially eliminates the risk of having an attacker eavesdrop on the current credentials because those will never be used again. Using a strong cryptographic hash function, a string of passwords is generated using a user passphrase as the seed value. S/Key and OPIE use message digest algorithms that make it cryptographically infeasible to derive the *next* password from the current one. Because each password is related to the previous one, the passwords are used in the reverse order for authentication to further decrease the possibility that attackers can derive a password based on the password history.

The Pluggable Authentication Modules (PAM) framework is a suite of shared libraries and configuration files that allow a system administrator to manage the authentication of multiple network applications using a single utility and a set of configuration files. This simplifies the work of administrators and developers alike because new network applications don't have to include source code to perform user authentication. Instead, they need only invoke one of the loadable modules included in the PAM library.

Appendices

- Other Sources of Information
- PAM Module Reference

Other Sources of Information

The following Internet sites should be part of your morning Web-browsing routine. This is not meant to be an all-inclusive list of resources, but it is comprehensive enough to ensure that you are as informed as you need to be in order to stay ahead of the security threats.

Security Trade Associations

www.sans.org   Founded in 1989, The SANS Institute is a 96,000-strong cooperative research and education organization for security professionals and system and network administrators. This site offers useful resources for security education, certification, publication, and news updates.

NOTE Don't forget to order your Network Security Roadmap poster from the SANS Web site. It should be on every Linux administrator's wall.

www.gocsi.com   This site is the home of the Computer Security Institute, publisher of several industry surveys and publications, including the Frontline end-user awareness newsletter. They offer a number of seminars and put on two yearly conferences on network and information security.

Linux Information Sites

www.linuxsecurity.com   This site is a good clearinghouse for security information on the Linux operating system. Useful features include Today's Tip, a daily news section, and a well-organized set of resources, including reviews, security advisories, and in-depth articles.

www.lwn.net   This site is home to the Linux Weekly News. Although not its exclusive focus, security is well covered in this frequently updated site.

Linux Vendor Sites

www.redhat.com/support/errata   Red Hat's site contains links to the security advisories, package enhancements, and bug fixes for each of the Red Hat Linux distributions, dating back to Version 4.0.

www.calderasystems.com/support/security   Just the facts: This site contains security advisories for Caldera's eDesktop and eServer distributions and information about security patches and fixes.

www.debian.org/security   Debian's Security Information site contains current and archived security alerts dating back to 1998 and information about security fixes for the Debian distribution. It also includes information about PGP keys and instructions on how to join the mailing list.

www.suse.de/security   SuSE's Security Announcements Web site includes security advisories, PGP keys, security patches, and information on SuSE's two mailing lists, one for security discussions and another for announcements of security updates.

www.turbolinux.com/security   This site contains security updates and fixes for TurboLinux and links to two security mailing lists, one for a discussion of security issues related to TurboLinux distributions and one for receiving security alerts and updates.

Security Advisories

www.cert.org   The original security advisory clearinghouse, the CERT Coordination Center is located at the Software Engineering Institute, a federally funded research and development center operated by Carnegie Mellon University. CERT studies security vulnerabilities, provides incident response services, and publishes security advisories on their Web page and via their mailing list.

csrc.nist.gov   This site is home to the National Institutes of Standards and Technology's Computer Security Resource Center. This is a good resource for security testing, certification, validation, and advanced cryptographic research. This Web site includes information about the Advanced Encryption Standards (AES), which is the long-awaited replacement for the aging Data Encryption Standard (DES).

Security Magazines

www.scmagazine.com   Read in more than 50 countries, SC Magazine is the security publication with the largest circulation. Three different editions are available: North American, International, and Asia Pacific. The useful Info Security News Service (Infosecnews, for short) provides the daily industry news, including vulnerability bulletins. Qualified applicants are eligible for free subscriptions.

www.infosecuritymag.com   Information Security magazine is a good combination of feature articles and product reviews. Contributors to this magazine include top industry experts. The Security Wire news page is updated daily. Qualified applicants are eligible for free subscriptions.

Security Mailing Lists

www.cert.org/contact_cert/certmaillist.html   With a subscribed base of over 100,000 e-mail addresses, the CERT Advisory mailing list is the single most effective resource for staying abreast of security vulnerabilities. All messages are PGP-signed for authenticity.

www.securityfocus.com/bugtraq/archive   The BugTraq mailing list is a moderated list of information security vulnerabilities. There's a bit more subjective information and general discussion than the CERT mailing list, but it's useful to subscribe nonetheless.

lists.gnac.net/firewalls   The Firewalls mailing list is a forum for the discussion of Internet firewall security systems and related issues, including the design, construction, operation, maintenance, and philosophy of Internet firewall security systems.

www.nfr.com/mailman/listinfo/firewall-wizards   The Firewall-Wizards security mailing list is a moderated list of firewall- and security-related issues maintained by security pioneer Marcus J. Ranum. The list topics tend to be mostly conceptual, although there are often practical topics being discussed.

Appendices

B

PAM Module Reference

This appendix provides implementation details for a select number of Pluggable Authentication Modules (PAMs). Chapter 13, "Strong User Authentication," describes the Linux PAM feature in detail and explains how to use the PAM modules to control client authentication for network applications. This appendix will help you decide which modules will be most effective in assuring the security of your Linux server.

Each module-specific section in this appendix describes the functionality of the module, the management group to which the modules applies, and the module's configuration arguments and includes examples illustrating the module's suggested use.

Overview

PAM modules perform four categories of authentication tasks, called *management groups:*

Authentication PAM establishes whether the user is who they claim to be. PAM will prompt the user for a name or password if necessary for authentication. This can be achieved using a simple method like standard username/passwords, a more complex method such as challenge-response authentication, or a time-based hardware token card.

Account   PAM provides verification services based on the account information. This management group concerns itself with questions like the following: Has the user password expired? Does this user belong to the right group to be allowed access to a particular service?

Password   PAM takes care of any necessary updates of the authentication token associated with the user. Once the user is authenticated, this management group prompts a user for a new password if the previous password has expired.

Session   PAM does a number of things in preparation for granting the user access to the resources or right before the service is to be withdrawn. Session management tasks include logging events, mounting home directories, etc.

More information about these management groups is available in Chapter 13.

PAM consults a configuration file for each type of network service to authenticate. These configuration files are named /etc/pam.d/*service*, where *service* is the name of the network application to be configured (e.g., ftp, Samba, and sshd). The /etc/pam.d/other file is always consulted after the service in question.

Each line in the configuration files has the following format:

```
module_type    control_flag    module_path    arguments
```

These fields have the following meanings:

module_type   A PAM module can be one of four types; these types correlate to the management groups described earlier in this appendix:

- auth
- account
- session
- password

control_flag   Since PAM modules are often stacked and executed in sequence, the *control_flag* field determines what effect the success or failure of a single module should have on the overall authentication result returned to the application. This field can have one of the following values:

- required: Failure in this module results in overall authentication failure. Execution continues to the remaining modules.
- requisite: This value means the same as required, but execution of the module sequence halts if the result is a failure.
- sufficient: Success in this module is enough to result in an overall authentication success. If no other required modules are in the sequence, execution stops.
- optional: Success of this module is not necessary for overall success.

module_path   This field includes the path name of the dynamically loadable object file associated with the module itself, for example, `/lib/security/pam_access.so`.

arguments   This field is a list of command-line arguments passed to the loadable module when it is invoked by PAM. This is an optional field, since many loadable modules do not take any command-line arguments. Each module-specific section in this appendix lists the arguments for that module.

The *pam_access* Module

This module provides login access control based on a number of customizable parameters, including the user's login name, host or domain names, Internet addresses or network numbers, and even terminal line names for logins from directly connected terminals. The pam_ access module controls which user can log in from which place. Both login successes and failures are logged through the `syslog` facility.

The pam_access module is used for account management tasks. It accepts only one argument, *accessfile*, which defines the absolute path to the file containing pam_access configuration information. As an example, assume that you use pam_access authentication for the login facility by specifying the following line in `/etc/pam.d/login`:

```
account required pam_access.so accessfile=/etc/security/access.conf
```

In this example, the *accessfile* argument is defined as `/etc/security/access.conf`, which is the default. So in this case, the argument is not actually required but including it in the `/etc/pam.d/login` file makes a more complete example. (Because it is the default, this section will refer to the file defined by the *accessfile* argument as `access.conf` throughout the rest of this discussion.)

When a login is attempted, the `access.conf` file is scanned for the first entry that matches the source of the request. The `access.conf` file uses the following syntax:

permission:*users*:*origins*

These fields have the following meanings:

permission   The *permission* field contains either a + (plus sign) to grant access to the listed users or a - (minus sign) to deny them access.

users   The *users* field identifies who is attempting to gain access. It is a list of one or more of the following:

- Login names
- Group names
- The keyword ALL, which matches everything

- The keyword EXCEPT, which is used in conjunction with other values to except some values from the previously defined set, e.g., ALL EXCEPT

- A pattern of the form *user@host* that matches when the login name matches the *user* part and when the *host* part matches a local machine name

origins The *origins* field identifies from where the access attempt is originating. Combining the *users* field and the *origins* field gives the pam_access module control over who logs in and from where they login. This field contains a list of one or more:

- Linux tty names for non-networked logins

- Host names

- Domain names, which must begin with a period (.)

- Host addresses

- Internet network numbers, which must end with a period (.)

- The keyword ALL, which matches anything

- The keyword EXCEPT, which is used in conjunction with other values to except some values from the previously defined set, e.g., 192.168.12 EXCEPT 192.168.12.251

- The keyword LOCAL, which matches any host name that does not contain a period (.)

Let's see some example lines from the access.conf file that illustrate how *permission*, *users*, and *origins* values are combined to create access controls. The following line disallows console logins to all but a few accounts:

```
-:ALL EXCEPT wheel shutdown sync:LOCAL
```

The next line disallows logins from users in the privileged wheel group, unless those users log in from a host that can be reached without using a fully qualified domain name or from a host in the domain sybex.com:

```
-:wheel:ALL EXCEPT LOCAL .sybex.com
```

The next line means that some accounts are not allowed to log in from anywhere:

```
-:control01 control02 service fieldsvc :ALL
```

The *pam_cracklib* Module

The pam_cracklib module provides strength checking of passwords before they are accepted. This module prompts the user for a password and checks its strength against a system dictionary and a set of rules for identifying potentially vulnerable password choices. By default, pam_cracklib prompts for a single password, checks its strength, and then, if it is considered strong, prompts for the password a second time to verify that it was typed correctly the first time.

In addition to the checks to which the cracklib library submits a potential password, the pam_cracklib module also checks that the password is not:

- A palindrome: Is the new password a palindrome of the old one?

- A simple case change: Is the new password simply the old one with only a change of case?

- Too similar: Is the new password too much like the old one? This is primarily controlled by one argument, difok, which defines the minimum number of characters by which the new password must differ from the old; this defaults to 10 characters or 1/2 the size of the new password, whichever is smaller. To avoid the lockup associated with trying to change a long and complicated password, difignore is available. This argument can be used to specify the minimum length that a new password needs to be before the difok value is ignored. The default value for difignore is 23.

- Too simple: Is the new password too small? This is controlled by five arguments: minlen, dcredit, ucredit, lcredit, and ocredit. (See the description of these arguments later in this section.)

- Rotated: Is the new password a rotated version of the old password?

- A password that has already been used: Was the password used once already by this user? Note that Linux stores previously used passwords in the file /etc/security/opasswd.

If all of these checks succeed, the password is passed on to subsequent modules to be installed as the new authentication token.

A typical pam_cracklib entry in the /etc/pam.d/system-auth file has the following syntax:

```
password control_flag pam_cracklib.so arguments
```

The arguments to be passed to the pam_cracklib module can be one or more of the following:

- debug: This argument makes the pam_cracklib module write debug information to syslog. Note that even with this option set, pam_cracklib does not write password information to the log file.

- type=XXX: This argument replaces the word UNIX with the value defined for XXX in the following prompts: "New UNIX password:" and "Retype UNIX password:".

- retry=*N*: This argument is the default number of times that this module will request a new password (for strength checking) from the user. The default is 1. If after *N* times the user does not enter a password that passes the strength test, the module terminates. Using this argument can be increase the default *N* times.

- difok=*N*: This argument changes the default of 10 for the number of characters in the new password that must not be present in the old password. In addition, if half of the characters in the new password are different, then the new password will be accepted anyway.

- minlen=*N*: This argument sets the minimum acceptable size for the new password plus one. In addition to the number of characters in the new password, credit (of +1 in length) is given for each different kind of character (other, upper, lower, and digit). The default for this parameter is 9, which is good for an old-style Unix password where all characters are of the same type of character. But a default of 9 may be too low to exploit the added security of an MD5 system. Note that there is a pair of length limits in the cracklib library itself, a "way-too-short" limit of 4, which is hard-coded in and a defined limit (6) that will be checked without reference to minlen. If you want to allow passwords as short as five characters, either don't use this module or recompile the cracklib library and then recompile this module.

- dcredit=*N*: This argument is the maximum credit for having digits in the new password. If you have less than or *N* digits, each digit counts +1 towards meeting the current minlen value. The default for dcredit is 1, which is the recommended value for a minlen value of less than 10.

- ucredit=*N*: This argument is the maximum credit for having uppercase letters in the new password. If you have less than or *N* uppercase letters, each letter counts +1 towards meeting the current minlen value. The default for ucredit is 1, which is the recommended value for a minlen value of less than 10.

- lcredit=*N*: This argument is the maximum credit for having lowercase letters in the new password. If you have less than or *N* lowercase letters, each letter counts +1 towards meeting the current minlen value. The default for lcredit is 1, which is the recommended value for a minlen value of less than 10.

- ocredit=*N*: This argument is the maximum credit for having non-alphanumeric characters in the new password. If you have less than or *N* other characters, each character counts +1 towards meeting the current minlen value. The default for ocredit is 1, which is the recommended value for a minlen value of less than 10.

- use_authtok: This argument is used to force the pam_cracklib module to not prompt the user for a new password but to use the one provided by the previously stacked password module.

Let's see some examples of entries in the file /etc/pam.d/system-auth that illustrate the use of the pam_cracklib module. The following line takes all the defaults for pam_cracklib, but allows the user three attempts at providing a strong password:

```
password required pam_cracklib.so retry=3
```

The next example defines passwords to include at least 14 bytes, with extra credit of two bytes for digits and two bytes for others. The new password must include at least three bytes that are not present in the old password:

```
password required pam_cracklib.so minlen=15 dcredit=2 ocredit=2
difok=3
```

The *pam_deny* Module

The pam_deny module always returns a negative authentication result to the application through the PAM framework. As such, it might be suitable for using for default entries to ensure a deny-all authentication stance.

Entries in the /etc/pam.d/other file have the following format:

```
module_type control_flag pam_deny.so
```

This module takes no command-line arguments. For pam_deny, the *module_type* value can be one of the following:

- account
- auth (for authentication)
- password
- session

The following lines are examples of the use of pam_deny in the /etc/pam.d/other file:

```
auth       required      pam_deny.so
account    required      pam_deny.so
password   required      pam_deny.so
session    required      pam_deny.so
```

These four entries prevent the user from gaining access to the system via any applications that use PAM's authentication, account, password, and session management groups.

Appendices

The *pam_group* Module

The pam_group module assigns group membership based on the user's name and the terminal that they are attempting to access, and it takes into account the time of day at which the request is made.

The pam_group module does not provide user authentication. Instead, it grants group memberships to the user during the credential phase of the authentication module. Group memberships are based on the service the user is applying for. The group memberships are listed in text form in the /etc/security/group.conf file, which includes lines (rules) of the following format:

```
services ; ttys ; users ; times ; groups
```

These fields have the following meanings:

- *services*: This field is a list of service names that are affected by this rule.
- *ttys*: This field is a list of terminal names that indicates those terminals to be covered by the rule.
- *users*: This field is a list of usernames to which this rule applies.
- *times*: This field is a list of times to which this rule applies. The format of each element is a day/time range. The days are specified by a sequence of two-character entries. For example, MoTuSa indicates Monday, Tuesday, and Saturday. Note that repeated days unset each other; in other words, MoTuMo indicates Tuesday, and MoWk means all weekdays except Monday. The valid two-character combinations are:
    - Mo: Monday
    - Tu: Tuesday
    - We: Wednesday
    - Th: Thursday
    - Fr: Friday
    - Sa: Saturday
    - Su: Sunday
    - Wk: All weekdays
    - Wd: All weekend days (Saturday and Sunday)
    - Al: All seven days of the week

The time range part of the *times* field is a pair of 24-hour times in the format *HHMM*, separated by a hyphen that indicates the start and finish times for the rule. If the finish time is smaller than the start time, it is assumed to apply on the following day.

For example, Mo1800-0300 indicates that the permitted times are Monday night from 6 P.M. to 3 A.M. the following morning.

- *groups*: This field is a list of groups to which the user should be granted membership if the other four fields are found to match the request.

Note that the pam_group module works in parallel with the standard Linux /etc/group file. If the user is granted membership to any groups based on the behavior of pam_group, they are granted in addition to those entries in /etc/group.

The pam_group module takes no command-line arguments. The format of the /etc/pam.d/login file is as follows:

```
account     control_flag     pam_group.so
```

Consider the use of the pam_group module with the following entry in the /etc/pam.d/login file:

```
account  required        pam_group.so
```

Use the previous line with the following /etc/security/group.conf examples:

- Running /bin/bash on ttyS0, the user operator acquires membership to groups wheel and privileged:

```
/bin/bash ; ttyS0 ; operator ; * ; wheel, privileged
```

- Running /bin/bash on ttyS*, any user acquires membership to the daystaff group, as long as the login is made between 9 A.M. and 6 P.M.:

```
/bin/bash ; ttyS* ; * ; Wk0900-1800 ; daystaff
```

The *pam_limits* Module

The pam_limits module sets limits on the system resources that can be obtained in a user session. The pam_limits module restricts the resources granted to successfully authenticated users, according to the limits defined in the configuration file (typically the /etc/security/limits.conf file). This configuration file contains lines of the type:

```
domain type item value
```

These fields have the following meanings:

- *domain* can be one of the following:
  - a username
  - a group name, with @*group* syntax
  - the wildcard *, for the default entry

- *type* can be one of the following:
  - hard for enforcing the hard limits. These limits are set by the superuser and enforced by the Linux kernel. The user cannot raise his requirement of system resources above such values.
  - soft for enforcing soft limits. These limits are ones that the user can move up or down within the permitted range by any pre-existing hard limits. The values specified with this token can be thought of as default values for normal system usage.
- *item* can be one of the following:
  - *core*: Maximum core file size (KB)
  - *data*: Maximum data size (KB)
  - *fsize*: Maximum file size (KB)
  - *memlock*: Maximum locked-in-memory address space (KB)
  - *nofile*: Maximum number of open files allowed
  - rss: Maximum resident set size (KB)
  - *stack*: Maximum stack size (KB)
  - *cpu*: Maximum CPU time (minutes)
  - nproc: Maximum number of processes allowed
  - *as*: Address space limit (KB)
  - *maxlogins*: Maximum number of logins allowed for this user
  - *priority*: The priority to run user process with
- *value* is a numeric or alphabetic literal corresponding to one of the *items*.

Entries in the /etc/pam.d/login file have the following format:

    session   *control_flag*   pam_limits.so   *arguments*

The valid command-line arguments for the pam_limits module are as follows:

- debug: Use verbose logging to syslog.
- *configuration*: This argument is the absolute path to the file containing configuration information for this module. The default is /etc/security/limits.conf.

Consider the use of pam_limits with the following entry in the /etc/pam.d/login file:

    session   required   pam_limits.so   configuration=/etc/limits.conf

Use the previous line with the following /etc/limits.conf examples since you have used the configuration argument to change the default of /etc/security/limits.conf:

- The following line uses pam_limits to restrict the core file size to 0KB for all users:

```
*               soft    core            0
```

- The next two lines use pam_limits to restrict the maximum number of processes to 20 and the number of logins to 4 for members of the staff group:

```
@staff          hard    nproc           20
@staff          hard    maxlogins       4
```

- The next line imposes a soft rss limit of 10000KB for username alice:

```
alice           soft    rss             10000
```

The *pam_pwdb* Module

The pam_pwdb module provides a generic interface to the Password Database library (pwdb). The use of the pam_pwdb module varies according to the management group in question:

Account   When used as an account function, the pam_pwdb module establishes the status of the user's account and password. In the case of the password, pam_pwdb may offer advice to the user on changing their password, and it may even delay giving service to the user until they have established a new password.

Authentication   When used as a authentication function, the pam_pwdb module determines under what conditions the password provided by the user should be used to authenticate them to the requested service.

Password   When used as a password function, the pam_pwdb module updates the user's password. Using libpwdb, this module can move the user's password from one database to another.

Session   When used as a session function, the pam_pwdb module logs the username and the service type to syslog. Messages are logged at the beginning and at the end of the user's session.

The pam_pwdb module is typically used in services like /etc/pam.d/login, and its syntax is as follows:

```
module_type control_flag pam_pwdb.so arguments
```

The arguments you can use with the pam_pwdb module vary according to the management group in question.

Appendices

Account   The arguments for the account management group are as follows:

- debug: This option makes the pam_pwdb module write diagnostic information to syslog.

Authentication   The arguments for the authentication management group are as follows:

- debug: This option makes the module write diagnostic information to syslog.

- try_first_pass: This argument forces the pam_pwdb module to attempt the previous stacked authentication module's password in case that satisfies this module as well.

- use_first_pass: This argument forces the pam_pwdb module attempt to use the previous stacked authentication module's password and effectively never prompts the user for one. Note that if no password is available or the password is not appropriate, the user is denied access altogether.

- nullok: By default, the pam_pwdb module does not permit the user access to a service if their password is blank. The nullok argument overrides this default.

- nodelay: By default, the pam_pwdb module requests a delay-on-failure of the order of one second. The no_delay argument discourages the authentication component from requesting a delay should the authentication as a whole failure.

- likeauth: This argument makes the pam_pwdb module return the same value when called as a credential setting module and as an authentication module. This is useful to allow libpam take a sane path through the authentication component of your PAM configuration file.

Password   The arguments for the password management group are as follows:

- debug: This option makes the module write diagnostic information to syslog.

- nullok: By default, the pam_pwdb module does not permit the user access to a service if their password is blank. The nullok argument overrides this default.

- not_set_pass: This argument informs the pam_pwdb module that it is not to pay attention to or make available the old or new passwords from or to other stacked password modules (other authentication modules present in the same service).

- use_authtok: This argument forces the pam_pwdb module to set the new password to the one provided by the previously stacked password modules.

- try_first_pass: This argument forces the pam_pwdb module to attempt the previous stacked authentication module's password in case that satisfies this module as well.

- use_first_pass: This argument forces the pam_pwdb module attempt to use the previous stacked authentication module's password and will effectively never prompt the user for one. Note that if no password is available or the password is not appropriate, the user is denied access altogether.

- md5: Use the MD5 algorithm to encrypt the password.
- bigcrypt: Use Compaq's C2 extension to the conventional Linux crypt function to encrypt the password.

Session   No arguments are required for the session management group.

In /etc/pam.d/login, you can use pam_pwdb to make sure that the incoming user's account and password is still active:

```
account   required      pam_pwdb.so
```

You can also use the pam_pwdb module in the authentication stage. The following example allows the use of a password from a previously stacked module:

```
auth      required      pam_pwdb.so try_first_pass
```

The *pam_rootok* Module

The pam_rootok module allows the root user to gain access to a service without having to enter a password. The pam_rootok module authenticates the user if their user ID is set to 0 (the standard Linux user ID for root).

The pam_rootok module takes one command-line argument, debug, that makes the module write diagnostic information to syslog. The entries in the /etc/pam.d/su file have the following format:

```
auth control_flag module_path [debug]
```

The following lines in /etc/pam.d/su allow the root user to su to a regular user without having to issue a password while writing diagnostic information to the syslog utility via the debug argument:

```
auth      sufficient    pam_rootok.so   debug
auth      required      pam_unix.so
```

The *pam_securetty* Module

The pam_securetty module checks to make sure that the root user is logging in from a secure terminal. If root is not logging in from a secure terminal, authentication for root fails unless PAM_TTY (the environment variable containing the terminal descriptor for the request) is set to a string listed in the /etc/securetty file. For all other users, it succeeds.

To force the root user to use a secure terminal, add the following directives to /etc/ pam.d/login as the first line in the file:

```
auth      required        pam_securetty.so
```

The *pam_unix* Module

The pam_unix module is the standard Unix authentication module. It uses standard calls from the system's libraries to retrieve and set account information as well as to perform authentication. Usually this is information is obtained from the /etc/passwd file, and from the /etc/shadow file as well if shadow is enabled.

The arguments available on the pam_unix module vary according to the management group in question.

Account   The arguments for the account management group are as follows:

- debug: This option makes the module write diagnostic information to syslog.
- audit: This option forces additional (more pedantic) information to be written to syslog.

Authentication   The arguments for the authentication management group are as follows:

- debug: This argument makes the pam_unix module write diagnostic information to syslog.
- audit: This argument forces additional (more pedantic) information to be written to syslog.
- use_first_pass: This argument forces the pam_unix module attempt to use the previous stacked authentication module's password and effectively never prompts the user for one. Note that if no password is available or the password is not appropriate, the user is denied access altogether.
- try_first_pass: This argument forces the pam_unix module to attempt the previous stacked authentication module's password in case that satisfies this module as well.
- nullok: By default, the pam_unix module does not permit the user access to a service if their password is blank. The nullok argument overrides this default.
- nodelay: By default, the pam_unix module requests a delay-on-failure of the order of one second. The nodelay argument discourages the authentication component from requesting a delay should the authentication as a whole fail.

Password   The arguments for the password management group are as follows:

- debug: This argument makes the pam_unix module write diagnostic information to syslog.

- audit: This argument forces additional (more pedantic) information to be written to syslog.
- nullok: By default, the pam_unix module does not permit the user access to a service if their password is blank. The nullok argument overrides this default.
- not_set_pass: This argument informs this module that it is not to pay attention to or make available the old or new passwords from/to other stacked password modules.
- use_authtok: This argument forces this module to set the new password to the one provided by the previously stacked password module.
- try_first_pass: This argument forces the pam_unix module to attempt the previous stacked authentication module's password in case that satisfies this module as well.
- use_first_pass: This argument forces the pam_unix module to attempt to use the previous stacked authentication module's password, and effectively never prompts the user for one. Note that if no password is available or the password is not appropriate, the user is denied access altogether.
- md5: This argument is used to force the module to perform password encryption with the MD5 algorithm instead of with the conventional Linux crypt function.
- nodelay: By default, the pam_unix module requests a delay-on-failure of the order of one second. The nodelay argument discourages the authentication component from requesting a delay should the authentication as a whole fail.
- bigcrypt: This argument forces the module to encrypt more than the first eight characters of a password with Compaq's 'C2' extension to the standard Linux crypt function.
- shadow: This argument denotes that the encrypted passwords are kept in the /etc/shadow file.
- nis: This argument denotes that Sun's Network Information System (NIS) should be used for setting new passwords.
- remember=N: This argument takes one subargument, the number of previously used passwords to remember (save) for each user. Linux stores these passwords in /etc/security/opasswd to keep the user from using a recently selected password.

Session   No arguments are required for the session management group.

The file /etc/pam.d/system-auth typically contain entries of the following type:

```
auth        sufficient      pam_unix.so md5 shadow
auth        required        pam_deny.so
account     sufficient      pam_unix.so
```

Appendices

```
account     required      pam_deny.so
password    required      pam_cracklib.so retry=3
password    sufficient    pam_unix.so use_authtok md5 shadow
password    required      pam_deny.so
session     required      pam_unix.so
```

The entries in the preceding example illustrate the use of the pam_unix authentication module as a sufficient module, backed up by pam_deny as a required module, so that requests that cannot be properly authenticated are not granted.

Both the auth and password modules (the fifth and sixth lines in the preceding example) invoke pam_unix with the md5 and shadow options. Note that in the password module (the sixth line), pam_unix features the use_authtok argument, which forces the module to set the new password to the one provided by the pam_cracklib module (stacked directly on top of pam_unix).

Index

Note to the Reader: Throughout this index **boldfaced** page numbers indicate primary discussions of a topic. *Italicized* page numbers indicate illustrations.

Index

Index

Index